Beyond Soviet Studies

Beyond Soviet Studies

Edited by Daniel Orlovsky

WW Published by The Woodrow Wilson Center Press
Distributed by The Johns Hopkins University Press

Woodrow Wilson Center Special Studies

The Woodrow Wilson Center Press
Editorial Offices
370 L'Enfant Promenade, S. W.
Suite 704
Washington, D.C. 20024-2518 U.S.A.
telephone 202-287-3000, ext. 218

DK
38
B45
1995

Distributed by
The Johns Hopkins University Press
Hampden Station
Baltimore, Maryland 21211
order department telephone 1-800-537-5487

Printed in the United States of America

⊗Printed on acid-free paper.

9 8 7 6 5 4 3 2 1

Library of Congress Cataloging-in-Publication Data

Beyond Soviet studies / edited by Daniel Orlovsky.
        p.   cm. — (Woodrow Wilson Center special studies)
    Includes bibliographical references and index.
    ISNB 0-943875-69-2 (pbk. : alk. paper) : $24.95
    1. Former Soviet republics—Historiography. I. Orlovsky, Daniel
T., 1947-   . II. Series.
DK38.B45   1994
947' .0072—dc20   94-41117
                                                               CIP

The Woodrow Wilson International Center for Scholars

The Center is the living memorial of the United States of America to the nation's twenty-eighth president, Woodrow Wilson. Congress established the Woodrow Wilson Center in 1968 as an international institute for advanced study, "symbolizing and strengthening the fruitful relationship between the world of learning and the world of public affairs." The Center opened in 1970 under its own board of trustees.

Woodrow Wilson Center Special Studies

The work of the Center's Fellows, Guest Scholars, and staff—and presentations and discussions at the Center's conferences, seminars, and colloquia—often deserve timely circulation as contributions to public understanding of issues of national and international importance. The Woodrow Wilson Center Special Studies is intended to make such materials available by the Woodrow Wilson Center Press to interested scholars, practitioners, and other readers. In all its activities, the Woodrow Wilson Center is a nonprofit, nonpartisan organization, supported financially by annual appropriations from the U.S. Congress, and by the contributions of foundations, corporations, and individuals. Conclusions or opinions expressed in Center publications and programs are those of the authors and speakers and do not necessarily reflect the views of the Center staff, Fellows, trustees, advisory groups, or any individuals or organizations that provide financial support to the Center.

Contents

Foreword

Blair A. Ruble

When historians in the coming century chronicle the field of Soviet studies, they will mark the early years of the 1990s as a turning point. The rapidly changing nature of the field's object of study has challenged all the major assumptions that once held together a common enterprise. This volume is the result of a series of six seminars convened at the Kennan Institute between July 1992 and February 1993 to examine the magnitude of those challenges. Similar gatherings five, ten, twenty years from now would undoubtedly involve a somewhat different cast of characters. The very existence of a discernible community of scholars focusing on the societies, cultures, and political and economic systems of the various states and territories that were under the control of the Soviet regime is in question at the moment. It is perhaps more important to observe that the various perspectives offered in this volume also reveal unprecedented opportunities.

Until recently, the study of the Soviet Union had remained largely outside the process of integration taking place in the international scholarly community. Walls separating communities of Soviet affairs specialists—national, ideological, disciplinary, and institutional—frustrated the evolution of a common language of discourse. Relatively few opportunities existed for the sharing of experience and ideas among diverse approaches to the study of the Soviet Union. As with so many other walls recently, these have crumbled with remarkable ease.

The political, economic, and social upheavals of the past half-decade have served as a catalyst for profound changes in the way specialists on the countries of the former Soviet Union conduct their business. Traditional methodologies for studying the Soviet Union, such as monitoring the order of officials atop Lenin's Mausoleum, have lost their meaning altogether. Meanwhile, researchers embrace previously rejected methodologies, such as public opinion polling, and explore once-taboo topics, ranging from "filling in the blank pages of history"

to contemporary afflictions of crime, poverty, environmental degradation, and inadequate medical care. The political, economic, and social
transformations of the past decade have uncovered an especially rich
laboratory for research examining the core issues of the social sciences
and humanities.

The creative response of the Soviet studies community to these new
research opportunities promises genuinely fresh insights into the realities of the societies under investigation, while simultaneously casting
new light on fundamental questions in the disciplines. These questions
lie at the center of the workshops out of which this volume has
emerged.

Each of the Kennan Institute seminars in the "Rethinking Soviet
Studies" series focused on a given set of concerns usually connected
with, but not limited to, particular disciplines: nationalities, society,
politics, economics, foreign policy, and culture. Participants at each
session represented a variety of research traditions and backgrounds.
Special effort was made to involve scholars at various career stages,
from graduate students through distinguished professors emeriti.
Scholars from the regions under investigation were invited to participate in each session as well. Although historical studies were not discussed independently, historians were active in every seminar so that
special attention was, in fact, paid to historical experience and issues of
historical research throughout the program.

The chapters and commentary contained in this volume represent a
sampling of the views presented on the future of the field once known
as Soviet studies. More than 130 specialists from nine countries representing all major social science and humanities disciplines debated the
precise contours of successor fields, disputed the relative merit of various source materials, argued about the most efficacious lines of future
research, and continued long-standing polemics over the appropriate
relationship between empirical and theoretical approaches to social
knowledge as well as between area studies and the "core" disciplines.
No single volume can hope to capture the intensity, dense complexity,
and rich diversity of these discussions. It is hoped that the materials
presented here will stimulate scores of equally fervent de-bates over
the future course of study of the societies, cultures, and political and
economic systems of the various states and territories that were under
the control of the Soviet regime.

Neither the seminars nor this volume would have been possible
without the generous support of the Ford Foundation. Behind-the-
scenes staff support carried the project through to completion. In particular, I would like to thank Daniel Abele and Monique Carroll Prin-

cipi of the Kennan Institute, whose stalwart efforts and unflagging energy carried this project through to completion with considerable élan. The Woodrow Wilson International Center for Scholars, of which the Kennan Institute is a constituent program, provided decisive institutional support throughout these activities. Members of the Kennan Institute's Academic Council were especially active in the formulation of the workshop program. In particular, Abbott Gleason, the council's chair, deserves special mention, as do council members Carol Avins, David Bethea, Richard Ericson, Ellen Mickiewicz, Alex Pravda, Judith Thornton, William Mills Todd, and Dean Worth. In the end, however, council member Daniel Orlovsky, the editor of this volume, provided the intellectual leadership and ensured the success of the entire venture. Professor Orlovsky deserves special credit for having transformed the vague musings of disoriented scholars and administrators into more highly refined and easily accessible essays.

The contributors to this volume should not be given the final word about the past and future of the Soviet studies field. Rather, they have established the broad outlines of a discussion that must continue in the months and years to come. As our colleagues from the lands that we study can attest, transitions are not easy to understand, especially when one is in the middle of a transitional period. But change can energize a community, fostering remarkable adaptations and innovations. The "Rethinking Soviet Studies" seminar series will be considered a success if it can prompt more profound deliberations in classrooms, conference halls, faculty clubs, and student cafeterias in the months and years ahead.

Introduction

Judging the Past, Charting the Future:
On Aquariums and Fish Soup

Daniel Orlovsky

The reference in my title is to Martin Malia's reference to "Sovietism,"
which may be loosely translated as the Soviet way of life or Soviet system: "It is easy to make fish soup out of an aquarium, but no one has
yet found a way to make an aquarium out of fish soup." Malia refers to
the total crisis in the Soviet Union and indeed the total crisis in Sovietology,[1] arguing at least on the issue of Soviet collapse and its aftermath quite sensibly that such a total crisis requires a total approach
(and not a piecemeal one) to solve it. Again, referring to the Soviet
demise, Malia argues that "such a situation, such a conundrum, is
without precedent in world history. And it will no doubt take a generation and a decade or two to improvise, while still in the soup, Russia's
return to a 'normal society.'"[2] Sovietology, too, is in the soup, in that its
subject matter has been transformed (though not completely) and its
methods and contributions have been questioned.

The violent confrontation in September 1993 between Boris Yeltsin
and his opponents centered in the Russian parliament and the Yeltsin
government's subsequent attempts to build a new constitutional and
economic order starkly reveal the legacies of the past and the complexities of building a new society in yet another revolutionary era in Russia and the other newly independent successor states of the Soviet
Union. All these developments demand that the field of Soviet studies
renew and revitalize its intellectual mission. This volume aims to contribute to this renewal and redefinition. It does not dwell on "who got
it right and who got it wrong" but offers what is intended to be helpful
and constructive criticism of the field from a variety of points of view
and sets out research questions for an uncertain, yet terribly compelling, future. Taken together, these essays and commentaries provide
the self-assessment of a significant portion of the profession of "Soviet
studies," a unique window into the mentalité of leading scholars at a
time of great uncertainty and sea change as the field faces its critics as
well as the transformation of the former Soviet Union that was the raison d'être of the profession's existence. In any enterprise of this sort,
the spirit of the activity is key, and here the contributions were expressed in a spirit of constructive and critical engagement with the for-

mer Union of Soviet Socialist Republics and its successor states rather than from distant and Olympian heights.

Beyond Polemics: Plan of the Volume

Does Soviet studies have a future as a coherent, organized academic field, especially one that goes beyond a name change and "damage control" or self-justification for even the most plodding products of the academic assembly line?[3] The essays, commentaries, and discussions produced for the Kennan Institute Seminars and edited for this volume show that the field faces extraordinary intellectual and institutional challenges but has opportunities just as extraordinary. The essays here do not pretend to provide comprehensive coverage of the range of possible issues surrounding either the history of the field or the agendas of the future. Nor do they take on in any systematic way (with the exception of Katherine Verdery's anthropological analysis of the collapse of communism) the question of the causes and meaning of the end of the Soviet Union and the Communist Party state.

Rather, the aim is to present at the outset Verdery's fresh view of the nature of communism as a system and the reasons for its collapse. Verdery's essay is expressed in strikingly original language, and her analysis strives to make connections in its emphasis on the social, the cultural, and the economic. In a similar spirit of trying something new, in this case highly critical of both the totalitarian school and modernization theorists, Michael Burawoy uses a neo-Weberian analysis of the post-Soviet economic scene to set out an agenda in the comparative political economy of transitions. Not everything in this volume is as intellectually ambitious, but the essays and commentaries that follow do provide a fresh and stimulating look at the intellectual challenges and possibilities from the vantage point of a creative group of scholars and fair-minded critics. Some of the essays emphasize the structures of the past as harbingers and shapers of the present and future, while others are more oriented toward that unknown future. Yet the majority of the essays and commentaries move beyond the polemics to new conceptions and questions, to imagining and reimagining the content of post-Soviet studies. This is a necessary and healthy exercise, even though one must recognize that scholarship is never "total," that changes in scholarly perspective and methods sometimes occur at a glacial pace, and that researchers of Russia and the successor states must assimilate both the massive changes that are unfolding in the wake of perestroika and the end of Soviet power and the new intellectual departures and challenges within the various academic disciplines themselves.

The Kennan Seminars raised many issues that will be part of the agenda for future scholarship in the field, issues that cannot and should not be ignored by scholars whatever their discipline, persuasion, or political point of view. Some of these issues are unresolvable—the age-old question of Russia's uniqueness, for example, the very point around which turns the debate on the meaning of revolution and the blindness of American Sovietology. But some issues should generate consensus. For example, no partisan in these debates denies the importance of comparative, historical, and theoretically informed studies of transitions in Russia and the successor states (to democracy, to the market, to mixed forms of economic and social institutions, etc.), which can inform and enrich the study of other societies and historical studies of the Soviet period in all its rich, if often repugnant, variety, with all its tragedies and, yes, even accomplishments. For example, political scientists must not just look to the present, exciting as it is, but also to the antecedents that are now shaping the emergence of new forms and institutions, antecedents in the Brezhnev and Khrushchev eras as well as in the more distant Stalinist past. For better or worse, unavoidably, the Soviet past now shapes the present. We need accurate maps of the layers of Russian society, of the occupational and demographic structure and the objective characteristics, views, and aspirations of all the social groups that have made up that society both before and after such turning points as March 1989, August 1991, or September 1993. These can be added, of course, to the pathbreaking studies now emerging about local politics, the nature of authority and power, and the new institutionalism in political and economic studies that show from the ground up the workings of new institutions, the "rules of the game," and the adaptations, accommodations, innovations of individuals, firms, and social units as they emerge from the indelible past. Moral judgments alone, though unavoidable, will not suffice. We must know how and why the system worked, how it operated as a social and cultural system.

The study of Russia and the successor states can make contributions to the disciplines. To make these contributions, however, there first must be a recognition that Soviet studies (including Sovietology) did exhibit sclerotic tendencies, that it did suffer not just from the difficulty of gaining access to sources, to institutions, and to the individuals who made them work but also at times from the lack of vision and imagination, theoretical sophistication, and comparative perspective that existed in the larger worlds of social science, history, and literary studies. Furthermore, Sovietology had disconnected itself from history and had dodged such tough questions as Russian uniqueness, the meaning of revolution, continuities across the divide of 1917, the nature of civil society, the power of spontaneous social forces, and the like. There was little comparison with Eastern Europe or with China, for example, that might have thrown patterns of development into sharper relief.

The Kennan Seminars were organized according to discipline and themes. Seminars were held during 1992–93 on the following topics (in chronological order of the meetings, not order of relative importance): national identity and nationalism; society; politics and political institutions; economics; foreign policy; and culture. In each instance, the Kennan Institute commissioned one or two papers that were meant to assess the state of the field and suggest directions for future research. The aim was to arrive at some judgments about the past, but, even more important, to begin to define intellectual agendas for the various disciplines and for the field of post-Soviet studies as a whole (should there be a common vision that there would continue to be a more or less distinctively defined "field"). In each case, we added commentators, including if at all possible at least one from outside the Russian-Soviet area. Papers were circulated in advance, and after formal comments the floor was given over to free-flowing discussion under the gentle but firm and directing hand of Blair Ruble. The organizers decided to integrate history into all the seminars rather than hold a separate discussion on the merits of "Soviet history."[4] Was this a success? It remains for the seminar participants and now the readers to decide.

Broadly speaking, the seminars were not simply an exercise in self-justification or damage control, though it must be said that self-criticism was more prevalent among some scholars than others. Political scientists, for example, and indeed many representatives of other disciplines, played down critiques of their inability or unwillingness to predict the rapid collapse of Soviet power. Thomas F. Remington provided the rationale for this constraint with his metaphor of earthquake prediction. Scientists cannot predict the exact, or even remote timing of earthquakes, despite vast knowledge of tectonics and the like, so why should social scientists be expected to do better in the far more subjective realm of political and social change? From the Kennan discussions, which of course included a sprinkling of representatives from outside the area of Russian studies, it is clear that mainstream American social science is unprepared to take on prediction as part of its project. There was a very small amount of time allotted to discussion of institutional matters pertaining to the future of the field—for example, funding, prospects for graduate study, access to archives, libraries (and preservation of their contents), and academic contacts in the new Russia and successor states. These matters proved to have relevance not just to the future of the field but also to our own capacity to analyze an emerging civil society in Russia and the successor states. There was much lively discussion, for example, about the question of scholarly contacts. Should Western scholars maintain their ties with the old Soviet institutions exclusively (Academy of Sciences and universities), or should we seek new formal relations with the various new institutes, associations, organizations, and individuals now engaged in social, political, and economic research, or with those who are actors in forging new political and social institutions? The answer is a clear yes, though there was heated discussion about whether relations ought to be even maintained with colleagues (in the eyes of some seminar participants, tainted colleagues; see the paper of Martha Brill Olcott and the unpublished remarks in discussion by Roman Szporluk, for example) whose careers had been made during the last decades of the Soviet regime. What is the proper role of scholars who are now involved through their scholarly vocation in the planning of current policy in Russia and the successor states, or who by their choice of collaborators become participants in local or national politics?

On a general level the papers and discussions identified several themes or agendas that cut across the boundaries of the disciplines. These include the need for more historical work within the social sciences, a new comparative social science, more explicit recognition of the role of theory and more effective use of theory, greater emphasis on process and transitions, a shift in cultural studies away from high culture to popular culture broadly conceived (with the possibility that cultural studies, rather than traditional literature departments, may be the home for a freshly conceived study of culture in Russia and the successor states), and a recognition of the validity of the Soviet cultural experience.

Alternative Explanations for the Collapse of Communism and New Theories for the Future

The essays by Katherine Verdery and Michael Burawoy underscore some theoretical shortcomings of Sovietology and offer new paradigms and metaphors that help both to explain the collapse of communism (Verdery) and to offer insights into the social and economic transitions of Russia's present and future (Burawoy) even while working within and against the analyses of such seminal thinkers as Moshe Lewin and Ken Jowitt.

Lewin in his own elegant essay sums up his deep sense of social spontaneity in Soviet history and the power of societal forces and social groups to shape history and even the acts of acknowledged great leaders, not to mention lesser individuals. He provides an excellent taxonomy of the changes in the Soviet regime over time and dwells on the importance of bureaucracy and statism in all its forms, including social allegiances to particular institutions and institutional points of view (*vedomstvennost'*) as a unifying and driving force in Russian and Soviet history alike. Lewin's reluctance to take on the present and future stems, it would appear, from his belief in the open-endedness of history, his sense that the best guide to the future would be to understand the structures of the past and to adopt a cast of mind or attitude toward social phenomena that would allow for at least the elimination of the most egregious simplifications and ill-founded predictions of commentators on today's Russia.

Burawoy opens with a penetrating critique of the totalitarian model that emphasizes the social and corporatist elements in the Soviet system that in his view have not been swept away by what he sees as the nonrevolution of August 1991. Burawoy's respectful but strong critique of Lewin provides scholarly debate of these issues at its best, since Burawoy uses Lewin's major contributions about the structural social forces at work in Soviet history and their impact upon the present to move beyond Lewin to a new formulation based upon theoretically informed historical sociology (so ably practiced by Lewin himself) and impressive fieldwork in the factories and financial institutions of post-Soviet Russia (and earlier in those of communist Hungary as well). The problem as Burawoy sees it is Lewin's use of an undertheorized, residual category termed "society," his implicit use of a modernization model, and his unwillingness to face the future. Burawoy provides instead a suggestive discussion of how the Soviet administrative command economy tended to reproduce itself under new and rapidly changing conditions and how what has since emerged can be best termed a form of merchant capitalism, marked by the search for profit in trade and commerce rather than pure production, as would be the case in more advanced forms of capitalism.

For Burawoy, there is a danger in the facile application of Western models to today's Russia. Civil society, to take one example, is a process, not a thing. Burawoy shows on the basis of his own investigations and work experiences in Russian factories and banks that the answer to the question of Russian uniqueness must be that Russia is at once unique *and* different. Nothing must be assumed by the investigator. The new opportunities for work on site in Russia and the successor states informed by an intense historical and theoretical sensibility will underscore the profoundness and depth of the Russian experience. Russia can offer keys to historical processes unfolding around the globe even as the history and models of change of other nations will shape our understanding of Russia. We must constantly rework, reshape, and reimagine the language and categories of narrative and of analysis as we try to keep pace with transformation and ask the most fruitful historical questions about a Soviet past that after it has ended is in some respects still very much alive in the present and doubtless will continue to shape the future.

Verdery deploys just such new categories and new language in her anthropological dissection of Leninist political culture and the causes of the collapse of Leninist regimes. Acknowledging her debt to Ken Jowitt on the inner workings of Leninist regimes,[5] Verdery first defines socialism as a system designed to provide a minimum standard of living for its people but also designed to prevent them from becoming consumers. The system was enforced not by the "internalized discourses of bourgeois society," to use Reginald E. Zelnik's apt phrasing of Foucault's concept, but by the apparatus of surveillance. Consumer consciousness was the domestic key to the unraveling of the system, a kind of Trojan horse that put pressure on the state and all but undid the formal and informal arrangements that held things together. Verdery goes on to show how, beginning back in the 1960s, the socialist world embraced the capitalist, forging a symbiotic relationship that profoundly destabilized the socialist states. This explanation challenges, of course, the idea that it was mainly the Reagan administration arms buildup of the early 1980s that caused the Soviet meltdown. Verdery introduces time as a metaphor for the conflict of the two world systems and argues that the Soviet system, a way of life (social, cultural, organizational) defined by a notion of messianic time very different from that of capitalism (speed up), became a prisoner of "simultaneity," or the clash of two temporal systems. Seen in this light, such policies initiated by Mikhail Gorbachev as "speeding up the tempo" (*uskorenie*) take on new significance. Zelnik, a leading historian of imperial Russia and its labor movement, is especially taken with the freshness of Verdery's categories and anthropological analysis. Although Zelnik finds Verdery's use of dossier production to be a somewhat "precious" reduction of the system of controls used by communist regimes, he is inspired by Verdery to think historically about the presence in late imperial Russia and today of contradictory or overlapping patterns of development and value systems (legality versus traditional authority, or civil society and the market versus collectivism, for example).

David Holloway's lucid discussion of the study of Soviet foreign policy illustrates most clearly the problems that Soviet studies had in relating to the mainstream social science disciplines. While the Soviet field was mired in debates about national interests versus ideology in the formation of Soviet policy, international relations (IR) theory had moved in new directions that emphasized the psychological and organizational constraints upon decision making. Lack of access to sources made such approaches impossible for researchers in the Soviet field, however. When political scientists working in the Soviet field used international relations models, they most often misused them and tended to see a stable, "normal" Soviet foreign policy establishment rather than its internal dynamics and contradictions. The constant focus on war and the nuclear issue perhaps caused scholars to miss the other options for change in a nuclear age. Holloway clearly sees a large historical component in the field of Russian foreign policy (and the successor states), but he also proposes that researchers raise the question of the connection between Soviet foreign policy and that of Russia and the successor states.[6] There is a major task ahead in defining the new states and their identities as IR actors, their national interests, and the nature of their diplomatic and other international institutions. From Holloway's perspective IR theory will have little to say about such matters. What will be the new framework of international relations? Will Ukraine and the Baltic states be drawn into the European orbit, and Central Asia into that of Turkey and Iran?

In his commentary, unpublished here, Mark Katz shifted the focus to the present and future foreign policies of Russia and the successor states. He argued that the methods of Sovietology can no longer be applicable to these new subjects, which by definition have new roles in new international systems. For Katz, information is now flooding in about the new foreign policy publics in these states and the new influences that combine to form national interests. Katz remained sensitive to history, however, and seemed to hope that democratization in Russia will lead to a renunciation of imperial traditions.

John Mearsheimer, a national security policy expert from outside the Soviet field (and chair of political science at the University of Chicago), responded aggressively to Holloway and the assembled specialists on Soviet foreign policy (he declined to publish his paper). He claimed that the consensus of experts in the international relations and foreign policy fields was that Sovietology was weak in this area for the following reasons: (1) ideology, which Mearsheimer elaborated by stating that the ideological component was too high, the cold war interfered, liberals hated communism, and there were many émigrés in the Soviet studies field; (2) government funding, which restricted independent thinking among Sovietologists; (3) the data problem, which Mearsheimer said was not as great as Holloway claimed though he did admit that government control of the data was a problem for researchers because the government had a vested interest in seeing the USSR in a certain way; (4) the isolated nature of Soviet studies in universities, which was a critique of the research centers and institutes for their provincialism and lack of cross-fertilization with other areas of the universities and for their shaping of graduate students as clones of themselves, fellow travelers in the propagation of sterile approaches to the Soviet Union; and (5), finally and most important, the antagonism toward theory, which Mearsheimer defined succinctly and without jargon as generalizations that apply across space and time, a practice that should be followed by all social scientists. Mearsheimer perceived professionalization as having produced an unhealthy bifurcation between those who supposedly do engage in theoretical approaches and those who do not. This is an artificial distinction, said Mearsheimer, a false dichotomy. Good political science will anticipate counterarguments, make assumptions explicit, pay attention to competing explanations, show subtlety and flexibility and not rigidity, and be prepared to admit that a particular approach or application might be wrong. These abilities, according to Mearsheimer, were lost in the Soviet field, which in any case must be judged by its performance with available data; ideology blocked the subtlety, and people felt they had the answers so debate was foreclosed, making it all the harder for good social science to enter into the field's mainstream.

No subject has raised greater passions than the nationality question. Here the field of Soviet studies has absorbed many blows from critics who quite rightly proclaim that social scientists and historians were Russocentric in their studies of the Soviet Union, that they accepted the Moscow line on the existence of something called a Soviet person or national identity, and that they even turned away from potential research on nationality questions out of fear of being denied access to the Soviet Union itself (on the International Research and Exchanges Board, or IREX, for example) or of offending their hosts. Nowhere, except on the issue of Stalinism, do we find a more pointed intellectual and moral indictment. The relatively small, hardy, but always endangered band of specialists in the various non-Russian nationalities were so marginalized by their career experiences that the scars remain visible to the present day, even at a time when a good many of these scholars are in public demand as never before and when they may be seen frequently on television, heard on radio, observed in the halls of government, and are most highly sought after for important conferences.

The papers by Martha Brill Olcott and Ronald Grigor Suny and the commentary of Gale Stokes frame the issues extremely well. From Russocentrism to the constant making and remaking of national identity (along the lines of Benedict Anderson's "imagined communities"),[7] to the broad and long-term process of decolonialization and the end of empires (emphasized by Kingsley de Silva in his unpublished commentary at the session), to the need for critical history of both the mythos of the nationalities and the uses to which nationalism has been put by political leaders sometimes rooted in the past (the easy transition of some Communist Party officials to leadership in the new nations), to the scholar's need for immersion in the language and culture of the new states and for seeing them as having been part of a Soviet past as well as in new frames of reference (Stokes's "framing units"), whether European, Turkic, Muslim, Scandinavian, or whatever—the breakup of the Soviet Union demands a new commitment to the ethnic and national units that have revealed both the great promise of national liberation and its capacity to generate nightmarish violence and exclusivity. Finally we should not forget the twin questions of new Russian national identity or identities[8] and the historical but fertile and far-reaching matter (all too quickly dismissed as ridiculous, as something that never existed) of how to analyze the Soviet identity (including the process of nativization, or *korenizatsiia*) that denizens of the postcommunist order are too quick to deny.

In addition to the calls for historical and comparative studies that view the Soviet period as an incubator of new nations with new interests (expressed in new terminologies for both dominant and minority ethnic groups) or of regional groupings, for recognition of the notion that national formation in the USSR offers the best clues as to its unraveling and the new course in national and ethnic development, and for fieldwork with links to anthropology and ethnic studies, the discussion also brought forth the notion that Russia provides a larger than usual example of a frontier society or a sequence of edges, of a massive meeting place of peoples constantly in the process of mutual influence and enrichment. New and reinvented nations and other formations must not be studied only in their pristine and self-defined isolation.

Despite James R. Millar's pessimistic views of the future of Russian area studies in the field of economics—a pessimism driven by loss of intellectual raison d'être as much as funding and the advent of "interlopers" or trained economists from outside the area studies nest or even worse from Russia itself who have obtained economics training—scholars in economics seemed extremely well poised to take advantage of the rapidly changing situation in Russia and the successor states.

Not only could economists point to a range of writings during the last years of the Soviet period in which the blatant and hidden contradictions and problems of the administrative-command economy were rather well described and analyzed, but the field had done more than other social science disciplines to maintain its standing within its own discipline of economics (and the subfields therein, such as comparative economics and development economics). In addition, resources were put into the training of a new generation of economics graduate students during the 1980s, students who could legitimately claim to be both economists and experts in Russian area studies and who have already gone on to important academic posts in major research universities. Christopher Clague's commentary from outside the Soviet area pushed the discussion back toward the intellectual orientation of the field. Clague, an expert in international trade, economic development, and the new institutional economics, sees in the post-Soviet laboratory great possibilities for increasing our understanding of both capitalism and transitions. He downplays the economists' failure to predict the communist collapse and parries critics of the field by claiming that far more serious was the profession's failure to predict the degrees of economic and social disruption and decline that have accompanied attempted transitions to market economies. Clague connects this failure to economists' lack of appreciation of the institutional and cultural foundations of market economies.

In addition to representatives of all the earlier and highly accomplished generations in Millar's scheme, we were fortunate to have had several of these younger scholars whose views are represented here in the commentary of Thomas J. Richardson of Yale University. Richardson is an optimist, preferring to believe in a continuing academic demand for economic analysis of the Eurasian land mass—Eastern Europe and the former Soviet Union. For one thing, it is not at all clear that relations between the United States and Russia will remain friendly. Moreover, the task of helping Russia to build a market economy and democracy, if that is our national goal, will be an important and ongoing agenda indeed. Further, while it is true that specialists in planned economies have gone the way of the dinosaur, there is a growing need for specialists in labor economics, public finance, industrial organization, development, and macroeconomics. Richardson sees Russian area specialists integrating their work even more closely now into the mainstream of economics.

Formal presentations at the seminars inspired lively and productive discussion about society, politics, and culture, and here it is helpful to underscore the content of some of that discourse. Participants emphasized such themes as history and the question of continuity or continuities, for example in the question of whether Soviet nationalism was simply a variety of Russian historical nationalism and empire or something new. New research agendas put forth included the need to study concrete groups and occupations in society, the need for new taxonomies and definitions and descriptions of social arenas, and demographic work on gender, ethnicity, mortality, health, social differentiation, the family, social welfare, and the like. Michael Burawoy reinforced this call by proclaiming the need to study "internal variations" among social and occupational groups as they live through the transition process. Coal miners, for example, have responded differently from steelworkers to the challenges and opportunities of the late 1980s and 1990s, and the same can be said for entire industry branches, such as lumber compared to coal or oil. There was a strong sense that mass beliefs might be of greater importance than formal ideologies, a point reinforced by the seminar on culture. Others argued for more work on the changing fortunes of the state, the ongoing role of state institutions in their social and cultural complexity, and the importance of institutional location and culture (*vedomstvennost'*) as an organizing social and political principle. They pointed to state formation and center-periphery relations, the obvious fact that power is flowing to the regions and that the Russian Federation is in danger of going the way of the Soviet Union, that it is subject to the secession of constituent republics and new and possibly debilitating local claims upon resources, taxes, and the like. The idea of civil society may be too value laden and determinist, too fixed (as opposed to its uncontrollable nature as so well described in Moshe Lewin's paper and previous works) for analytical purposes in the Russian and post-Soviet context. For example, we would have no trouble identifying the classic notion of civil society with the emergence or existence of the *Rechtsstaat*, or the rule of law. Yet we all too easily proclaim its existence in Russia (or Eastern Europe) when the rule of law cannot be seen even on the distant horizon, when there are multiple and fluid social formations, where there may be no single path forward—the "multiple trajectories," as stated in the unpublished comments of Michael Burawoy. Another fertile subject is language and its role in shaping reality and history. In this revolutionary or transition period there must be studies of new languages much like those done during the 1920s. Language must be seen as the harbinger of new social realities, new social systems. Along similar lines, Mark von Hagen, in unpublished comments, reported that at Columbia graduate students were less interested in studying transitions to markets and democracy than in studying (and promoting) the human rights of minorities and ethnic groups, the environment, science, public health, and social welfare. Boris Mironov, a distinguished Russian social historian visiting for the year as a Woodrow Wilson Fellow, raised the need for a Russian history of daily life (*Alltagsgeshichte* or *byt*), a move into the social psychology of the regime, its mass support and nonsupport.

"Bring Russia in and create a better sociology," proclaimed Michael Burawoy at the society seminar (though he might well have substituted political science, political economy or any of the social sciences); and indeed echoes of the same idea could be heard among all the social scientists. And the idea was central to David Joravsky's claim that we must not confuse the problems of Sovietology with those of the host social science disciplines (for Joravsky these tend to be narrow, behaviorist, and ahistorical). The idea that post-Soviet studies could contribute to the disciplines was stated again and again, by defenders and detractors of Sovietology.

Political science remains at the heart of the debate over Sovietology, and here, too, there are positive signs. On the one hand, Thomas F. Remington's fair-minded and thorough review of the literature and contributions of Kremlinology shows that the field was far from asleep and that it made many noteworthy, if sometimes tentative, contributions despite the unprecedented research obstacles. I suspect that the difficulties inherent in the study of Soviet politics did not make that field attractive to many talented individuals who were drawn into the study of Russian history, literature, and language. On the other hand, there is a new wave of energetic scholars out in the field, mapping the workings of new institutions and political processes, conducting interviews, gathering data that we never imagined might be possible. Scholars are now working in enterprises, government offices, and collective farms; they are tracing privatization in agriculture and business, and they monitor elections and public opinion. It might be better for a time to have theoretical sophistication or precociousness take a backseat to this refreshing and sometimes more mundane task of information gathering.

Support for Remington's defense of the field came from the eminent comparativist Gabriel A. Almond. Almond argues that even in the early 1970s specialists had understood the "tectonics" of the system quite well. But Almond does chide Sovietologists mildly for underemphasizing the elite's use of force in maintaining the system and for failing to notice the decline in willingness to apply force that signaled the system's demise. For Almond, this loss of coercive will affected the very instruments of coercion themselves. Almond further takes the political scientists to task for underutilizing the relevant parts of modern-

ization and development theory dealing with state and nation building. He elegantly states the established theorem that state and nation
building must precede the process of democratization. And he argues
forcefully that the Russian transition is unlike that of the third world or
southern tier countries, because Russia has few third world characteristics. Remington and Almond agree that, in the ongoing bargaining
process between old and emerging elites, Russia reveals and expresses
oscillation between participatory and technocratic-authoritarian elements.

Representing a younger cohort of political scientists, Joel Hellman
and Mark Saroyan, in comments not published here, drove home the
counterargument that Sovietology had suffered from its distance from
mainstream, sophisticated political science, especially from such approaches as the new institutionalism (a similar movement or method
may be found among economists). In his recent study, *Red Sunset*,
Philip G. Roeder argues for the primacy of politics and explains the collapse of the Soviet Union in terms of the unraveling of "constitutional"
arrangements between party leaders and the sectors of the bureaucracy
(broadly conceived) that had buttressed their power and provided stability and predictability, that indeed were at the very heart of Soviet
power.[9] This volume includes an essay especially prepared for it on the
new institutionalism in political science by one of its practitioners,
Scott A. Bruckner, formerly of the Social Science Research Council.
Bruckner aims to save the honor of positivist, model-building social
science as applied to the last years of Soviet rule and the post-Soviet
era. According to Bruckner, social science should very much be in the
business of prediction, or at least aiming toward such an end, but
above all it ought to be concerned with explanations of how human beings make decisions and the frameworks in which they are made.
Bruckner borrows the notion of transactional costs from economics,
starting from the assumption that actors are rational and appropriating
a definition of institution, from Douglass North, also an economist. Institutions are "the rules of the game in a society, or more formally . . .
the humanly devised constraints that shape human interaction," the
frameworks and codes that are meant to regulate and make transactions possible.[10] Bruckner goes on to apply his model to periods of both
stagnation and transition, with special focus on the building of credible
commitments and governance structures. As a recipe for future political studies, Bruckner is opposed to the collection of theoretically unin-
formed empirical data, as important as they may be for understanding
how things work.[11] Peter Solomon, in unpublished comments, answered the charge that Sovietology had abandoned a moral view by

raising the danger of a new determinism, a history freshly minted that will treat the collapse as inevitable, a situation of no alternatives that will close discourse about the hows and whys of this watershed event. Some took a coldly pragmatic view, as did Harvard sociologist Liah Greenfeld, in comments also unpublished, who claimed that Sovietology did not fail, it simply ended.

The discussion of culture was very lively, signifying the vibrancy of cultural studies among scholars across a broad spectrum of disciplines. As the spirited papers by Nancy Condee and Richard Stites so clearly reveal, there is strong interest—one might even call it a movement—toward the study of popular culture and the overall history of Soviet culture, but a Soviet culture reconceived as a system of beliefs and symbols, the entire array of messages received by the population over time and especially at the crisis nodes during the demise of the Soviet Union and at present, as new codes and messages are produced and received by society. Important points were raised in the unpublished comments on this session. Katerina Clark argued that Slavists needed to break out of their isolation and parochialism, that they had to reexamine the borders of inquiry, both spatially and temporally. In her own work, for example, she has found that the 1920s cannot be understood without its resonances throughout the entire period from 1910 to 1940 and that Soviet culture of the New Economic Policy era was embedded in a Central European cultural vision that moved along a Berlin–Moscow–St. Petersburg/Leningrad axis. The American studies model might be appropriate, she offered, but in any case the notion of Russian particularism needed to be rethought, as did the notion that the study of greater numbers and more cultural activities or products would mean better Slavic cultural studies. Alfred Rieber echoed this last point by claiming that we have been obsessed with Russia's uniqueness and, therefore, guilty of isolation. The future demands, he argued, the study of Russian culture in relation to Europe, Greece, and Islam and the need to listen to the nondominant voices in Russian culture. George Gerbner criticized the papers for deemphasizing, or paying too little attention to the collapse of the Soviet Union and its causes, the reason that we were rethinking Soviet studies in the first place. According to Gerbner we need a holistic approach (we dare not say total), one that emphasizes new cultural conditions and institutions, especially the media, and that sees culture as a system of messages governing social relations, a totality of signification of all languages—visual and verbal. The media, particularly television but also the press, helped to accelerate the breakup of Soviet power, but now there are new institutions subject to global markets and a loss of internal support for other cultural institutions.

Gerbner argued that it was futile to study only one aspect of the media or culture (say, television or film or popular music) and that a more fruitful approach would recognize that the experience of modern popular culture is most like a religious experience and deserving therefore of similar methods of analysis. Social life is a total cultural experience requiring the monitoring and analysis of the entire cultural environment, or all the messages received from individuals from all sources within given units of time. Coming from another world, that of cultural anthropology, Jennifer Rayport of the University of Chicago proclaimed the need for theoretically informed fieldwork and the study of daily life (*byt*) now possible to degrees unimagined in the recent past. There seemed to be much hostility to traditional English and comparative literature departments for holding back Slavists in the struggle for scarce university resources and some disappointment with Slavic departments mired in the traditional study of high culture and written texts. The professional lives of the growing popular culture advocates can be highly restricted in the world of a Slavic department, where it may be hard to teach courses related to one's research (though these might attract many undergraduates), and there is a very real problem in the realm of graduate studies, where there was consensus that drastic modifications are needed in courses of study leading to the Ph.D.

Dissent from the popular culture agenda was led by Dean Worth, Victor Terras, and William Mills Todd III, in comments all unpublished. Worth objected strenuously to any attempt to set an agenda for the field, arguing that agenda setting goes against the spirit of scholarship and would curb creativity. Further, the Slavic field must not focus on the twentieth century to the exclusion of earlier periods and particularly of old Russian culture, the foundation of it all. We must work to ensure lasting results, Worth argued, not a body of work nullified by tomorrow's news. William Todd called for spark, energy, and moral relevance, proclaiming that until Russian studies speaks with the moral and political charge of cultural studies it must remain peripheral. But he did insist that some of the agenda called for in the papers by Condee and Stites was already long under way in the universities, that the cadre of theoretically informed scholars whose work was on a par with literary and cultural studies in other fields was larger than one might think, and that these accomplishments illustrated that study of the classic texts and authors must continue, a return in some senses as noted by Victor Terras to the structure of culture approaches of the prerevolutionary decades. Todd and the paper givers and commentators all called for new education for the professorate—seminars and workshops on how to integrate and use new cultural materials, new technologies, new approaches and the all-important need to keep language teaching as a priority, though informed by new cultural materials. The session also called for a heightened awareness of the impact of internationalization and penetration of the market within Russia, with their attendant loss of support for traditional cultural endeavors and the in telligentsia and the difficulties in the production and distribution of cultural artifacts and the like.

In this manner the discussions grew out of the fertile soil of the formal papers and commentaries. Their essence amounted to a set of themes common to all the disciplines, a set of topics or questions to guide future research that includes an even greater emphasis on cultural and social factors, the mapping of new institutions and their work and how values shape politics and economics even as they in turn influence social consciousness and identity. Scholars agreed that a desired goal is "understanding" rather than the ability to predict, a balance between grasping the deep structures and the rule of contingent factors in history and the problem of aging, including the role of personalities. They also aimed to use the Russian example, the breakup of the Soviet Union, to generate new theories and methods and imaginative approaches that could be integrated into social science or could contribute to its general development and practice. They called for attention to history and the emergence of new ideologies and identities. They saw a need to trace the emergence of new international subsystems among the former Soviet republics, especially their foreign policy interests, economic relations, and political and cultural ties. The unprecedented breakup of this unprecedented empire will lead to new irredentisms, boundaries, and nationalisms. The role of the military will require very close scrutiny, as there seemed to be no unified military voice in strategic matters or in larger policy making. Finally, the field must be watchful of intellectual self-limitation and compartmentalization. Cultural studies and social history, for example, may lead in interest at this time, but their practitioners should not be closed to the findings and subject matter of scholars working in foreign policy or politics. The list is long but indicative of the intrinsic interest and importance of post-Soviet realities in Eurasia. The soup becomes more aromatic, maybe not such a bad place to be at all.

Beyond Soviet Studies: Historical Postscript

Historical problems permeate much of the debate over Soviet studies. How can we define revolution? Was there a revolution under Mikhail

Gorbachev, or in August 1991? Are there analogies to the February and October Revolutions of 1917? On the issue of predictability, were the analyses of Sovietologists so fundamentally flawed as to render the field blind to the coming change? Finally, what caused the demise of the USSR and the communist regime (now also a historical problem)?[12] There are no easy answers to such questions, but I offer a few observations that may help in framing future discussions. As already noted, most Kennan Seminar participants rejected the idea that social science was in the business of prediction (Thomas Remington's analogy of "underlying tectonics" sums it up), although Michael Burawoy dissented vigorously from this point of view; for him good social science always predicts by its very nature and then assimilates history to predict again. A more concrete issue was that of the logic of the often misunderstood and oversimplified totalitarian model and especially the notion of inevitability of the Soviet collapse and the "new democratic revolution." This is not the place for a full discussion of the totalitarian model or models,[13] but if we assume, as do some proponents of that model, that a totalitarian state is indeed a completely interconnected set of institutions, a unique, or very rare historical phenomenon, then such a system cannot by definition be reformed piece by piece, gradually, or in stages. No part may be changed significantly because each element—political, economic, social, cultural—is so interwoven as to be inseparable and intractable. But the same thing is often said about the pre-1917 tsarist autocracy, namely that all the parts were connected and the problem with reform (the Great Reforms of the 1860s and 1870s, or Piotr Stolypin's reforms, for example) was that the government could not change things in one or several sectors without working to reform the entire system, that the abolition of serfdom, for example, or agrarian reform in general, entailed a whole range of accompanying reforms—of local government, civil rights, legal affairs, economics, the military, and more. Of course, defenders of unsubtle totalitarian models will fall back and claim that the twentieth-century totalitarian regime, and especially the Soviet Union, is qualitatively different from any other form of state, that it is not subject to the same historical laws, that it is beyond the realm of comparative politics and history. But this is an unprovable claim that lies in the realm of philosophy (and idealism to be more specific). When this point of view is applied to the Gorbachev–August 1991–Yeltsin era, the Gorbachev reforms were doomed as a matter of historical necessity.

Yet all revolutions have created the perspective in which previous reform efforts appear doomed. The powerful old regimes in history appear either invincible and stable or at least in crisis, but reformable. By the logic of the totalitarian school, the successful revolution of Boris Yeltsin and democracy signifies the absolute unreformability of the Soviet regime, with its party and social and economic system and the necessity of their collapse. It would follow by historical analogy that the successful revolution of V. I. Lenin and the Bolsheviks, or even of the February democrats (liberals and socialists) implies the absolute impossibility of the reform of the autocratic regime of Tsar Nicholas II. Yet it is a cornerstone (even an article of faith) of liberal—not to mention conservative or nationalist—discourse about Russia's 1917 Revolutions that the regime of the tsar was indeed reformable and that it in fact was being reformed and transformed into a parliamentary regime resting upon civil society. Signs of this transformation included the Stolypin reforms, the emergence of autonomous social groups, and the development of middle-class culture, entrepreneurial attitudes and organizations, and the limited or constitutional monarchy. Some of the critics of Gorbachev and skeptics about Soviet reform often hold steadfastly, when they write of Russian history, to the idea of a modified constitutional monarchy moving ever closer to European norms that was destroyed by the contingent factors of world war and conspiratorial intelligentsia. Here they would claim that Soviet totalitarianism was unique in history and not at all to be compared to tsarism (a brand of authoritarianism that at least allowed the existence of nascent civil society). Granted, the Soviet experience was in so many ways tragic. The point is, however, that reforming regimes may or may not turn revolutionary and the process of renovation and reform once engaged leads to uncertain outcomes in large measure determined by a variety of intervening conjunctures and events. But the critics of Sovietology alluded to here hold that the Soviet Union is historically unique, not subject to universal patterns of change and not even describable in the language of historical analysis.[14] The answer is again to be sought in perspective; people at the time did not believe tsarism to be weak enough to collapse in five bloodless days. And once it did, very few had the sense that "utopia" would come to power, or that five-year plans, antikulak campaigns, and bloody purges would be unleashed.

Revolutions are inherently unpredictable processes marked by surprising and unpredictable events. Even in September and October 1917, Lenin demanded that the Bolsheviks seize power immediately because he believed that the conditions for a successful coup could very likely be lost by either a German advance or some new strategy of Premier Aleksandr Kerensky and the Provisional Government. After the July Days, it appeared that the Bolsheviks were significantly weakened and the Provisional Government strengthened. Was this situation only a surface manifestation that could not stand up to the powerful social forces at work, or was it an indication of contingency, of the fact that different individual decisions might have saved the Provisional Government and hence the February Revolution? There is no doubt that the events of the past ten years, including the demise of the Soviet Union, amount to a revolution. We have witnessed a revolution no less profound than that of 1917–21 (or perhaps 1917–29). The Soviet empire is no more, and the antiliberal, antimarket, socialist agenda of Soviet-style communism is now rubble. What is even more surprising, at least in terms of comparative history of revolutions, is the fact that this revolution occurred when the Soviet Union was not at war and in fact after it had begun to scale down significantly its overseas commitments. We are now witnessing the working out of this revolutionary process, now presenting itself in terms of discourse directly opposed to those of 1917–21. Now the rush is to establish the market and capitalism, to proclaim the victory of democracy, to change the habits and manner of life of an entire population brought up under one set of institutions and symbols (and language). The attempt to build democracy and capitalism, to establish the market, and to change the everyday life (*byt*) of this vast nation is itself revolution, no less so than the Bolshevik destruction of entire social classes, the market, and establishment of the administrative-command system. But where should we date the beginning of the revolution? Did it happen with the failed August 1991 coup, or can we push the date back to the June 1990 election of Boris Yeltsin as president of Russia, or to the Nineteenth Party Conference at which Gorbachev launched his own ambivalent coup against his own party? Or do we want to push it even further back to the beginning of the Gorbachev years and Gorbachev's initial calls for perestroika and glasnost, his advocacy of a return to the true Leninist spirit of the October Revolution, which in Gorbachev's terms meant a return to his own mythology of a popular, Leninist revolution and democratic soviet power, decentralized, participatory "democracy," a kind of permanent revolution of newly legitimized state and social power that could renovate and renew the country (within the existing framework or "constitution")?

When talking about today's revolution in Russia, we tend to forget that in 1917 there were two revolutions, a February one marked by the collapse (implosion) of the old regime and the establishment of a liberal and then broadly socialist democratic order that had its own revolutionary agenda: the establishment of rule of law, breaking the power of bureaucracy and police, civil rights, autonomy for the nationalities, self-government, and the like. The February Revolution aimed to make its revolution permanent through a constituent assembly to be elected by the most democratic electoral law ever used in Russian history. Perhaps the best way of viewing Gorbachev was as a conscious maintainer and renovator of the system (yet one who was most certainly unaware of the consequences of his actions and of the power of history), similar to the great Russian statesman and administrator Stolypin, and an unconscious revolutionary who most certainly unleashed the forces of radical transformative change (in terms of both domestic policy and the "new thinking" in foreign policy abetting the collapse of the Soviet Union's Eastern European empire) that resulted in the end of the USSR and the still open-ended process we witness today. We are still in the midst of this revolution; the outcomes are still to a large extent open just as they were for some years after the October Revolution. Though the logic, ideology, and revolutionary experience of the Bolshevik Party (1917–27) doubtless predisposed it toward certain authoritarian structures and policies, Josef Stalin or the Soviet government still did not have to opt for collectivization or any other extreme mobilizing measures that subsequently marked the tragic history of the Soviet Union. Even if we concede that the general path toward capitalism and democracy are now chosen, now irreversible, still the exact manner, the relative participation and power of state and society, the tempo and physiognomy of change remain to be worked out. A look at contemporary China should be enough to convince. Hence the importance of our subject—the need to redefine, revive, and restore Russian-Soviet studies, the need to have the best possible sense of the future based on solid understanding of the past, including the Soviet past. Even the most impressive analysis of high elite politics (Yeltsin and the democrats versus the former Congress of People's Deputies or defenders of corporate authoritarian interests, for example) is not enough. It cannot substitute for and must be complemented by studies that embrace the many layers of state, society, and nation. We are dealing with revolution and transformation, a transition on a scale and with implications rarely seen in world history.[15] The post-Soviet field must be up to this task; it must recognize its weaknesses and strengths, its failings of imagination and sensitivity, and it must formulate new, clear objectives that can speak to academic disciplines and the wider public alike. Scholars in post-Soviet studies have a rare opportunity to chronicle and analyze the later stages of this new Russian revolution as it unfolds.

No matter how repugnant or "foreign" the Soviet experience must seem, it still must be understood in all its workings, cultural codes, patterns of authority, and social dynamics. The Kennan discussion produced a strong sense that whatever the future may hold, it will be very profoundly shaped by the immediate past, by the Soviet past, by failed dreams, by a vast panorama of unprecedented human mobilization, by seventy years of administrative-command economy, by the abolition of the market, by bureaucratization, and by hostility to the liberal institutions associated with abused concepts such as civil society.

Notes

I wish to thank Richard Stites, Lewis Siegelbaum, Reginald Zelnik, Abbott Gleaver, Blair Ruble, Dan Abele, and Joe Brinley of the Woodrow Wilson Center Press for their incisive commentaries on various drafts of this essay. I also thank the Kennan Institute staff, and especially Monique Principi for her valiant labor in organizing the workshops, Peggy McInerney for her efforts in recording and transcribing, and Dan Abele for wise counsel throughout and for helping to conduct the often delicate negotiations with scholars about their participation and contributions. Blair Ruble did his usual masterful job of chairing the sessions at the Kennan. Mildred Pinkston of the SMU History Department worked miracles with a most difficult manuscript. Finally, thank-you to all the participants who made the seminars a rewarding experience.

¹I use "Sovietology" here to describe the research of scholars (in academe, government, research institutes, and any other organizations) in the social sciences and humanities who do research on the Soviet period, 1917–91, and on Russia and/or the successor states after 1991 with an aim of understanding the workings of the current regime in power (or its immediate predecessor) and its supporting social and political institutions. The term "Soviet studies" here has a broader connotation to include historical and cultural studies that are less focused on the present.

²Martin Malia, "From under the Rubble, What?" *Problems of Communism* 41, nos. 1–2 (1992): 91.

³Peter Rutland has already used "damage control" to describe the attitudes of the political scientists at the Kennan Institute Seminar on politics. "Sovietology: Notes for a Post Mortem," *National Interest* no. 31 (1993): 109–22.

⁴See Daniel Orlovsky, "The New Soviet History," *Journal of Modern History* 62, no. 4 (1990): 831–50. There is no doubt that a field emerged in the 1980s that can be called "new Soviet history," just as there is no doubt that some of the sharpest polemics surrounding Soviet studies have revolved around the findings of some writers of that history; see the recent works of Martin Malia, Robert Conquest, or Richard Pipes, three very different historians, in terms of method and subject matter. Still the primary goal of the Kennan Seminars was to address the disciplines most directly concerned with present and future. We had a sense that all the seminars would call forth heated exchange about history, about the need to integrate historical perspectives into analysis of present and views of the future, and about whether the historical profession (or at least historians of the Soviet era, an era that can now be studied as a closed epoch, like, for example, Nazi Germany, the Weimar Republic, or the Byzantine Empire) was least at risk of disappearing or losing its moorings due to the collapse of Soviet power.

⁵Ken Jowitt, *New World Disorder: The Leninist Extinction* (Berkeley: University of California Press, 1992).

⁶David Holloway particularly emphasizes the new archival findings pertaining to the cold war and gave the example of documents showing Josef Stalin's personal approval given to the Koreans to begin war in 1950 and the major role played by his death in ending the conflict.

⁷John B. Dunlop, *The Rise of Russia and the Fall of the Soviet Empire* (Princeton: Princeton University Press, 1993).

⁸See especially the works of John Dunlop, who at the seminar argued that there was little continuity between the Russian and Soviet empires, that the Russian Empire was not based upon ethnicity (Russification came very late in its history), that Soviet Russia was not the same thing as Russia as it was driven by ideology much more than by the inherited national identity, and that in historical terms the Russians were not an imperial people. In the Soviet era they saw other nationalities as being privileged. On the question of new Russian identities, Dunlop identified four: (1) reds and browns—that is, die-hard communists and the right; (2) atlanticists; (3) democratic *gosudarstvenniki* or statists; and (4) Eurasians, who wish to keep the Slavs and Muslim-Turkic peoples together. See John Dunlop, "Russia: Confronting a Loss of Empire," in *Nation and Politics in the Soviet Successor States*, ed. Ian Bremmer and Ray Taras (Cambridge: Cambridge University Press, 1993), 43–72. For Dunlop's arguments on the qualitative differences between the Russian and Soviet empires, see his review of *The Hidden Nations: The People Challenge the Soviet Union*, by N. Diuk and D. Karatnycky, *American Political Science Review* 86, no. 1 (1992): 262–64.

⁹Philip G. Roeder, *Red Sunset: The Failure of Soviet Politics* (Princeton: Princeton University Press, 1993). On the post-Soviet problems of state building and the nature of the Yeltsin government, see Peter J. Stavrakis, "State Building in Post-Soviet Russia: The Chicago Boys and the Decline of Administrative Capacity," Kennan Institute Occasional Paper 254 (Washington, D. C., 1993). The author documents the failure of the Gaidar government to create new institutions, amounting to the decline of the state.

¹⁰Douglass C. North, *Institutions, Institutional Change and Economic Performance* (Cambridge: Cambridge University Press, 1990), 3. See also Mancur Olson, *The Rise and Decline of Nations: Economic Growth, Stagflation, and Social Rigidities* (New Haven: Yale University Press, 1982); James G. March and Johan P. Olsen, *Rediscovering Institutions: The Organizational Basis of Politics* (New York: The Free Press, 1989).

¹¹An excellent example of the new institutionalism is Joel Hellman, "Breaking the Bank: Bureaucrats and the Creation of Markets in a Transitional Economy" (Ph.D. diss., Columbia University, 1993). Some recent examples of solid and deep empirical fieldwork include Michael Burawoy's work in factories, mines, and banks; Cynthia Buckley's work in Siberian collective farms, Kathryn Stoner-Weiss's work on local government performance in Nizhnyi Novgorod, Yaroslavl, Saratov, and Tiumen'; Peter Stavrakis's work on state building and the bureaucracy; and the very important work of Stephen Wegren on contemporary agriculture based largely on extensive fieldwork in Kostroma (and also well informed by both Russian and Soviet history and comparative models drawn from the agricultural sector in third world countries). On agrarian policy see Stephen K. Wegren, "Agricultural Reform in the Nonchernozem Zone: The Case of Kostroma Oblast," *Post Soviet Geography* 33, no. 10 (1992); Wegren, "Two Steps Forward and One Step Back: The Politics of an Emerging New Rural Social Policy in Russia," *Soviet and Post Soviet Review* 19 (1992): 1–51; Wegren, "Rural Reform and Political Culture in Russia," *Europe-Asia Studies* 46, no. 2 (1994): 215–41.

¹²Alexander Dallin has written an excellent analysis of the causes of Mikhail Gorbachev's downfall and response to the "essentialist" argument in "Causes of the Collapse

of the USSR," *Post Soviet Affairs* 8, no. 4 (1992): 279–302.

[13]See Abbott Gleason's forthcoming study of totalitarianism in the twentieth century, to be published by Oxford University Press in 1994.

[14] Here Richard Pipes and Martin Malia unite, the advocates of Russian political culture, material conditions, institutions, the nature of the intelligentsia versus Marxism as the cause of the tragic utopia in power.

[15]The literature on transitions to democracy is very large, and already much ink has been spilled on the applicability of this material to the post-Soviet and Eastern Europe cases. See Philippe C. Schmitter and Terry Lynn Karl, "The Conceptual Travels of Transitologists and Consolidologists: How Far to the East Should They Attempt to Go?" *Slavic Review* 53, no. 1 (1994): 173–85.

Part I

Social Perspectives on Soviet History, the Demise of Communism, and the Ongoing Transition

Chapter 1

What Was Socialism, and Why Did It Fall?

Katherine Verdery

The startling disintegration of Communist Party rule in Eastern Europe in 1989, and its somewhat lengthier unraveling in the Soviet Union between 1985 and 1991, rank among the century's most momentous occurrences. Especially because neither policymakers nor area specialists predicted them, these events will yield much analysis after the fact, as scholars develop the hindsight necessary to understanding what they failed to grasp before. In this essay, I aim to stimulate discussion about why Soviet-style socialism fell. Since answers to the question require understanding how socialism "worked," I begin with a model of this; I then suggest how it intersected fatefully with certain features of the world-system context.

What Was Socialism?

The "formerly existing" socialist[1] states of Eastern Europe and the Soviet Union differed significantly from each other—for instance, in the intensity, effectiveness, and span of central control, in the extent of popular support or resistance, and in the degree and timing of reforms. I opt, nevertheless, for a single model of them. The resemblances within socialism were more important than its variety, for analytic purposes, much as we can best comprehend French, Japanese, West German, and U.S. society as variants of a single capitalist system. Acknowledging, then, that my description applies more fully to certain countries and time periods than to others, I treat them all under one umbrella.

For several decades, the analysis of socialism has been an international industry, employing both Western scholars and Eastern dissidents. This industry has lately received a massive infusion of new raw materials, as once-secret files are opened and translations appear of research by local scholars (especially Polish and Hungarian) into their own declining socialist systems.[2] My own taste in such theories is "indigenist": I have found most useful the analyses of Eastern Europeans concerning the world in which they lived. The following summary, which is subject to revision as new material appears, owes much to that work.[3] Given temporal and spatial constraints, I will compress elements of a larger analytical model.[4] I will emphasize how production was organized and the consequences of this for consumption and for markets, themes that afford the best entry into why party rule crumbled much faster than anyone expected.

PRODUCTION

Socialism's fragility begins with the system of "centralized planning," which the center neither adequately planned nor controlled.[5] Central planners would draw up a plan with quantities of everything they wanted to see produced, known as targets. They would disaggregate the plan into pieces appropriate for execution, estimating how much investment and how many raw materials were needed if managers of firms were to fill their targets. Managers learned early on, however, that not only did the targets increase annually, but the materials required often did not arrive on time or in the right amounts. So they would respond by bargaining their plan: demanding more investments and raw materials than the amounts actually necessary for their targets. Every manager, and every level of the bureaucracy, padded budgets and requests in hopes of having enough, in the actual moment of production. (A result of the bargaining process, of course, was that central planners always had faulty information about what was really required for production, and this impeded their ability to plan.) Then, if managers somehow ended up with more of some material than they needed, they hoarded it. Hoarded material had two uses: it could be kept for the next production cycle, or it could be exchanged with some other firm for something one's own firm lacked. These exchanges or barters of material were a crucial component of behavior within centralized planning.

A result of all the padding of budgets and hoarding of materials was widespread shortages, for which reason socialist economies are called *economies of shortage*.[6] The causes of shortage were primarily that people lower down in the planning process were asking for more materials than they required and then hoarding whatever they got. Underlying their behavior was what economists call *soft budget constraints*—namely, if a firm was losing money, the center would bail it out. In our own economy, with certain exceptions (such as Chrysler and the savings and loan industry), budget constraints are *hard*—if you cannot make ends meet, you go under. But in socialist economies, it did not matter if firms asked for extra investment or hoarded raw materials; they paid no penalty.

With all this padding and hoarding, it is clear why shortage was endemic to socialist systems and why the main problem for firms was not whether they could meet (or generate) demand but whether they could procure adequate supplies. So while the chief problem of economic actors in Western economies is to get profits by *selling* things, the chief problem for socialism's economic actors was to *procure* things. Capitalist firms compete with each other for markets in which they will make a profit; socialist firms competed to maximize their bargaining power with suppliers higher up. In our society, the problem is other sellers, and to outcompete them you have to befriend the buyer. Thus, our clerks and shopkeepers smile and give the customer friendly service because they want business; customers can be grouchy and it will only make the clerk try harder. In socialism, the locus of competition was elsewhere: your competitor was other buyers, other procurers, and to outcompete them you needed to befriend those higher up who supplied you. Therefore, in socialism it was not the clerks—the providers, or "sellers"—who were friendly (they were usually grouchy) but the procurers, the customers, who sought to ingratiate themselves with smiles, bribes, or favors. The work of procuring generated whole networks of cozy relations among economic managers and their bureaucrats, clerks and their customers. We would call this corruption, but that is because getting supplies is not a problem for capitalists; the problem is getting sales. In a word, for capitalists *salesmanship* is at a premium; for socialist managers, the premium was on *acquisitionsmanship*, or procurement.

So far I have been describing the clientelism and bargaining that undercut the party center's effective control. A similar weakness in vertical power relations emerges from the way socialist production and shortage bred workers' oppositional consciousness and resistance. Among the many things in short supply in socialist systems was labor. Managers hoarded labor, just like any other raw material, because they never knew how many workers they would need. Fifty workers working three eight-hour shifts six days a week might be enough to meet a firm's targets—if all the materials were on hand all month long. But this never happened. Many of those workers would stand idle for part of the month, and in the last ten days when most of the materials were finally on hand the firm would need seventy-five workers working overtime to complete the plan. The manager therefore kept seventy-five workers on the books, even though most of the time he needed fewer; and since all other managers were doing the same, labor was scarce. This provided a convenient if unplanned support for the regimes' guaranteed employment.

An important result of labor's scarcity was that managers of firms had relatively little leverage over their workers. Furthermore, because supply shortages caused so much uncertainty in the production process, managers had to turn over to workers much control over this process, lest work come to a standstill.[7] That is, structurally speaking, workers under socialism had a somewhat more powerful position relative to management than do workers in capitalism. Just as managers' bargaining with bureaucrats undercut central power, so labor's position in production undercut that of management.

More than this, the very organization of the workplace bred opposition to party rule. Through the party-controlled trade union and the frequent merger of party and management functions, party directives were continually felt in the production process, and, from the workers' viewpoint, they were felt as unnecessary and disruptive. Union officials either meddled unhelpfully or contributed nothing, only to claim credit for production results that workers knew were their own. Workers participated disdainfully—as sociologist Michael Burawoy found in his studies of Hungarian factories—in party-organized production rituals, such as work-unit competitions, voluntary workdays, and production campaigns; they resented these coerced expressions of their supposed commitment to a wonderful socialism.[8] Thus, instead of securing workers' consent, workplace rituals sharpened their consciousness and resistance. Against an official *cult of work* used to motivate cadres and workers toward fulfilling the plan, many workers developed an oppositional *cult of nonwork*, imitating the party bosses and trying to do as little as possible for their paychecks. Cadres often found no way around this internal sabotage, which by reducing productivity deepened the problems of socialist economies to the point of crisis.

The very forms of party rule in the workplace, then, tended to focus, politicize, and turn against it the popular discontent that capitalist societies more successfully disperse, depoliticize, and deflect. In this way, socialism produced a split between "us" and "them," workers and party leaders, founded on a lively consciousness that "they" are exploiting "us." This consciousness was yet another thing that undermined socialist regimes. To phrase it in Gramscian terms, the lived experience of people in socialism precluded its utopian discourse from becoming hegemonic—precluded, that is, the softening of coercion with consent.[9]

SURVEILLANCE AND PATERNALISTIC REDISTRIBUTION

Ruling communist parties developed a variety of mechanisms to try to obscure the fact of their nature from their subjects, mechanisms designed to produce docile subject dispositions and to ensure that discontent did not become effective opposition. I will briefly discuss two of these mechanisms: the apparatus of surveillance, and redistribution of the social product.

In each country, some equivalent of the KGB was instrumental in maintaining surveillance, with varying degrees of intensity and success. Particularly effective were the secret police in the Soviet Union, East Germany, and Romania, but networks of informers and collaborators operated to some extent in all. These formed a highly elaborate "production" system parallel to the system for producing goods—a system producing paper, which contained real and falsified histories of the people over whom the party ruled. Let us call the immediate product "dossiers," or "files," though the ultimate product was political subjects and subject dispositions useful to the regime. This parallel production system was at least as important as the system for producing goods, for producers of files were much better paid than producers of goods. My image of this parallel production system comes from the memoirs of Romanian political prisoner Herbert Zilber.

> The first great socialist industry was that of the production of files. . . . This new industry has an army of workers: the informers. It works with ultramodern electronic equipment (microphones, tape recorders, etc.), plus an army of typists with their typewriters. Without all this, socialism could not have survived. . . . In the socialist bloc, people and things exist only through their files. All our existence is in the hands of him who possesses files and is constituted by him who constructs them. Real people are but the reflection of their files.[10]

The work of producing files (and thereby political subjects) created an atmosphere of distrust and suspicion dividing people from one another. One never knew whom one could trust, who might be informing on one to the police about one's attitudes toward the regime or one's having an American to dinner. Declarations might also be false. Informers with a denunciation against someone else were never asked what might be their motive for informing; their perhaps-envious words entered directly into constituting another person's file—thus, another person's sociopolitical being. Moreover, like all other parts of the bureaucracy, the police, too, padded their "production" figures, for the fact of an entry into the file was often more important than its veracity.[11] The existence of the shadowy system of production could have grave effects on the people "processed" through it, and the assumption that it was omnipresent contributed much to its success, in some countries, in repressing unwanted opposition.

If surveillance was the negative face of these regimes' problematic legitimation, its positive face was their promises of social redistribution and welfare. At the center of both the party's official ideology and its efforts to secure popular support was *socialist paternalism*, which justified party rule with the claim that the party would take care of everyone's needs by collecting the total social product and then making available whatever people needed—cheap food, jobs, medical care, affordable housing, education, and so on. Party authorities claimed, as well, that they were better able to assess and fill these needs than were individuals or families, who would always tend to want more than their share. Herein lay the party's paternalism: it acted like a father who gives handouts to the children as he sees fit. The benevolent father–party educated people to express needs it would then fill and discouraged them from taking the initiative that would enable them to fill these needs on their own. The promises—socialism's basic social contract—did not go unnoticed, and as long as economic conditions permitted their partial fulfillment, certain socialist regimes gained legitimacy as a result. But this proved impossible to sustain.

Beyond its effects on people's attitudes, paternalism had important consequences for the entire system of production discussed above and for consumption; here I shift to the question of why consumption was so central in the resistance to socialism. A party that pretends to meet its citizens' needs through redistribution and that insists on doing so exclusively—that is, without enlisting their independent efforts—must control a tremendous fund of resources to redistribute. Nationalizing the means of production helped provide this, and so did a relentlessly "productionist" orientation, with ever-increased production plans and exhortations to greater effort.

The promise of redistribution was an additional reason, besides my earlier argument about shortages, why socialism worked differently from capitalism. Socialism's inner drive was to accumulate not (as in capitalism) *profits*, but *distributable resources*. This is more than simply a drive for autarchy, reducing dependency on the outside; it aims to increase dependency of those within. Striving to accumulate resources for redistribution involves things for which profit is totally irrelevant. In capitalism, those who run lemonade stands endeavor to serve thirsty customers in ways that make a profit and outcompete other lemonade stand owners. In socialism, the point was not profit but the relationship between thirsty persons and the one with the lemonade— the party center, which appropriated from producers the various ingredients (lemons, sugar, water) and then mixed the lemonade to reward them with, as it saw fit. Whether someone made a profit was irrelevant: the transaction underscored the center's paternalistic superiority over its citizens, that is, its capacity to decide who got more and less lemonade.

Controlling the ingredients fortified the center's capacity to redistribute things. But this capacity would be even greater if the center controlled not only the lemons, sugar, and water but the things they come from—the lemon trees, the ground for growing sugar beets and the factories that process them, the wells and the well-digging machinery. That is, most valuable of all to the socialist bureaucracy was to get its hands not just on resources but on resources that generated other usable resources, resources that were themselves further productive. Socialist regimes wanted not just eggs but the goose that lays them. Thus, if capitalism's inner logic rests on accumulating *surplus value*, the inner logic of socialism was to accumulate *means of production*.[12]

The emphasis on keeping resources at the center for redistribution is one reason why items produced in socialist countries so often proved uncompetitive on the world market. Basically, most of these goods were not being made to be sold competitively; they were being either centrally accumulated or redistributed at low prices—effectively given away. Thus, whether a dress was pretty and well made or ugly and missewn was irrelevant, since profit was not at issue; the dress would be "given away" at a subsidized price, not sold. In fact, the whole point was *not* to sell things. The center wanted to keep as much as possible under its control, because that was how it had redistributive power; and it wanted to give away the rest, because that was how it confirmed its legitimacy with the public. Selling things competitively was therefore beside the point. So, too, were ideas of "efficient" production, which for a capitalist would enhance profits by wasting less material or reducing wages. But whatever goes into calculating a profit—costs of material or labor inputs, or sales of goods—was unimportant in socialism until very late in the game. Instead, "efficiency" was understood to mean "the full use of existing resources," "the maximization of given capacities" rather than of results, all so as to redirect resources to a goal greater than satisfying the population's needs.[13] In other words, what was rational in socialism differed from capitalist rationality. Both are stupid in their own way, but differently so.

CONSUMPTION

Socialism's redistributive emphasis leads to one of the great paradoxes of a paternalist regime claiming to satisfy needs. Having constantly to amass means of production so as to enhance redistributive power caused party leaders to prefer heavy industry (steel mills, machine construction) at the expense of consumer industry (processed foods, or shoes). After all, once a consumer got hold of something, the center no longer controlled it; central power was less served by giving things away than by producing things it could continue to control. The central fund derived more from setting up a factory to make construction equipment than from a shoe factory or a chocolate works. In short, these systems had a basic tension between what was necessary to *legitimate* them—redistributing things to the masses—and what was necessary to their *power*—accumulating things at the center. The tension was mitigated where people took pride in the economy's development (that is, building heavy industry might also bring legitimacy), but my experience is that the legitimating effects of redistribution were more important by far.

Each country addressed this tension in its own way. For example, Hungary after 1968 and Poland in the 1970s gave things away more, while Romania and Czechoslovakia accumulated things more; but the basic tension existed everywhere. The socialist social contract guaranteed people food and clothing but did not promise (as capitalist systems do) quality, ready availability, and choice. Thus, the system's mode of operation tended to sacrifice consumption in favor of production and controlling the products. This paradoxical neglect of consumption contributed to the long lines about which we heard so much (and we heard about them, of course, because we live in a system to which consumption is crucial).

In emphasizing this neglect of consumption as against building up the central resource base, I have so far been speaking of the *formally* organized economy of socialism—some call it the "first" or "official" economy. But this is not the whole story. Since the center would not supply what people needed, they struggled to do so themselves, developing in the process a huge repertoire of strategies for obtaining consumer goods and services. These strategies, called the "second" or "informal" economy, spanned a wide range from the quasi-legal to the definitely illegal.[14] In most socialist countries it was not illegal to moonlight for extra pay—by doing carpentry, say—but people doing so often stole materials or illegally used tools from their workplace, or they might manipulate state goods to sell on the side. Clerks in stores might earn favors or extra money, for example, by saving scarce goods to sell to special customers, who tipped them or did some important favor in return. Also part of the second economy was the so-called private plot of collective farm peasants, who held it legally and in theory could do what they wanted with it—grow food for their own table or to sell in the market at state-controlled prices. But although the plot itself was legal, people obtained high outputs from it not just by virtue of hard work but also by stealing from the collective farm—fertilizer and herbicides, fodder for their pigs or cows, work time for their own weeding or harvesting, tractor time and fuel for plowing their plot, and more. The second economy, then, which supplied a large part of consumer needs, was parasitic upon the state economy and inseparable from it. It developed precisely because the state economy tended to ignore consumption.

It is clear from what I have said that whereas consumption in our own society is considered primarily a socioeconomic question, the relative neglect of consumer interests in socialism made consumption deeply political. In Romania in the 1980s (an extreme case), to kill and eat your own calf was a political act, because the government prohibited killing calves: you were supposed to sell them cheap to the state farm, for export. Romanian villagers who fed me veal (having assured themselves of my complicity) did so with special satisfaction. It was also illegal for urbanites to go and buy potatoes directly from the villagers who grew potatoes on their private plot, because the authorities suspected that villagers would charge more than the state-set price, thus enriching themselves. So Romanian policemen routinely stopped cars riding low on the chassis and confiscated produce they found inside.

Consumption became politicized in yet another way: the very definition of "needs" became a matter for resistance and dispute. "Needs," as we should know from our own experience, are not given; they are created, developed, expanded—the work especially of the advertising business. It is advertising's job to convince us that we need things we did not know we needed, or that if we feel unhappy, it is because we need something (a shrink, or a beer, or a Marlboro, or a man). Our need requires only a name, and it can be satisfied with a product or service. Naming troubled states, labeling them as needs, and finding commodities to fill them is at the heart of our economy.

Socialism, by contrast, which rested not on devising infinite kinds of things to sell to people but on claiming to satisfy people's basic needs, had a very unadorned definition of them—in keeping with socialist egalitarianism. Indeed, some Hungarian dissidents wrote of socialism's relationship to needs as a "dictatorship."[15] As long as the food offered was edible or the clothes available covered you and kept you warm, that should be sufficient. If you had trouble finding even these, that just meant you were not looking hard enough. No planner presumed to investigate what kinds of goods people wanted or worked to name new needs for newly created products and newly developed markets.

At the same time, however, regime policies paradoxically made consumption a problem. Even as the regimes prevented people from consuming by not making goods available, they insisted that under socialism, the standard of living would constantly improve. This stimulated consumers' appetites, perhaps with an eye to fostering increased effort and tying them into the system. Moreover, socialist ideology presented consumption as a "right." The system's organization exacerbated consumer desire further by frustrating it and thereby making it the focus of effort, resistance, and discontent. Anthropologist John Borneman sees in the relation between desire and goods a major contrast between capitalism and socialism. Capitalism, he says, repeatedly renders desire concrete and specific and offers specific—if ever-changing—goods to satisfy it. Socialism, in contrast, aroused desire *without* focalizing it and kept it alive by deprivation.[16]

As people became increasingly alienated from socialism and critical of its achievements, then, the politicization of consumption also made them challenge official definitions of their needs. They did so not just by creating a second economy to grow food or make clothes or work in after hours but also, sometimes, by public protest. Poland's Communist Party leaders fell to such protest at least twice, in 1970 and in 1980, when Polish workers insisted on having more food than government price increases would permit them. Less immediately disruptive were forms of protest in which people used consumption styles to forge resistant social identities. The black markets in Western goods that sprang up everywhere enabled alienated consumers to express their contempt for the system through the kinds of things they chose to buy. You could spend an entire month's salary on a pair of blue jeans, for instance, but it was worth it: wearing them signified that you could get something the system said you did not need and should not have. Thus, consumption goods and objects conferred an identity that set you off from socialism, enabling you to differentiate yourself as an individual in the face of relentless pressures to homogenize everyone's capacities and tastes into an undifferentiated collectivity. Acquiring objects became a way of constituting your selfhood against a deeply unpopular regime.

BUREAUCRATIC FACTIONALISM AND MARKETS

Before turning to why these systems fell, I wish to address one more issue: politicking in the party bureaucracy. Although this took different and specific forms in the different countries, it is important to mention the issue, for socialism's collapse owed much to shifts in the balance among factions that emerged within the party apparatus. Even before 1989, researchers were pointing to several forms of intraparty division.[17] One such division might be that between *ownership* and *management*, another between the people who oversaw the paperwork of administration and those "out in the field," intervening in actual social life.[18] We might then look for conflicting tendencies based in the different interests of these groups. Such conflicts might arise between the central "owners" or "paper-workers," on one hand, who might persist in policies that accumulated means of production without concern for things like productivity and output, and the bureaucratic managers or field-workers, on the other, who *had* to care about such things. Although the power of the system itself rested on continued accumulation, such tendencies, if unchecked, could obstruct the work of those who had actually to deliver resources or redistribute them. Without tangible investments and hard material resources, lower-level units could not produce the means of production upon which the party bureaucracy relied. If productive activity were so stifled by "overadministration" that nothing got produced, this would jeopardize the redistributive bureaucracy's power and prestige.

Thus, when central accumulation of means of production began to threaten the capacity of lower-level units to produce, when persistent imbalances between investment in heavy industry and in light industry, between allocations for investment and for consumption, and so on, diminished the stock of distributable goods, and when the center's attempts to keep enterprises from meddling with surplus appropriation obstructed the process of production itself, then pressure arose for a shift of emphasis. The pressure was partly from those in the wider society to whom not enough was being allocated and partly from bureaucrats themselves whose prestige and prospects of retaining power depended on having more goods to allocate. One then heard of decentralization, of the *rate of growth*, of *productivity*—in a word, of matters of *output*, rather than the inputs that lay at the core of bureaucratic performance. This is generally referred to as the language of "reform."

For those groups who became concerned with questions of output and productivity, the solutions almost always involved introducing mechanisms such as profitability criteria and freer markets. This meant, however, introducing a subordinate rationality discrepant with the system's inner logic and thereby threatening continued party rule. Market forces create problems for socialism in part for reasons treated implicitly or explicitly above (recall the contrast between demand-constrained capitalism and socialism's economy of shortage, as well as socialism's lack of interest in the salability of its products). But more broadly, markets create problems because they move goods *horizontally* rather than *vertically* toward the center, as all redistributive systems require. Markets also presuppose that individual interest and the "invisible hand," rather than the guiding hand of the party, secure the common good.[19] Because these horizontal movements and individualizing premises subverted socialism's hierarchical organization, market mechanisms had been suppressed. Reformers introducing them were opening Pandora's box.

Why Did It Fall?

My discussion of socialism's workings already points to several reasons for its collapse; I might now address the question more comprehensively. To do this requires, in my view, linking the properties of its internal organization (discussed above) with properties of its external environment as well as with shorter-term "event history." This means examining the specific conjuncture of two systems—"capitalist" and "socialist," to use ideal types—one encompassing the other.[20]

In event-history terms, the proximate cause of the fall of Eastern European and Soviet socialism was a public relations gambit by the Hungarian government on the eve of a visit by President George Bush—the dismantling of the barbed wire between Hungary and Austria. This enabled some East German tourists to extend their tour and thereby—because Mikhail Gorbachev refused to support Erich Honecker with Soviet troops—to bring down the Berlin Wall. We still need to explain, however, the conjuncture in which Hungary could score its public relations coup and Gorbachev could decide to refuse his troops. For that, we must wind up the static model I have offered and set it in its international context. This includes asking how socialism's encounter with a changing world capitalism produced or aggravated factional divisions within communist parties.

My discussion of socialism indicated several points of tension in its workings that affected the system's capacity for extended reproduction. Throughout their existence, these regimes sought to manage such tensions in different ways, ranging from Hungary's major market reforms in the 1960s to Romania's rejection of reform and its heightened coercive extraction. In all cases, managing these tensions involved decisions that to a greater or lesser degree opened socialist political economies to Western capital. The impetus for this opening—critical to socialism's demise—came chiefly *from within*, as party leaders attempted to solve their structural problems without major structural reform. Their attitude in doing so was reminiscent of a "plunder mentality" that sees the external environment as a source of booty to be used as needed in maintaining one's own system, without thought for the cost. This attitude was visible in the tendency of socialist governments to treat foreign trade as a residual sector, used to supplement budgets without being made an integral part of them.[21] Because of how this opportunistic recourse to the external environment brought socialism into tighter relationship with capitalism, it had fateful consequences.

The critical intersection occurred not in 1989 or 1987 but in the late 1960s and early 1970s, when global capitalism entered the cyclical crisis from which it is still struggling to extricate itself. Among capitalists' possible responses to the crisis (devaluation, structural reorganization, etc.), an early one was to lend abroad. Loans enabled recipients to buy capital equipment or to build long-term infrastructure, thereby expanding the overseas markets for Western products.[22] The loans became available just at the moment when all across the socialist bloc the first significant round of structural reforms had been proposed, half-heartedly implemented, and, because profitability and market criteria fit so poorly with socialism's rationale, largely abandoned. Instead of reforming the system from within, most party leaderships opted to meet their problems by greater articulation with the surrounding economy—importing Western capital and using it to buy advanced technology (or, as in Poland, to subsidize consumption), in hopes of improving economic performance. Borrowing, then, became a substitute for extensive internal reforms that would have jeopardized the party's monopoly over society and subverted the inner mechanisms of socialism. Thus the internal cycles of two contrasting systems suddenly meshed.

The intent, as with all the international borrowing of the period, was to pay off the loans by exporting manufactured goods into the world market. By the mid-1970s it was clear, however, that the world market could not absorb sufficient amounts of socialism's products to enable repayment, and, at the same time, rising interest rates added staggeringly to the debt service. With the 1979–80 decision of the Western banking establishment not to lend more money to socialist countries, the latter were thrown into complete disarray. I have already mentioned several features that made socialist economies inapt competitors in the international export market. The "plunder" stance toward external economies, the system's fundamental organization *against* notions of salability of its products, the shortage economy's premium on acquisitionsmanship rather than on salesmanship, the neglect of consumption and of producing to satisfy consumer needs with diverse, high-quality products—all meant that an adequate response to the hard-currency crisis would have catastrophic effects on socialism's inner mechanisms. To this was added the fact that socialist economies were "outdated": as Ken Jowitt put it, "After 70 years of murderous effort, the Soviet Union had created a German industry of the 1880s in the 1980s."[23]

In these circumstances, the balance of power tilted toward the faction within the Communist Party of the Soviet Union that had long argued for structural reforms, the introduction of market mechanisms, and profit incentives, even at the cost of the party's "leading role." The choice, as Gorbachev and his faction saw it, was to try to preserve either the Soviet Union and its empire (by reforms that would increase its economic performance and political legitimacy), or collective property and the party monopoly. He was ready to sacrifice the latter to save the former but ended by losing both.

While Western attention was riveted on the speeches of policymakers in the Kremlin, the more significant aspects of reform, however, were in the often-unauthorized behavior of bureaucrats who were busily creating new property forms on their own. The Polish sociologist Jadwiga Staniszkis describes the growth of what she calls "political capitalism," as bureaucrats spontaneously created their own profit-based companies from within the state economic bureaucracy. Significantly for my argument that socialism's articulation with world capitalism was decisive in its fall, the examples she singles out to illustrate these trends are all at the interface of socialist economies with the outside world—in particular, new companies mediating the export trade and state procurement of Western computers.[24] She sees as crucial the factional split between the groups who managed socialism's relations with the outside (such as those in foreign policy, counterintelligence, and foreign trade) and those who managed it internally (such as the party's middle-level executive apparatus and the KGB).[25] Forms of privatization already taking place by 1987 in Poland and similar processes as early as 1984 in Hungary[26] show the emerging contours of what Staniszkis sees as the reformists' goal: a *dual economy*. One part of it was to be centrally administered, as before, and the other part to be reformed through market or profit mechanisms and selective privatization of state property. The two were to coexist symbiotically.[27]

These forms of "political capitalism" arose in part by economic managers' exploiting the shortages endemic to socialism—shortages now aggravated to crisis proportions. In the new hope of making a profit, "political capitalists" (I call them "entrepratchiks") were willing to put into circulation reserves known only to them—which they would otherwise have hoarded—thus alleviating shortages, to their own gain. As a result, even antireformist Soviet and Polish bureaucrats found themselves acquiescing in entrepratchiks' activities, without which, in Staniszkis's words, "the official structure of the economic administration was absolutely unsteerable."[28] Contributing to officials' tolerance was rampant bureaucratic anarchy, a loss of control by those higher up, rooted in the "inability of superiors to supply their subordinates (managers of lower level) with the means to construct a strategy of survival."[29] Since superiors could no longer guarantee deliveries and investments, they were forced to accept whatever solutions enterprising subordinates could devise—even at the cost of illicit profits from state reserves. Entrepratchiks soon began to regard the state's accumulations much as Evgenii Preobrazhensky had once urged Soviet leaders to regard agriculture: as a source of primitive accumulation. They came to find increasingly attractive the idea of further "privatization," so important to Western lenders.

It is possible (though unlikely) that socialist regimes would not have collapsed if their hard-currency crisis and consequent intersection with capitalism had occurred at a different point in capitalism's cyclicity. The specifics of capitalism's own crisis management, however, proved unmanageable for socialist systems. Without wanting to present recent capitalism's "flexible specialization" as either unitary or fully dominant (its forms differ from place to place, and it coexists with other socioeconomic forms), I find in the literature about it a number of characteristics even more inimical to socialism than was the earlier "Fordist" variant, which Soviet production partly imitated. These characteristics include small-batch production; just-in-time inventory; an accelerated pace of innovation; tremendous reductions in the turnover time of capital via automation and electronics; a much-increased turnover time in *consumption* as well, with a concomitant rise in techniques of need-creation and an increased emphasis on the production of *events* rather than *goods*; coordination of the economy by finance capital; instantaneous access to accurate information and analysis; and an overall decentralization that increases managerial control (at the expense of higher-level bodies) over labor.[30]

How is socialism to mesh with this—socialism with its emphasis on large-scale heroic production of means of production, its resources frozen by hoarding (no just-in-time here!), its lack of a systemic impetus toward innovation, the irrelevance to it of notions like "turnover time," its neglect of consumption and its flat-footed definition of "needs," its constipated and secretive flows of information (except for rumors) in which the center could have no confidence, and its perpetual struggle to retain central control over all phases of the production process? Thus, I submit, it is not simply socialism's embrace with capitalism that brought about its fall but the fact that it happened to embrace a capitalism of a newly "flexible" sort. David Harvey's schematic comparison of "Fordist modernity" with "flexible postmodernity" clarifies things further: socialist systems have much more in common with his "Fordist" column than with his "flexible" one.[31]

Let me add one more thought linking the era of flexible specialization with socialism's collapse. Increasing numbers of scholars note that accompanying the change in capitalism is a change in the nature of state power: specifically, a number of the state's functions are being undermined.[32] The international weapons trade has made a mockery of the state's monopoly on the means of violence. Capital's extraordinary mobility means that as it moves from areas of higher to areas of lower taxation, many states lose some of their revenue and industrial base, and this constrains their ability to attract capital or shape its flows. Capital flight can now discipline *all* nation-state governments.[33] The coordination of global capitalism by finance capital places a premium on capital mobility, to which rigid state boundaries are an obstacle.

This has two consequences for the fall of socialism. First, within socialist countries those groups whose structural situation facilitated their fuller participation in the global economy now had reasons to expand their state's receptivity to capital—that is, to promote reform. Second, the extent to which socialist states controlled capital flows into their countries may have made them special targets for international financial interests, eager to increase their opportunities by undermining socialist states. These internal and international groups each found their chance in the interest of the other. It is in any case clear from the politics of international lending agencies that they aim to reduce the power of socialist states, for they insist upon privatization of state property—the basis of these states' power and revenue. Privatization is pushed even in the face of some economists' objections that "too much effort is being invested in privatization, and too little in creating and fostering the development of new private firms"—whose entry privatization may actually impede.[34]

No Time for Socialism

Rather than explore further how flexible specialization compelled changes in socialism, I will summarize my argument by linking it to notions of time. Time, as anthropologists have shown, is a fundamental dimension of human affairs, taking different forms in different kinds of society. The Western notion of a linear, irreversible time that consists of equivalent and divisible units, for instance, is but one possible way of conceptualizing time and living it. A given cultural construction of time ramifies throughout its social order, as calendars, schedules, and rhythms establish the very foundation of daily existence (which is why elites, especially revolutionary ones, often manipulate them) and affect how people make themselves as social beings.

Capitalism exists only as a function of time—and of a specific conception of it. Efforts to increase profits by increasing the velocity of capital circulation are at its very heart. Thus each major reorganization of capitalism has entailed, in David Harvey's term, "time-space compression"—a shrinking of the time horizon of private and public decision making, whose consequences encompass ever-wider spaces owing to changed communications and transport technology.[35] The inner logic of socialism, by contrast, placed no premium on increasing turnover time and capital circulation. Although the rhetoric of Stalinism presented socialism as highly dynamic, for the most part Soviet leaders acted as if time were on their side. (When Nikita Khrushchev said, "We will bury you," he was not too specific about the date.) Indeed, I have argued that in 1980s Romania, time—far from accelerating—was being gradually *slowed down*, flattened, immobilized, and rendered nonlinear.[36]

Like the reorganization of capitalism at the end of the nineteenth century, the present reorganization entails a time-space compression that we all feel as a mammoth speedup. Yet the socialism with which it interacted had no such time-compressing dynamic. In this light, the significance of Gorbachev's perestroika was its recognition that socialism's temporality was unsustainable in a capitalist world. Perestroika reversed Soviet ideas as to whose time definition and rhythms were dominant and where dynamism lay—no longer within the socialist system but outside it, in the West. Gorbachev's rhetoric from the mid-1980s is full of words about time: the Soviet Union needs to "catch up," to "accelerate" its development, to shed its "sluggishness" and "inertia" and leave behind the "era of stagnation." By "the latter half of the seventies . . . the country began to lose momentum. . . . Elements of stagnation . . . began to appear. . . . A kind of 'braking mechanism' affect[ed] social and economic development. . . . The inertia of extensive economic development was leading to an economic deadlock and stagnation."[37] Change has suddenly become an "urgent" necessity. These are the words of a man snatched by the compression of space and time.

Even as Gorbachev spoke, new time–space-compressing technologies were wreaking havoc on the possible rhythms of his and other leaders' control of politics, as Radio Free Europe made their words at once domestic and international. Soviet leaders could no longer create room for themselves by saying one thing for domestic consumption and something else for the outside world; they were now prisoners of simultaneity. The role of Western information technology in undermining socialism was evident in the spread of Solidarity's strikes in 1980, news of which was telephoned out to the West and rebroadcast instantly into Poland via Radio Free Europe and the BBC, mobilizing millions of Poles against their party. The revolutions of 1989 were mediated similarly.

I am suggesting, then, that the collapse of socialism came in part from the massive rupture produced by its collision with capitalism's speedup. If so, it would be especially useful to know something more about the life experience of those people who worked at the interface of these two temporal systems and could not help realizing how different was capitalism's time from their own. Bureaucrats under pressure to increase foreign trade and foreign revenues, or importers of computer equipment, would have discovered that failure to adapt to alien notions of increased turnover time could cost them hard currency. They would have directly experienced time-annihilating Western technologies, which effected a banking transaction in milliseconds as opposed to the paper-laden hours and days needed by their own financial system. Did the rise of "profitability" criteria in the command economy owe something to such people's dual placement? Did they come to experience differently their sense of themselves as agents? My point, in short, is that the fall of socialism lies not simply in the intersection of two systems' temporal cycles but rather in the collision of two *differently constituted temporal orders*, along with the notions of person and activity proper to them.

If socialist economies had not opened themselves to capital import and to debt servicing, perhaps their collision with capitalist speedup would have been less jarring, or would at least have occurred on more equal terms. But the capitalist definition of time prevailed, as socialist debtors bowed to its dictates (even while postponing them), thereby aggravating factional conflicts within the elite. Because its leaders accepted Western temporal hegemony, socialism's messianic time proved apocalyptic. The irony is that had debtor regimes refused the definitions imposed from without—had they united to default simultaneously on their Western loans (which in 1981 stood at more than $90 billion)[38]—they might well have brought down the world financial system and realized Khrushchev's threatening prophecy overnight. That this did not happen shows how vital a thing is a monopoly on the definition of social reality, and it should give pause to those impatient to move beyond capitalism.

Notes

This paper was prepared as a lecture for the Center for Comparative Research in History, Society and Culture, at the University of California, Davis. I am grateful to those who invited me—William Hagen, G. William Skinner, and Carol Smith—as well as to members of the center's seminar. I also received helpful advice from Ashraf Ghani. Reprinted with permission of *Contention* 3, no. 1 (1993), edited by Nikki Keddie and published by Indiana University Press.

[1]Cf. Rudolph Bahro's "actually existing socialism" in *The Alternative in Eastern Europe* (London: Verso, 1978).

[2]See especially Elemér Hankiss, *East European Alternatives* (Oxford: Oxford University Press, 1990); Agnes Horváth and Árpád Szakolczai, *The Dissolution of Communist Power: The Case of Hungary* (New York: Routledge, 1992); Jadwiga Staniszkis, *The Dynamics of the Breakthrough in Eastern Europe: The Polish Experience*, trans. Chester A. Kisiel (Berkeley: University of California Press, 1991); Staniszkis, *The Ontology of Socialism* (Oxford: Oxford University Press, 1992).

[3]See, in particular, Pavel Campeanu, *The Origins of Stalinism: From Leninist Revolution to Stalinist Society* (Armonk, N.Y.: M. E. Sharpe, 1986); Compeanu, *The Genesis of the Stalinist Social Order* (Armonk, N.Y.: M. E. Sharpe, 1988); Ferenc Fehér, Agnes Heller, and György Márkus, *Dictatorship over Needs: An Analysis of Soviet Societies* (New York: Basil Blackwell, 1983); George Konrád and Ivan Szelényi, *The Intellectuals on the Road to Class Power: A Sociological Study of the Role of the Intelligentsia in Socialism* (New York: Harcourt, Brace, Jovanovich, 1979); Janos Kornai, *The Economics of Shortage*, 2 vols. (Amsterdam: North-Holland Publishing Co., 1980).

[4]See Katherine Verdery, "Theorizing Socialism: A Prologue to the 'Transition,'" *American Ethnologist* 18, no. 3. (1991): 419–39.

[5]This section draws upon Michael Burawoy's discussion in *The Politics of Production* (London: Verso, 1985), as well as the sources listed in 3.

[6]See Kornai, *Economics of Shortage*.

[7]See Burawoy, *Politics of Production*, chap. 4.

[8]Michael Burawoy and János Lukács, *The Radiant Past: Ideology and Reality in Hungary's Road to Capitalism* (Chicago: University of Chicago Press, 1992), chap. 5.

[9]Cf. Burawoy, *Politics of Production*.

[10]Andrei Şerbulescu (Belu Zilber), *Monarhia de drept dialectic* (Bucharest: Humanitas, 1991), 136–38.

[11]These observations show how fraught is the use of files in assessing fitness for political office, as in the Czech practice of "lustration."

[12]Campeanu, *Genesis of the Stalinist Social Order*, 117–18.

[13]Horváth and Szakolczai, *Dissolution of Communist Power*, 77–78.

[14]See István Gábor, "The Second (Secondary) Economy," *Acta Oeconomica* 14, nos. 3–4 (1979): 291–311; Steven Sampson, "The Second Economy in Eastern Europe and the Soviet Union," *Annals of the American Association of Political and Social Science* 493 (1986): 120–36.

[15]Fehér, Heller, and Márkus, *Dictatorship over Needs.*

[16]John Borneman, *After the Wall* (New York: Basic Books, 1990), 17–18.

[17]E.g., Leslie Benson, "Partynomialism, Bureaucratism, and Economic Reform in the Soviet Power System," *Theory and Society* 19, no. 1 (1990): 92; Burawoy and Lukács, *Radiant Past,* 90–92, 96–100; Campeanu, *Genesis of the Stalinist Social Order,* 143–57; Horváth and Szakolczai, *Dissolution of Communist Power,* 204–5; Konrád and Szelényi, *Intellectuals on the Road,* 153; Jadwiga Staniszkis, "Patterns of Change in Eastern Europe," *East European Politics and Societies* 4, no. 1 (1990): 80.

[18]Campeanu, *Genesis of the Stalinist Social Order,* 143–57; Horváth and Szakolczai, *Dissolution of Communist Power,* 204–5.

[19]Horváth and Szakolczai, *Dissolution of Communist Power,* 48–49.

[20]See also Terry Boswell and Ralph Peters, "State Socialism and the Industrial Divide in the World Economy," *Critical Sociology* 17, no. 1 (1990): 3–34; Valerie Bunce, "The Empire Strikes Back: The Evolution of the Eastern Bloc from a Soviet Asset to a Soviet Liability," *International Organization* 39, no. 1 (1985): 1–46; Daniel Chirot, "After Socialism, What?" *Contention* 1, no. 1 (1991): 29–49.

[21]Paul Hare, "Industrial Development of Hungary since World War II," *East European Politics and Societies* 2, no. 1 (1988): 115–51.

[22]David Harvey, *The Condition of Postmodernity* (Oxford: Blackwell, 1989), 184.

[23]Ken Jowitt, "The Leninist Extinction," in *The Crisis of Leninism and the Decline of the Left,* ed. Daniel Chirot (Seattle: University of Washington Press, 1991), 78.

[24]Jadwiga Staniszkis, "'Political Capitalism' in Poland,'" *East European Politics and Societies* 5, no. 1 (1991): 129–30.

[25]Staniszkis, "Patterns of Change," 79–83.

[26]David Stark, "Privatization in Hungary: From Plan to Market or from Plan to Clan?" *East European Politics and Societies* 4, no. 3 (1990): 364–65.

[27]Staniszkis, "Patterns of Change," 77–78.

[28]Staniszkis, "'Political Capitalism,'" 131.

[29]Staniszkis, *Dynamics of the Breakthrough,* 164.

[30]See Harvey, *Condition of Postmodernity,* 156, 164, 340–41.

[31]Ibid., 340–41.

[32]E.g., Eric Hobsbawm, *Nations and Nationalism since 1780: Programme, Myth, Reality* (Cambridge: Cambridge University Press, 1990), 181–83; Charles Tilly, *Coercion, Capital, and European States, A.D. 990-1990* (Oxford: Blackwell, 1990).

[33]Harvey, *Condition of Postmodernity,* 164–65.

[34]Peter Murrell, "Privatization Complicates the Fresh Start," *Orbis* 36, no. 3 (1992): 325.

[35]Harvey, *Condition of Postmodernity,* 147.

[36]Katherine Verdery, "The 'Etatization' of Time in Ceausescu's Romania," in *The Politics of Time,* ed. Henry Rutz (Washington, D.C.: American Ethnological Society, 1992), 56–57.

[37]Mikhail Gorbachev, *Perestroika: New Thinking for Our Country and the World* (New York: Harper and Row, 1987), 5, 6.

[38]Bunce, "Empire Strikes Back," 39.

Commentary:

Not the Juice But the Juicer

Reginald E. Zelnik

Scholars struggling to keep up with the kaleidoscopic changes now taking place in the former Soviet Union and Eastern Europe are often careful to end their articles with an exact date of submission, lest tomorrow's unexpected events cast a shadow over their scholarship by the date of publication. Mikhail Gorbachev is unlikely to stay in power—but he stays; he will never allow the Berlin Wall to fall—but it falls; there will never be a free election while Gorbachev remains in power—but Boris Yeltsin is freely elected president of the Russian republic; a coup is out of the question—but there's the coup (but wait, it's gone!); the collapse of Soviet power will mean civil war—but there's no civil war, not in Russia, not yet (September 23, 1994); the significance of the referendum is. . . . And so it goes, with the right prediction often based on the shallower analysis, the wrong one on the deeper, as wish and thought, emotion and scholarship, are stirred together into the language of academic ratiocination. One is reminded of the nervous father in a Ring Lardner story, who, lost at the wheel of his car in the forests of New York City, responds to a suggestion from his overzealous son: "'Shut up,' he explained!"

Wisely, in her thoughtful and thought-provoking essay, "What Was Socialism, and Why Did It Fall?" Katherine Verdery eschews prediction (what comes next, she said in an earlier version, is "anybody's guess") and even avoids much commentary on the present situation—so no need for a date at the end of her article! Instead, she uses the dramatic events of recent years to explore in depth and, I would add, with neither tears nor laughter, the deeper structure of the communist system, probing as she does so for the underlying causes of its demise while remaining alert for the nonstructural input from human agents. The result is one of the most compelling statements of the problem I have read.

Before reviewing the steps of Verdery's analysis sequentially, I would call attention to her very controlled use of language, specifically her self-conscious effort to deploy a terminology that carries a minimum of ideological or emotional baggage, lest the charged language of the various "camps" that have dominated the Sovietological debate get in the way of clarity. For example, she steers clear of "Leninism," while drawing heavily (and, as always, with generous acknowledgment) on Ken Jowitt's studies of the "Leninist" phenomenon; and she avoids "totalitarianism," neither attacking nor defending the term, though clearly harboring no illusions about the enormous punitive power of the old communist security apparatus. (For an example of the debasement of language that now surrounds the term, see the May 1, 1993, AP report of die-hard communists and Russian ultranationalists protesting against Yeltsin's "totalitarian" regime.) None of this is to deny that Verdery's findings will be greeted more warmly in some camps than in others, but it is a strength of her essay, as I hope to show, that it pushes us all in the direction of a different, less-loaded, less-tendentious (and less-tedious) language of analysis.

As the title suggests, the essay is subdivided into two main problem areas. As to what socialism was, Verdery, while recognizing the wide variations that existed among the communist countries of Europe (let alone those of East and Southeast Asia), sensibly uses the Soviet Union as her basic model, the system from which the others, all dating from the postwar period, were derivative. She is also correct in noting that the USSR was the country where the Communist Party had the greatest "legitimacy," by which I think she means that there was the least popular sentiment that the regime was imposed from without by alien arms. (She might have added that to the extent that Communist Party legitimacy was revitalized by the patriotic engagements of World War II, at least among ethnic Russians, the same could be said of Yugoslavia, at least among ethnic Serbs.) Hence it is by probing the character of Soviet socialism, the "Ur-socialism" (or the *Ur-existing* socialism) that we can best get to the character of its unwilling progeny.

As an anthropologist, Verdery predictably draws upon the testimony of the natives—she calls this approach "indigenist"—the major source of information about the world in which they lived. But insofar as this method can take her only so far, especially in light of the many self-contradictory tales these natives tell, she needs some kind of conceptual framework to help her assess the credibility and organize the insights of her informants into a useful pattern, lest she fall into the polemical trap I have observed so many times—the abrupt ending of an argument about the Soviet system by calling on the authority of what natives believe: if they call it "totalitarian" (or "democratic" or "Judeo-Masonic"), then it must be totalitarian (or as Russians say, if he calls himself a mushroom, we'll put him in the mushroom box!).

The framework Verdery uses to pattern and make sense of her ethnographic information about "actually existing socialism" (socialist theory as such is of little interest to her) is provided by the system of centralized planning and distribution and by its points of intersection with Soviet methods of police control. Almost from the outset, though mainly implicitly, she measures that system against the old standard model of party domination and control, but unlike other critics of that model, she does so not to test the limits to which the system was cruel or benign but to uncover its structure, functions, and internal weaknesses and contradictions.

Drawing heavily on the work of Michael Burawoy, Verdery concludes that the centralized planning system was hardly a planning system at all but rather a system of hoarding, padding, and barter, based on the systemic scarcity of materials and the need for "planners" and production managers to protect themselves from unforeseen shortages. Though essentially inefficient, the system was perpetuated by the political center's desire to protect each unit of the system from the consequences of its own inadequacy. Far from being the summum of economic rationality it proclaimed itself to be, Soviet socialism squandered resources, mainly at the expense of its own citizens.

Paradoxically, however, this inefficient system "worked"; it worked, that is, in the limited sense that for many years, for decades, it managed to provide minimum satisfactions to almost everyone involved in the production process, with only one important reservation. It was important that these producers, from management down to the lowliest production-line worker, not begin to think of themselves as consumers. For it was the consumer, Verdery argues, who was deliberately excluded from even the meager advantages derived from the system; the consumer was the odd man out (in practice, more often than not, the odd woman), scraping fawningly for what he (usually she) could procure, using bribery, flattery, whatever means were at hand. Of course, as Verdery must understand, the consumer-producer distinction functions at a certain level of abstraction, for in reality the consumer and producer are sometimes one and the same person, in which case what Verdery is talking about is not just a conflict within the hierarchical structure of society but a conflict within one's self-identity, with satisfaction possible only insofar as people are able to suppress or control their desire for new worldly (no pun intended!) goods or, perhaps more accurately, their desire and capacity to choose among such goods.

Within certain limits, Verdery argues convincingly, the worker qua worker benefited from this system. Viewed as a raw material in short supply, the worker (unlike Verdery, I would stress the skilled worker here, again mainly male) had to some extent to be pampered by the Soviet manager, kept on hand even when the plant was idle lest he be missing when the plant was working at full capacity. (Analogous practices occurred during earlier stages of the industrial revolution, the capitalist one, that is, including the one in late-nineteenth-century Russia.) This was Soviet full employment, providing an objective point of reference for what Verdery does call, with measured irony, I am sure, a kind of workers' state (as well as for the old workers' joke about the communist social contract: "We pretend to work and they pretend to pay us"). But however satisfactory this arrangement was to workers in the short or medium run, it was bound to feed their cynicism in the long run and to promote what Verdery calls "an oppositional cult of nonwork." Certainly the failure of miners and other Soviet workers to rally to the cause of a party-state that had flattered and coddled them so long was in part attributable to the state of affairs that Verdery describes.

If the system of production was loosely held together by a minimally beneficial social contract (including the social safety net that Verdery subsumes under the notion of "socialist paternalism"), its threads were too loose to survive in the absence of a tight political superstructure, what Verdery calls the "apparatus of surveillance." Of course, she does not mean the subtle surveillances that Michel Foucault attributes to the internalized discourses of bourgeois society, but a far grosser system of internal espionage ("the production of [personal] files") that kept the Soviet and Eastern European populations divided and defensive. Although it does no irreparable damage to her basic line of argument, I find Verdery's novelistic emphasis on dossier production (and overproduction), based on the memoirs of a Romanian political prisoner, a little too precious to be useful. What counted in the end (including for her prisoner) was the police's power of arbitrary arrest, with or without a dossier—even whimsically, at the high (or low) point of the Stalinist system; this was the power that gave the dossier system its terrorizing underpinnings.

Where does "society" fit into Verdery's schema? To be sure, she again eschews the dull, conventional, timeworn problematic (Did society exist under the communist system?—Of course it did!), but implicit in the logic of her analysis is the notion that popular expectations were constantly shaping, reshaping, and especially restricting the options available to an otherwise powerful state. Not only did privileged workers have this capacity, but even the average consumers of state paternalism had it; however passive they were trained to be, however dependent on the state for the definition of their needs, consumers nevertheless were able to force the state to design and limit its much-beloved productionist goals so as to maintain a minimal storehouse of wearable and edible goods (rarely goodies)—"distributable resources," in Verdery's terms—to pass out among them. This was the lemonade. Lemonade socialism (conceptually clearer, I think, than goulash). Yet, the regime's self-esteem and self-definition depended not so much on possession of the lemonade as of the lemons and the juicers.

This analysis shows in a fresh and insightful way how the system functioned at the level of its political economy—that is, badly—but with the wherewithal for longevity, and where the points of friction and weakness were should the system be faced with tough new challenges and be forced to innovate creatively. The toughest challenge came, according to Verdery, from the outside, not, as is usually claimed, from Ronald Reagan's Star Wars project but from a deeper and more extensive conjunctural confrontation with Western economies ("the specfic conjuncture of two systems"). (Verdery could have integrated the Star Wars factor into her scheme, I believe, but that is another matter.) The pivotal moment came in the late 1960s–early 1970s, when rather than face up to the need for radical reform, with the attendant risk (to put Verdery's complex argument much too concisely) of empowering the Soviet consumer by attending to privately generated needs and filling them with quality products, the Soviet leadership opted for a strategy of compensating for its deficiencies by entering into friendlier economic relations with the capitalist world, essentially by borrowing large sums of capital with which to shore up a tottering system without remodeling its structure (without perestroika, let us say). Verdery seems to suggest, but is not very clear on this point, that the alternative, an internally driven reform campaign (a pre-Gorbachev perestroika?) would have weakened the foundations of the system and led to its collapse, though at what pace and with what differential outcomes are not explained. Possible alternative trajectories are not sketched in, leaving me with some doubts as to the explanatory power of her provocative notion that socialism's deadly "embrace" with capitalism just at a time when capitalism was redesigning its "temporal order" is what brought about its fall. Was the collision between "capitalist speedup" and socialism's "messianic time" the necessary condition for socialism's demise, or was an earlier effort to resolve the system's contradictions "internally" just as likely to collapse into a similar endgame? The answer should be clarified.

In any case, it is a matter of historical record, not counterfactual, that the conditions Verdery describes eventually split the Soviet and other communist parties into reformist and reactionary camps. The same conditions also created, extended, intensified, and multiplied nonparty values and desires among the populace, especially for forbidden fruit (not just lemons), and ultimately culminated in Gorbachev's reformist regime, one, I would add, that among its many accomplishments (its failures have been well researched), permitted the historical losers, yesterday's gods, to slip from the stage of power feebly and undramatically, without a Valhalla. As a historian I commend Verdery for introducing contingent "events"—Hungary's decision to lower the barbed wire on its Austrian frontier, and Gorbachev's refusal to rescue Erich Honecker with Soviet troops—into her story. She is of course right that only by grasping the conjuncture within which these events occurred are we able to understand the historical rationality of such decisions, but she is wrong to allot them an equal order of importance or probability. It is hard to imagine something like the Hungarian decision not taking place in Eastern Europe under these circumstances. It is all too easy, however, to imagine a very different, much more adventurous and perilous decision by Gorbachev (or his replacement?) had discussions in the Kremlin taken a different but historically familiar turn. It will surprise me very much if we fail to learn some day, perhaps from archives, that the decision not to use force in East Germany (or elsewhere) was a close call and came at the end of a bitter, divisive debate. Had the other fork in the road been taken, Verdery might be writing not of why socialism failed, but of why its escalating internal crisis led to dangerous military adventure (as many Kremlinologists used to predict).

What is the relevance of Verdery's analysis to the important issues raised in the writings of Peter Reddaway, most notably his interview in the journal *Contention* and at greater length and more analytically in a thoughtful essay in the *New York Review of Books*.[1] And beyond the Reddaway argument, in what ways should her analysis help us rethink some of the broader historical and political issues that continue to torment students of the region, especially of the former Soviet Union and, more specifically still, of Russia? Reddaway's most powerful and impassioned point has been, at its base, a plea (to Yeltsin and to his supporters, especially abroad, i.e., here) for modesty and restraint in the pursuit of capitalism, an unfettered market economy, approaches based on "economic shock therapy" (EST). Reddaway draws on his vast knowledge of the Soviet past and the Russian present to suggest a number of economic, social, and cultural resistances to an excessively rapid reversal of engines, a time-machine-like movement back to the capitalist future. Recast in Verdery's (and David Harvey's) terms—and I take deliberate liberties at the almost certain risk of rebuttal or denial—Reddaway seems to be saying that the "time-space" compression that Verdery attributes to recent capitalism not only could not be absorbed by the Soviet-type personality but that the Russian cultural type as it exists today is still so grounded in the personality formation produced by seventy-five years of hothouse existence under the old system that the best that can be hoped for is a gradual, step-by-step, phase-by-phase movement across political-economic time zones, lest the passengers experience ruptured eardrums or much worse. Or, to shift the image somewhat, he in effect reminds us that no astronaut or cosmonaut has been launched into orbit without months and years of preparation in simulated space travel. The people who worked in Verdery's module, though they experienced the impact of powerful new forces, were hardly prepared or even preparing for a rapid ascent into the world of laissez-faire, free markets, and a consumer driven social order, in short—EST.

Thus the Verdery analysis, or at least my own peculiar reading of it, strengthens Reddaway's case, already a credible one, particularly in light of his impeccable credentials as a defender of the victims of Soviet oppression and, as far as I can gather, a defender in principle of market economies, a man with no personal or intellectual stake in the survival or defense of Soviet "socialism." Even Verdery's explication of the growing role of the "second economy" does little to undermine his case, for far from being a school for free enterprise, as she points out, the second economy has to a large extent been parasitic on the first. (Her important point about the dependency of the superproductive private plot on resources siphoned off [my euphemism] from the collective farm is a telling one.) If consumer demand has increased over time, especially the demand for higher quality Western or Western-like goods, even this change in consciousness, important as it was to the decline and fall of the system, was largely defined as a (negative) dependent variable of the system, that is, as a defiant quest for external markers of nonsocialist identity in the presence of a discredited communism.

As a historian of Russia, I would like to suggest that another dimension of this issue is worthy of exploration in the context of the debate over Russia's readiness for the plunge into a market economy. Deep beneath the Soviet version of the socialist system described by Verdery there lies a long history of Russian cultural attitudes, the structure of Russian mentalities over a much longer *durée* than the life of the Soviet system as such. This subject is enormously complicated and does not lend itself to easy generalization. Many pages of good history have and will be written about the rise of entrepreneurship during the last decades of imperial Russia, the appearance on the scene of private corporations, the development of corporate law, the Russian version of the independent farmer (the yeoman if you like him, the kulak if you don't), and many other related phenomena that imply that a market culture was starting to take root. More broadly, many pages have been written, and many more are in the works, that reveal the early signs of an embryonic democratic political culture, grounded in legality (*zakonnost'*), aborning in the womb of the troubled Russian Empire (not to mention other, more "advanced" areas of Eastern Europe). Whether one believes that a more liberal democratic order fosters a freer economy, or that a free economy is the necessary foundation for such a political order, or—closer to the historical truth, I believe—that the two often work in harmony with one another without a clear, one-directional causality (Max Weber's "elective affinities"), there is plenty of evidence that Russia had the historical wherewithal to progress in these directions. But while keeping this positive, progressivist picture in mind, we cannot forget that the best of this historical work also reveals the deep and pervasive antipathy to market values that continued (and apparently continues) to survive in the Russian political culture: the anticapitalism that not only suffused the entire political left but penetrated the liberal center and the right as well; the family-based collectivism of the peasant commune (in no way to be confused with centralist, productionist communism but nonetheless hostile to the values of liberal individualism, including those of the farmer-separator of the Stolypin era); the powerful egalitarian ethos of industrial workers, still operative even in the mining communities that are supportive of Yeltsin; and the elitist cultural prejudices against the "crass" materialism and consumerism of the West, characteristic of such politically diverse groups and individuals as Aleksandr Herzen, the Slavophiles, the populists, the antidemocratic right of various shadings, and, to take a contemporary example with superb anticommunist credentials, Aleksandr Solzhenitsyn. Although I cannot possibly be sure, even Yeltsin's commitment to the free market strikes me as a recently learned strategic position rather than a positive personal commitment with deep roots in his own past experience. In short, even if and when the thick topsoil layer of "socialist" experience described by Verdery has been removed, Russians (and many others) will have to confront the enormous challenge of a deeper layer of precapitalist, if not anticapitalist, permafrost. I do not believe that Peter Reddaway is asking Russians not to face this inevitable challenge, but he is asking them to be realistic and, in a sense, unheroic in the way they go about it, and asking us to allow them to be so. Russia has experienced more than its share of sacrifice and "heroism." While serious economic reform cannot await the full establishment of a new political order, building democratic institutions in a new spirit of negotiation and compromise, pluralism and tolerance, including, above all, the willingness to lose by the rules as well as win by the rules, should be Russia's highest priority.

Our part of the capitalist West, which, as Verdery points out, has been going through its own conjunctural pains (a major factor in her explanatory mechanism), may soon engage in its own redistribution of goods (not lemonade, but vaccines, insurance premiums, and medical assistance) through the avenue of the state, but based on the democratic exercise of political power. How a nation combines the market with its social needs is not the defining element in the characterization of a polity, how it *chooses* to design that combination, the *process* of decision making, is. Here I find Reddaway too cautious. As he says in his *Contention* interview, it is not in our power to save democracy in Russia (a "grandiose idea"), but we do have a moral imperative to be as supportive of Russia's very fragile democracy as we can be. In the long run, it is more important than the mix of what is sure to be some kind of mixed economy, a mix, after all, that can always be changed and changed again through the democratic process.

Notes

Reprinted with permission of *Contention* 3, no. 1 (1993), edited by Nikkie Keddie and published by Indiana University Press.

[1]Peter Reddaway, "Russia in Crisis," *Contention* 2, no. 3 (1993): 1–7, and Peter Reddaway and Yelena Bonner, "Yeltsin and Russia: Two Views," *New York Review of Books*, April 22, 1993, 16–18.

Chapter 2

Society, Past and Present, in Interpreting Russia

Moshe Lewin

This presentation begins from a reaction against the "rush for the instantaneous" that characterizes many people in the field these days—an approach that contaminated even historians and people not known previously for being prone to hasty improvisations. It is understandable that "the present" that opened up to us in such a big way works like a powerful magnet, but "the present" is, of course, a subject for many fields of scholarship—and it is not just "a moment." It always comes from somewhere and is moving somewhere, and it presents us with serious methodological problems that have to be handled if what we mean is an in-depth study. What themes to select, what should be the appropriate time span in the so-called present—and why—would be a scholar's approach and contribution. I wonder whether the flood of publications on perestroika and its aftermath is meeting this elementary precondition of our trade. (This may be one of our themes in the discussion.)

Next, I did not understand my task to be an empirical or theoretical study of today's society. I make, of course, different forays into the current situation—and more should be done in the discussion—but my emphasis is on a search of criteria and ideas concerning longer-term developments that contributed to the making of the current crisis. One more point, quite obvious by now, is worth mentioning: the USSR is gone. Hence there is no Sovietology anymore. There is, at best, a former Sovietology. Everyone is free either to mourn or celebrate this fact, but one thing does not go away, namely, the *history* of the USSR. And if this stays, so does the history of thinking about it, that is, its historiography. Soviet history and historiography are far from being as closed, solved, or uninteresting as some seem to have concluded.

Events as monumental as the ones we are observing in Eastern Europe demand hard thinking—and quite a lot of rethinking—of what we thought and wrote about the USSR, what we did right, and where we might have been mistaken. And this is not easy to do. Rethinking can be a shattering affair, it can destroy establishments, authorities, and careers, and it may demand considerable mental and intellectual retooling—the learning and relearning that is, at least formally, the feature of any scholarship. But rethinking is easier to state or preach—or repent by the beating of somebody else's chest—than to apply in practice. Powerful psychological, intellectual, and institutional forces fight to maintain prevailing paradigms, and—believe it or not—they often succeed. If rethinking is not done seriously when the circumstances call for it, the health of the whole profession may be in question.

Today, access to Russia—its sources, archives, people, and institutions—allows massive studies and research in history and all the social sciences. Nonetheless, conditions are still difficult, and there can be political slippages and obstacles. Barring such mishaps, new avenues are available for many scholars to do important work we could not do before. Will there be enough resources for it and a national interest for maintaining this field on the same scale?

For the moment things seems to be booming in "former Sovietology"—numbers of "experts" are mushrooming, instead of one USSR we are facing fifteen nations—so, on the face of it, there is much more to do for many more people. But considering that the one was a superpower and that the fifteen are not, and that Russia itself is in for a prolonged decline, and also that the only superpower—the United States—is itself experiencing a malaise and its international vistas may be in the process of being curtailed for lack of means, will there be a flow of funds, now when the superpower competition is wound down, into the study of Russia and the other new players in the area? Curtailment is a somewhat intricate, even chilling thought—and I do not wish to insist—but attitudes and programs for actions, in case such a prospect materializes, should be devised. One of the best strategies would consist of achieving acceptance in the general scholarly world and with the knowledgeable general public (readership) by a display of quality, sound methodology, and creativity.

The Past Is Not a Hideout . . .

The impact on world affairs caused by the downfall (or meltdown) of Soviet power is the subject of a big, ongoing discussion. But let me at least signal another interesting problem, nearer to the direct professional concerns of our field: what will be the impact of the current changes on our knowledge and interpretations of large nodal points of the Russian past, for example, the downfall of the tsarist regime, the revolutions, and the making and unmaking of the Soviet system? We have been handicapped by not having in Russia a powerful community of professional colleagues, like those present for historians of France and Germany, to provide points of departure or bodies of historical knowledge to match and contribute to. The emergence of such a professional community in Russia will take some time, adding to our preoccupations an extremely interesting but complex, even painful *problématique* (itself deserving scholarly studies) concerning the emergence, or reemergence, of historical, social, and human sciences over there. How is it coming about, under what influences, and how much of the old, or from abroad, helps or hinders developments? For the moment the hampering factors are overwhelming. At its outset the Russian brouhaha produced "a rush to Russia" in the West and a mushrooming of self-appointed "experts," fresh from a month-long visit to Russia followed by an increased gullibility about Russian intellectuals' interpretations of their past and present. This is to forget that in the prevailing atmosphere of heightened emotions, the Russian intelligentsia operates the biggest gossip mill in the world and exports its product as "analysis." Russian political thought is still strongly dominated by a powerful "mechanical swerve" and quite a bit of archaic McCarthyist anticommunism that rejects the recent past (and blackens it completely) and "rehabilitates" wholesale the pre-1917 system and other previously banned things. The indispensable and salutary reaction against previous orthodoxies, lies, and taboos does not automatically consecrate its products, especially when they lead to the fallacy of "ahistoricism"—a very damaging illness in scholarship, politics, and culture. We can study and understand such reactions—but those are, precisely, reactions, not scholarship, which is still in its infancy—however interesting some articles and works may be individually. To view them as scholarship would be a trap for us. Now, as in 1917–20, a whole ruling nexus has gone or is going away, a new way of doing and running things, "a new world" is promised, but not too many people believe in it, and many, on the contrary, are naive enough to think that the best way to run away from the nearer past consists in taking shelter in an invented and redecorated earlier glory—say of St. Petersburg or the Romanov dynasty. The reality is that the new institutions are being built up—on a much larger scale than in the 1920s—by the apparatchiks formed by the previous regime. Most of the parties are run and journals are edited by intellectuals formed in and by the previous regime. Many of the previous institutions were "normal." Their experience, mode of organization, contacts, and operation were not just pathologies. They often were legitimate and fulfilled needs, even if "the system" was diseased. Therefore, not all in the past was sinister. The previous regime bequeathed continuities—good or bad is another story—as well as a new social structure, an urban society different from the tsarist past. New social classes were in the making under the previous regime, but also a huge bureaucracy. They and much of their bureaucratic practices will remain. The same applies to the intelligentsia, with its warts and all, previously a mainstay of the regime and now engaged in a painful process of becoming something else. It is interesting for us to study Russians as they rethink and revise, but we should not adopt their conclusions too hastily because they are often products of emotions, or complicated psychological defense mechanisms, and will be revised once again. The currently fashionable admiration, say for Piotr Stolypin, for the Whites, for the Russian right wing, for the church, for the tsarist couple—is it here to stay? Or the powerful distaste for everything that was on the left? The past, as many will "rediscover," is treacherous—simply because it does not go away. We should help the serious scholars (and each one of us knows at least some excellent ones) and avoid patronizing attitudes, but hallucinations, emotionalism, mediocrity, and ignorance (there are plenty of them) should be seen for what they are.

The Impediments to Knowledge

In a different, though related register, important lessons can be learned by examining the history of the Western, especially of American Sovietology, compared, say, to the pre–World War I German *Ost-Wissenschaft* or to the German studies as practiced in the United States. Among the factors that harmed Sovietology was, first, its politicization, that is, the powerful impact of the cold war and its pressure to have a Russia tailor cut to its needs, facilitated by the fact that it was not a very "likable" system. A second factor was the phenomenon of ethnocentrism, strongly opposed and deplored by many scholars for making one's own system into the model of all history and the criterion for evaluating other nations, the future, and the truth. Cold war images produced a special political demand to show a one-sided moral superiority, making the two competing systems into exponents of the ultimate and contradictory values of "good" versus "evil." Still a third factor should be mentioned, although it has nothing to do with the cold war. History and the social sciences are hampered by artificial divides that stem from a widespread academic departmental routine, advantageous in some ways but often pernicious: advantageous, because specialization is a very sharp tool; pernicious, because in reality, societies and systems are complicated entities. The fact is that fragmented scholarly disciplines cannot handle the broad sweeps of social change and trends, and the Soviet crisis is yet another proof of this fact. This crisis is "global"; it is one of a whole "system." Separate disciplines, on their own, are not equipped to handle complexes like this.

"Politicization" as troublemaker is not necessarily a reproach made to political science or scientists. First, historians, too, sometimes more than others, have on their record and conscience a long history of serving all kind of regimes, leaders, and myths. Serious political scientists, on the other hand, are aware of sociology, history, and other disciplines. But being aware does not mean having a drink together. Awareness is about "depoliticization" of their own (or any other) field, first in the direct sense of keeping a distance from current political moods and pressures and, in a deeper sense, of keeping the definition of the field, its separateness, from hardening into very rigid frontiers. Any such hardening is ominous; the definition of a field should be flexible and open-ended, responsive to its specificity and autonomy but aware of their relative character, or else it is sclerosis. Among other negative influences in Soviet history, we should also mention ideology, which is highly exaggerated and poorly understood and results in a widespread unilinearity of interpretation, a tendency to see the system in a state of fixity, a kind of substantive sameness all through. Misapplied, totalitarian theories have the same results and contribute to a main weakness of many interpretive studies—the elimination of "society" from much of the analysis.

For me "society" is the whole human aggregate and its interrelations, and those are patterned in various ways. Without such patterns life would be impossible. Terms like "system," "structures," and "classes" are indispensable for analyzing patterned entities; further and finer subdivisions and conceptual categories are equally indispensable, provided they are not arbitrary constructs. It is also quite useful to look at the broad social entities as an interplay of the essential dimensions of human life. Yet *interplay* is certainly not easy to handle, and its difficulty explains why we go for one particular dimension, especially when we believe that it is a crucial one (say, culture, economy, politics) and then maintain (erroneously) that it gives us the whole that matters in any given time. We are hearing frequent calls to emphasize the "cultural" dimension (for some it is reality par excellence and the only one), and there is certainly a wealth of insight to gain from it, especially when culture happens to be a dimension that suffuses everything else. Yet even the cultural dimension cannot replace all the others and be, as it were, turned against all of them. That again would lead into a fallacy, with results similar to exaggerating the principle of specialization—fragmenting what is not fragmented at all, subsuming a multidimensional reality in one, engendering thereby the fragmentation and impoverishment of our understanding. Finally, the cultural dimension encourages a quite fashionable doubt or denial of the validity of historical (or any other) knowledge. This doubt goes with slogans like "the end of history," or, on the other side of the political spectrum, the cultural construction of reality.

This is the right context to propose some friendly warnings against the sirens of "deconstruction." What looks sophisticated and therefore attractive is, in fact, a recurrent phenomenon in the history of scholarship, and again, of culture. The grasping of human reality (that is, all change and flux) is a matter of a continuous intellectual battle, closely intertwined with politics and ideology, and we witness some periods in which a caesura occurs and reality is questioned. In this case the real theoretical, professional, and methodological difficulties that human sciences encounter are magnified and transformed, and yet academics deny their validity. The role of ideology and politics in the scholarship and professional life of the same fields is interpreted as their essence, their basic malleability. The result is a free-for-all, and in some conceptions, no more than a domain of unverifiable personal perceptions or, at best, some results of "intersubjectivity." Interestingly enough, the most "radical" of such "postmodernist" expressions come, in this country, from the departments of English—often with a strong verbal nerve or chutzpah, and self-defeating loss of historical perspective. History is declared to be "dead," in addition to being "finished"— which comes from yet another perspective.

These people become enamored in "texts" that become the only "reality." For some, even the idea of an "author" of a text is constraining and "authoritarian." It is hubris, to my mind, notably because these ideas seem to imply—even without saying so—that they can beget themselves, they do not need to have any parents. And in any case, it would be difficult to actually prove that those parents existed, not least because "proving" is a false pretense.

All those tendencies we enumerated—specialization, unidimensionality, and finally the dissolving of all reality into "reading individuals" (with tenure, if possible)—are interesting problems. They belong to the combined fields of sociology of knowledge, of different branches of philosophy, and to studies of the history of culture. We cannot deal with them except by reiterating the point of departure: relations between specialization and theory need to be addressed to overcome the effects of anomalies that contribute to losing the sense of complicated historical entities. This loss made us commit a variety of omissions and made us vulnerable to this overpoliticization of a field that needed badly to stay away from the changing interests of political strategies. So the essential traits of what for me was fallacious, from the outset, included immutability, "linear simplification" (Lenin = Stalin, party =

totalitarianism), the refusal of change and even of history, blindness to the complexities of social and cultural development, and lack of ideas like "social system" and "process." These tendencies did not prevent many of our colleagues in different domains of Soviet studies from producing good work, but they did shape the prevailing opinions in politics, in the media, and all too often in the classroom. Those are therefore elements of a critical assessment.

Society: Lost and Recovered

My own approach is a personal example of trying to cope with historical entity. Synthesis is an ever-elusive aim, but this is what is needed. When people hear "social" they get upset, suspecting the elimination of the political and of the state; when they hear "system" (or "structure") they are troubled, suspecting the elimination of the individual, the specific, the subtle, and the personal. It is true, as said, that people who go for one aspect, or dimension, however important, do tend to exclude other components; thus we got "society with the politics out" or, not less one-sidedly, "politics with society out." What guides me in my efforts to grasp these complicated interconnections is the following: it is society that has economic and political institutions and produces values, cultures, leaders, and personalities. "Personality" and its action are social phenomena; personality does not exist, so to speak, in a vacuum. It is a social product, and this takes nothing away from its potency, originality, or, as the case may be, mediocrity. Hence, whatever aspect of society is studied—legitimately—it is always enmeshed in other aspects. Whatever we study is done by people and is organized and led by elites. Whatever the society, it depends on resources, and those, among others, involve battles for political power and authority. For example, although the family has been considered for a long time an important social category, in the past our scholarship accepted uncritically the notion than men run society. Today, however, we view gender also as an important social and historical category, and understand better that this is equally an all-societal dimension. That is how I see that social element in history in all simplicity, which amounts also to an enormous complexity, to be realized and mastered.

I like to use the term "bedrock" for the essential features of the societal configuration in a particular period, always and everywhere involving the full measure of the political, and these features change from one period to another, in our case even quite hectically. The "bedrock" was one in the middle of the New Economic Policy (NEP); it became different, more differentiated toward the later 1930s. The development and growing complexity continued until, basically, the whole social landscape changed fundamentally, as we can see for ourselves. At this stage the "bedrock" idea begins to lose some of its value; the large-scale urban societies are too complex to be analyzed in terms of a few key factors, however massive. One thing remains, though, that circles the whole seventy years: a full reversal of the main developmental vectors of this system.

Let me explain. It all began with the bulk of society being composed of a rather primitive, not very dynamic peasantry, facing an action-oriented bureaucratic state, and ended with a complex urban society, pushing for change, facing a stagnating bureaucratic state—quite a turnover! This is what I mean by the reversal of the developmental vectors. This approach was attuned to spontaneity and to processes in what appeared, essentially, a state-guided, planned action. Spontaneity helps to correct the overemphasis on the role of agencies like the party as well as the place of personality. The downfall of tsardom was, of course, not V. I. Lenin's work and not everything in the Revolution was of his doing. The radicalization of the masses and the failure of democratic parties were crucial factors, and they were not of Lenin's making either. I would add a more controversial point: a civil war was in the cards, against the Provisional Government or the Constituent Assembly, and a scenario visible in microcosm in the victory over L. G. Kornilov could have brought the Bolsheviks to power through the defense of the assembly or brought back to power the so-called Whites, at least for a time.

The Civil War and the destruction of capitalism and of the economy happened against the background of a capitalist sector already in the process of folding down before October 1917. But we also should be reminded that the behavior of peasants -as tillers and as soldiers—was a powerful factor that made some of the next steps possible or unavoidable.

What the new Soviet state (that was, in its earlier stages, a quite wretched organization) was doing during the Civil War and the New Economic Policy was only partly action and partly reaction to what was happening, or else plain drift. Incidentally, even competent authors, when dealing with the years 1918–20, do not even notice the Civil War raging in the country and speak only about the Bolsheviks and their regime. But without the other side (or sides), there is no history of the country or of the Bolshevik regime. Many longer-term trends and processes stemmed precisely from the Civil War, including the bureaucratization, the "apparatization," of the party. A man like Josef Stalin could and did know how to use these processes, but his and the regime's actions were not just pure policy, design, or plan. We were fascinated with state power and especially Stalin, who was doing things "from above," and this view seemed to be the key to the whole phenomenon, hence actually self-explanatory. But study shows that actions "from above" were followed by cascades of counteractions "from below" and from many other directions, including from the upper layers of the ruling crust. These actions again caused new responses from the top that sense in the unruly and convoluted social reality, in the societal flux, nothing less than "sedition." This sense was specific to Stalinism, which had problems living with the results of its own actions.

I tried to conceptualize the troubles of the tsarist system as a clash of the "agrarian nexus" (peasantry, nobility, and the tsarist court) with capitalist development. The Revolution destroyed both but inherited the peasant part of the nexus and produced a state of a considerably different social complexion, namely a plebeian dictatorship, soon to become incompatible with its agrarian base. I always spoke of a twentieth-century state facing an eighteenth-century peasantry—just to underline the gap, without claiming any precision in this choice of "centuries."

The Intricacies of Stalinism

The Stalinist period, its accelerated effort to take the eighteenth century into the twentieth, initially produced a social chaos that nevertheless took on less-formless contours of a basically three-layered "bedrock": poorly collectivized peasants plus freshly urbanized and industrialized peasants, a working class predominantly using hands rather than machines, and a *praktiki*-dominated (trained on the job, not in specialized schools) management and state apparatus. Here is the soil in which "Stalinism" flourished and got finally implanted as a hallucinatory terrorist state, enjoying immense support yet behaving as if permanently menaced by treason.

This support—or eventually its denial—still demands analysis, and a subtle one at that. Reading numerous biographies and autobiographies of the system's grandees and luminaries, we can rarely find one who was not accused, imprisoned, or on the brink of catastrophe. And yet the honest ones among them would say, even today, when they repudiated Stalin (the writer Konstantin Simonov is an excellent example) that they also admired him and believed in him. There is plenty here for fine social psychology, comparative historical analysis, and reflection about women and men of our times.

In any case, experience during the war showed that most of the rural population did not live in fear of purges, but in the cities—especially in institutions and among influential intellectuals—such a fear must have been widespread. Yet plenty of support existed, as did a massive phenomenon—still unstudied as far as Russia goes—of open and especially confidential denunciations. Both are important societal phenomena, and so was another that I always pointed to—the massive flood of complaints, either oral or, in millions of cases, in letters about and against injustices. We have therefore to think about the history of those years in terms of more than just "Stalinism," and this, too, deserves discussion and a few more remarks here.

It is important to show that even in (and despite) the worst features of Stalinism, there existed elements of "emancipation" because the hectic Stalinist industrial development brought up from rural Russia—and in contrast to it—new forms of social mobility, education, professionalization, and urbanization, and though such "emancipation" is not about democracy and human rights, it does introduce into the system something new. The very one-sided traditional dependence on the state is quite potently supplemented by a growing dependence of the state on this new social complexity that keeps pressing for ever more autonomies all over the system. A despotic rule cannot accept precisely this pressure because it is *samotek* (elemental) "sabotage." This conception explains how a pathological system perverted the most natural results of social change that were pertinent to our century.

The whole development of the Stalinist system can best be interpreted in this light, never forgetting the elemental and spontaneous flows and outcomes. Leaders make errors of all kinds—so did Stalin—but one has to learn how to distinguish trends from errors. Was there error in allowing the emergence of a rather sinister despotic system? There was, but spontaneous trends were also at work that either enabled it or made it at some point inescapable. The origins and the making of Stalinism—a complex phenomenon—can be refined by introducing the confluence of three features, deeply seated in the national tradition: an authoritarian patriarchalism inherent in the rural mentality; the autocratic political tradition of tsarism; and the despotic features that were ingrained in the smokestack industry that was being pushed mightily and forcefully. Finally, these three features were topped by a political despotism and its cult. The elemental social flux of the 1930s has to be added as indispensable historical context to this confluence of sociohistorical authoritarian traditions to explain the reemergence of the peculiar version of an agrarian despotism with very archaic features, but (hectically) endowing itself with modern industrial and warfare technology. This, of course, is Stalinism, a phenomenon centered on a personality, but far from just being a one-man historic show.

From a Despot to "Bureaucratic Absolutism"

Continuing the "spontaneity" theme, we can discern an analogous trio of will, drift, and trend at work in the making of a bureaucratic administrative routine, under and after Stalin and also in the working of an economy that was—it is true—state created, but once put on the rails generated a powerful momentum of its own in the form of widespread self-defensive and self-serving practices and deep disproportions and imbalances that policies tried to master but to no avail. The development of an urban society and its effects are another mighty example of essentially spontaneous processes. To summarize: both the making and the downfall of the system were not due to any particular individual's error either.

We are therefore fully attuned now to powerful shifts of huge segments or sectors in the social system, heading in incompatible, or reciprocally blocking, directions, and whenever such incompatible, crisis-making shifts occurred, slippages or worse—systemic crises—followed. The downfall of tsarism, the revolutionary upheaval, the Stalinist phenomenon, its unmaking, and finally the downfall of the Soviet system and of the old empire it inherited can and should be studied in this light. Not the same layers, not the same type of shifts were operating in each case, but elemental shifts, nevertheless, were producing ruptures, crises, and new realities. Today, as before, solutions demand, of course, conscious actions, but a spontaneous activity did and will go on and will contribute to the making of a postcrisis system, probably with greater effect than these conscious policies.

During the twentieth century, as a result of the overall development and change in the social context, at least four quite distinct varieties of political regimes emerged and succeeded each other. The Civil War produced war communism—the first version of the mono-party system that was an advance over the crumbling tsarism because it was a regime capable of being a state building agency.

It is clear to me that the NEP, based initially, to a large extent, on anti-war communism premises, was still a one-party system, with emphasis on "party." The next steps, supported by trends advancing quite strongly during the same NEP, produced a new configuration in which what is called "the party" still existed but in name only. The system became, in the 1930s, a Soviet-style despotism that appeared first as "an agrarian despotism," borrowing much from the tsarist past but with different means at its disposal—and this is to me not a "one-party system" anymore, for there was no *political* party there at this stage. Next, after Stalin, a new model of rule appeared, presided over by a bureaucratic ruling class that restored, on the face of it, some kind of organism called "party"—in essence a specific administrative agency to take care of essential state business. In any case, it all had, again, an important advantage over the decaying Stalinism because this form could respond better not just to the needs of the bureaucracy but also to many of the requirements of a changing society, broader elites, and a new international environment. (Nikita Khrushchev's de-Stalinization, e.g., was no trifle in this context.) But this bureaucratic ruling class, perched on a foundation inherited from Stalin's industrialization, soon hardened into its final shape of "bureaucratic absolutism," about which some more ideas in a moment.

A focus on social development with its attention to spontaneity permits us to understand better the vagaries of ideology. Many considered ideology as the regime's "original sin"—namely, as some intellectuals keep hammering, the presence of a societal project, an ideological design to be imposed in order to liberate, but then invariably leading to enslavement. Such constructs miss the whole point. The so-called design kept changing and even multiplying and finally actually disappearing entirely, to be replaced by several other ideologies. They had to coexist, in their defense of a simple status quo, with hundreds of thousands of smart students deriding the "diamat" and the road "to communism stage two." Ideological transformations were quite clear already in Lenin, but others who claimed to be his heirs ended up singing the anthem about this "Velikaia Rus'" that "united forever the free republics" (Stalin, probably, wrote this one himself). So, which "design" or "societal project" should we talk about? And, more important, what system?

Thus a broader view of social development encompassing the state and its ideology shows that this ideology has a history, too, and can point to the presence of several formulas, changing their colors and content. Finally, a much-sharper problem becomes ripe: how to define what this system really was, how to classify it. With ideology overemphasized and its essence actually misconstrued, the problem seemed to be covered by the system's own claim to being socialist, with a counter ideological correction from abroad that it was "totalitarian"—and all seemed to be settled.

A good analytical procedure begins it search of basic definitions by studying social realities; it does not start with ideology. From this point of view the so-called Soviet, or communist phenomenon—both terms being obviously misleading—can be seen as belonging to the class of historical phenomena that combine "underdevelopment" with "statism"—a genus of the bureaucratic species. Stopping the movement toward market mechanisms in the economy might have had in the minds of the actors involved a socialist ring to it, but in fact it just lodged the country in a precapitalist stage (socialism was supposed to be postcapitalist?) bringing it—when compared to Western countries—into a sui generis detour that it tries to overcome today.

Who Assimilates Whom in a Historical Game?

We have no space for and can only hint at very suggestive and hotly debated themes in German history that can be of help to us. According to the so-called Sonderweg school in German history, the explanation of Germany's problems, notably the veering into Adolf Hitler's state, lay in the prevalence in the past of powerful, premodern, feudal forces that controlled the state and had deep roots in society. The development of capitalism and of a vast *Bürgertum* failed, supposedly, to overcome these blockages to democracy—among them Junkers, the state bureaucracy, the army, and the court with their deeply seated nationalism, militarism, expansionism, and antisemitism. But other interpretations, when describing the powerful economic development of Germany, point to a different reading of events. It is true that the conservative state complex and its ideologies did incorporate and "contaminate" the different bourgeois layers. But the army, bureaucracy, and Junkers, pushed by economic and military interests, did in fact become themselves imbued with interests and some values of the capitalist sectors, especially heavy industry. Against the background of a speedy transition from a deeply rural to a modern industrial economy, capitalist in character, the "exchange" of values and ideologies was a two-way street: if there was "feudalization" of the bourgeoisie by the values of the conservative forces that dominated the state and by a deeply seated devotion to "statism," there also was the "embourgeoisement" of the conservative elites, notably through the Junkers' becoming agrarian capitalists on their estates. I would mention a less-talked-about but successful integration into the system of even its so-called red menace—namely, the social democracy and the working class.

We can observe parallel phenomena in the Soviet period that also fit my general "bedrock" conception. The broad picture shows here, too, a transition from an agrarian system, of which Stalinism is the last stage, to the next, an urban-industrial one. "Statism," both as ideology and as actual prevailing role of the state, is here equally present. Whatever the differences in patterns, this is Stalinism with its mixture of old and new. We can show how the system could successfully instill (Bolshevize, Sovietize, Stalinize) wanted values into strata that did not normally espouse them—the peasantry in the countryside, the industrializing and urbanizing peasantry, the bourgeois specialists, and the growing layers of specialists (intelligentsia) of Soviet minting. As a counterpart to the taming of social democracy in Germany, we can point to the destruction of the party's left—on one plane, but even more potently, the transformation of the whole party, the carrier, initially, of the Revolution— into an administration and finally, the emasculation of this political administration by its transformation into a sector, however important, of the state bureaucracy. The fast changes, especially in the last thirty years, made the presumably one-sided instilling of the regime's values into a two-way process (in fact, it was never really a one-way street) and finally into a presumably one-way street again, but in the opposite direction. Apparatus values began to lose their grip. Values of a growing urban society now beamed into the apparat and the party (not to mention the well-known *meshchanstvo* [petty, bourgeois, urban society], so powerful in the apparat, in the form of a frenetic consumerism, among others), dissolved their ideological unity, introduced ever more political pluralism (however incipient) into their ranks, and, above all, denied them the power of productive zeal—exposing the incredible inadequacies of an overgrown bureaucratic mastodon.

Once again, a peculiar twist in this history makes its appearance. The bureaucratic system that mushroomed under Stalin was nevertheless extremely vulnerable because it was the main target of Stalin's "demonization" of politics. But once he was out of sight, the bureaucratic upper crust finally did crystallize into a full-fledged ruling class, enjoying a monopoly of power, including power over economic assets and the managing of culture, to form a system I call (borrowing from Arthur Rosenberg) "bureaucratic absolutism." Like much else in Soviet history, the source of success contained also the root of the demise. Bureaucratic absolutism was dangerously, even mortally, bugged by an inability to innovate and to renovate or reform itself. The key to this inflexibility lay partly in the past but also in this combination of absolute power in the hands of a bureaucracy. Neither element had anything to offer to the mightily—I would say torrentially—changing social setting that spelled complexity, outgrowing a system created in and for a still rural, even if hectically industrializing, environment.

One particular feature in the "bedrock" notion is the problem of "the curse of Russian history," which expressed itself in getting out of underdevelopment by a combination of "extensive" methods operated primarily by the state and begetting, especially under the Soviet system, an "expanded" and stagnation-prone statism. This all too "successful" bureaucratization ended up in preempting most of the functions that had to be exercised autonomously by an increasingly complex society. The granting of autonomies (the aim of any development by the standards of most modern ideologies) was thwarted. Hence there was an inability to reform and move on into a new state adequate to handling problems at the close of the century. Hence there was stagnation and the lamentable and powerful underdevelopment again and the persistence of "the curse": the *shag vpered, dva shaga nazad* (one step forward, two steps back), a recurrent and debilitating feature. Hence there occurred the downfall of the system and the ongoing deep crisis.

What is in store? The menace, a "Brazilian" version—a state capitalism under the aegis of a social alliance of former apparatchiki and former black marketeers—is looming large. The combination of policies of the weak governments in place, with a crucially important spontaneous process to which we do not pay enough attention, and lack of sufficient forces to counteract the more unpalatable outcomes is the reality of the moment. A powerful democratic, left-leaning public opinion and parties are missing so far, and without such a countervailing force, Russia may become successfully "marketized" as well as remain retarded—again. Can this curse be overcome this time?

An interesting, even puzzling feature of the latest development is the character of the system's downfall. The system did not succumb to popular pressure, uprising, or even a movement like the Polish Solidarity. It fell of its own weight, and so did its lamentable belch, the so-called putsch. This fall occasioned a massive crisis but without any civil war—a lucky stroke, no doubt, because it has avoided bloodshed. But there was also no alternative force or leadership that a strong opposition or a side in a civil war would represent. In fact, obvious alternatives were successfully prevented from emerging by the previous system. Even Solidarity, a powerful opposition, was a movement based on sheer negation. It was not a carrier of a different regime, and it fell apart once the other side left the scene. Avoiding a witch hunt is also part of the same set of circumstances, but the lack of one also makes continuity with the previous cadres and their traditions more direct and more potent.

Conclusion

I leave the argument at this point without a summary. The debate will probably allow one, but so much is ahead, so much is open-ended in today's Russian crisis, that a continuous "introduction" is more to the point. The only conclusion can be that the crisis today is not the first, and each of them was one of a kind. Nevertheless the crises can and should be studied comparatively. There are some common features, and, if discovered, they could help in understanding how the current situation relates to longer waves in the past and how it differs from earlier turning points.

Chapter 3

From Sovietology to Comparative Political Economy

Michael Burawoy

In the opening issue of *Post-Soviet Affairs*, its editor, George Breslauer, surveys Sovietology under the daring title "In Defense of Sovietology." He opens auspiciously with summaries of two opposed perspectives within Sovietology—the "totalitarian model" of Martin Malia and the "societal model" of Stephen Cohen. But rather than engage in their debate, he dismisses them both for misreading the history of the field, which, he asserts, is much more ecumenical and diverse than either allow. He proceeds to locate Sovietologists in an impressive typology, according to their images of state and society. He concludes that, if there is a central debate, it is between inductive studies of microcomponents of a political system and deductive projections of a macrosystem's evolution.[1]

Thus, Breslauer's attempt to set the historical record straight turns out to be strangely ahistorical. It is as though nothing has happened in the last three years. To an outsider it seems to be a case of fiddling with matches while Moscow burns. Instead of adjudicating between two major orientations to Soviet development in the light of recent world historic events, or instead of presenting his own alternative perspective, Breslauer scolds these gladiators for caricaturing the field. My problem is not that Sovietology failed to anticipate the collapse of communism. Indeed, the arguments of many suggested that the Soviet order could not last. No, my complaint is that in Breslauer's review of Sovietology there is little attempt to come to terms with that collapse, let alone use past studies to project where Russia and the other former republics may now be going.[2] How is it that a defense of Sovietology ends up being a celebration of its irrelevance—in short a crushing indictment?

Debates Locked in the Past

Rather than dismiss the clash between "societal" and "totalitarian" perspectives, I reexamine each for the light they shed on Sovietology's difficulty in grappling with the transition from socialism to capitalism. Martin Malia and Moshe Lewin are two celebrated historians, strongly identified with opposed views in the debate. Moreover, Malia's "From under the Rubble, What?"[3] and Lewin's essay in this volume represent their attempts to come to terms with the present. As will become apparent, although the disintegration of "communism" is at the center of their concerns, strangely neither has much to say about the present, let alone about the future. This first part of the paper asks what it is about Sovietology that might contribute to such silences, while the second part sketches out an approach, which I loosely call "comparative political economy," to studying contemporary transformations in Russia. In so doing I take up Breslauer's challenge to integrate deductive theorizing about systemic change with more inductive case study analysis of processual change.

THE REHABILITATION OF TOTALITARIANISM

Martin Malia's essay simultaneously diagnoses the dissolution of the Soviet Union and the failure of Sovietology. He pursues a relentless denunciation of revisionist Sovietology for giving too much credence to the liberalizing and rationalizing tendencies of the Soviet order. Revisionism's worst offenders dared to imagine historical possibilities that would have taken the Soviet Union toward a market socialism or social democracy. Others, almost as heretical, defended such intimations of modernization as "developmental authoritarianism" and "institutional pluralism." Moshe Lewin, in particular, faces the drums for suggesting that perestroika laid the basis for democratization.

> The point is made that Gorbachev introduced *glasnost'*, parliament and elections, and these reforms depended upon the Soviet regime's earlier success in industrializing, urbanizing, and educating the country—a position that derives from the corpus of Moshe Lewin's writings, as these are summed up in his *The Gorbachev Phenomenon* of 1988. In short, despite all the acknowledged horrors of communist history, the system produced the resources for transforming itself. Thus, Russia's transition to democracy was an evolutionary, not a revolutionary process.[4]

For Malia the collapse of communism was the real revolution—a fundamental break with the singular, monolithic order that encompassed the entire Soviet period. In his view the idea of socialism is a contradiction in terms and the attempt to build it is profoundly irrational. It could not possibly contain the seeds of self-transformation in a democratic direction.

For Malia, then, there is nothing modern about Soviet society. It was a totalitarian society, unreformable and untransformable—a monstrous order whose goal was "building socialism" and whose means were the dictatorship of the apparat. It could only be sui generis—"a qualitatively new departure in human affairs."[5] Extinction was inscribed in its genetic code "born of the October overturn of 1917."[6] It was only a matter of time before the mythology of a radiant future would be revealed as a lie and the Soviet edifice would collapse under its own contradictions. Far from rejuvenating communism, as the revisionists thought, perestroika killed it and thereby demonstrated that Soviet society was incompatible with any modernizing tendency. The extinction of totalitarianism leaves post-Soviet Russia free to move forward to the freedoms of markets and democracy.

In trying to dispel one mythology—the Soviet Union as a modernizing society—Malia is forced to create another, the mythology of total destruction. The mythology follows from the denial of any autonomous realm for the social.[7] The Soviet order is reduced to a combination of "partocracy" and ideocracy,[8] that is, to the dictatorship of the party in the service of building socialism. The dissolution of the party, therefore, is "tantamount to dissolving the system itself,"[9] and abandoning the "idea of socialism" signals the collapse of its moral order. Thus, the real Russian Revolution took place not in 1917 but in 1991 when communism "came crashing down in one all-embracing revolution."[10] "The basic components of the system—the party, the plan, the police and the Union—were not transformed; they were abolished, and in the short span of three months after August."[11] And what was left? "Communism left in its wake, as a poisoned legacy to the democratic August Revolution, nothing but rubble—in the most literal sense of that word."[12] But the evidence of the senses suggests otherwise. Anyone who ventures into Russian society knows there has been no revolution. The party may have formally disappeared, but its leadership is still in power. Liberal democracy may reign, but it has limited relevance so long as the apparat rules. To be sure, "building socialism" is no more, market ideology abounds, the streets have become bazaars, and galloping inflation has replaced old securities, but the old administered economy has been slow to change. Indeed, as I shall argue, the Soviet economic order has, in specific ways, even consolidated itself. The union remains, if not on paper, in the continuing economic ties that were established over seventy years. As to the police, they may be muted, but Malia deceives no one in declaring their abolition. In the conventional meaning of the word, therefore, there was no revolution in 1991. This is the first time a regime has collapsed without being followed by revolution. Massive mobilization and extension of political participation—the hallmark of revolution and certainly the hallmark of the period between February and October 1917—is simply absent both now and before August 1991.

Malia, of course, is not concerned with what is actually going on in Russia today. He is interested in celebrating the collapse of communism and the advent of a world made safe for private property, the market, and liberal democracy. He talks piously of a "normal society" arising from the rubble of the old but has no way of gauging the road forward to "true modernity" because he has no point of departure, because in his totalistic view all the institutions of Soviet society collapsed together and at once.[13] Thus, the first mythology he creates, that of total destruction, ineluctably gives rise to a second mythology—the utopian fantasy that Russia can be whisked up into modern capitalism. It is not the Soviet Union but his apocalyptic theory of communist disintegration that has turned to rubble.

IN DEFENSE OF SOCIETY

My conclusion would, presumably, please Moshe Lewin, who has devoted his scholarly life to revealing the shortcomings of the totalitarian model.

> Though the term served quite well in its ideological function, it was useless as a conceptual category. It did not have much to say about where the system came from, where it was heading, what kind of changes it was undergoing, if any, and how to study it critically and seriously. In fact, the term was, in this context, itself "totalitarian" in its empty self-sufficiency: it did not recognize any mechanism of change in the Soviet Union and had no use for even a shadow of some historical process.[14]

Lewin opposes the unidimensional reduction of Soviet society to the state with a multidimensional view that includes both state and society. However despotic, however total its power, the state always creates and depends upon "society" and with it a realm of spontaneity that evades party supervision. With this more complex analytical framework, Lewin offers an appealing history of the present. In his essay in this volume he summarizes the argument developed at length in his scholarly writings: "It all began with the bulk of society being composed of a rather primitive, not very dynamic peasantry, facing an action-oriented, bureaucratic state, and ended with a complex urban society, pushing for change, facing a stagnating bureaucratic state." Soviet society had its own dialectical logic. The state, from being a force of development of society—from peasant to urban society—becomes a fetter. Here is an answer to the double puzzle: how, against all odds, did the Soviet Union last as long as it did, and in the process even become a superpower, and why, when it looked so enduring, did it collapse so unexpectedly?

In offering a theory of the rise *and* fall of the Soviet Union, Moshe Lewin is way ahead of the field. Still, the danger of being locked in combat against an alternative interpretive framework is that it limits one's own. Countering the totalitarian model with its paramount focus on the state system and its formal apparatuses of power and ideology, Lewin introduces the concept of society. The social becomes a sensitizing concept, alerting us to gaps, omissions, and silences. As such it suffers from being ill-defined as everything external to the state. Indeed, Lewin argues that it lies within the state, too. It is, in short, a residual category, and like other residual categories—the informal as opposed to the formal, the second economy as opposed to the first—its theoretical fruit comes from highlighting what is missing rather than conceptualizing the totality of what exists.

Thus, in Lewin's usage the social takes on very different meanings. On the one hand in the opposition state-society, it encompasses networks of social relations, the family, informal groups, the more nebulous public opinion as well as civil society, seen as autonomous organization and even as broad a concept as urban society. On the other hand, in the opposition plan-spontaneity, the social ranges from individual acts of exit, such as quitting one's job or fleeing to the city; to individual acts of resistance, such as restricting output, hiding resources, offering bribes, or slaughtering one's own cattle; to collective acts of resistance such as the creation of samizdat or public protest against the destruction of the environment. Important as these observations are to demonstrate the shortcomings of the totalitarian model, once made they exhaust the utility of such a broad concept of society. Sociology has long taught us that intended action has unintended consequences, that punishment-centered bureaucracies stimulate resistance, that bureaucracies in adapting to their environment experience goal displacement. These sociological truisms should be points of departure, not points of conclusion. We need to go beyond them if we are to understand the dynamics of any modern society.

Trapped by the totalitarian model into formulating the dynamics of society as the interaction of state and society, Lewin leaves key problems of the collapse unresolved: "An interesting, even puzzling feature of the latest development is the character of the system's downfall. The system did not succumb to popular pressure, uprising, or even a movement like the Polish Solidarity. It fell of its own weight, and so did its lamentable belch, the so-called putsch." If the system's downfall was a development internal to the party, albeit in response to the transformation of society, we need to understand more about the internal dynamics of the party, how it was able to go as far as it did, and how it was not able to contain the momentum it unleashed.

Ambiguous theorizing encourages opportunism. Thus, when writing in 1987 Lewin scoffs at those who question the flexibility of the Soviet system: "But most of these misconceptions are trifles compared to the widespread misperception of an inherent weakness stemming from an almost sclerotic institutional grid that cannot but be what it is and, finally, is destined to go under."[15] Now he writes: "Bureaucratic absolutism was dangerously, even mortally, bugged by an inability to innovate and renovate or reform itself." Lewin succumbs to the fallacy of retrospective inevitability in which an event that appears beyond the realm of possibility before it occurs becomes natural and inevitable after it happens. When it comes to the development of theory, it is better to problemize one's mistakes rather than conceal them behind inconsistency.

Its problems notwithstanding, Lewin's theory is unique in its attempt to encompass the origins, dynamics, and disintegration of the Soviet order on the basis of careful historiography. It is precisely what Breslauer is looking for: building macroanalyses out of microprocesses. And yet, when it comes to the genesis of the new post-Soviet order, Lewin offers no more than a gesture: "Today, as before, solutions demand, of course, conscious actions, but a spontaneous activity did and will go on and will contribute to the making of a postcrisis system, probably with greater effect than these conscious policies." To be sure this system is more than Malia's rubble, but how much more? The limitations are, once again, rooted in the undertheorized, residual category of society. But there is also a failure of sociological nerve. Lewin's historical analysis surely points to the following unstated thesis: the withering away of the party-state, rather than creating a mountain of rubble, reveals a sturdy structure of society.

In other words, Lewin implicitly presents us with a challenge: to spell out the nature of that sturdy structure. In taking up the challenge, albeit in a preliminary way, I return to Lewin's treatise on the historical and political origins of Soviet economic debates in the 1960s.[16] In this work, which owes much to N. I. Bukharin, he shows how reforms to rectify the patent inadequacies of the command system demanded recognition of a plurality of interests, regulation of the regulators, the expansion of markets, and greater autonomy for enterprises. Liberalizing the economy was tantamount to creating a rudimentary civil society.

I take these ideas forward in examining the economic basis of post-Soviet society.

FROM SOVIETOLOGY TO TRANSITOLOGY

Still the puzzle remains: why the silence about the present? Perhaps, it is too much to ask historians, burdened as they are by the past, to turn round and face the future. Perhaps. But it is also the case that the legacy of Sovietology creates its own obstacles to carrying forward an understanding of the past into the post-Soviet future. Sovietology, by definition, deals with the Soviet Union, defined by its uniqueness, by its formal characteristics. Their disappearance means that Sovietology can indeed only study the past. Even those who studied the more spontaneous, enduring elements of Soviet society have lost their bearings as the debates that propelled their scholarship evaporate. The raison d'être of the societal model depended on the totalitarian perspective, and when the latter loses its relevance so does the former.

Sovietology was born and grew in an ideological bubble. It lagged behind theoretical developments in social sciences and received them only in a heavily mediated fashion. It was unable to encounter the society it studied except through specially chosen academics, censured media, or bitter dissidents. It constructed its object as sui generis so that comparisons with other societies only served to emphasize its difference. Equally problematic, it eschewed internal variations, both within the Soviet Union and between different Soviet societies—the sort of comparative study that could provide some empirical basis for serious analyses of change. Now that the bubble has burst it is possible, nay necessary, for scholars of Russia to become "normal" and reenter the community of social scientists, to explore comparisons with a view to seeking out both similarity and difference, and to take advantage of the possibility of direct, unmediated contact with Russian society.

In their desperate search for a quick theoretical fix, former Sovietologists have been tempted to turn to their old ally, modernization theory. Whether the Soviet Union was fundamentally antimodern or whether modernity proved its undoing, the use of models, often fictitious, of Western capitalism dominated Sovietology. The Soviet Union was either fundamentally different from the West or the imperatives of industrialism were ineluctably causing it to converge on the West. In the same way interlopers are now capturing the field with their designer capitalism. They are riveted to where Russia must go—market economy and liberal democracy—rather than from where it is coming or where it might be arriving.

In its celebration of the end of history, modernization theory promotes one road forward. Countries can take it or leave it. In fact, of course, it is less a matter of choice than of conditions. In the obsession with destiny, modernization theory overlooks the specific origins from which societies, classes, economic sectors, and enterprises struggle with the Soviet legacy, and it overlooks the differential advantages and disadvantages of very late development in a world capitalist order. In short, where Russia and its erstwhile satellites are actually going is repressed.[17]

To open the historical imagination to the multiplicity of futures, it is necessary to deploy an appropriate comparative framework—one that is sufficiently general as to encompass very different epochal transitions and at the same time sufficiently precise as to highlight the specificity of the Soviet transition. In short, if the first task of this essay is to give some specificity to the concept "society," the second task is to do so in a comparative manner.

Toward a Comparative Political Economy of Transition

In studying the transformation of the old order and the genesis of a new order, we are looking at something historically quite novel— the transition from some form of socialism, I would call it state socialism, to some form of capitalism, yet to be determined. In beginning such an enterprise it seems appropriate to look for historical analogies that might guide our investigations. Many who study the transition in Eastern Europe, for example, have turned to "democratic transitions" in Latin America.[18] Such comparisons are obviously less appropriate to Russia in view of the latter's position in the world order, but even more important because they deemphasize the significance of state socialism's administered economy. They tend to focus on the political and to see this in terms of divisions within the ruling class and how these affect the relation between ruling class and popular classes. The economy gets short shrift. Instead of analogies to Latin America that miss the double transformation, simultaneously economic and political, of state socialism, I propose to compare the Russian transformation with other epochal economic transitions.

REINSTATING MODERNIZATION THEORY: THE OPTIMISTIC SCENARIO

Twice in this century Russia has attempted a historic transition: first, a transition from what we may call a specifically limited Russian capitalism to socialism, and second, a transition from a specifically Soviet socialism back to capitalism. These transitions seem unequivocal grist for the mill of modernization theory: there is but a singular road to the radiant future, and the Soviet detour was a mistake of historic proportions. Still, such a conclusion presumes that the prospects for the present transition are more propitious than for the earlier one. These are good grounds for defending this proposition.

First, the economic backwardness of Russia at the time of the October Revolution, with some 85 percent of the population still rural, made any conception of transition hard to comprehend unless it would receive considerable support from revolutions in the West. Second, such revolutions did not in the end take place, and Russia found itself not only with a backward economy but encircled by hostile capitalist nations only too ready to feed internal resistance to the revolutionary order. The Civil War left Russia economically more backward than before the Revolution. There was, in Lewin's words, a ruralization of society.[19]

Third, even though the Bolsheviks managed to survive the Civil War, they still faced huge internal enemies of socialism, namely the massive peasantry, an increasingly alienated and war-weary working class, and bureaucratic resistance. The Bolsheviks tried to reintegrate society through the extension of the party, appealing to bourgeois experts and opening the economy to market forces. But in the end the party lost faith in the New Economic Policy (NEP).

Fourth, there were no available models of actually existing socialism that might inform any transition. Instead there were only vaguely formulated utopian principles. According to the prevailing Marxist social Darwinism, capitalism was inevitably doomed and socialism would be its inevitable successor. It had not been important to examine socialism's nature, its feasibility or viability, since its superiority to capitalism was as predetermined as its inevitability. Russia had to explore this emptiness with painful improvisation.

Fifth, the form of socialism Russia would finally stumble upon at the end of the 1920s was not the product of any doctrinaire Marxism but, as Lewin has shown, was "discovered" piecemeal. It was based on state organized terror that not only demobilized, destroyed, and atomized any resistance but was specifically aimed to disable party and bureaucracy. It was not a form that could last for long, but it did bring Russia into the industrial world, however clumsily and however costly.

Sixth, a specifically new ruling ideology quite distinct from bolshevism—Marxism-Leninism—summoned and justified the sacrifices necessary to build a class society based on central appropriation and distribution of surplus. This society was so patently at odds with its legitimating ideology that eventually even the leadership could not believe in it. Without belief in its own ruling ideology and without the nerve to restore a reign of terror, the party apparat disintegrated in the face of even the weakest challenge.

The character of the transition to Soviet society contrasts vividly with the present transition back to capitalism. First, for better or worse, Russia has been brought into the industrial world. If the agrarian problem has not been solved, at least the agrarian transition has been made. The peasantry has been destroyed, notwithstanding efforts to restore it.

Second, instead of being surrounded by hostile nations feeding opposition to the new internal order, Russia finds itself entering a capitalist world, jubilant that the old enemy is joining the fold. International finance in the form of Western banks, the World Bank, and the International Monetary Fund are bent on the most rapid transition possible, even at the cost of destroying the Soviet economic foundation. A token liberal democracy is propped up by making Western support contingent on its survival.

Third, without support from the outside, the forces opposed to a market economy and liberal democracy are much weaker than the opposition the Bolsheviks faced. After seventy years of "socialism" no one has the energy to put up much resistance to the invasion of the market—although apprehension mounts daily as to where it will all end and whether tomorrow will ever bring an improvement in living standards. Having been subject to the trials and tribulations of a shortage economy, Soviet citizens are easily seduced by the glamours of consumerism. It has taken over the media—the newspapers, the radio, the television, the arts, the cinema—and the streets from hawkers to bazaars to exclusive stores. From the outside it looks irresistible, and so all are banging at its doors.

Fourth, capitalism already exists; it does not have to be invented. Russia is surrounded by a variety of capitalisms—some more attractive than others—that actually work. This situation makes the capitalist future more certain even if at the same time life itself becomes much less secure. It will be neither necessary nor possible to enter into wholesale deception of the population in order to convince people that capitalism is really here.

Fifth, the very existence of a variety of capitalisms makes it plausible that Russia will develop a capitalism to suit its specific conditions and legacies. Thoughts of third world capitalism are repressed in favor of redoubled efforts to mimic American institutions. However, when foisted onto a very different economic base, they have unanticipated consequences, throwing leaders and their foreign advisers into confusion. Initial failures can lead to the search for alternatives based on the experience of other countries.

Sixth, market ideology seems to thrive on the inequalities and injustices that capitalism creates. Indeed, unlike state socialism, capitalism does not require any legitimating ideology. It reproduces itself of itself. Those within have to peddle faster and faster to avoid being flung into the crowds clamoring to get in.

If it is true that the rise of capitalism has more chances of enduring stability than the earlier rise of socialism, a second question rears its head: will the Russian transition be more or less successful than other transitions to capitalism? Considering this question requires a very different comparative framework, which I develop in embryo in the remainder of the paper. I first explore analogies between transitions to capitalism from feudalism and from state socialism, in particular why in both merchant capital should play a key role. Turning from origins to destinies, I delineate two historic roads to capitalism—English and Japanese—and consider whether Russia might follow either. I then explore comparisons with other latecomers to capitalism and the barriers to their development posed by the capitalist world system. Finally, I turn away from such determinism by highlighting the combined and uneven movement toward capitalism within Russia.

THE RISE OF MERCHANT CAPITAL

A major contention in the debate over the transition from feudalism to capitalism revolves around whether merchant capital was a dissolvent of feudalism or whether feudalism had an endogenous dynamics of its own that led to its demise.[20] There is the subsidiary question of whether that endogenous dynamics is largely of a demographic character or whether in fact it is better understood in terms of class struggle.[21] What is clear, however, is that feudal classes coexisted quite happily with merchant capital. While merchant capital provided for the needs of feudal dominant classes, it also depended upon feudal states for protectionist policies in trade. The symbiotic relation between merchant capital and feudalism was possible because merchant capital grafted itself onto preexisting systems of production without undermining them.[22] It was, in Karl Marx's terms, not interested in the production of increased surplus value but in extracting profit by selling dear and buying cheap. Or in Max Weber's terms, merchant capital, like adventure capital, was not concerned with the rational organization of formally free labor. Both Marx and Weber saw a revolutionary gap between merchant capital and modern bourgeois capitalism. Whereas the former had a natural affinity with feudalism, the latter was fundamentally incompatible with it.

I argue similarly that in the Soviet Union the disintegration of the party-state gives rise to merchant capital and not modern capitalism. The parallel is persuasive because, under state socialism, as under feudalism, the organization of production assumed an independence from the process of distribution. Specific political and ideological mechanisms were necessary to exact tribute or rent as a means of sustaining the dominant class but also to coordinate the economic system as a whole. An economic system based on merchant capital in which profit is guaranteed through political mechanisms emerges quite naturally from both feudalism and state socialism.

In pursuing this analogy it is, therefore, necessary to begin with the legacy of the past, with a model of the state socialist economy based on central appropriation and redistribution of surplus. The party-state that runs the central planning apparatus seeks to maximize what it appropriates from and minimize what it redistributes to economic units. Enterprises have the opposite set of interests, maximizing what is redistributed to them and minimizing what they give up. The relations of appropriation and redistribution work through a system of bargaining—more or less coercive—conducted in the idiom of planning. Three features of this administered economy are important for our discussion.

First, in order for planning to work at all, centrally devised goals become specified through a system of delegation to ministries, then to conglomerates, and finally to enterprises. This system gives the economy a *monopolistic character*, since production of the same goods and services by many different enterprises is more difficult to coordinate. Duplication is viewed as wasteful. Monopolies are further consolidated by the emergent system of hierarchical bargaining over targets, success indicators, and resources. Enterprises seek to increase their power with the center through expansion and the monopoly of the production of scarce goods and services.[23]

Second, in the absence of hard budget constraints defining economic failure, the compulsion to expand leads to an insatiable appetite for resources and thus a shortage economy.[24] Each enterprise faces constraints from the side of supply rather than, as is usually the case with a capitalist enterprise, from the side of demand. Enterprises, therefore, seek to incorporate the production of inputs into their structure and circumvent the command economy by entering into informal relations with their suppliers. This semilegal system of lateral *barter relations* is organized by party and *tolkachi* ("pushers" who expedite these semilegal relations).[25]

Third, within the framework of an administered economy, workers exercise considerable *control over the shop floor* for two reasons.[26] On the one hand, under a regime of shortage, effective work organization requires flexible adaptation to uncertainty of inputs—machinery and raw materials. On the other hand, together with policies of full employment, shortages of labor give workers the power to resist managerial encroachments on their autonomy. The result is a compromise in which workers try to realize the plan so long as managers provide the conditions for its fulfillment and a minimal standard of living. The enterprise presents a united front in bargaining upstairs for the loosest plan.

What happens to a command economy when the party disintegrates and the center no longer commands? I will consider each dimension of the model in turn. First, far from collapsing, *preexisting monopolies are strengthened*. No longer subject to control either from the party or ministries, their monopolistic tendencies are unfettered. Many enterprises respond to being cut off from ministries by creating their own vertical organizations to capture supplies more effectively or by swallowing up competing organizations by denying them access to supplies.[27] Furthermore, local conglomerates protect the interests of enterprises in a given industry by acting like huge trading companies with a monopoly over specific resources and products. Turning to the second dimension, the breakdown of the party-state leads to an *increase in lateral exchanges* that had previously been strictly controlled by ministry and party. Trading relations between enterprises in a shortage economy where money is of limited value increasingly take the form of barter. A given enterprise is, therefore, the stronger the more universally desired and therefore the more barterable are its products.[28]

The third dimension of our model concerns the political regime of the firm. The decomposition of central planning gives enterprises considerable autonomy to deal with an increasingly uncertain environment. The common interest that bound together different groups within the enterprise against the central planning apparatus evaporates and in its stead *different fractions of management enter into battles over economic strategies*.[29] In this process workers continue to be without effective representation, but each managerial group presents its strategy in terms of the interests of all employees. Seeking the support of workers is more than a tactic in a political struggle; it is a particularly pressing need since workers assume even *greater control of the shop floor*. Under the Soviet order, workers already possessed considerable control over the production process due to social guarantees that gave them power, to the autonomous work organization necessary for adapting to shortages, and to management's interest in plan fulfillment and obtaining supplies rather than regulating work. With the collapse of the party, supervision at the workplace became even weaker and managers even more attentive to problems of supply and barter. The result was the expansion of worker control over production.

On the one hand, these three sets of changes can be seen as deepening distinctive features of the old order.[30] On the other hand, they can be seen as the rise of merchant capital, since the driving force behind the strategies of enterprises and conglomerates is the *maximization of profit through trade*, by selling dear and buying cheap. Merchant capital does not have its own distinctive system of production but grafts itself onto preexisting systems of production without necessarily altering them. Just as historically merchant capital tended to reinforce feudal forms of production, so I argue similarly that in Russia the expansion of trade has conserved rather than dissolved the Soviet enterprise. In effect, managers of enterprises and conglomerates "put out" work, not to families, but to work collectives within the enterprise. Rather than seeking to transform production, managers struggle to maximize returns on the products produced. That is to say, industrial production is subordinated to merchant capital rather than the other way round. Again, like merchants of the European cities, Russian top managers advance their profits from trade through political regulation. Managers use the close ties with governmental organs that they inherited from the Soviet order to protect their subsidies, credits, and export licenses and at the same time to stifle independent capital accumulation.

If the command economy disintegrates into a network of conglomerates that act as trading companies, extracting profit on the basis of commerce and taking advantage of politically bargained price differences, then the question becomes: will this form of capitalism turn into something resembling modern capitalism? In the historical case of Western Europe, it was indeed a difficult path from merchant to modern capitalism. Where merchant capital developed earliest, in the Italian city-states, it held back the development of modern capitalism. Only under the quite peculiar circumstances of English agriculture did merchant capital give way to modern capitalism and thus establish the basis of the industrial revolution. One may ask equally, but perhaps more provocatively, whether Russia will get stalled in the stage of merchant capital, just as it earlier got stalled in the stage of state socialism.

TWO ROADS TO MODERN CAPITALISM?

By convention, there are two paths from feudalism to capitalism: the one from below, which involved the creation of an independent small-scale bourgeoisie that responded to the market by transforming the character of production, and the one from above, in which the state sponsored and organized the transformation of preexisting large-scale merchant capital.[31] Former Soviet societies have attempted analogous paths of transformation. On the one hand, they have encouraged the development of a dynamic private sector based on small enterprises that develop outside the state sector. This model was most successful in Hungary, where a wide-ranging second economy was cultivated in the twenty years before the collapse of communism.[32] The present task is to continue the transfer of resources from the state sector to the private sector. Now that the protective role of the state has been replaced by the gales of an international economy, the danger lies in the strangulation of the private sector. Even with protection, the legacy of the second economy provides too fragile a basis for autocentric capital accumulation.[33]

On the other hand, where private enterprise did not enjoy such room for expansion under state socialism, the transformation of state enterprises becomes the more important question. Thus, whereas the distinctiveness of socialist Hungary lay in its economic experiments, the distinctiveness of Poland, notwithstanding its private agriculture, has centered on its mobilized industrial working class and their leaders' call for rapid transition to a market economy through free trade and the privatization of industry. Poland has become the (very problematic) showpiece of the World Bank's "shock therapy." One of the major points of contention in this model has been how to avoid "nomenclatura capitalism" in which apparatchiki become the new capitalist class by a simple transfer of property rights.[34]

Both patterns can be observed in Russia. Under perestroika, a plethora of new organizational forms were created, from the small-scale cooperatives to "small enterprises" and joint ventures. Most were attached to and dependent upon state enterprises that monopolized access to materials and equipment.[35] Typically, cooperatives were created within state enterprises to reduce levels of taxation, to introduce more flexible distribution of wages, or to avoid the system of state orders. When they were created as separate organizations, it was usually to facilitate trade between enterprises; only rarely did they develop into independent units of production. Reforms beginning in January 1992, on the other hand, have sought to transform the economy as a whole under a state-directed program. The government liberalized prices and opened the country to international market forces with a view to sorting out efficient from inefficient enterprises. Concurrently the government moved ahead with privatization plans, ordering the rapid transformation of state enterprises into joint stock companies.

In evaluating these reforms, attention is riveted to quantitative decline as measured by inflation, productivity, budget deficits, rising cost of living, and unemployment. However, these economic indicators cannot tell us where and when the economy will hit the bottom of its trough and whether subsequently it will assume a steady ascent. Answers to these questions depend on the economic institutions established. For all the attention paid to transforming state socialist economies, there is little discussion of the institutional forms of capitalism. The end point is assumed to be a market economy along Western lines –the textbook utopia of private ownership, free movement of factors of production, and perfect competition. Political and economic debate concerns the "best" strategy to accomplish this singular goal. Historical perspective suggests that strategy determines the goal, that different patterns of transition give rise to different capitalisms. American capitalism, which grew up from below, is profoundly different from Japanese capitalism, which was sponsored from above, and both are far removed from the textbook utopia. Comparison of these two forms of actual existing capitalism adds a new dimension to the transition debate.[36]

In the United States a financial model of self-accumulation has led to corporate mergers across industries. The typical American company raises capital by floating shares. As a result, it is responsive to its widely flung shareholders, whose common interest lies in maximizing dividends. Here profit reigns above all else. The stock market is, therefore, more influential than the state in guiding corporate strategy. By contrast, the Japanese economy is dominated by groups of interdependent enterprises within a single industry. Each group, or *kieretsu*, is bound together by interlocking directorships and mutual stock ownership. The major shareholders of a given enterprise are other enterprises in the same *kieretsu*, having an interest in their long-term prosperity rather than short-term profits. Moreover, each *kieretsu* is organized around a large bank responsible for obtaining and allocating credit and a trading company that secures supplies and distributes products. Instead of profit, market share is the driving force behind capital accumulation. In the Japanese order, the state rather than the stock market becomes the effective organizer of the economy. It does so through orchestrating incentives, through capital formation, research funding, taxation, and by controlling the inflow of foreign capital.

These comparisons underline just how different are the organizing principles of two major capitalist economies and how both diverge from textbook models. Given the historically specific circumstances within which each system emerged, "choosing" one or other or some combination is out of the question. Adopting strategies is not like buying goods in a supermarket. Still, studying these different economies does provide lessons and opens the imagination to a third (communist) road to capitalism. As a point of departure for such a discussion, it is worth considering the proposition that a Japanese rather than an American model is more relevant to post-Soviet circumstances. First, even in the United States, the Japanese model is widely regarded as better adapted to and more effective in modern world conditions. Second, Japanese rather than U.S. economic history is simply more relevant to the Soviet experience. The legacy of *zaibatsu* corporations, the intimate connection between state and economy (reflected in the mobility of high officials between the two), and Japan's late entry to capitalism after a period of isolation all fit the historical context of the Soviet Union. Third, if I am correct in my theory of the rise of merchant capital with its pursuit of profit through trade, then the Japanese model offers a better corrective to those tendencies than the American one, which, ironically, suffers from a similar mercantile sickness.

Yet, in practice, the Russian government has followed the advice of American devotees of the free market economy. With its eyes on (unlikely) Western credits, the Russian government tried to persuade a skeptical world, and perhaps itself as well, that it had really turned its back on the past and that it could put into practice fashionable theories of free trade and monetarism. Accordingly, the new Russian government followed the model of the World Bank, hitherto adopted in small agrarian societies with their governments often propped up by American economic and military aid. The reforms were inaugurated with the dramatic price liberalization of January 1, 1992. The idea was to weed out unprofitable enterprises by subjecting them to international competition. However, so that the situation would not get out of hand, the prices of some basic goods were still controlled. Finding themselves in a very difficult financial situation, the enterprises that produced these basic goods began to refuse to pay for supplies. Refusal led to refusal until seemingly every enterprise was claiming bankruptcy. Faced with a collapse of the economy, the government lost its nerve, turned its back on monetarism, and flooded the economy with a huge issue of credits. While merchants were able to make windfall gains from galloping inflation, most of the population suffered from declining standards of living as wages lagged behind prices. In August 1992, desperate to maintain some credibility for his economic reforms, Boris Yeltsin introduced his voucher system, which would simultaneously console the population and lead to the rapid privatization of means of production. Since it was not clear what to do with the vouchers, most people stored them away or sold them for less than their nominal value, thus further fueling inflation. The experience confirms the old adage that there is no market road to a market economy.

The mistake was to underestimate the autonomy of the economy and the capacity of its networks of huge conglomerates to sabotage economic policy. The case of banking is instructive.[37] A key dimension of the American model of capitalism is its independent banking system, regulated by the Federal Reserve Bank. In 1991 before the August events, the then Soviet state bank was turned into an "independent" Russian central bank and its separate branches were turned into commercial banks. Three types of commercial banks emerged in Russia— the original economic branch banks dominated by the agricultural bank and industrial construction bank, pocket banks created by large conglomerates, and "independent" banks created from scratch. More or less free to engage in financial transactions, banks sought the most profitable means of playing the credit and money markets. Given the rate of inflation, they extended credit to commercial operations rather than to investment projects. They tried to turn the cheap credit being dispensed by the central bank into higher-yielding loans to private commerce. As founders and major shareholders of the banks, state enterprises wanted to partake in the profits from speculative trading in money and credit. In short, banks lubricated and deepened the system of merchant capital. Their profits have risen in direct proportion to the descent of the economy as a whole.

The lesson is obvious: the growth of markets depends upon the environment in which they are planted. Recoiling from the old system, the government seeks to inaugurate a market economy overnight, adapting the institutions and models of a society with a fundamentally different economic structure. It tries to cultivate capitalism by decree, ignoring the existing institutional soil in which it must take root. As a result, the government throws itself back into the hands of the conglomerates, and the pillars of the Soviet economy are strengthened, not weakened. However unpalatable ideologically, might not the government have been better advised to recognize from the start the strength of the conglomerates and on that basis work toward a state-guided, Japanese-type economy? Would looking East rather than West have made that much difference? Are the obstacles to a transition to capitalism more fundamental than impatience, zealousness, and strategic error on the part of government? Is the successor post-Soviet state equipped to mimic Japanese-style capitalism? To these questions we turn next.

THIRD ROAD TO THE THIRD WORLD?

The danger of focusing on the goal of transformation—on the different models of advanced capitalism that might inspire government policy—

lies in underplaying the legacy of the past. This danger should be amply apparent by now. But such a futuristic focus can also underestimate the significance of external factors. Thus, it might be argued that drawing an analogy between the Soviet transition and the Western transition from feudalism to capitalism is flawed at the outset because the international economic context is so profoundly different. It is one thing to be the first to make the transition or even to be a latecomer who manages it under severe protective policies; it is quite another matter to be the last to make the transition. Indeed, rather than look to the United States or Japan, it might be better to look to third world countries for Russia's likely destiny. Here theories of development and underdevelopment are relevant.

Responding to the euphoric modernization theory that expected and recommended third world countries to recapitulate the first world's stages of development, underdevelopment theory argued to the contrary that newcomers will have to find their own road to modernity and that the world capitalist system in fact bars their way forward. In this view capitalism in the West developed and continues to develop at the expense of third world countries. That is to say, underdevelopment was created by the transfer of surplus from periphery to core, from satellite to metropolis.[38] Thus, international capital operating in the guise of merchant capital, often working through a local comprador bourgeoisie, was held responsible for extracting resources from colonies or third world countries at exploitative rates of exchange. Furthermore, merchant capital would extract agricultural or mineral surplus from third world countries but without transforming indigenous forms of production, that is, without fostering a transition to modern capitalism.[39]

One cannot but be struck by parallels with changes taking place in Russia. In the rush to take advantage of "free trade," Russian entrepreneurs seek to maximize exports, selling arms and raw materials abroad since other goods are not competitive. They divert wood, coal, gas, oil, aluminum, and even steel from the local market and dump these materials on the world market at low prices. In theory, there is a system of quotas and licenses that controls exports, but this system has enough loopholes and is sufficiently loosely supervised to allow plenty of room to maneuver for those with good connections. They work through intermediary "firms" from Western countries, often of very shady economic and even legal standing. Indeed, sometimes, when it comes to payment, these foreign firms are found to be nonexistent.

What happens to the foreign currency that is accumulated from such sales? In theory, 50 percent is supposed to be bought by the Central

Russian Bank, but there are many ways around this. A considerable but unknown amount is deposited in Western banks; estimates vary, but between $4 and $15 billion left Russia in 1992. A high proportion is converted into Western consumer goods, which are then returned to Russia and sold at prices lower than international prices, handed out to employees of the exporting enterprise, or distributed as bribes for the intermediaries who helped to organize the barter. Often, when trade involves processed goods, the Western receiving firm will insist on quality levels that require further purchases in the West. Thus, after a furniture factory had signed a contract for bed frames with a Swedish enterprise, the latter insisted that the factory use a water-based lacquer unavailable in Russia. The factory had to import the lacquer, eating away at its profits. The result of all these operations is that very little foreign exchange is used for new investment or machinery.

Despite Russia's vast resources, foreign investment is similarly insignificant. Only the most "adventurous" or "unscrupulous" foreign businesses are prepared to risk working through a vast maze of personal contacts.[40] In the face of political and economic uncertainty, they demand immediate returns on their capital, which usually involves exporting raw materials. In the words of one of the directors of a huge wood conglomerate, Russia is becoming a "banana republic." In short, international trade props up a Russian merchant class with its Western bank accounts and consumer durables, while productive investment in enterprises declines dramatically. Trade, whether local or international, does little to develop the economy, confirming the worst prognoses of underdevelopment theory.

Still, the bleak hypotheses of underdevelopment theory have come under theoretical and empirical assault, holding out lessons for Russia. Underdevelopment theory stands accused of merely inverting modernization theory, of replacing an erroneous teleological optimism with an equally erroneous teleological pessimism in which the only conceivable road to development becomes the very problematic one of insulation from the world capitalist system. Industrial growth in the so-called newly industrializing countries (NICs), such as Brazil, Mexico, South Africa, Taiwan, and South Korea, pointed to the limitations of the determinism of underdevelopment theory. Theories of dependent development arose to explain such "anomalies" by focusing on the political dimension of development, in particular the capacity of the state to sponsor and guide development.[41]

Where there was a strong multinational presence, as in Latin America, the role of the state was to manufacture developmental alliances among state, domestic, and international capital. Even so, Latin America has been much less successful in avoiding the traps of underdevelopment than Asian NICs, where direct foreign investment and landed elites were much weaker, giving the state more room to forge alliances with domestic capital. In South Korea and Taiwan the legacy of Japanese colonialism established a strong industrial infrastructure, while postwar aid and protection under U.S. political hegemony sponsored a program of import substitution. These two externally induced factors, following on each other, nurtured the accumulation of domestic capital and a strong state. Together they engineered the export-led growth behind the Asian miracles. Again the state was crucial to economic development, in particular, its insulation from political pressures, the technical expertise of its bureaucrats, its capacity to create a politically stable environment, and its control of incentives, credits, and taxation to elicit capitalist conformity to development plans.[42]

Russian recapitulation of the Asian model is out of the question, but it is still instructive to compare the Soviet and post-Soviet states with the developmental state whose "embedded autonomy" assures both independence from enterprises as well as access to market incentives to shape their evolution.[43] The Soviet economic system is usually considered to have been under the command of a strong state, but it is becoming increasingly clear that this was far from reality. The relationship between state and economy, between central organs of planning and enterprise, was a bargained relation of mutual interdependence over which the state had only partial control. The capacity of the post-Soviet state to guide the transformation of the economy becomes more limited as enterprises become more independent and the bargain relation disappears. At the same time, it has not managed to shed the Soviet interpenetration of state and economy in favor of an autonomy insulated from political and social lobbies. It turns out that direct control of the economy based on state ownership of the means of production was easier to accomplish than the delicate mechanisms of indirect control that work through market relations and private ownership.[44]

Contrary to conventional wisdom, Russia has inherited a weak state and a resilient economy, which explains why its attempts to introduce a market economy go awry and why shock therapy seems to redound to the benefit of the very economic forces it is designed to undermine. What strength the party-state had was based on its monopoly of redistribution, and from this position of strength it could under some circumstances sponsor capitalist development. Indeed, in Hungary just such a process began to take place more than twenty years before the collapse of communism. Physical planning gave way to fiscal planning, and enterprises were given more autonomy to decide their production profile, to reinvest their profits, and to find supplies. Prices were slowly decontrolled to match real market prices so that shortages of consumer goods, still so familiar in the Soviet Union, disappeared in the 1970s. At the same time, a thriving second economy, based on productive enterprise, grew in symbiosis with the state sector. Collective farms were allowed to sponsor and share the profit of independent industrial workshops. State enterprises in industry began to stimulate the growth of self-organized cooperatives that could relieve bottlenecks in production as well as provide additional revenue for the enterprise and wages for workers. All these changes took place in a relatively protected environment, of a party-state and established trading relations among the COMECON countries. If the Hungarian party-state was able to guide the development of a mixed economy, it is now losing that capacity, buffeted by international markets and domestic political forces. There, too, merchant capital has won a new lease on life.

Even more striking is the expansion of capitalism under the auspices of Chinese communism. If there is a successful third road, that is a communist road, to capitalism, it may not be through an attempted revolutionary break with the past, which in this case seems only to re-create the past, but through nurturance from within.[45] Or to adapt an unhappy Marxian metaphor, capitalism grows best within the womb of socialism. And one can presume that the offspring will be quite distinctive.

MICROFOUNDATIONS OF MACROPROCESSES

The foregoing discussion has provided different frames for studying what is, after all, a historically unique transition. It is necessary, therefore, to indicate how one might systematically pursue the questions raised in the analogical comparisons. What follows is brief and intended to be only suggestive. It takes as its point of departure the conclusion laid out above of a weak post-Soviet state and an institutionally resilient economy, calling for an analysis of the actual workings of this resilient economy and its response to state policies.

Here we face considerable methodological problems. Most economic analyses rely on aggregate figures, which present a uniformly bleak picture of galloping inflation, declining production, falling standards of living, and increasing inequality. Reliance on these figures leads to the pessimistic conclusion that what exists is natural and inevitable. Only governmental intervention as a deus ex machina can reverse the direction of change. The reification of statistics that obscures the social processes which produce them corresponds to the reification of government policy that ignores the social and economic context in which it operates.

Macroindices inevitably obscure the unevenness of microchange. They cannot reveal how the unintended consequences of state policies are produced or why such consequences vary not only by regions and sectors of the economy but also within such broad categories by enterprise and even within enterprises by department. We should start from below not from above. By comparing internal variations, by asking why change assumes different patterns in different contexts, we can identify the mechanisms and responses that lead to success here and failure there. In this way we can arrive at a more profound understanding of the composition of forces moving the Russian economy.

As I have said, the comprehension of microprocesses cannot be inferred from aggregate statistics. It requires an altogether different research strategy, quite new to the Russian scene, namely, the enterprise case study. Only careful, detailed investigation of single economic units, from a comparative perspective, can lead to an understanding of the conditions and interests that motivate different strategic responses to changes in the political and economic environment. As more case studies are included, it is possible to reconstruct and refine the mutual determination of micro- and macroprocesses. However, such extended case studies lead toward a comprehension of the broader economy only when they are based in a theoretical framework. I shall illustrate the technique with examples from research conducted in Russian enterprises—six months in 1991, two months in 1992, and six months in 1993—that was informed by and indeed contributed to the theoretical framework laid out in previous sections.

We can begin with a comparison of two enterprises that responded in very different ways to the disintegration of the party state and central planning.[46] The first, a rubber factory (Rezina) in Moscow, found it very difficult to survive, while the second, a furniture enterprise (Polar) in northern Russia, thrived on the new conditions. The rubber factory was an ancient factory whose employees, mainly women, worked in dungeonlike conditions for very low wages. The factory relied on the demand for a vast assortment of rubber products from major state enterprises. At the same time it faced a severe crisis of supply since rubber production depended on chemicals from all over the Soviet Union. The problem was not only shortage of crucial inputs but also of their transportation. As Rezina's output fell in 1991 and as the external environment ceased to exercise control over or offer benefits for the enterprise, its managers began to battle with each other over the best strategy for the enterprise to follow. Different parts of the enterprise pursued independence from the center by becoming an *arenda* (leasing arrangement) enterprise, forming themselves into a "small enterprise," or creating their own "cooperatives." The crisis of the enterprise compelled different shops to pursue innovative strategies, while the productive autonomy of each shop, that is, the lack of dependence on other shops, made such divergent strategies possible. Their common dependence on the single subenterprise that produced the basic material for all rubber production—resin—held the enterprise together, although competition for this resin often developed into internecine warfare between shops.

The furniture enterprise that produced wall systems in northern Russia was entirely different. It was eminently successful, the best-paying enterprise in Arctic City, housed in a modern new building, boasting a showroom and a polished, cohesive managerial team. The factory was the only producer of wall systems in the republic, wall systems that in 1991 were not available in the shops. They were a consumer item always in demand and therefore offered great opportunities for barter, whether cars for managers or sugar and sausage for workers. Here lies the first secret of its success. The second secret lies in the character of the product itself—made out of simple and for the most part locally available materials and using a very simple production system that cut up sheets of pressed wood into panels, covered them with textile paper, drilled holes, and then varnished them. There was a very limited variation in the final product. If the shop floor was ceded to the brigades, the overall design of the factory lay in the hands of management. There was no organizational basis for departments to pursue their own independence through *arenda* agreements, small enterprises, or cooperatives. Given their monopoly of the production of such a hot item as wall systems, there was no need for this factory to undertake the sort of innovations that made the difference between the life and death of the rubber factory.

There was another crucial factor in Polar's success, namely, its relation to the republic's wood conglomerate. The conglomerate brought together all enterprises in the wood industry, from the lumber camps to the wood-processing factories. The furniture factory was a key and potentially lucrative member of the conglomerate. Backing Polar's plans for the production of bed frames for export, the conglomerate had invested in expensive German machinery (bought before the collapse of the Soviet Union), paid for by earnings from the export of raw wood. The conglomerate in effect redistributed resources from the lumber camps to the furniture factory in the hope that the return would benefit everyone. The lumber camps depended on the conglomerate for markets, supplies, and the possibility of new machinery and so had to agree to relinquish control of their wood at relatively unfavorable prices.

Competition within conglomerates between enterprises can be very intense. The Vorkuta Coal conglomerate is a case in point.[47] The executive apparatus of the conglomerate controls the distribution of state subsidies and export quotas that are the lifeblood of the individual mines. The criteria of distribution are not based on profitability but on the cost of production and the type of coal—criteria sufficiently ambiguous to leave considerable space for political struggle within the conglomerate. The more costly the production and the lower the grade of coal, in principle, the greater the subsidies, so that the more-profitable mines support the least-profitable. In the context of an emerging merchant capital, this arrangement gives rise to bitter struggles for independence, which the conglomerate can contain only by virtue of its monopolistic access to state subsidies.

We can move one step further toward the macrolevel by comparing the way the two conglomerates mediate relations between state and enterprise. In 1992 the wood conglomerate had its ties to the Russian government cut and price controls lifted so that criteria of profitability became more important in governing relations between enterprises. It has weaker control over prices and fewer resources to redistribute. Vorkuta Coal, however, remains heavily subsidized, and its price is subject to state regulation. State orders are still in effect for 83 percent of production. The conglomerate represents the common interests of the mines when it bargains with the Russian government for subsidies (including higher wages) and export quotas (bartering 17 percent of coal for Western consumer durables). The conglomerate's bargaining power with the state is enhanced by the militancy of workers, although this power can be disruptive at individual mines. The heavily politicized and publicized miners' strikes of 1989 and 1991, which brought Yeltsin to power, provide a credible threat that the conglomerate and the so-called independent trade union use to demand wage increases. At the same time the mines know that the Russian government could cut off their subsidies altogether, and Vorkuta Coal's survival will be threatened by the cheaper coal from the Kuznetsk Basin.

These case studies reflect the first phase of merchant capital in which lateral relations between enterprises expand through barter. With the consolidation of the reforms of 1992, in particular price liberalization and privatization, the economy has entered a second phase of transition, which can be called primitive finance capital. Despite inflation of 25 percent a month, 1993 has witnessed the substitution of monetary transactions for barter. Banks, as mediators of monetary transactions, are spreading like weeds, flourishing in an environment of cheap government credit and expanding commerce. Although banks themselves have undergone a major transformation toward a modern capitalist enterprise in both their internal organization and their relations to clients, the effect is to stimulate the expanded reproduction of merchant capital in the wider economy. As in the phase of merchant capital, so in the phase of finance capital the decline in investment continues, and there is little incentive to pursue profit through the transformation of production. Privatization, far from promoting the rise of hard budget constraints, has facilitated the rationalization of soft budget constraints. Through banks, central and regional governments dispense credits to all and sundry, just as before they used to allocate materials, machinery, and labor. There is no reason to believe that building a financial infrastructure will itself transform the Soviet economy into modern capitalism.[48]

Conclusion

In this short paper I have tried to develop and extend Moshe Lewin's insights into the centrality of society in Soviet history. Just as Lewin studied the legacy of the Russian rural nexus in the postrevolutionary period, so I have pointed to the legacy of the Soviet industrial nexus in the post-Soviet period. I have shown how the withering away of the party-state revealed a resilient economy, frustrating and turning to its own purposes efforts at a rapid transition to capitalism. In studying what is reproduced and what disappears one also gains new insights into what was important in the past. Certainly, it would seem that studies of the Soviet Union exaggerated the importance of the party and the strength of the state. The collapse of the party-state will inevitably lead to substantial rewriting of Soviet history, and I suspect the shift will be more in Lewin's direction than in Malia's.

I have also tried to show the importance of comparative analysis. To highlight commonality without losing particularity is, of course, a delicate operation. In many scholarly studies of the Soviet Union the tendency was toward emphasizing its uniqueness, whereas more recently the field has been invaded by those who obliterate history in a search for quick generality. I have tried to straddle the tension by using *analogical* comparisons with other major epochal transitions to generate questions for *systematic* comparisons between and within state socialist societies. Comparisons presuppose theory, the more explicit the better. I have taken advantage of preexisting theories of transitions from capitalism to socialism and from feudalism to capitalism, of development and dependency as well as of the Soviet economy. In line with Lewin's studies of historical contingency, I have suggested how those theories might be extended to open up the range of possible futures.

Any epochal change gives rise to new bodies of social theory. The Russian Revolution and the consolidation of the Soviet Union divided the development of Marxism into two divergent paths. It prompted the transformation of the social sciences more generally, making Western thinkers more self-conscious about the virtues and defects of the market. The defeat of fascism in the Second World War led to self-confident celebration of the virtues of democracy in which the Soviet Union became anti-Christ. The crumbling of the totalitarian empire has already given rise to a second wave of modernization euphoria. Like the first wave, it is more than likely to end up in disillusionment, but unlike the first wave, instead of leading to the renaissance of Marxism, it is just as likely to herald the end of confidence in modernity *tout court* and cement the exploration of postmodernity.

Undoubtedly, we have witnessed only the beginning of the reunderstandings that will spring from examining the post-Soviet world—reunderstandings of the transitions to socialism, as well as to capitalism, and more generally of the processes of development and underdevelopment. But who will undertake these reconstructions? Will it be those who have made the Soviet Union their lifework, or interlopers who come after them and stand on their shoulders to offer grand speculations with little intimate understanding of what has been? While debate is still in flux, Sovietologists have a chance to turn their field into a leading rather than a dying edge of social science—but only if they cease to be Sovietologists.

Notes

I should like to thank George Breslauer, Lewis Siegelbaum, Peter Evans, and Daniel Orlovsky for their comments. The research that informs this essay was funded by the McArthur Foundation and the National Science Foundation and covers events up to June 1993.

[1] George Breslauer, "In Defense of Sovietology," *Post-Soviet Affairs* 8, no. 3 (1992): 197–238.

[2] Elsewhere Breslauer has written about the "present." See, for example, "Reflections on the Anniversary of the August 1991 Coup," *Soviet Economy* 8, no. 2 (1992): 164–74. However, my point is that in *defending Sovietology*, he makes only passing reference to the present, while his discussions of the present virtually ignore traditional studies of the Soviet Union.

[3] Martin Malia, "From under the Rubble, What?" *Problems of Communism* 41, nos. 1–2 (1992): 89–106.

[4]Ibid., 103.

[5]Ibid., 102.

[6]Ibid., 104.

[7]Ibid., 101.

[8]Ibid., 93.

[9]Ibid., 90.

[10]Ibid., 93.

[11]Ibid., 103.

[12]Ibid., 91.

[13]Ibid., 91.

[14]Moshe Lewin, *The Gorbachev Phenomenon*, expanded ed. (Berkeley: University of California Press, 1991), 3.

[15]Moshe Lewin, *The Gorbachev Phenomenon*, 1st ed. (Berkeley: University of California Press, 1988), 9.

[16]Moshe Lewin, *Political Undercurrents in Soviet Economic Debates* (Princeton: Princeton University Press, 1974).

[17]Lewin's "history of the present" is another version of modernization theory. In his study of the collapse of the Soviet Union, the past is seen as leading to a singular present and history loses its contingency. He tries to keep up with the changing present by altering his theory. Instead of the theory of contingency that marked his studies of the rise of Stalinism and collectivization, he now offers us contingency of theory.

[18]For example, Adam Przeworski, *Democracy and the Market: Political and Economic Reforms in Eastern Europe and Latin America* (Cambridge: Cambridge University Press, 1991).

[19]In my rendition of the rise of the Soviet order I have borrowed from Moshe Lewin, *Russian Peasants and Soviet Power* (London: George Allen and Unwin, 1968); Lewin, *The Making of the Soviet System* (New York: Pantheon, 1985).

[20]Rodney Hilton et al., *The Transition from Feudalism to Capitalism* (London: Verso, 1976).

[21]T. H. Aslon and C. H. E. Philpin, eds., *The Brenner Debate: Agrarian Class Structure in Pre-Industrial Europe* (Cambridge: Cambridge University Press, 1985).

[22]Maurice Dobb, *Studies in the Development of Capitalism* (New York: International Publishers, 1947).

[23]See, for example, Alec Nove, *The Soviet Economic System* (London: George Allen and Unwin, 1977); Tomas Bauer, "Investment Cycles in Planned Economies," *Acta Oeconomica* 21, no. 3 (1978): 243–60.

[24]Janos Kornai, *The Economics of Shortage*, 2 vols. (Amsterdam: North-Holland Publishing Co., 1980).

[25]Joseph Berliner, *Factory and Manager in the USSR* (Cambridge, Mass.: Harvard University Press, 1957); Jerry F. Hough, *The Soviet Prefects: The Local Party Organs in Industrial Decision-Making* (Cambridge, Mass.: Harvard University Press, 1969).

[26]Vladimir Andrle, *Workers in Stalin's Russia* (New York: St. Martin's Press, 1988); Walter Connor, *The Accidental Proletariat* (Princeton: Princeton University Press, 1991); Donald Filtzer, *Soviet Workers and Stalinist Industrialization* (Armonk, N.Y.: M. E. Sharpe, 1986); Holubenko, "The Soviet Working Class," *Critique* 4, no. 4 (1975): 5–26.

[27]Simon Johnson and Heidi Kroll, "Managerial Strategies for Spontaneous Privatization," *Soviet Economy* 7, no. 4 (1991): 293. See also Heidi Kroll, "Monopoly and Transition to the Market," *Soviet Economy* 7, no. 2 (1991): 143–74.

[28]Michael Burawoy and Pavel Krotov, "The Soviet Transition from Socialism to Capitalism: Worker Control and Economic Bargaining in the Wood Industry," *American Sociological Review* 57, no. 1 (1992): 16–38.

[29]See Michael Burawoy and Kathryn Hendley, "Between Perestroika and Privatization: Divided Strategies and Political Crisis in a Soviet Enterprise," *Soviet Studies* 44, no. 3 (1992): 371–402.

[30]Simon Clarke, "Privatization and the Development of Capitalism in Russia," *New Left Review*, no. 196 (1992): 3–28.

[31]Hilton et al., *Transition from Feudalism to Capitalism*.

[32]See, for example, Alec Nove, *The Economics of Feasible Socialism* (London: George Allen and Unwin, 1983); David Stark, "Coexisting Organizational Forms in Hungary's Emerging Mixed Economy," in *Remaking the Economic Institutions of Socialism : China and Eastern Europe*, ed. Victor Nee and David Stark, with Mark Selden (Stanford: Stanford University Press, 1989); 137–68; Nigel Swain, *Hungary: The Rise and Fall of Feasible Socialism* (London: Verso, 1992); Ivan Szelenyi, *Socialist Entrepreneurs* (Madison: University of Wisconsin Press, 1988).

[33]Istvan Gábor, "Modernity or a New Kind of Duality?" in *The Unofficial Legacy of Communism: The Ironies of Transition in Eastern Europe*, ed. G. M. Kovács (New Brunswick: Transaction Publishers, forthcoming).

[34]Michal Federowicz and Anthony Levitas, "Polish State Enterprises and the Properties of Performance," *Politics and Society* 19, no. 4 (1991): 403–37; Levitas, "The Trials and Tribulations of Property Reform in Poland: From State-Led to Firm-Led Privatization, 1989–1991" (paper presented at the conference "The Political Economy of Privatization and Public Enterprise in Eastern Europe, Asia and Latin America," Brown University, April 1992); Jadwiga Staniszkis, *The Dynamics of the Breakthrough in Eastern Europe: The Polish Experience*, trans. Chester A. Kisiel (Berkeley: University of California Press, 1991).

[35]Anthony Jones and William Moskoff, *Ko-ops: The Rebirth of Entrepreneurship in the Soviet Union* (Bloomington: Indiana University Press, 1991).

[36]In making the following comparison between the United States and Japan I have drawn on Neil Fligstein, *The Transformation of Corporate Control* (Cambridge, Mass.: Harvard University Press, 1990); Chalmers Johnson, *MITI and the Japanese Miracle* (Stanford: Stanford University Press, 1982); Rodney Clark, *The Japanese Company* (New Haven: Yale University Press, 1979); Michael Gerlach, *Alliance Capitalism* (Berkeley: University of California Press, 1992); John Zysman, *Governments, Markets and Growth* (Ithaca: Cornell University Press, 1983).

[37]See Joel Hellman, "Bureaucrats vs. Markets?" unpublished paper, Department of Political Science, Columbia University, 1991; "The Revenge of the Past: Building Market Institutions in Soviet-Type Economies" (paper presented at the annual meeting of the American Political Science Association, Chicago, September 3–6, 1992).

[38]The classic formulations are Paul Baran, *The Political Economy of Growth* (New York: Monthly Review Press, 1957); Andre Gunder Frank, *Latin America: Underdevelopment of Revolution* (New York: Monthly Review Press, 1969); Samir Amin, *Unequal Development* (New York: Monthly Review Press, 1976); Immanuel Wallerstein, *The Modern World System* (New York: Academic Press, 1974).

[39]Geoffrey Kay, *Development and Underdevelopment* (New York: St. Martin's Press, 1975).

[40]See, for example, the many articles in both the Soviet and Western press on the spoils from Russian oil and aluminum deals that flowed to the infamous international commodities trader, Marc Rich, who is wanted by the U.S. Justice Department on a fifty-one count indictment for fraud, racketeering, and tax evasion. "Rich, Influential and Very Dangerous," *Izvestia*, June 2, 1992; "Artem Tarasov, Marc Rich and Others," *Izvestia*, July 8, 1992; "Again on the Mysteries of 'Big Business,'" *Izvestia*, August 3, 1992; "How the USW Hit Marc Rich Where It Hurts," *Business Week*, May 11, 1992; "How Rich Got Rich," *Forbes*, June 22, 1992; "Rich Pickings," *Independent Magazine*, March 27, 1993.

[41]See Fernando Cardoso and Enzo Falletto, *Dependency and Development in Latin America* (Berkeley: University of California Press, 1979); Peter Evans, *Dependent Development: The Alliance of Multinational, State and Local Capital* (Princeton: Princeton University Press, 1979).

[42]See Frederic Dedyo, ed., *The Political Economy of New Asian Industrialism* (Ithaca: Cornell University Press, 1987), Gary Gerafti and Donald Wyman, *Manufacturing Miracles* (Princeton: Princeton University Press, 1990).

[43]For analyses of the "developmental state" and "embedded autonomy," see Dietrich Rueschmeyer and Peter Evans, "The State and Economic Transformation: Toward an Analysis of the Conditions Underlying Effective Intervention," in *Bringing the State Back In*, ed. Dietrich Rueschmeyer, Peter Evans, and Theda Skocpol (Cambridge: Cambridge University Press, 1985), 44–77; Peter Evans, "The State as Problem and Solution: Predation, Embedded Autonomy, and Structural Change," in *The Politics of Economic Adjustment*, ed. Stephan Haggard and Robert Kaufman (Princeton: Princeton University Press, 1992), 139–81; Vedat Milor, *The Comparative Study of Planning and Economic Development in Turkey and France* (Madison: University of Wisconsin Press, forthcoming); Gary Hamilton and Nicole Biggart, "Market, Culture, and Authority: A Comparative Analysis of Management and Organization in the Far East," *American Journal of Sociology*, Supp. (1988): 52–94.

[44]This is the argument of Kiren Chaudhry, "The Myths of the Market and the Common History of Late Developers," *Politics and Society* 21, no. 3 (1991): 245–74.

[45]Victor Nee, "Organizational Dynamics of Market Transition: Hybrid Forms, Property Rights, and Mixed Economy in China," *Administrative Science Quarterly* 37, no. 1 (1992): 1–27; Andrew Walder, "Corporate Organization and Local State Property Rights: The Chinese Alternative to Privatization" (paper presented at the conference "The Political Economy of Privatization and Public Enterprise in Eastern Europe, Asia and Latin America," Brown University, April 1992).

[46]Burawoy and Hendley, "Between Perestroika and Privatization"; Michael Burawoy and Pavel Krotov, "The Soviet Transition from Socialism to Capitalism: Worker Control and Economic Bargaining in the Wood Industry," *American Sociological Review* 57, no. 1 (1992): 16–38.

[47]Michael Burawoy and Pavel Krotov, "The Rise of Merchant Capital: Monopoly, Barter, and Enterprise Politics in the Vorkuta Coal Industry," *Harriman Institute Forum* 6, no. 4 (1992).

[48]These conclusions are based on six months' research into banking in northern Russia during the first half of 1993.

Part II

Nationalism and National Identities

Chapter 4

Rethinking Soviet Studies:
Bringing the Non-Russians Back In

Ronald Grigor Suny

The series of crises in the late 1980s and early 1990s that led to the collapse of the Soviet Union and the evaporation of the "socialist choice" were matched by a parallel crisis in the field of Soviet studies. Enjoying a new celebrity, pundits flourished in the fertile fields between predictions and postmortems, while scholars observed the creative chaos of the post–Soviet Union with concern about their more traditional enterprise. The limitations of Sovietology have been well surveyed—overemphasis on stability and stagnation of the old regime and the resultant failure to predict the kinds of reforms initiated by Mikhail Gorbachev; obsession with the political and a lack of attention to the social and cultural; excessive focus on the Russian center with consequent neglect of the non-Russian peoples.[1] One might also mention the overhasty leap to model building without adequate empirical underpinning (a practice only in part and only in the early years of the profession necessitated by inaccessibility and lack of sources); the shaping of the field by the cold war division of East from West, left from center and right; the conditioning of research by sources of funding and policy needs of sponsors; and the generational differences between the field's founders and those who came after and sought to "revise" their mentors' orthodoxies.[2] Yet too often the urge to overthrow and rebuild (here I am showing my age) has led to a dismissive, even derisive, attitude toward the real achievements of fifty years of academic writing on the USSR. That record is varied and uneven, but even in the polarized years of the cold war serious engagement with the difficulties of an unknown world produced studies of great power. For all the limitations of the totalitarian model—its rush to assimilate Stalinism into fascism, its narrow focus on the leader and politics at the top, its inability to deal with change within the system, its blindness on the national question—fundamental aspects of the Stalinist regime were illuminated by scholars, such as Merle Fainsod and Zbigniew Brzezinski, writing in this tradition. Though one might legitimately take issue with the fatalism of the totalitarian approach and its original reading of Stalinism as the culminating point of the Soviet revolution, one should at least acknowledge that some of its proponents, like Brzezinski or Alex Inkeles,

Clyde Kluckhohn, and Raymond A. Bauer, did attempt to adjust the model to fit ever-shifting realities and were able to produce extremely suggestive works, like *The Soviet Bloc* and *The Soviet Citizen*, that provided both analyses of change and a range of prospective evolutions. In its various incarnations, the totalitarian approach was tied to the restructuring of political alliances and loyalties after World War II and may have had a pernicious influence that reached far beyond scholarship. But it never totally dominated scholarship itself, even in the most frigid years of the cold war, and within the totalitarian school there were those, like Inkeles and Bauer, who focused on society as much as on the state and wrote, however briefly, on the nationality problem.[3] Finally, as pretentious as the totalitarian model's claims to explanatory completeness may have been, one can agree with Alexander J. Motyl that "the radical rejection of totalitarianism as a conceptual mode pushed Sovietology away from theory; to a certain degree it may be argued that, in ridding themselves of the bath water, Sovietologists also threw out the baby."[4]

Whatever the ultimate failure to predict indicates about social science in general and Sovietology in particular, for several decades the major empirical historical and sociological work on the USSR was carried out in a foreign community of scholars, working under difficult circumstances of limited access to primary sources. The quite extraordinary monographic literature of the 1970s and 1980s, particularly in Russian history, testifies to the ability of the "children" and "grandchildren" of the founders to develop their own scholarly agenda, reconceptualize Western thinking of such contested issues as the Revolution of 1917 and the viability of the New Economic Policy, and deepen understanding of the imperial state and nobility, the revolutionary movement, the costs of collectivization, and the purges. Even though government and many scholars were deeply invested in an unmodulated condemnation of all Soviet policies and practices, no intellectual consensus or single discourse was ever imposed on Russian-Soviet studies, and after the 1950s, a healthy and relatively tolerant exchange characterized the field. Against those who collapsed the whole Soviet experience into Stalinism or saw an unbroken continuity between V. I. Lenin and Josef Stalin, the work of Isaac Deutscher, Moshe Lewin, Robert C. Tucker, and Stephen F. Cohen offered an alternative picture of the varieties of Bolshevism and possible trajectories. In my own experience, a teacher like Alexander Dallin provided a welcome skepticism about the harder-line visions of the cold war world. And for all the criticism directed at them, revisionists of various types remained a vital part of a professional dialogue—so much so that many conservative critics of Sovietology in their post-Soviet reassessment see "revisionism" as the hegemonic reading of Soviet history among Western scholars by the mid-1970s.[5]

Soviet Nationality Studies: From Cold War to Hot Wars

Besides the chasm that for most of the forty-five years since the Second World War separated Soviet scholars from Western scholars, another hard-to-bridge gap divided those Western scholars studying non-Russians from those doing Russian history and Soviet politics. Just as it had been acceptable until recently for historians to treat all humankind as if it were male, so the study of imperial Russia and the Soviet Union could be treated unapologetically as if these empires were homogeneously Russian. For the first several decades the central concerns of mainstream Sovietology had to do with politics, economic growth, and foreign policy, and sociologists, applied anthropologists, and social psychologists played the most important roles in the founding moments of postwar studies of the USSR. Along with political scientists and political historians, they focused almost exclusively on the party and regime studies. Studies of nationalities were left to émigrés with strong emotional and political affiliations with nationalist movements, whose personal experiences with the brutalities of Stalinism indelibly colored their writing. Studies of non-Russians, so often pungently partisan and viscerally anticommunist, were relegated to a peripheral, second-rank ghetto within Soviet studies and associated with the right-wing politics of the "captive nations."

Until the turn toward social history in the late 1960s and 1970s, concentration on the state left society relatively—though not entirely — ignored, and the legacy of the totalitarian approach encouraged seeing the non-Russians as objects of political manipulation and central direction, sometimes as victims of Russification, sometimes as pathetic, archaic resisters to the modernizing program of the central authorities. Nationalities were homogenized; distinctions between them and within them were underplayed; and political repression and economic development, with little attention to ethnocultural mediation, appeared adequate to explain the fate of non-Russian peoples within the Soviet system. Since studying many nationalities was prohibitively costly and linguistically unfeasible, one nationality (in the case of the Harvard Project on the Soviet Social System, the Ukrainians, "clearly the outstanding candidate for this purpose") was chosen to stand in for the rest.[6]

Though in the locus classicus of the totalitarian model—Carl

Friedrich and Zbigniew Brzezinski's *Totalitarian Dictatorship and Autocracy*—nationalities were not mentioned as potential "islands of separateness," along with family, church, universities, writers, and artists, in time the non-Russian nationalities were conceived of as possible "sources of cleavage" in the Soviet system and, therefore, of significance.[7] As Inkeles and Bauer wrote in 1961:

> Much attention has been given to the nationality problem as perhaps the weakest link in the chain of Soviet armor. Interest in the question has been intensified because exiled representatives of the national minorities have been extremely vocal in calling attention to the nationality question and its potentialities as a focus for psychological warfare. Indeed some of those leaders have gone so far as to insist that they can, if given sufficient resources, foment internal revolutions and successful independence movements among those of their own nationality inside the Soviet Union.[8]

Though the thrust of their findings emphasized the salience of social class, Inkeles and Bauer noted:

> National and ethnic membership constitutes a basis for loyalties and identifications which cut across the lines of class, political affiliation, and generation. Nationality could, therefore, easily be a major determinant of the attitudes and life experiences of the individual and consequently a central element in the functioning of Soviet society.[9]

Here the social was at least introduced, but social and ethnic were contrasted and seen as largely opposed to one another. Later studies would demonstrate how variety among nationalities in economic well-being and differential access to social resources could create complex patterns of class-ethnic complementarity in which the social and ethnic would combine to reinforce cleavages between rulers and ruled.[10]

When attention was turned to non-Russians in the early postwar years, the dominant Western conclusions stood in stark contrast to the Soviet claim to have solved the "national question." Émigré scholars from the Soviet Union, with their unique experience and linguistic endowments, were key in the generation of information and analysis of the non-Russian nationalities. The Institute for the Study of the USSR, founded in 1950 in Munich and secretly funded by the Central Intelligence Agency until it was closed in 1971, published a series of monographs, symposia, and periodicals in which the brutalities and horrors of Bolshevik repression during the Civil War and the Stalinist period and the excesses of police rule were carefully documented.[11] But the polemical style and inflamed language of many of the texts compromised their value as scholarship. In a collection of essays entitled *Genocide in the USSR: Studies in Group Destruction,* Soviet nationality policy as a whole was treated exclusively as a series of cultural, demographic, and social genocides. Like the term "Red Fascism," the use of the neologism "genocide" linked Stalinism to the universally despised nazism, and the accompanying imagery of inevitable expansionism generated by totalitarianism, with any negotiation with such an adversary considered appeasement, was applied to considerable effect to the major existing threat to the West. Genocide, it was argued, was "one of the inevitable concomitants" of Soviet totalitarianism. "Various forms of genocide may disappear and new ones may appear, but the practice itself must continue, irrespective of changes in the leadership of the Communist regime. It cannot be relinquished as a Soviet means to its goal until the Communist totalitarian system itself comes to an end."[12]

Published after Stalin's death, well into the period of Nikita Khrushchev's reforms, works like this became part of the debate about the possibilities of change within the Soviet system and Western strategic responses to an unyielding communist threat. Ironically, the efforts of Western political scientists, in particular, to improve the totalitarian model occurred as the very Stalinist system on which it was based was in the process of political reform.[13]

Whether expressed in the extremely charged language of the Munich institute or the more modulated words of the influential Walter Kolarz or Richard Pipes, the Bolshevik Revolution and the Soviet state were presented as a fundamentally imperial arrangement, a colonial relationship between Russia and the borderlands.[14] The Revolution and Civil War were conceived as a series of conquests of ethnic peripheries by the Russian communist center, with legitimacy and morality on one side and cynical manipulation of ideals in the interest of naked power on the other. In his remarkable survey of the Revolution in the non-Russian regions, Pipes wrote with great sympathy for the nationalist perspective, though he often overestimated the degree of popular nationalism and political coherence of the non-Russian populations, particularly in his discussion of Central Asia. The activities and proclamations of nationalist leaders or writers were used as indicators of the attitudes of whole peoples, and the widespread support for socialist programs, particularly in the early years of the Revolution and Civil War, was played down. Moreover, by not treating the Baltic countries, where Bolshevik strength, particularly among Latvians, was considerable, the role of foreign intervention in the victory of the nationalists decisive, and the pragmatism of Lenin in recognizing the indepen-

110 RONALD GRIGOR SUNY

dence of Poland, Finland, Estonia, Latvia, and Lithuania notable, Pipes reduced the interconnected complexities of civil and ethnic warfare to a simple picture of military expansionism from Russian center to non-Russian periphery.

Deservedly respected as a synthetic treatment of the histories of dozens of nationalities, Pipes's encyclopedic account dealt primarily with politics and parties. A stronger social historical approach, as I have written elsewhere, would have led to different emphases. Much of the social history of the 1970s and 1980s depicted the Revolution in the central Russian cities as a struggle between increasingly polarized social classes, or at least an intense pulling apart of the *verkhi* (top) and the *nizy* (bottom) of society, while historians of the borderlands traditionally emphasized ethnic rather than social struggles and failed to illuminate the ways in which the two were connected. Yet in multinational regions, social conflicts were very often conceived in ethnic terms and given cultural meanings that obscured the sources of conflict.[15] The Revolution and Civil War can be seen as a single experience that engulfed the millions of Russians and non-Russians in both a common maelstrom of imperial collapse and social revolution. Bolshevism was not everywhere the enemy of non-Russian actors, but it was seen by many as the preferred alternative to a national independence promoted by a small nationalist elite in the name of a peasant majority. The difficult choice for both Russians and non-Russians was whether to support the central Soviet government and the Revolution as now defined by the Leninists or to accept a precarious existence in alliance with undependable allies from abroad with their own agendas. Ethnic considerations were always bound up with estimations of the relative advantages to be gained from the options available, which in turn were influenced by the cultural determinants of interest calculations.

The conception of the Soviet Union as an empire certainly makes comparative sense, but the nature of this peculiar empire requires more detailed investigation. The product of migration as much as conquest, ideological as well as economic interconnection, both the tsarist and Soviet empires were remarkable in the ways they contributed to the formation of nations within them. Like Pipes, most scholars writing on the Soviet peoples treat nationality as an unproblematic category and national consciousness and nationalism as natural reflections and expressions of a national essence that needs little historical explanation. Though Pipes demonstrates that the full mobilization of many peoples was accomplished only with great difficulty, if at all, the assumption seems to be that it was only a matter of time before nationalism spread beyond the intelligentsia, that its absence may be explained by political immaturity or the effectiveness of Bolshevik propaganda. The authenticity and legitimacy of the nationalists' formulations are never in doubt, and they are opposed to the artificiality of the Communists' claims. Though his story goes up to 1923 and the foundation of the Soviet Union, Pipes includes no discussion of Soviet policies directed at preservation and development of national cultures within the USSR. Indeed, in the decade following Pipes, few discussions of Soviet nationality policy dealt with the *korenizatsiia* (nativization) policies of the Soviet party-state in the 1920s, with the notable exception of the work of Mary Matossian on Armenia.[16]

A discordant note in the chorus of voices of the 1950s and early 1960s that echoed the nationalist vision of the communist world was the work of Inkeles, Bauer, and Kluckhohn, whose

> most important and striking findings on the nationality problem cast serious doubt upon the assertions most often made by émigré nationality leaders concerning the central role of nationality status in determining the attitudes of Soviet minorities. The basic social and political values of our respondents, their attitudes toward the Soviet regime, and their life experiences were on the whole strikingly little determined by their nationality as compared with their social origins or their class position in the Soviet system. On most questions a Ukrainian or Georgian lawyer's or doctor's responses are more like a Russian lawyer's or doctor's than like a Ukrainian or Georgian peasant's. And the same goes for the Russian member of the intelligentsia as against the Russian peasant. . . . Thus, we may conclude that basically a man's nationality is not a good predictor of his general social and political attitudes in the Soviet system, but rather that these attitudes are better predicted by knowledge of his occupation or social class.[17]

The major conclusion of the Harvard Project—"that ethnic identity is of comparatively minor importance relative to social class membership as a predictor of the individual's life chances, his attitude toward the regime, and many of his general socio-political values"[18]—was not taken to mean that nationality was irrelevant in all matters. Though there was "little evidence of gross discrimination in life chances which the Soviet regime provides to youths of Ukrainian as against Russian origin when the background the of two was otherwise comparable," there were differences between occupational achievements "with more restricted opportunity and lesser rewards being the apparent lot of the Ukrainians."[19] The salience of nationality was felt more by Ukrainians than Russians when it came to marriage and family life. Ukrainians were also about twice as likely as Russians to recommend dropping an atom bomb on Moscow.[20] One-third of Ukrainians interviewed were very pro-Ukrainian and more anti-Russian than anti-Soviet; another third showed some nationality consciousness on some issues but not on others; and a final third exhibited no visible anti-Russian feeling, did not experience discrimination on the basis of nationality, and were unconcerned about the national question. "Our data indicate that it is primarily the older people who are knowledgeable about and identified with Ukrainian culture and folklore, which indicates some success for the regime's effort to suppress knowledge of certain historical figures and events. Even more important, however, is the fact that the younger, well-educated respondents are least likely to charge the regime with mistreatment of the Ukrainian people."[21]

In retrospect, two other aspects of the Harvard Project are noteworthy. First, the evaluation of Soviet nationality policy on the part of the refugees interviewed was not wholly negative. "Refugees from the less well-developed areas point to the positive achievements in the direction of racial equality, increased educational opportunities, and technological and industrial advance. The regime has claimed and received credit in the eyes of many non-Russians for improved medical facilities, the increased literacy rate, the growth of the theater and cinema, and other developments."[22] Muslims, however, more than any other large minorities,

> feel deprived of their cultural heritage. Furthermore, the relative isolation from the center of many Moslem groups and the wide gulf between their culture and that of the European Russian probably facilitate the relative endurance of a Moslem subsociety in the villages which is both an actual and a potential source of passive resistance to Soviet and Russian penetration. However, resistance groups within the USSR are atomized. . . . Russification and diminishing of strong nationality feeling have proceeded rapidly during and since World War II, owing to the movements of peoples, liquidation of dissident leaders, industrialization, and increased literacy in Russian.[23]

A second conclusion was that the USSR was a relatively stable society and that the nationality issue was not one that threatened that stability.

> Time is mainly on the side of the regime as far as the nationality issue goes, particularly because of the trend among the youth noted above. Population transfers and purges of the national, political, and cultural leaderships, while increasing the resentments

of articulate elements in the national populations, have even further reduced the possibility of their raising an effective opposition against the regime. Most of the various minority borderlands are increasingly dependent on Moscow because of more and more economic specialization. Local situations in some cases (e.g., Armenian fears of the Turks and jealousy of a strong Georgia) also reinforce ties to the center. Most of all, the drift through time is enhanced by larger processes which tend to destroy folkways and nationality feelings, such as urbanization, industrialization, and increasing Union-wide literacy in Russian. Project data show rather dramatically the extent to which, even a decade ago, attitudes had become homogenized along social class rather than nationality lines. However, the very process of minimizing national differences in the USSR produces resentments, especially in the trouble spots of the moment.[24]

The work of Inkeles, Bauer, and Kluckhohn was a model of applied social science—coolly detached, mildly critical of existing paradigms, and cautious in its predictions. Much of the Manichaean moralism of the totalitarian school had been left behind.[25] Yet *The Soviet Citizen* was decidedly a product of a particular moment in Western social science. It was already marked in its conclusions by modernization theory, the idea that industrialization and urbanization were fundamental in shaping the life experience and psychology of the Soviet peoples. It also flirted with convergence theory and the assumption that industrial societies, both democratic and totalitarian, had common features.

> The distinctive features of Soviet totalitarianism have for so long commanded our attention that we have lost our awareness of an equally basic fact. The substratum on which the distinctive Soviet features are built is after all a large-scale industrial order which shares many features in common with the large-scale industrial order in other national states of Europe and indeed Asia. . . . Many of the general features of the modern industrial order are remarkably close to the special features of the Soviet system.[26]

But Inkeles and Bauer saw neither an incompatibility between totalitarianism and industrialism nor the likelihood of a "managerial-revolution." And on the nationality front there was little prospect of the national republics becoming "that tinder box, which so many have asserted them to be."[27]

Toward the end of the 1960s Western Sovietology became less one-sided and provided a more balanced picture of successes and failures—to be sure, on balance, still negative in its judgments. The post-*Sputnik* appreciation of Soviet economic and technical achievements and the notion of a society, however alien, that seemed in some ways to be becoming more like ours contributed to a reading of the Soviet experience as an alternative model for development. New possibilities for research in the USSR—and eventually outside of Moscow and Leningrad—and the availability of a wider range of contact and information, most notably the results of the 1959 census, affirmed the sense of a society in transition. "The verdict of the objective student," wrote Erich Goldhagen in his introduction to *Ethnic Minorities in the Soviet Union* in 1968,

> on the historical performance of the Soviet Government in the treatment of ethnic minorities under its rule cannot be rendered in clear-cut and unicolored terms. . . . Among the minorities, material achievements, impressive as they are in many cases, have been attended by intellectual and cultural constrictions and the tailoring of their identities, and all have been exposed to the pressures of Russification. Yet all we know about the Soviet minorities suggests that their ethnic personalities are alive and that their muteness is a tribute to the efficiency of the totalitarian Leviathan rather than a sign of the absence of collective aspirations. If the incipient, feeble, and struggling trend toward pluralism in Soviet society increases, then these aspirations may assert themselves and profoundly affect the shape of Soviet society.[28]

The tension between the new interest in change and pluralistic aspects within the Soviet system, on the one hand, and older assumptions of the universalism of central command and domination, on the other, is evident in an influential article published in the same volume, by John Armstrong.[29] Adopting a modified functionalist approach, Armstrong began with assertions that the Soviet elite was committed "to maintain control of the decision-making process in the present Soviet Union and to expand the power of the USSR as widely as possible" and that this commitment in turn required "a unified national culture" that must be Russian.[30] Given those aims, much of nationality policy and its effects on non-Russians is understood to be central manipulation calculated to realize the goals of the regime. Armstrong went beyond the customary treatment of "Soviet nationality policy, and, indeed, the entire ethnic problem in the USSR, as a single, homogeneous phenomenon" and outlined a number of "functional types of ethnic groups." One of the great accomplishments of the Soviet system, claimed Armstrong, is the absence of an "internal proletariat" made up of ethnic migrants. More characteristic are the "mobilized diasporas"—educated, mobile ethnicities, like Jews and Armenians—that help in the modernization project.

Armstrong contrasted them to "younger brothers," nationalities close to the dominant ethnic group culturally but low in social mobilization, for example, Belorussians and Ukrainians. "State nations," those like the Baltic peoples and the Georgians with "strong traditions of national identity," were distinguished from the "colonials" just entering the transition to modernity, such as Soviet Muslims.[31] Armstrong's schema are instructive, but his "view from the dictatorship" does not include consideration of ethnic elites within republics with their own agenda, not to mention the variety of cultural and social evolutions taking place among non-Russians that diverged from the stated goals of the central regime.

Reflecting the interest in the 1960s in problems of "development," Alec Nove and J. A. Newth collaborated on a provocative study, *The Soviet Middle East*, to test Soviet economic and social achievements against those of its neighbors to the south. On the question of industrialization, Nove and Newth argued that association with Russia had been a net benefit for the southern republics.

> Given that capital was relatively very scarce, given also the much richer untapped resources in Siberia and parts of European Russia and the Ukraine, it followed that, if economic rationality alone were adopted as a guide, there would be very little industry in [the Central Asian and Transcaucasian] republics. In a free-enterprise setting, in a huge free trade area within the USSR's present borders, it is very doubtful if there would be rapid industrial growth in these regions. They have benefited, therefore, not only from being part of a much larger whole, but also, or even particularly, from the fact that the Government of the USSR had an industrializing ideology, equated social progress with industry, and paid special attention to the development in formerly backward areas.[32]

In the areas of education and other social services the southern republics also benefited from Soviet policies. In the area of finance, "by and large, with the possible exception of Azerbaijan, the republics contributed a less than average amount, *per capita*, to the revenue of the Soviet Union" and "were permitted to retain a more than average proportion of all-Union revenues raised in their territories, to finance economic and social development. . . . The Russian connection, membership of a large and more developed polity, greatly facilitated such social and economic progress as was achieved in these areas."[33] Soviet-style development was distinct from Western-style imperialism.

Far from there being any economic exploitation, it is reasonable on the evidence to assert that industrialization, especially in Central Asia, has been financed with money raised in Russia proper. In other words, capital has tended to move to those outlying under-developed areas and there has been virtually no counterbalancing move of remittances of profit or interest, because in the Soviet Union capital grants are not repayable and do not bear interest. . . . This may be contrasted with the very substantial remittances of profits to capitalist companies from Latin-America. No reasonable person can doubt that industrial growth would have been less rapid without Russian capital and Russian skills.[34]

Reluctant to call the relationship between center and periphery "colonial" in the sense of economically exploitative, Nove and Newth, nevertheless, pointed out that all real decision-making power rested with Moscow. "Therefore, if we do not call the present relationship colonialism, we ought to invent a new name to describe something which represents subordination and yet is genuinely different from the imperialism of the past."[35] However distinctive Soviet imperialism was, its emphasis on development would have been familiar to imperialists of other empires, and the form of that development was decided almost exclusively in the center, with the needs of the empire paramount and those of the indigenous peoples secondary.

The opening of the Sovietological discussion occurred simultaneously with the arrival of a new generation of younger scholars, most born in the United States, the greater academic professionalization of Soviet studies, and a lessening of the conformist ideological pressures of early years. The work and career patterns of this generation soon routinized into three or four years of graduate study at university, followed by a research year in the Soviet Union, and a year or two of writing up the dissertation. However one's research interests might be connected with non-Russians, teaching appointments were defined as Russian or Soviet (read, Russian), and almost all nationality specialists had to teach more broadly. In many ways, they carried a double burden: maintaining their field specialization and keeping up with the central interests of Soviet studies, which provided employability, an audience for their work, and a certain legitimacy.

The monographic literature of the 1970s and 1980s was part of a larger academic discourse that, in the wake of the dismantling of the totalitarian model, sought new paradigms for understanding the Soviet Union. The emphasis on Kremlinology and model building of political science of earlier years made way for more empirical and historical studies, while historians turned from high politics and institutions to an obsessive interest in social history. While there was no guarantee

that the social historical turn would lead to attention to non-Russians—
consider the groundbreaking work of Moshe Lewin, which assiduously left out non-Russians—a number of political scientists and sociologists turned toward non-Russians to deal with problems generated
from disciplinary concerns.[36] Zvi Y. Gitelman's discussion of the *Evsektsiia* (the Jewish section of the party), for example, was both grounded in
modernization theory and sensitive to the different models of development used in different periods of Soviet history.

> Without denying the usefulness of the totalitarian model in ex-
> plaining much of Soviet history, we might find it more enlighten-
> ing to view the first decade of Soviet power as a period in which
> an authoritarian regime attempted to mobilize social and eco-
> nomic resources for the purpose of rapid modernization, political
> integration, and political development. . . . The modernization
> strategy of the Bolsheviks in the 1920s differed substantially from
> the Stalinist pattern of modernization and in many ways resem-
> bled the "nationalist revolutionary" pattern as seen, for example,
> in Mexico and Turkey.[37]

Gitelman's story, like that of Gregory J. Massell, who explored the same
period in Central Asia, was one of Communist Party failure "to combine modernization and ethnic maintenance," largely because of the
poor fit between the developmental plans of the party and the reservoir
of traditions and interests of the ethnic population. Evkom (commis-
sariat for Jewish National Affairs) and Evsektsiia had set out to destroy
the old order among the Jews, Bolshevize the Jewish workers, and reconstruct Jewish life on a "socialist" basis, that is, "establishing the dictatorship of the proletariat on the Jewish street."[38] Jewish Communists
were relatively successful in eliminating Zionism and Hebrew culture,
"new and tender growths on Russian soil," and in encouraging Yiddish
culture, but they failed to "eradicate religion, so firmly rooted in Jewish
life."[39] Bolshevism also failed to understand nationalism, and by the
1930s the party subordinated all ethnic concerns to the overall program
of rapid state-dictated industrialization. In Central Asia, as Massell
demonstrates, the failure to mobilize women as a "surrogate proletariat" with which to overturn the patriarchal social regime led to a curious accommodation with traditional society.

> A revolution in social relations and cultural patterns evidently
> could not be managed concurrently with large-scale political, or-
> ganizational, and economic change. . . . Political institutionaliza-
> tion and stability as well as a modicum of economic growth had
> to be purchased at the price of revolutionary and ideological pu-

rity and of a lower rate of social transformation. This implied a willingness, on the part of the regime, to tolerate distinctly uneven development in political, economic, and socio-cultural spheres—indeed, a willingness to leave pockets of antecedent life-styles relatively undisturbed, if necessary, for an indefinite period of time.[40]

This kind of complexity, which included greater appreciation of the need for attention to chronology, periodization, change, and increased awareness of contradictions and improvisations in Soviet policies (rather than the steady working out of an a priori Marxist blueprint), characterized the best work in nationality studies through the 1970s and 1980s. Exemplary in telling a story far messier and contradictory than had been told during the cold war was a widely read article by Teresa Rakowska-Harmstone.[41] Using a "dialectical" approach to explain the "increasingly assertive ethnic nationalism among the non-Russian minorities," she illustrated how "powerful integrative forces . . . released through the process of industrialization and the accompanying expansion of mass education and intensive socialization" were countered by "the retention of a federal administrative framework" that "safeguarded the territorial loci and formal ethnocultural institutions of most minorities, thereby preserving the bases for potential manifestations of national attitudes."[42] Distinguishing between "orthodox" and "unorthodox" nationalism, the first permitted within the system, the second advocating secession, independence, and/or the rejection of the system's ideological mold, she demonstrated how indigenous ethnic elites in the republics sought "sources of legitimacy in their own unique national heritage" and established ties with their own nationality through the skillful manipulation of permissible "nationalism." The consolidation of ethnic power and consciousness in many (though by no means all) of the non-Russian republics was challenged continually by "the continued political, economic, and cultural hegemony enjoyed by the Great Russian majority and the national chauvinism manifested by this group vis-à-vis the minority nationalities."[43] Whatever the policy goals of the regime (sblizhenie, or rapprochement; sliianie, or full merger), whatever the expectations that social mobilization and economic growth would blunt the edge of minority nationalism, in actuality national cohesion and nationalist expression were growing and were "on a collision course with party policies."[44]

An explosion of empirical studies—by, among others, Barbara A. Anderson and Brian D. Silver, Hélène Carrère d'Encausse, Murray Feshbach, Rasma Karklins, Gerhard Simon, and Victor Zaslavsky—benefited from the greater availability of Soviet statistics and the work of Soviet colleagues like Iurii Arutiunian and Iulian V. Bromlei.[45] A general rise in interest in ethnicity and ethnic studies in the 1970s and 1980s brought new scholars and new resources into the field of Soviet nationality studies. Armenian studies programs and endowed chairs were established at Harvard, UCLA, Columbia, Michigan, Fresno State, and other universities. Institutes of Ukrainian studies were founded at Harvard and Alberta. A chair in Estonian studies was funded at the University of Toronto. Along with the development in knowledge of the variety of ethnic processes in the Soviet Union, several scholars, like Gail W. Lapidus and Alexander J. Motyl, encouraged broader conceptual thinking about the problem of nationality in the USSR.[46] Through the 1980s a series of volumes, under the general editorship of Wayne Vucinich, appeared in the Hoover Institution Press's series Studies of Nationalities in the USSR.[47] Praised by reviewer David D. Laitin as "the best historical and contextual accounts of Soviet nationalities available in English," they failed in his view, to develop a shared theoretical conceptualization of the problems of nationality and nationalism.

> For Olcott, once national boundaries are historically constituted, they remain relatively fixed; that is, national identifications are eternal. . . . Meanwhile Allworth opens his study of the Uzbeks by asking: "How will the creation of a corporate, retrospective nationality where none existed before affect people when it is politically motivated and applied and executed by outsiders?" (p. 4). He answers that a politically imposed category can take on social meaning by virtue of state action (chap. 11) and of the strategic activity of intellectuals who found it useful to call themselves Uzbek (pp. 229–31)—this in combination with a fear of Tatar domination over Central Asia that pushed Uzbek intellectuals away from a broader identity (p. 180). National traditions, that is, are created out of struggle; they are not a primordial given. Finally, Suny looks for answers in social analysis: the various Georgian nationalist movements are seen as the design of particular classes or coalitions of classes, aimed at securing wealth or legitimate domination. In sum, nationalities are variously presented in the volumes as primordially real, historically reconstituted, or socially organized—without any synthesis to reconcile these distinct visions.[48]

For all its extraordinary achievements, Soviet nationality studies was not prepared for the "rise of nations" in the USSR and the collapse of the union. Though some scholars, like Robert Conquest and Carrère d'Encausse, warned of the coming nationality crisis in the USSR, most others would have answered Alexander Motyl's question in the title of his book, *Will the Non-Russians Rebel?* as he did.

> Structural grounds for opposition are there: latent conflict tendencies are inherent in the ethnic pattern of domination of the Soviet Russian state. In time, if economic decline and ideological erosion set in and outside interference continues, behavioral reasons for rebellion may accumulate. At some point, non-Russians may massively want to rebel. But will they? As long as the public sphere is occupied and, more important, as long as the KGB remains intact, the deprivatization of antistate attitudes will be problematic, antistate collectivities and elites will be unlikely to mobilize, alliances between workers and intellectuals will not materialize, and rebellion, revolt, and insurrection will be well-nigh impossible. Because they cannot rebel, non-Russians will not rebel.[49]

Motyl was both wrong and right. In fact, non-Russian peoples, beginning with the Armenians and the Baltic peoples, did rebel and in that rebellion further weakened the central state's authority and legitimacy. In the end, the erosion of central power and the unwillingness of Gorbachev to use violence against the population made possible the massive ethnic oppositional movements that unraveled the Soviet system.

Where to Go, What to Do: The Future of "Soviet" Nationality Studies

"Soviet" nationality studies have now come to the center of both professional and public political attention. One might refer to this—forgive the chauvinism—as the "post-Karabagh syndrome." The expansion of awareness of non-Russians in the late Soviet period and in the early post-Soviet period has been accompanied by a variety of initiatives from government, universities, foundations, and exchange programs to expand the possibilities for research in the newly independent republics. One might mention only the formation of the International Research and Exchanges Board (IREX) Advisory Group on Central Asia and the Caucasus, the opening of an IREX office in Erevan, and IREX's new program supporting individual advanced research opportunities in the Baltics, Georgia, and the Commonwealth of Independent States. The number of graduate studies from what might be described as "nonethnic" backgrounds interested in Central Asia, the Caucasus, Ukraine, and elsewhere has exploded in recent years, and students working on primarily Russian topics have been sensitized to the need to look at multinational and ethnic factors in their work. Ethnicity has joined class and gender as part of the grand triad of references of which historical and social scientific thinking must be aware.

Like so many other fashionable turns in Sovietology, so this recent move toward the non-Russians has been dictated by policy requirements and the interests of funders.[50] Yet in the post–cold war environment nonconformist thinking is more easily tolerated, and members of the academy who might have been marginalized or disregarded in the more frigid years of East-West confrontation now find themselves addressing official audiences. Whether ideology is dead or not is less important than that policymakers believe it is no longer relevant in a period of democratic capitalist triumph. With the communist menace buried, officialdom is willing to listen even to dissonant voices that help it understand the current power of nationalism, predict the future of the decolonized Soviet bloc, or foresee new dangers from postnationalist fundamentalisms.

A number of suggestions might be made on the future of work in nationality studies.

First, the insights of particular ethnocentric studies must somehow be married to broader comparative and theoretical perspectives in cultural studies, political science, and sociology.[51] The evident turn toward history should be encouraged. Many practitioners in Sovietology have already demonstrated how historical case studies can enrich the field. From sociologists like Gregory J. Massell to political scientists like Zvi Gitelman, Robert C. Tucker, and Stephen F. Cohen, older modeling tumbled before the empirical texturing provided by histories that accented the metamorphoses of the Soviet system. With the recent opening of the Central Party Archive in Moscow and widening access to both central state and regional archives, historical research offers fertile ground for generalizations, new conceptualizations, and the development and testing of theory. Comparative studies of nationalities might investigate why some have moved more rapidly than others toward assertion of sovereignty and declaration of independence. The whole problem of formation of nations within the USSR, an essentially historical project, is fundamental to understanding the trajectories, ambitions, and self-conceptions of the post-Soviet nations. Everything from borders to literary languages has been historically constructed, rather than naturally determined, and the present moment offers a unique opportunity to find investigators and funding for such explorations.

That research should not be confined to the period after 1917, however, for one of the glaring lacunae in Russian-Soviet studies has been the undevelopment of prerevolutionary investigations of non-Russians, particularly in a comparative, multiethnic, or empirewide context. There have been no major studies of imperial nationality policies or of the differentiated effects of imperial state economic policies on non-Russians since the initial probes by Hugh Seton-Watson and a few intrepid monographists a generation ago. The "making of the tsarist empire" is a topic ready for its researchers.

Second, the new opportunities for work in the field should encourage the development of approaches to nationality studies that were limited in the past, namely survey research and anthropological fieldwork. One of the most suggestive treatments of a non-Russian people in the 1980s was Caroline Humphrey's work on the Buryats of Siberia, which underlined the uneven transformative effects of Soviet collectivization and the persistence and adaptation of cultural forms and kinship patterns.[52] Discovering patterns not unlike those uncovered by Tamara Dragadze in her study of a Georgian village, Humphrey showed how

> the communal values, inherent in the working of a collective farm, have the effect of supporting parochialism and local ties. . . . On some occasions such as the wedding ritual or the *suurkharbaan* games, units of the collective farm even take over the functions of the earlier kin groups. More common, however, is a dual and parallel maintenance of two different kinds of communal group, purely Soviet on the one hand, and "Buryat" (or more correctly Buryat-Soviet) on the other.[53]

From her fieldwork in the northern Ob River region in Siberia, Marjorie Mandelstam Balzer observed how even a very small ethnic group, the Khanty, were able to adapt themselves selectively to the large Russian-Soviet milieu but without complete cultural disintegration. For smaller peoples biculturalism proved to be a viable response to the pressures of the multiethnic, Russian-dominated Soviet environment.[54]

Third, borrowing methodologies from other disciplines or attempting cross-disciplinary study seems self-evidently to be a laudable and innocent enough enterprise. This has been one of the major strengths of the area studies approach. But in fact the "historical turn" in anthropology and the "anthropological" or "cultural turn" in history have led to considerable intellectual uncertainty about the approaches of both fields. The poststructuralist and postmodernist innovations have at one and the same time opened up new ways of thinking about identities and categories that appeared fixed and clear and divided the profession between those anxious about relativist and discursive erosion of unexamined fixities and those anxious to undermine old certainties.

In its largely atheoretical treatment of nationality, much of Sovietological thought has either accepted uncritically a commonsensical view of nationality as a relatively observable, objective phenomenon based on a community of language, culture, shared myths of origin or kinship, and perhaps territory—or not thought about the question. Nationalism, in what I have referred to elsewhere as the "Sleeping Beauty" view of nationality and nationalism, was seen as the release of denied desires and authentic, perhaps primordial, aspirations. This view contrasted with a more historicized view that has gradually gravitated toward a postmodernist understanding of nationality as a constructed category, an "imagined community." The latter, or "Bride of Frankenstein" view of nationality and nationalism, which has hegemonized academic writing outside of Sovietology in the last decade, argues that, far from being a natural component of human relations, something like kinship or family, nationality and the nation are created (or invented) in a complex political process in which intellectuals and activists play a formative role.[55] Rather than the nation giving rise to nationalism, it is nationalism that gives rise to the nation.[56] Rather than primordial, the nation is a modern sociopolitical construct.

The emphasis in Soviet studies on a priori nations that have reawakened in the Gorbachev era to put forth their long-repressed demands has had the regrettable effect of suppressing study of the formative influence of the seventy-year-long Soviet period. Seldom adequately evaluated, except negatively, by most Western writers and by the nationalists now in power in many of the non-Russian republics, the Soviet period was in fact the incubator of new nations that were formed in part as a result of contradictory Soviet policies (e.g., *korenizatsiia*, or the "rooting" of national cultures, particularly in the 1920s, followed by Stalinist Russification) and in spite of them. Unfortunately, at the very moment when opportunities for most interesting research are opening up, when the possibility of working more closely with colleagues in the post-Soviet world has become a reality, the triumph of anticommunist nationalism has also meant the victory of a certain reading of history and the potential exclusion of other readings. New political requirements at the moment of establishing ethnic claims to territory and statehood may foreclose conceptualizations that threaten the essentialist understanding of the antiquity and solidity of nations.

Examples of the kind of thinking of which scholars should be most suspicious are particularly prevalent in the media. In an article on the Armenian-Azerbaijani conflict, entitled "In the Caucasus, Ancient Blood Feuds Threaten to Engulf 2 New Republics," Serge Schmemann of the *New York Times*, for example, referred to

> images of unavenged deaths and ancient hatreds, of tribal passions that 70 years of enforced Communist harmony failed to quell. . . . Artsakh, [Khachatur B. Simonyan] declares, using the ancient Armenian name for Nagorno-Karabakh, is indisputably Armenian and nonnegotiable. "Do you know when the first Turk set foot on Karabagh?" he thundered with disdain. "Only in 1752! How can they claim that these are their lands?"
>
> That he should consider 240 years so negligible begins to explain why a mere 70 years of Soviet peace failed to still ancient passions. . . .
>
> To Nagorno-Karabakh belongs the distinction of being the first tribal conflict to break through the enforced Soviet peace. That was four years and more than 2,000 casualties ago.[57]

Rather than an "ancient tribal" conflict, the war in Karabagh can be read as a multilayered struggle over territory and national identity that has as much to do with cultural and social constructions of what makes up Armenia and Azerbaijan in the twentieth century as it does with older narratives, with who Armenians and Azerbaijanis conceive themselves to be after seventy years of Soviet state making, and how each people defines the "other" that it is ready to annihilate. Though there have been numerous conflicts between Armenians and Azerbaijanis in this region, there have been long periods of coexistence and collaboration as well. Few historians would excuse Serge Schmemann if he attributed the first and second world wars, fought within twenty years of one another and by the same adversaries, to the same causes or to ancient tribal antagonisms that could be read back into primordial Gallic or Gothic origins.

Scholars of Russia, the Soviet Union, and the post-Soviet area would benefit enormously from the insights of those critics of intellectual traditions that have separated Russia and "the East" from the "more advanced" or progressive or civilized West. Russia and the Eastern bloc, not to mention the non-Russian areas of Transcaucasia and Central Asia, have been the victim of an Orientalist disdain for a backward society and state formation that maliciously deviated from the normal, natural path of world civilization. As Edward Said has pointed out, thinking about the non-West is really a way of understanding and conceiving "the West." In such a perspective the non-Western other, be it

Russia or the Middle East, is seen as inferior and alien, and it can then be intellectually and perceptually, if not politically, dominated. The evident acceptance of such an idea of deviation from civilization and historically constructed inferiority by post-Soviet intellectuals has created a community of consensus between American conservatives and Russian "democrats," but the confidence with which difference between the communist experience and the normal path of civilization is declared only masks profound epistemological difficulties and unexamined political assumptions. "The East" has not only connotated weakness and inferiority, but mystery and danger. At this moment when fundamentalist Islam occupies the space left by Marxism-Leninism, when the Green Menace has replaced the Red Menace and the threat from Russia appears to have dissipated, all the cultural apparatus remains in place to restore old fears and suspicions should there be a change in government or a restored military.[58]

Fourth, in much of the past writing on Soviet nationalities, non-Russian communities have been treated as homogeneous, relatively coherent groups facing the Russian other. Predictions by the 1970s included the notion that *homo islamicus* would stand against *homo sovieticus*. But just as the Soviet Islamic world proved to be far from homogeneous, so many of the republics found themselves divided internally, and on closer focus even within ethnicities divisions along class, gender, generational, and regional lines can be observed. The vertical integration of the nation, which had been proposed by nationalists as the more authentic social alliance in opposition to horizontal class solidarities, has often proven to be quite fragile. The clearest case is Georgia, where interethnic struggle evolved into intraethnic civil war, but in Armenia, Azerbaijan, Lithuania, Ukraine, and the Central Asian republics deep political cleavages have also emerged now that the Russian imperial enemy has been displaced. Among the most serious cleavages have been those between old political classes, often made up of former communists remade as nationalists, and rival elites; between cosmopolitan intellectuals and more popular nationalist forces; between more intensely nationalist regional elements and more assimilationist or accommodationist groups; and between religious fundamentalists and secular modernizers. Strange and seemingly unpredictable alliances between ethnic and social groups have been formed in the new context of states dominated by a formerly repressed nationality. Russian and non-Russian minorities (e.g., Poles and Russians in Lithuania) in multinational fronts confront nationalities seeking to become hegemonic in their "homeland."

Fifth, clearer definitions and distinctions must be made in our thinking about nationality and nationalism. A common vocabulary may be an impossibility, but some collaboration and agreement in the use of common terms would enhance further discussion. Here again comparative studies are most important, and the field of post-Soviet studies must be linked with the broader field of ethnic studies. The relative neglect or complete omission of the work of Fredrik Barth, Donald L. Horowitz, Harold Isaacs, Anthony D. Smith, and other theorists of ethnic identity and conflict is glaring in Soviet nationality studies.[59] The problem we are studying is no longer confined to a demonstration of the weaknesses and failings of Soviet-style regimes in the area of nationality policy but rather the consequences of empire and the difficult postcolonial transition from authoritarianism to democracy, from an imposed hegemonic culture to the construction of national cultures.

Sixth, for all its orientation on policy making and the Russian center, Soviet studies in the past managed largely to avoid discussion of Russians as a nationality and Russian nationalism as a cultural and political expression of underdeveloped nationhood. Exceptions to the rule, like Frederick C. Barghoorn, John B. Dunlop, Roman Szporluk, and Alexander Yanov only made more apparent the silence both of scholarship and of the Russians themselves.[60] Like the largest non-Russian nationality, the Ukrainians, the Russians are in the throes of an intense national formation in which neither the boundaries of the nation nor the degree of inclusion and exclusion of populations has yet been determined. Here the processes of constructing identities, affiliations, and loyalties, of projecting images of enemies, and of formulating "national interests" are under way with no certain end in sight. A period of political competition among rival definitions of the nation lies ahead as the Russian republic—not unlike the other republics—struggles with a more exclusively ethnic (*russkaia*) notion of nationhood and a more inclusive (*rossiiskaia*) idea of citizenship.

The variety of Russian nationalisms—ranging from Russophilic nostalgia for a lost past to authoritarian and neofascist movements—and the phenomenon of Russian national state building in the post-Gorbachev period have heightened the need for distinctions between various kinds of nationalisms. Certainly an imperialist nationalism of a Vladimir Zhirinovskii must be distinguished from the self-deterministic nationalisms of Rukh or the Pan-Armenian National Movement.[61] If the various functions of nationalism—as mobilizer of disparate strata and diverse regions around the "nation," defender of ethnic privileges and advantages, or claimant to recognition of existence, legitimacy, and security—are uncritically homogenized, analysis of the variety of nationalist movements is rendered impossible.

Seventh, while nationalists might gloat that the idea of *sovetskii narod*, that "meta-ethnic entity" projected as the Soviet future by communist theorists and ethnographers, has died an ignominious death, one of the consequences of empire has been the ethnically mixed population that resulted from intermarriage and migration within the USSR. The 65 million former Soviet citizens who live outside their nominal "homelands" (25 million of whom may consider themselves ethnically Russian); partners in or children of ethnically mixed marriages; the so-called *russkoiazychnye* (Russian speakers); and millions who still identify with a country that no longer exists all defy easy categorization into ethnic nationality. Even in many of the non-Russian peoples a deep imprint of "sovietism" (*sovkovost'*)—of habits and expectations, values and ways of thinking—is not quickly erased.[62] This extraethnic formation had a reality of its own, which needs to be studied, if only because supraethnic "nationalities," like the American or Swiss, present vital alternatives to the more ethnically determined nationalities.

Finally, the future of nationality, nationalism, and nationhood needs to be considered in all its multidimensionality and contradictions. The twentieth century appears to have been a century when nationality, far from melting away in the pot of capitalist or socialist modernization, emerged as a potent form of social cohesion, consciousness, and allegiance. Given the legitimacy of the contemporary discourse of national self-determination, both in its Wilsonian and Leninist variants, the drive of nationalism in this century toward recognition of nations as states has an unquestioned authenticity and authority. But both on the road to sovereignty and after achieving it, ethnic nations have often attempted to achieve full empowerment of the dominant ethnic group through ethnic homogenization. Democracy, defined as both majority rule and legal protection of minorities, has often been the victim of nationalist movements in power.

At the same time, the other great secular trends of the twentieth century—the transnational nature of modern capitalist economies, the internationalization of the division of labor, mass migrations, the homogenization of pop culture over the globe, and the consequent compromise of state sovereignty—have challenged the viability of homogeneous ethnic states. As Eric J. Hobsbawm observed,

"The nation" today is visibly in the process of losing an important part of its old functions, namely that of constituting a territorially bounded "national economy" which formed a building block in the larger "world economy," at least in the developed regions of the globe. Since World War II, but especially since the 1960s, the role of "national economies" has been undermined or even brought into question by the major transformations in the international division of labour, whose basic units are transnational or multi-national enterprises of all sizes, and by the corresponding development of international centers and networks of economic transactions which are, for practical purposes, outside the control of state governments.[63]

Lest this sound like one more variant of economic determinism and another "Marxist" failure to appreciate the independent variables of demography, politics, and culture, one might also note the current migration of peoples from south to north, east to west, so threatening to relatively homogeneous nations like those in Northern Europe; the flow, not only of commodities, but of money, American culture, and information and technology; the creation of a global culture, an international legal system, and extranational media networks—all of which compromise the agendas of single ethnicity states.[64]

Just as an integration of "Russian" studies and the study of non-Russian peoples seemed about to break through, the collapse of the Soviet Union and the Soviet bloc into constituent national states threatens, not only to reinforce the division of ethnic Russian from non-Russian studies but to explode the whole concept of "Russian-Soviet and East European" area studies. As parts of the former USSR gravitate in one direction toward Scandinavia, in another toward Central Europe, and in a third toward the Middle East, scholars are increasingly doubtful about the conceptual unity or intellectual justification for an area studies approach. A disciplinary approach may be more tantalizing for political scientists and sociologists studying contemporary developments, but the attraction toward disciplines and away from area studies presents both advantages and disadvantages. Area studies was never a discipline with its own field theory but always an interdisciplinary arena in which investigators from a variety of disciplines could work more deeply with combined knowledge of language, culture, history, economics, as well as politics and sociology. Because the "Soviet" region retains its historical heritage of half a millennium of imperial connection, for historians area studies needs little justification. Given the legacy of Russian and Soviet hegemony, historians will necessarily be concerned with more than a single ethnicity. No history of Georgia or Tajikistan is possible without a larger focus. But neither, it can certainly be argued, can any meaningful contemporary study hope to understand present and future trends without knowledge of that complex, interethnic "Russian-Soviet" past. However the area may be defined in the future—"Eurasian," "post-Soviet," "postcommunist"

studies are only some of the suggested possibilities—it remains meaningful as a loose unit for study, an intellectual location for exchange of
information and ideas (institutionalized in the American Association
for the Advancement of Slavic Studies, or AAASS, and the field's journals), and a powerful claimant on state and university funding.

Nationality studies in general is now a growth industry. In the postcommunist world the evident power of ethnic political claims in mobilizing masses of people to the point of civil war and ethnocide requires
a major reassessment of our approaches to nationality and nationalism.
No longer a problem of the Soviet bloc, no longer to be framed only as
colonial struggles against multinational empires, nationality studies is
part of the larger field of postcolonial studies. The problem of our times
is embedded in the vital issues of decolonization and the transition
from authoritarian to democratic polities. How nationalism in the former Soviet bloc will perform will be connected with the particular un-
derstandings of the nation that national elites will generate. Here scholars of the Soviet and post-Soviet experiences can play a significant role
in shaping the visions of emerging national leaderships, not by pander-
ing to their preferred views of themselves but by challenging the unexamined myths and assumptions that have too often paved the roads to
Karabagh and South Osetia, Transdniestria and Sarajevo, and are already constructing signposts on the way to Narva and Crimea, Kazan
and Dushanbe.

Notes

My gratitude to the members of the seminar at the Kennan Institute who read and
criticized the original draft of this paper. Special thanks to Teresa Rakowska-Harmstone
and Aram Yengoyan, who were kind enough to provide me with extensive written comments.

[1]For two recent assessments of the death of communism and the crisis of Sovietology,
see Theodore Draper, "Who Killed Soviet Communism?" *New York Review of Books*, June
11, 1992, 7–8, 10, 12–14; Stephen R. Gaubard, ed., "The Exit from Communism," *Daedalus*,
special ed. (Spring 1992). A highly influential earlier discussion of the profession and its
problems was Stephen F. Cohen, *Rethinking the Soviet Experience: Politics and History since
1917* (New York: Oxford University Press, 1985).

[2]A recent treatment of the connection of intelligence agencies and the Russian studies
community can be found in Sigmund Diamond, *Compromised Campus: The Collaboration of
Universities with the Intelligence Community, 1945–1955* (Oxford: Oxford University Press,
1992), especially the two chapters on the Russian Research Center of Harvard University
(50–110), where Diamond discusses the regular reporting by university officials to the
Federal Bureau of Investigation and the quiet removal of H. Stuart Hughes from the administration of the center because of his connections with Henry Wallace's presidential
campaign of 1948. In an interview one of the early members of the center, sociologist Tal-
cott Parsons, remembered that "there was an avoidance of getting what you might call

political fireballs onto the staff, either pro- or anti-Soviet. I remember, for one year, as a visitor they had Isaac Deutscher here, but, of course, he is an old Trotskyite and therefore was very anti-Stalin" (76).

³Raymond A. Bauer, Alex Inkeles, and Clyde Kluckhohn, *How the Soviet System Works: Cultural, Psychological and Social Themes* (Cambridge, Mass.: Harvard University Press, 1956; New York: Vintage Books, 1961); Zbigniew K. Brzezinski, *The Soviet Bloc: Unity and Conflict* (Cambridge, Mass.: Harvard University Press, 1960; rev. and exp. ed., 1967); Alex Inkeles and Raymond A. Bauer, *The Soviet Citizen: Daily Life in a Totalitarian Society* (Cambridge, Mass.: Harvard University Press, 1961).

⁴Alexander J. Motyl, *Sovietology, Rationality, Nationality: Coming to Grips with Nationalism in the USSR* (New York: Columbia University Press, 1990), 5.

⁵See, for example, the essays by Richard Pipes, Martin Malia, and Robert Conquest on "Sins of the Scholars," *National Interest* 31 (Spring 1993): 68–98.

⁶Inkeles and Bauer, *Soviet Citizen*, 339.

⁷"To this day, one can read in the Soviet press virulent denunciations of 'bourgeois-nationalists' in the national republics, and periodic purges of such resisters are a common feature of the Soviet scene. . . . But after all is said and done, the most this sort of activity does is to maintain the self-respect of those participating because of the shared common danger." Carl Friedrich and Zbigniew Brzezinski, *Totalitarian Dictatorship and Autocracy* (Cambridge, Mass.: Harvard University Press, 1956; rev. ed., New York: Frederick A. Praeger, 1965), 282.

⁸Inkeles and Bauer, *Soviet Citizen*, 339.

⁹Ibid.

¹⁰See, for example, the revealing study by Nancy Lubin, *Labour and Nationality in Soviet Central Asia: An Uneasy Compromise* (Princeton: Princeton University Press, 1984), in which she concludes that "economic strains are growing among a rapidly expanding and relatively immobile population. Labour surpluses are growing and affecting the Central Asians to a greater degree than the Europeans. . . . The combination of growing economic strains and relatively low native participation in the economy's most modern spheres would suggest that political unrest might follow, and be articulated in ethnic terms" (225).

¹¹Among the institute's periodical publications were *Azat Vatan, Backauscyna, Bielaruski Zbornik, Caucasian Review, Der Christliche Orient, Derqi, East Turkic Review, Kavkaz, Ob"edinennyi Kavkaz, Suchasna Ukraina, Turkeli, Ukrainsky Zbirnik*, as well as the *Vestnik instituta*.

¹²Institute for the Study of the USSR, *Genocide in the USSR: Studies in Group Destruction* (Munich: Institut zur Erforschung der USSR, 1958), 19.

¹³Doubts about the efficacy of the model in the light of Nikita Khrushchev's reforms led to a scramble for alternatives, such as Allen Kassof's "administered society: totalitarianism without terror," and a move toward integrating the study of Soviet-type societies into a comparative politics approach. See, for example, Frederic J. Fleron Jr., ed., *Communist Studies and the Social Sciences: Essays on Methodology and Empirical Theory* (Chicago: Rand McNally, 1969); Jerry F. Hough, *The Soviet Union and Social Science Theory* (Cambridge, Mass.: Harvard University Press, 1977).

¹⁴Walter Kolarz, *Russia and Her Colonies* (New York: Frederick A. Praeger, 1952); Richard Pipes, *The Formation of the Soviet Union: Communism and Nationalism, 1917–1923* (Cambridge, Mass.: Harvard University Press, 1954). For variations on the theme of em-

pire, see also Olaf Caroe, *Soviet Empire: The Turks of Central Asia and Stalinism* (London: Macmillan, 1953; New York: St. Martin's Press, 1967); Robert Conquest, *The Soviet Deportation of Nationalities* (London: Macmillan, 1960), reprinted and expanded as *The Nation Killers: The Soviet Deportation of Nationalities* (London: Macmillan, 1970); Hugh Seton-Watson, *The New Imperialism* (London: The Bodley Head, 1961); and outside of scholarship, U. S. Congress, Senate Committee on the Judiciary, *The Soviet Empire* (Washington, D.C.: Government Printing Office, 1958; rev. ed., 1965).

[15]Ronald Grigor Suny, *The Revenge of the Past: Nationalism, Revolution, and the Collapse of the Soviet Union* (Stanford, Calif.: Stanford University Press, 1993).

[16]Mary Matossian, *The Impact of Soviet Policies in Armenia* (Leiden: Brill, 1962).

[17]Bauer, Inkeles, and Kluckhohn, *How the Soviet System Works*, 238–39.

[18]Inkeles and Bauer, *Soviet Citizen*, 351.

[19]Ibid., 347.

[20]Ibid., 353.

[21]Bauer, Inkeles, and Kluckhohn, *How the Soviet System Works*, 239–40.

[22]Ibid., 243.

[23]Ibid., 236.

[24]Ibid., 243.

[25]Some writers find the loss of the "solid moral ground" of the totalitarian model regrettable. (See, for example, Motyl, *Sovietology, Rationality, Nationality*, 8.) Others are convinced that in divided, violence-prone pluralistic societies where a woman's reproductive choice is seen by some as murder of a child, moral vacuums may be more salutory than solid moral grounds.

[26]Inkeles and Bauer, *Soviet Citizen*, 383–84.

[27]Ibid., 372–73. See also, Alex Inkeles, "Soviet Nationality Policy in Perspective," in *Russia under Khrushchev: An Anthology from Problems of Communism*, ed. Abraham Brumberg (New York: Frederick A. Praeger, 1962), 300–21.

[28]Erich Goldhagen, Introduction to *Ethnic Minorities in the Soviet Union* (New York: Frederick A. Praeger, 1968), xiv.

[29]John Armstrong, "The Ethnic Scene in the Soviet Union: The View of the Dictatorship," in ibid., 3–49.

[30]Ibid., 5.

[31]Ibid., 3.

[32]Alec Nove and J. A. Newth, *The Soviet Middle East: A Model for Development?* (London: George Allen & Unwin, 1967), 45. For an interesting contrast, these conclusions might be compared to those of Vsevolod Holubnychy, who argued that "wholly inexplicable gaps" in economic development existed among Soviet republics, with the Russian republic faring better than the rest, and that its success confirmed the image of a colonial relationship between Russia and the non-Russian republics. "Some Economic Aspects of Relations among the Soviet Republics," in *Ethnic Minorities in the Soviet Union*, ed. Goldhagen, 50–120.

[33]Nove and Newth, *Soviet Middle East*, 97.

[34]Ibid., 114.

[35]Ibid., 122.

[36]Among them are Zvi Y. Gitelman, *Jewish Nationality and Soviet Politics: The Jewish Sections of the CPSU, 1917–1930* (Princeton: Princeton University Press, 1972); Gregory J. Massell, *The Surrogate Proletariat: Moslem Women and Revolutionary Strategies in Soviet Central Asia, 1919–1929* (Princeton: Princeton University Press, 1974); Ronald Grigor Suny, *The Baku Commune, 1917-1918: Class and Nationality in the Russian Revolution* (Princeton: Princeton University Press, 1972).

[37]Gitelman, *Jewish Nationality and Soviet Politics*, 3–4, 6–7.

[38]Ibid., 491.

[39]Ibid., 492.

[40]Massell, *Surrogate Proletariat*, 408–9.

[41]Teresa Rakowska-Harmstone, "The Dialectics of Nationalism in the USSR," *Problems of Communism* 23, no. 3 (1974): 1–22.

[42]Ibid., 1–2.

[43]Ibid., 10.

[44]Ibid., 21.

[45]Barbara A. Anderson and Brian D. Silver, "Estimating Russification of Ethnic Identity among Non-Russians in the USSR," *Demography* 20, no. 4 (1983): 461–89; Anderson and Silver, "Equality, Efficiency, and Politics in Soviet Bilingual Education Policy, 1934–1980," *American Political Science Review* 78, no. 4 (1984): 1019–39; Hélène Carrère d'Encausse, *L'empire éclaté* (Paris: Flammarion, 1978), published in English as *Decline of an Empire: The Soviet Socialist Republics in Revolt* (New York: Harper and Row, 1975); Carrère d'Encausse, *The Great Challenge: Nationalities and the Bolshevik State, 1917–1930* (New York: Holmes & Meier, 1991); Murray Feshbach, "The Soviet Union: Population Trends and Dilemmas," *Population Bulletin* 37, no. 3 (1982): 1–44; Rasma Karklins, *Ethnic Relations in the USSR: The Perspective from Below* (Boston: Allen & Unwin, 1986); Gerhard Simon, *Nationalismus und Nationalitatenpolitik in der Sowjetunion: Von der totalitaren Diktatur zur nachstalinschen Gesellschaft* (Baden-Baden: Nomos Verlagsgesellschaft, 1986); Victor Zaslavsky, *The Neo-Stalinist State: Class, Ethnicity and Consensus in Soviet Society* (Armonk, N.Y.: M. E. Sharpe, 1982); Iurii Arutiunian, *Sotsial'noe i natsional'noe: Opyt etnosotsiologicheskikh issledovanii po materialam Tatarskoi ASSR* (Moscow: Nauka, 1973); Iulian V. Bromlei, *Sovremennye etnicheskie protsessy v SSSR* (Moscow: Nauka, 1975). See also Mark Beissinger and Lubko Hajda, eds., *The Nationality Factor in Soviet Society and Politics: Current Trends and Future Prospects* (Boulder, Colo.: Westview, 1989).

[46] Gail Warshofsky Lapidus, "Ethnonationalism and Political Stability: The Soviet Case," *World Politics* 36, no. 4 (1984): 355–80; Lapidus, "The Nationality Question and the Soviet System," in "The Soviet Union in the 1980s," ed. Erik P. Hoffmann, *Proceedings of the Academy of Political Science* 35, no. 3 (New York, 1984): 98–112; Alexander J. Motyl, *Will the Non-Russians Rebel? State, Ethnicity, and Stability in the USSR* (Ithaca: Cornell University Press, 1987); Motyl, *Sovietology, Rationality, Nationality*.

[47]Alan Fisher, *The Crimean Tatars* (Stanford: Hoover Institution Press, 1978); Azade-Ayse Rorlich, *The Volga Tatars: A Profile in National Resilience* (Stanford: Hoover Institution Press, 1986); Martha Brill Olcott, *The Kazakhs* (Stanford: Hoover Institution Press, 1987); Toivo U. Raun, *Estonia and the Estonians* (Stanford: Hoover Institution Press, 1987); Ronald Grigor Suny, *The Making of the Georgian Nation* (Bloomington and Stanford: Indiana University Press, in association with Hoover Institution Press, 1988); Edward A. Allworth, *The Modern Uzbeks, From the Fourteenth Century to the Present: A Cultural History*

(Stanford: Hoover Institution Press, 1990); Audrey Altstadt, *The Azerbaijani Turks* (Stanford: Hoover Institution Press, 1992).

[48]David D. Laitin, "The National Uprisings in the Soviet Union," *World Politics* 44, no. 1 (1991): 141.

[49]Motyl, *Will the Non-Russians Rebel?* 170. For another prediction that the collapse of the "empire" would not take place—if the center held—see Laitin, "National Uprisings in the Soviet Union," 173 75. For the opposite viewpoint, see Robert Conquest, ed., *The Last Empire: Nationality and the Soviet Future* (Stanford: Hoover Institution Press, 1986).

[50]The effect of policy requirements should not be understood as universally pernicious. Besides funding much academic research of great quality and value, government has sponsored the activities of investigators, like Paul Goble, formerly of the Department of State, currently with the Carnegie Foundation, or Murray Feshbach, formerly of the Department of Commerce, whose publications provided valuable information to academic researchers. But the agenda of government cannot be supportive of the full range of independent scholarship, which may include work "subversive" to the policies of particular states and critical of dearly held assumptions of people in power. My point here is that the policy tail has too often wagged the scholarship dog.

[51]For a passionate appeal for comparative nationality studies, see Alexander J. Motyl, "'Sovietology in One Country' or Comparative Nationality Studies?" *Slavic Review* 48, no. 1 (1989): 83–88.

[52]Caroline Humphrey, *Karl Marx Collective: Economic Society and Religion in a Siberian Collective Farm* (Cambridge: Cambridge University Press, 1983).

[53]Ibid., 441; Tamara Dragadze, *Rural Families in Soviet Georgia: A Case Study in Ratcha Province* (London and New York: Routledge, 1988).

[54]Marjorie Mandelstam Balzer, "Ethnicity without Power: The Siberian Khanty in Soviet Society," *Slavic Review* 42, no. 4 (1983): 633–48.

[55]Suny, *Revenge of the Past*, 3–4.

[56]Eric J. Hobsbawm, *Nations and Nationalism since 1780: Programme, Myth, Reality* (Cambridge: Cambridge University Press, 1990); Benedict Anderson, *Imagined Communities: Reflections on the Origin and Spread of Nationalism* (London: Verso, 1983, rev. ed., 1991).

[57]Serge Schmemann, "In the Caucasus, Ancient Blood Feuds Threaten to Engulf 2 New Republics," *New York Times*, July 8, 1992, A3.

[58]Edward Said's work has been particularly important in reconceiving the concepts of "the East" and "the West" and in forcing scholars to see the ever-present power of a pervasive imperial discourse. See his *Orientalism* (New York: Pantheon Books, 1978) and *Culture and Imperialism* (New York: Alfred A. Knopf, 1993).

[59]Fredrik Barth, ed., *Ethnic Groups and Boundaries* (Boston: Little, Brown, 1969); Donald L. Horowitz, *Ethnic Groups in Conflict* (Berkeley: University of California Press, 1985); Harold Isaacs, *Idols of the Tribes: Group Identity and Political Change* (New York: Harper & Row, 1975); Anthony D. Smith, *Theories of Nationalism* (London: Gerald Duckworth, 1971, 1983); Smith, *The Ethnic Revival* (Cambridge: Cambridge University Press, 1981); Smith, *The Ethnic Origins of Nations* (Oxford: Basil Blackwell, 1986).

[60]Frederick C. Barghoorn, *Soviet Russian Nationalism* (New York: Oxford University Press, 1956); John B. Dunlop, *The New Russian Revolutionaries* (Belmont, Mass., 1976); Dunlop, *The Faces of Contemporary Russian Nationalism* (Princeton: Princeton University Press, 1983); Dunlop, *The New Russian Nationalism* (New York: Nordland, 1985); Roman

Szporluk, "History and Russian Nationalism," *Survey* 24, no. 3 (1979): 1–17; Alexander Yanov, *The Russian New Right: Right-Wing Ideologies in the Contemporary USSR* (Berkeley: Institute of International Studies, 1978). See also "Russian Nationalism Today," *Radio Liberty Research Bulletin*, special ed., December 19, 1988.

[61]The importance of these distinctions was impressed on me in conversation with Lowell Barrington.

[62]The popular term *sovok* (literally, "dustpan") is used to refer to the Soviet Union, the Soviet way of life, or a Soviet person.

[63]Hobsbawm, *Nations and Nationalism since 1780*, 173–74.

[64]See, for example, Mike Featherstone, ed., *Global Culture: Nationalism, Globalization and Modernity* (London: Sage, 1990).

Chapter 5

Soviet Nationality Studies between Past and Future

Martha Brill Olcott

Who Are We, and What Is It We Do?

The breakup of the Soviet empire in Eastern Europe, the fall of the Communist Party of the Soviet Union (CPSU), and the collapse of the USSR as a juridical entity provide scholars of what once was called Soviet studies with some extraordinary challenges. Although there is widespread public perception—shared in part by all of us in the field—that we somehow collectively failed, in that the end of the USSR came so suddenly and so apparently unheralded, only a small part of that challenge is the necessity to see where we "went wrong," if indeed we did. In fact, despite the ease with which journalists could make good copy in the days after the coup by quoting the various suddenly false predictions by certain of the field's luminaries, the predictive record of the discipline is rather good and will probably seem even better as relationships among the shards of the Soviet Union continue to evolve.

Our discipline evolved—and, more important, was funded—because society perceived a defensive necessity to understand the Soviet Union, in the hopes of somehow anticipating future Soviet moves. Although it is just seven years since Mikhail Gorbachev first announced his policy of glasnost, which has subsequently flooded us with more information than an army of scholars could digest in a lifetime, we tend to forget that Soviet studies grew and evolved in an atmosphere of intense secrecy. Following Soviet politics, Winston Churchill is said to have remarked, was like watching a bulldog fight take place under a carpet; and it was to us that it fell to attempt to interpret those thrashing bulges and muffled growls, mostly so that we would have some warning, should the fight suddenly burst out upon us. The carpet has now dropped away, however, and the bulldog fight proceeds in full view. Society no longer needs us simply to fumble at Soviet secrecy, trying to make out shapes beneath. The question is whether society needs us at all.

Part of the process of answering that question will be to decide who we are, as scholars, and what it is we do. This is not a wholly new problem, as the way in which most of us make our livings will suggest. Save

135

for those who work strictly in intelligence analysis—many of whom have their own difficulties to work through about where their work stands in relationship to our "scholarship"—most of us have served two masters, combining Soviet-related work with participation in a broader context of the social sciences and humanities, generally in higher education. We are, most of us, Soviet scholars and university and college faculty members attached to our various departments. That fact has always required us to balance the interests of area studies with the needs of disciplinary research, a problem that the nature of funding opportunities and the makeup of selection committees usually made more concrete than abstract. However, since a good deal of American higher education itself was predicated upon the bipolar world that also shaped our work, our second "master" is changing as well. People do not go to college now for the reasons they once did; nor do they study their subjects as they once did. The relationship between higher education and society is also changing, even as ours is. It is far from clear, for example, that government will continue to subsidize higher education to the degree that it did when we were trying to "catch the Russians," and it certainly is clear that, even if it does, the fields to receive support will change. It is not surprising, then, that another part of the challenge before us will be to redefine our relationship to higher education.

In the past, those of us who have been gathered by the Kennan Institute to participate in this project did "Soviet studies," a nomenclature that despite our sometimes strong ties to colleagues in our disciplines, grouped our efforts in a way that set our research apart from theirs. Today we have to ask ourselves whether this is still true and whether the most expedient use of our talents and energies is for us to continue to study together.

The problem is serious. Our personal and professional inclinations would be to try and preserve the field of Soviet studies; not only are we used to working together, but our professional associations and funding committees are also organized for "Soviet studies." A part of this inclination is inertia; it is, after all, the nature of bureaucracies to seek their own continuation. However, there are also sounder reasons to consider continuing as a unit. The Soviet Union was a single place for seventy years, so that the various problems of its dismemberment will show common features in each of its constituent parts. Moreover, many of these features will also be found in the postcommunist states of Eastern Europe, the traditional "ally" with which Soviet studies was always linked.

Of course, in considering that option, we must at minimum change the adjective for what we do; of necessity, that will also change who we are. Names are important, and they help shape reality; the nature of an activity is defined in part by what we call it. If we as specialists choose to pursue retaining a common identity, then we are implying that the parts of the former Soviet Union share a common identity as well. On which part will we focus? Will we emphasize the European identity of the former Soviet Union over its Asian one? Will the former Soviet Union be a part of the Christian world or of the Muslim world? Or, like Nursultan Nazarbaev, will we imagine that the area can be a bridge between the two continents and two cultures?[1] Or will we agree that the former Soviet Union shared a former common identity but does not now share a future one? The choice is substantive, because where the latter accepts that the pieces can move farther apart, the former argues by implication that they should be moving toward new forms of integration.

Nationality Studies or Ethnic Studies?

What we call things also matters when we talk about the subfields of Soviet studies. I consider myself to be a specialist on Soviet nationality problems, not on Soviet ethnic problems. To say this is to make a political statement. Although different scholars offer different definitions of the terms and disagree on how these groups are formed and sustained, there is a general agreement that the term "nationality" is linked to peoples with aspirations of statehood and the term "ethnic groups" is not.[2] Soviet and Western usage of the terms has been different. Even after Josef Stalin himself was long discredited, Soviet scholars stuck to Stalin's definitions of nations, nationalities, and peoples, based on distinctions that were largely geopolitical in nature.

"Nations" were defined as large, economically viable blocks of people who have historic homelands and unique, distinctive cultures; in recognition of their status the Soviet rulers awarded them their own "sovereign" republics. "Nationalities" are fewer in number and often lack either economic viability or precisely definable homelands; their political rights were considered to have been satisfied with "semisovereign" autonomous territories. The term "peoples" was used much as we often use "ethnic groups," to designate kin-based cultural communities; these were granted rights of cultural self-preservation on their allotted territories.[3]

Although these rights of peoples were enshrined in the 1922, 1936, and 1977 constitutions, neither Soviet scholars nor Soviet policymakers ever seriously believed that the various Soviet national and ethnic communities possessed real cultural autonomy, much less actual sovereignty.[4] However, the Soviet Union being what it was, the tension between reality and the dreamworld of official life could never be explored in public. In the Brezhnev years this tension grew more pronounced, until the Soviet academic world was expected to address it. Soviet authors produced dozens of books on nationality and interethnic relations in this preglasnost period, but although many of them substantially expanded the body of existing knowledge about individual nationalities and advanced the debate on the national identity, ethnic consciousness, and the interrelationship of tradition and culture, none of them could challenge the "Leninist" theory about nationality and social behavior that underpinned Soviet policies.[5]

As a result, "nationalism" remained a pejorative term. In a socialist society, nationalist loyalties had to be subordinated to internationalist ideals or the common good would be threatened. Scholars were not allowed even to address the basic tension in V. I. Lenin's teachings, which held both that nationality would die away in the new order and that rights of national self-determination were to be endorsed.

These restrictions meant in practice that, although each of the major Soviet nationalities had been given its own republic, they were not free to run them according to nation-based criteria. Nation and nationality were central defining categories in Soviet political life, since every Soviet citizen had to indicate a nationality on his or her internal passport, but Soviet scholars were effectively barred from using Western theories of nationality to explain political conditions in their own country. Western theories argue, by implication if nothing else, that independence is a legitimate aspiration for nationalities. Even though each of the Soviet nationalities had a constitutional "right" to secede from the USSR, it was unthinkable that this right could ever be exercised, not least because there was no constitutional mechanism for doing so.

Instead of exploring the meaning of nationality, Soviet historiography had to authenticate each of the Soviet "nations" by writing histories to demonstrate its longevity and historic association with the land that Moscow had awarded it. Historians likewise provided histories for "nationalities" and "peoples" that made clear why these lesser groupings were not "nations."[6]

Despite this proliferation of national histories, part of the "proof" of a purported "flowering" of national cultures, Soviet scholarship and policy formation alike also demonstrated strong Russocentric biases. Even as it was granting some right of cultural preservation to each of the peoples, the CPSU simultaneously demanded partial Russification of the entire Soviet population as necessary to the successful integration and orderly functioning of the Soviet state. This policy, too, was defended by party ideologists and justified by scholars on the "scientific" grounds that Russian is a culture of civilization, a bridge to science and technology.

Thus Soviet scholars found it far more congenial to use ethnicity as the focus of their empirical research. This focus enabled them to fit Soviet theory and practice into Western scholarship without also stumbling into unwanted political quagmires. Soviet scholars could acknowledge that ethnic consciousness could have a political dimension and ethnic groups could have political agendas, but they could also then assert that ethnic groups which wished to break up their current states were advocating "separatism" and not "national liberation."

Why Did Nationality Studies Do Better?

Western "Soviet nationality" studies rejected the premise that nationality and ethnicity were interchangeable in the Soviet context. Indeed, the field had its origins in a desire to illustrate and advocate those who saw themselves as "captive nations," held in the Soviet Union against the national will.

Certainly we had no universally accepted criteria of nationality; nor were most of us active in either émigré action committees or U.S. intelligence operations. Still, most of us accepted as a given that the Latvians, Lithuanians, and Estonians were not just nationalities but peoples whose nation-states had been illegally usurped. The Ukrainians, Georgians, and Armenians were also assumed to be historic nations whose rights were being abused, although this assumption did not imply an endorsement of their rights to statehood.

There was less unanimity with regard to the nationhood of Azerbaijanis, Tatars, Belorussians, and Moldavians, while the five Central Asian nationalities were generally understood more as the creation of Soviet rule than as a logical outcome of local history. It was also commonly agreed that the other Soviet nationalities, Stalin's "peoples," were distinct ethnic communities and not surpressed nations. Our research on these peoples focused more on the denial of religious and cultural rights than on the denial of statehood.

Without question, Western studies of Soviet nationality problems had deficiencies. Virtually everything we produced suffered from our inability to live freely among the people we were studying or to have open access to their archival and historical legacy. This lack of access aggravated our overdependence on Russian language sources, increasing our tendency to become Russocentric ourselves, even if only unconsciously.

Ironically, the ideological bias of the field ran very much in the other direction. Dominated by scholars whose ethnic roots lay in their area of research, nationality studies often tended to overstate the case for national independence, painting rosier pictures of what might have been, if not for the Bolshevik Revolution, than history really justified. In addition, most of our work could have been written with more and better use of theory, in a way that better enabled us to engage in intellectual debate with colleagues outside our field but within our discipline. All that admitted, it must also be said that, on the whole, Soviet nationality studies saw far more clearly than did any other subfield of Soviet studies the imminent demise of the international state subsystem we were all studying.[7]

This insight was achieved primarily because we saw the Soviet Union as an empire, while colleagues in other subfields were less willing to do so. While most of the Soviet studies field focused on communism as a flawed ideological system and studied the special features of communist rule, the ways in which this ideology warped political, social, and economic life in the USSR, the central question for Soviet nationality studies was the illegitimacy of Russian rule forced upon non-Russians.

USSR: State or Empire?

Although the nationalities subfield was rife with divisions, the arguments were never over whether the Soviet Union could survive indefinitely. We argued over when, and how, the USSR would begin to disintegrate. We all shared a belief in the lasting emotional power of nationalism, although we never satisfactorily answered the question of how it was transmitted from generation to generation. We agreed, too, that national consciousness was fluid, simultaneously elastic and rigid. We were never able to go further, however, to show how nationalism is shaped by circumstances, or to predict the process of politicization. These were the questions over which our disagreements arose, and not always on strictly methodological grounds. Those of us in the subfield sharply disagreed as to the nature of communist rule itself, and whether communist ideology and Soviet structures could penetrate traditional nationally oriented societies. The debate demanded a fundamental examination of communism as an ideological system and the nature of nationalism. Stalin, of course, had decreed against national communism in the USSR in the late 1920s and condemned it again in Eastern Europe in the late 1940s. However, bloody though the results of his fiat may have been, the fiat itself left unresolved the basic question of whether a person could be both a nationalist and a communist.

Today this question has acquired a new context and so taken on immediacy. Throughout the former Soviet Union former communists are claiming to be both old-time and newly converted nationalists, presenting us with the need to assess whether these political chameleons can create stable regimes. In the past we failed to achieve consensus on whether communism and nationalism were flexible enough to become intellectually compatible, either for certain individuals or in a particular elite group. If they were not, were those who professed to accept both ideologies false nationalists or false communists?

These debates led to the subfield's other major disagreement, over the "real" nature of communist rule in localities where the Soviet-enforced limitations on field research made it impossible to develop empirically founded conclusions. Given that we could not agree on how to define "communists" and "nationalists," it is not surprising that we could never agree on whether communist structure had penetrated into traditional society. This disagreement gave rise to some of the fundamental questions of the field. Was there one Ukraine or two? Was the Communist Party leadership in the Baltic republics loyal to Moscow? What was the relationship between the religious and political elites in Central Asia?

In a sense we shared more than we might care to admit with our former Soviet colleagues. "Soviet nationality" studies was implicitly grounded in social science theory, although the relevant theories were not necessarily cited in our works. Like the Soviets, we favored theories of collective social behavior over those that focus on the individual actor, with the difference that nation, not class, was the unit that seemed to us to offer the greatest explanatory power.

How Can We Define the "Common Good"?

Now some of those Soviet scholars who earlier wrote in defense of socialism, like Galina Starovoitova or Valerii Tishkov, have themselves become democratic activists. However, although their politics have changed, they remain critical of nationalism. The nationalism that they once argued violates internationalism is now seen, in its elevation of group rights, as a peril to individual freedoms.

Anyone who has taken, to say nothing of taught, an introductory course in government knows how rich and complex is the debate in democratic theory about how to assign priority between individual and collective rights.[8] One of the ways in which democratic theory attempts to minimize the tension between the two sorts of rights is through the concept of "common good."

The definition of "common good" in the post-Soviet context is one of the pressing questions we face. If we assume, as I do, that the USSR was an empire, which is now breaking up, there is no longer a "common good" to be defined for the former USSR as a whole. Each of the states that is emerging will have a "common good" to define for itself. Part of the process will be to find a balance between individual and collective rights which works in the cultural context of that nation.

The international community, of course, will retain the same authority to monitor this process as it has asserted in other states. It will attempt to guarantee that states do not define "common good" in a way that leaves minority populations outside the commonweal, thus violating human rights on solely ethnic grounds. That authority, however, ought to be based upon a clear understanding of a new "common good" specific to each new nation and not to an outdated "common good" encompassing the entire USSR. Specifically, Russians should not be allowed to continue the privileges they once enjoyed as colonizers but rather be encouraged to assume their new position as minority members of new states.

The new standards ought to be applied to Russia as well. If the world permits Russia to claim the international property of the USSR, then it ought to require that Russia also assume the social and economic burdens of the former colonizer as well. If Russia wants to claim that it was colonized, and so has no responsibility to the new republics, then it should not be allowed to claim exclusive control of the property that once belonged to all fifteen republics alike. So far the Russian government has played this issue both ways, leaving Russia looking very much like a colonial power, as many of Russia's minority nationalities and peoples are charging.

What Role for the Russians?

Many Russians reject this state-specific definition of "common good" because it clashes with the "common good" of the Russians living outside the Russian Federation. Russians inside and outside of Russia proper still claim a special position for themselves, justifying their assertion in different ways. Russian communists argue that the USSR was a multinational state and so should be succeeded by another multinational state dominated, as was the first, by Russians. Russian nationalists argue that Russian labor built the Soviet Union, thus conveying to Russians the right to continue their control of most of the former empire. Russian democrats argue that, while they have no imperial ambitions and want only to create a society in which all peoples enjoy equal rights, Russians best understand democratic traditions and so it is they who will do the best job of introducing and preserving democracy everywhere in the former Soviet Union.

All of these positions share an unstated assumption that the division of the territory of the USSR into nation-states is a mistake, not only for Russians but for the entire international community. Threaded through the arguments of all these groups is the hope (sometimes stated outright) that formation of new nations is a phase which will pass, to be followed by the birth of a new multinational state, democratic or not, as the inclination of the group arguing it dictates, that will replace and stabilize the fifteen separate states currently developing.

As a field we face a real danger that we may come to share this Russian agenda. Soviet studies has always been ideological, sharply defined by anticommunism. The wellsprings of our anticommunism, though, were various. For many of us our anticommunism was fueled by Russophilia. We saw the CPSU as antithetical to prerevolutionary Russian cultural values, many of which we romanticized as badly as did the Russian dissident nationalists with whom we worked and associated.

With the USSR gone, these people are no longer dissidents, and we can associate with them openly, just as the former Soviet colleagues who earlier vilified or shunned us can now seek us out. The same is true for most of the former Soviet Union, making it possible for us to come to know well non-Russians whom earlier we had to study at a remove. Yet to personify earlier sympathies and interests increases the risk that we may glorify non-Russian nationalism. The way in which our field developed, however, and our personal predilections, make it an even greater risk that we will accept even more than we did in Soviet times the "objectivity" and "expertise" of our Russian colleagues, and especially the democrats.

The Russian democrats, after all, "speak our language" figuratively as well as literally, and the Slavic-speaking, secular, and pro-Western society that they envision throughout the territory of the former Soviet Union is one that would feel familiar, even congenial, to us. Each time Boris Yeltsin falters, the editorial pages of the principal newspapers in the United States are filled with articles written by leading scholars demanding greater U.S. support for his beleaguered government. The problem is that his reform program may not be the sort of society most former Soviets, including most Russians, want. To demonstrate that, and document it, is a real contribution that new social science research could make, using the techniques of empirical research to study the support base for democratic values in the former USSR.

Questions for Study, Old and New

Obviously, it will take years to do conclusive studies on these questions. While we are waiting, though, we should not ignore the wealth of existing literature that offers some important cautions. The extensive literature on the process of democratization in Latin America points up the problems of democraticization in authoritarian societies,[9] while the literature on decolonization in Africa and the Middle East attests to the recurrent paradox of "secularization"—-that what one culture defines as secularization is understood by another contiguous culture as economic domination.[10]

In a similar vein, we must begin to work closely with our colleagues in fields that have now become parallel to our own. As Latvians, Lithuanians, and Estonians aspire to become Northern Europeans, as Ukrainians, Belorussians, and Moldovans strive to be Central Europeans, as Azerbaijanis look toward Turkey, and as Central Asians orient themselves increasingly to Muslim Asia, we who claim expertise in these once-Soviet areas and nationalities now have an obligation to master at least the secondary literature that has sprung from study of the regions to which these various new nations are now beginning to orient themselves. Some changes are already visible; regional studies associations are broadening their programs to include sessions on former Soviet border areas.

However, by far the greatest task facing us is to strive to master the regions we are studying. None of us should be exempt from traveling to the regions we claim to study, living there and studying their languages, as once we did the Russians. We should push the profession to equate expertise with actual experience, including in the very practical sense the funding that would encourage senior faculty and people with families, and not just graduate students at the dawn of their careers, to live a time in the new republics and to pursue usable knowledge of the new "state languages."

We should take particular caution that lack of funding or lack of desire to face field conditions not allow a new form of Russian "gate keeping" to replace the Soviet closed countryside of the past. There are already far too many joint Russo-American projects under way, purporting to study situations in one or another of the new republics through projects funded by Americans but designed and conducted by Russians rather than by scholars indigenous to the republic of study. Too many of the Russian scholars who are now working on "nationality" themes still suffer from "great power chauvinism," believing that local scholars cannot function without Russian direction and support.

In fact, although they frequently do not have the same familiarity with the literature of our disciplines as do the more familiar colleagues from Moscow and Leningrad, many of the scholars in the newly independent states are as well qualified as Russians, while also possessing far deeper understanding of their own societies than either we or the Russians can presume to claim. Moreover, just as we have more to gain from their expertise, these non-Russian scholars have more to gain from us, as they are introduced to social science techniques and theories now current in the world.

The expertise of the non-Russians will be increasingly valuable if the breakup of the USSR continues to evolve, making the new states grow ever further apart. If there is no reintegration, then "Soviet studies" will inevitably cease to exist as a separate field. Russia is large enough, and important enough, to make it quite likely that "Russian studies" will continue to exist as a subfield, but those of us whose work relates primarily to non-Russian societies will increasingly find our colleagues in other configurations and associations as we "migrate" toward other regional subfields or perhaps leave area studies entirely.

"Soviet Studies" in the Post–Cold War World

For better or worse, the existing shape of American academia makes the question of what we call ourselves, and the manner in which we associate, not entirely a theoretical consideration. As a specialist on Central Asia, I am still barred from seeking research funds from most Middle East regional studies associations. In much the same way Baltic specialists find it hard to find research support among existing organizations of Europeanists. For the time being, Central Asianists and Balticists alike must solicit "Soviet" funds. Furthermore, although the breakup of the USSR and the creation of the new states have spawned some increased funding, research money in general is likely to become more difficult to obtain, as soon as the novelty and confusion of the breakup have worn off. The system of education in the United States was shaped in greatest part by the conditions of the competition between the United States and the USSR. The huge expansion of research facilities in universities and in the private sector was funded in express response to a perceived "Soviet threat." Basic science and engineering programs were obvious recipients of this divergence of societal resources because of the contributions these disciplines could make, or were assumed capable of making, to our defensive capacity.

However, the social sciences, too, benefited from "post-*Sputnik* funding." Influenced by the natural sciences and encouraged by significant new incentives for the development of empirical research, social science wanted to play a role, arguing that if we were successful in finding universal laws of human behavior, then we could not only predict behavior but even modify it.

Soviet studies in particular never existed independent of politics. The cold war gave us the money that sent most of us through graduate school and that in one way or another paid for virtually all the research that we have done since. Society set these funds aside to combat the threat we believed Moscow posed, not just to our ideology but to our way of life. Now, however, not only is the communist threat vanished, but our way of life itself is widely considered to be in crisis, as Americans question the values and purpose of our society in a way they did not when our discipline was forming. More important, and more fundamental, society also has less money than it once did, to say nothing of a greatly increased awareness of the deferred maintenance costs we have accrued over the decades by ignoring other of our needs. All this means that, with the end of the cold war, a reexamination of the basic premises of the American educational system is inevitable.

Area Studies or Disciplinary Research?

In the social sciences, especially, there is a basic difference between disciplinary and area research, which the reorganizations and shrinking available research funds of the future will affect. Disciplinary research favors microanalytic analysis over macroanalytic, because microanalytic studies are always able to show better control of detail, reducing the interference of extraneous factors to a minimum. In political science, for example, *how well* something is measured is at least as important as *what* is measured.

Area studies makes the opposite assumption, sometimes to an equal flaw. Favoring macroanalytic over microanalytic concerns, encouraging microanalytic research only when results can serve as a model or otherwise provide conclusions with universal application, area studies can tend to reward generality at the expense of methodological refinement.

Ideally, of course, the two approaches work in tandem. Those who build models or theories based solely on secondary literature, with a grounding in a specific area, sometimes do so based on gross misreadings of the history or culture of the peoples about whom they are generalizing. On the other side, those who work in an exclusively area-defined context are sometimes ignorant of lessons already drawn from comparable cases and so wind up replicating knowledge, not extending it.

Obviously, an integrative approach to research, with teams of generalists and area specialists, is probably the ideal solution. Many of our professional conferences and workshops are already beginning to be organized along these lines. However, to fund a series of long-term multiyear collaborative projects involving large teams of scholars would not only go against the tradition of individual or small group collaboration that has long dominated in American humanities and social science research but would be prohibitively expensive.

That last point cuts to what may be the central issue in the entire question of the future of "Soviet studies": what will society perceive to be our service, and what it will be willing to pay to receive that service? It would be a great injustice, to society and to ourselves, if we used artificial means to establish a justification for our continued existence, such as manufacturing some new variation on a "Soviet threat" or asserting some kind of intellectual disciplinary unity that in fact no longer exists.

Whether or not Soviet studies survives, there will continue to be work that needs to be done. Many of the works of the earlier Sovietologists will continue to be read, since they remain the best explanations of many features of the former Soviet system that we are apt to have, perhaps for a decade or more. The simple volume of the historical material that opening archives has presented to researchers is going to mean that well-written, closely researched, thoughtful books are going to take many years to write. The continued timeliness of many of the earlier nationality studies is even greater, for they are frequently the only sources—biased and even occasionally inaccurate though they may be—that we presently possess for the study of once-neglected, suddenly important regions.

For those of us studying the nationalities and nationalism in the successor states to the Soviet Union, though, the demands of the future will be even greater. New nations will be emerging, thick with problems and challenges for policymakers, challenges that will be intensified by the configurations and constellations of other nations—new and old—into which they may form. We specialists in these neglected areas must be prepared to teach in universities and to fill the new policy formation and assistance provision positions that shifting political configurations will produce.

In doing so, though, we will once again face the same dilemmas that stood before those in Soviet studies. Will our responsibility be to describe what is occurring in these new societies, or will we be called upon to play some sort of role in their evolution, attempting through aid or threat, coercion or encouragement, to influence the course of their development? Will we be adding the specificity of expertise on one area to the development of some overarching theory of human political and social behavior, or will we be extending our own nation's understanding of a particular nation, the better to guard ourselves against it, or the better to profit from doing business with it?

Ultimately, of course, it is not we who will answer these questions, but the evolution of what it is we study. The twentieth century is ending as it began, with great empires of the past breaking up and the peoples and nations of Europe and Asia struggling to define countries that will satisfy their longings for independent nationhood. These struggles are setting the stage for the political dramas to come, to which our disciplinary dramas will be a pale but necessary shadow.

Notes

[1] Nursultan Nazarbaev makes this point with great regularity. For an example, see his speech in *Kazakhstanskaia pravda*, December 16, 1992.

[2] In this regard it is useful to contrast the discussion of nationalities found in the introduction of John Breuilly, *Nationalism and the State* (Chicago: University of Chicago Press, 1982), with that of ethnic groups found in Crawford Young, *The Politics of Cultural Pluralism* (Madison: University of Wisconsin Press, 1976), chap. 1.

[3] See Iulian Bromlei, *Ocherki teorii etnos* (Moscow: Nauka, 1973), chap. 1.

[4] See *Istoriia natsional'no-gosudarstvennogo stroitel'stva v SSSR 1917-1978*, 2 vols. (Moscow: Mysl', 1979).

[5] For a summary of this literature, see Iulian Bromlei, *Etnosotsial'nye protsessy: Teoriia, istoriia, sovremennost'* (Moscow: Nauka, 1987), chap. 9.

[6] For an example, see *Voprosy istoriografii i istochnikovedeniia Kazakhstana* (Alma Ata: Nauka, 1988).

[7] Two examples of works that anticipated the collapse (although in a nonprognasticative way) were Hélène Carrère d'Encausse, *Decline of an Empire: The Soviet Socialist Republics in Revolt* (New York: Harper and Row, 1975); and Alexander J. Motyl, *Will the Non-Russians Rebel? State, Ethnicity, and Stability in the USSR* (Ithaca: Cornell University Press, 1987).

[8] See, for example, Robert Dahl, *A Preface to Democratic Theory* (Chicago: University of Chicago Press, 1956); Carole Pateman, *Participation and Democratic Theory* (Cambridge: Cambridge University Press, 1970).

[9] See Robert A. Packenham, *The Dependency Movement* (Cambridge, Mass.: Harvard University Press, 1991).

[10] See, for example, Robert H. Jackson, *Quasi-States, Sovereignty, International Relations and the Third World* (Cambridge: Cambridge University Press, 1991); Stephen Haggard, *Pathways from the Periphery: The Politics of Growth in Newly Industrialized Societies* (Ithaca: Cornell University Press, 1990).

Commentary:

Framing Post-Soviet Nationality Studies

Gale Stokes

The collapse of communism in the Soviet Union and Eastern Europe has sent a shiver of apprehension down the collective spine of the Soviet and East European scholarly community. Since, as Martha Brill Olcott writes, "Soviet studies . . . never existed independent of politics," how can post-Soviet studies continue to find a political justification that will keep the funding coming? This practical fear is very real, but the framing issue facing scholars is even more difficult. How can nationality studies survive without the Soviet Union to provide its academic or cultural umbrella? Or, more broadly, what will constitute the unit of study now that the Soviet empire no longer exists?

One of the assumptions of the latter question is that we adequately understood the unit of study while the Soviet Union did exist. Both Olcott and Ronald Grigor Suny suggest that perhaps we did not. They are in a good position to make this criticism because they themselves never concentrated on those issues deemed central by the majority of practitioners. They have never looked on the Soviet Union as Russia writ large, and they have well understood how damaging that widespread perception was to a nuanced understanding of the Soviet Union. Suny suggests in his comments a new danger—that the emergence of the new nations from the Soviet Union will be interpreted too narrowly in two senses. First there is the possibility—it is more than possibility, actually; it is well nigh a certainty—that newly independent nations will re-create their own versions of the whiggish interpretations of history which have been the standard fare of nationalist historians since the nineteenth century. Suny calls this the "Sleeping Beauty" notion of nationalism: having been overborne for centuries by a foreign oppressor (the Soviet yoke as the substitute for the Mongol yoke, the Ottoman yoke, or the Norman yoke), the virtuous nation is now ready to step forward in its pristine and youthful originality.

Presumably Western practitioners will not be too deeply involved in this enterprise. But they may succumb to the second temptation, which is to keep their focus too narrow. Suny points out that the new national entities of the former Soviet Union can be seen as participating in the post–World War II period of "decolonialization and the transition from authoritarian to democratic polities." He is absolutely correct about this, but the process actually started before World War I, when all four of the great European empires of the nineteenth century collapsed. This collapse was brought about not by national liberation movements of the postwar decolonialization but by the inability of those empires to sustain their increasingly archaic structures in the face of the social challenge of industrialization. In a sense, this is what caused the collapse of the Soviet Union as well—the inability of a rigid imperial structure to retain the minimal amount of flexibility a polity needs to survive in the postindustrial world. Suny is quite right that the best studies of the significance of the rise of nationalism in the former Soviet Union will embed themselves somewhere in these large processes.

The relationship of nationalism to decolonialization can be approached in this way, and so can the problem raised by Olcott of why communists often have proven to be vigorous nationalists in the post-Soviet (post-1989) era. My approach to these issues starts with the observation that the eighteenth-century roots of both nationalism and Stalinism lie in the view that the popular will has a unitary, homogeneous nature. The idea that the people are one is consistent with the classical view that there are three types of governance—government by the one, by the few, and by the many. In each case the king, the aristocracy, or the demos is understood to speak with one voice. For Jean-Jacques Rousseau and the leaders of the French Revolution, the people's will and political sovereignty were both indivisible. Neither of them countenanced any sort of pluralism, despite the obvious fact, well recognized by their contemporary James Madison, for example, that in reality individuals have an enormous variety of viewpoints, which they often are prepared to defend with violence. The constitution that Madison and his colleagues wrote for the United States took human contentiousness into account by parceling out sovereignty both horizontally and vertically. This distribution of power made for a messy system, but one in which the constant struggles for power at various levels and in numerous arenas created a rich variety of open spaces for the exercise of individual freedom and diversity. In the Anglo-American style of nationalism, the nation was authentic because it represented free individuals.

The eighteenth-century idea that the will of the people is a single, knowable entity had little impact in the United States, but in Europe it remained alive and well, traveling two separate but related routes out of the Enlightenment. The first was the road that led to Stalinism. The proletariat was Karl Marx's translation of the people-as-one into material form, the class that would ultimately become the world's sole class and impose its just regime. V. I. Lenin agreed, but he considered the actual working class fickle and subject to temptation. He therefore placed his confidence in the vanguard party, whose single correct position on any given question represented the true interests of humanity. And of course Josef Stalin took Leninism one step further by claiming that the entire general will, the whole rationality of the proletariat and the vanguard party, resided in his person. This reductio ad absurdum of eighteenth-century rationalism turned Stalin into the personal embodiment of the people—the people as one person, so to speak.

Nationalists took a different route. They translated the people-as-one into the idea of the homogeneous nation whose will the nationalists claimed to understand. This style of nationalism differed fundamentally from that of Anglo-American nationalism. In ethnic nationalism the people derive their dignity from their participation in the overarching idea of the nation, and membership in the group is seen as a primordial quality.[1] This idea is just as totalitarian in its implications as the Stalinist redaction of Marx, and it is one of the defining characteristics of modern nationalism, but it remained well hidden in the nineteenth century, just as it did among the Soviet nationalities under Leninism and Stalinism. Under the rule of empires nationalism appeared to be a liberal phenomenon because it sought self-determination, equal treatment, and cultural freedom. At a time when the concept of "the people" was being expanded to cover workers, women, and minorities, these demands seemed to accord well with the principle of popular sovereignty. But when the nationalists came to power in the twentieth century, they quickly demonstrated that they were no pluralist democrats. The worst of them, such as those at work in the former Yugoslavia, Georgia, Armenia, and Azerbaijan, continue to maintain that their people is a homogeneous whole with a single interest. Ethnic nationalism is attractive to former communists because its vision of a uniform and disciplined society in which leaders define what constitutes the popular will mimics the totalitarian pretensions of Stalinism. This quality may also have constituted nationalism's strength as an anticolonial ideology. It fought fire with fire. The antipoliticians of the 1970s and 1980s in Eastern Europe understood this. Their hope was to avoid the politicization of all life that is characteristic of the totalitarian project by creating a civil society of self-activated individuals and small groups. They feared that creating a political party with a program and conspiring to overthrow the state on behalf of that program would only result in the creation of a new kind of oppression. As Adam Michnik put it, those who wish to storm the bastille will end by building their own bastilles. Whereas nationalism may well be antithetical to colonialism, it is also antithetical to democracy. In the post-

1989 world, to paraphrase Karl Kraus, nationalism is the disease of which it professes itself to be the cure.

This irony makes the task of scholars investigating the dynamics of the breakup of the Soviet Union, as well as the confusing situation that has followed it, much more difficult than it was before the breakup. The need for critical history, in the German sense, is now much greater than it was before 1989 because the stakes have gone up. No longer is the story of the former Soviet nations a sideshow of Russian oppression. Now the danger of oppression is integral to the nation itself. But the critical investigator will not find it easy to express this view, since few former Soviet nations will want to hear "objective" history about themselves.

Still, this is what must be done. Nothing would be more self-defeating than unconsciously to adopt the nationalists' claim that nations are coherent and homogeneous. That would simply reinforce the totalitarian thrust of ethnic nationalists. As the Bosnia war has proven, it is very easy to fall into essentialist rhetoric ("Serbs are primitive," "Croats are fascists"). Those who slip into this discourse of homogeneity are only lending support to the point of view that is in good measure the cause of the fighting.

It is even easier to pass off Balkan and Transcaucasian antagonisms as "ancient hatreds" and their fighting as "tribal warfare." These nineteenth-century expressions of condescension place the combatants on a precivilizational, almost subhuman level. They are presented as not yet having emerged from some supposedly primitive level of civilization reached by the superior Europeans. Under this interpretation the differences among the Serbs, Croats, and Muslims are quasi-genetic, so ingrained in their psyches that no amount of negotiation will disabuse them. This rhetoric of condescension releases those who use it from having to analyze the situation in ways they would use elsewhere and frees them from the responsibility to act.

The first step in acting responsibly, therefore, is to use ordinary analytical tools when discussing Eastern European and former Soviet nations, rather than treating them as mysterious emanations of an unclean spirit, as the Primary Chronicle characterized the approaching Mongols in the thirteenth century. The admonitions of both Olcott and Suny toward this end are quite salutary. What, then, is the framing unit for our future studies? Whose "common good," as Olcott puts it, are we to consider primary? By subtitling his article, "Bringing the Non-Russians Back In," Suny proposes using the growing sophistication in nationality studies to enrich our understanding of the Soviet Union and the Russian Empire. One can hardly object to this project. But Suny is a historian, and for those involved in historical studies, whether they be anthropologists, political scientists, or historians, the framing problem is simple—the Soviet Union will always exist as an entity for historical study, as does the Russian Empire and even Kievan Rus. For social scientists, however, the problem is much more severe. They cannot "bring the non-Russians back in" to their studies of current affairs because they have nothing to bring them back into. This is precisely the problem. The old framing unit is gone.

In this century Europeans murdered at least 25 million of themselves in ways that are just as brutal and obscene as those now in use in Bosnia, and they did it over very similar issues, such as, for example, whether Alsace and Lorraine should be part of France or whether Germans should be permitted to ethnically cleanse Poland. But after the war the Europeans did find a way to bury the hatchet some place other than in each other's skulls. The 25 million deaths were not *entirely* in vain. By taking advantage of the destruction of the old society in 1945 to construct a new one, Western Europeans created structures that have contained the passions that created the two world wars. The European Union has become a vast, nonstop negotiating machine based on the principle of pooled sovereignty. Whereas nationalists continue to advocate homogeneity and unique sovereignty, in the European Union the sovereignty of member countries is no longer inviolate in certain specified areas of concern. Each country has voluntarily delegated bits and pieces of its control over some affairs to the larger community. Today when France and Germany have disputes, they take them to one or more of the scores of established negotiating nodes in the European Union rather than thinking about war. This change could happen only because in 1945 the Western Europeans were able to start afresh with the memory of the catastrophes of the previous thirty years vivid in their minds.

The Soviet Union and Yugoslavia were not voluntary associations, and that is precisely why they broke up. And neither the former Soviets nor the Yugoslavs had the "advantage" of suffering a crushing military defeat. They experienced no *stunde null* from which they could start anew in 1945, and they are not experiencing one now (although other Eastern European countries may be). Stalin isolated Eastern Europe and the Soviet Union from the possibility of rethinking their relationships with the rest of Europe at a time when the structure of European interactions was in a state of flux and rapid creative change. The question today is whether Europe will find the generosity, the broadness of vision, and the originality to draw its neighbors to the east into a system of pooled sovereignty. Only if this happens can we hope for a stable Europe over the next generation. We have plenty of experience with unique sovereignties and homogeneous nationalism to know what will be the consequences of failure.

Given some leadership, it is at least possible to conceive of a system of pooled sovereignty someday linking Eastern Europe as far as Ukraine with Western Europe in a very large cooperative entity. Because of its size, however, it is difficult to imagine Russia entering into such a system, and because of their remoteness and their cultural differences, it is even more difficult to imagine the Transcaucasian and Asiatic states entering directly into such a system. The Europeans, who have not found the strength to respond to chaos in the former Yugoslavia, a country that borders on some of them, are not going to care much about remoter regions. This conclusion may be unjust, it may be Europocentric, it may be shortsighted, but it is very likely to be true.

It seems to me, therefore, that there are three, or perhaps four, separate units of interest that will frame the work of social scientists over the next period. The main one is simply Europe, which I extend to Ukraine. This Europe has two historically distinct regions, East and West, and a very large number of separate cultures, people, and histories. But this very large entity does have at least the possibility of coherence. Russia, stretching from Europe to the Pacific, is a unit in its own right, huge, potential, diverse, and yet historically coherent. And finally there are the southern states of the former Soviet Union, not really European, not really Asian. Their framing unit may well be the Black Sea, where Turkey has taken the lead in attempting to draw together the region into an economic entity. In all these cases, of course, the framing unit is only a reference point, a potential community of affiliation, a combination of possible linkages; it is not a hegemonizing authority, or at least it should not be. All the proposals that Suny makes for the study of the Soviet Union and the Russian Empire are valid for studies of the nationalities existing in some other framing unit as well.

Finally, there is the practical problem of funding. Despite the importance of reconceptualizing what I have called framing units, one is forced to admit that the real framing element may well be not intellectual or geopolitical but financial. At this point we do not know what will happen to the proposals under consideration for funding what used to be called Soviet and East European studies. But as an empirical matter, it is highly likely that the outcome of those struggles will determine the agendas of a good number of scholars over the next generation.

Whatever the outcome of the funding debate may be, I wholeheartedly support Olcott's insistence that scholarly investigation of former

Soviet national entities, whatever the framing unit, be rooted in a thorough knowledge of the language, culture, and history of specific places. All human activity is intrinsically interesting. Especially in today's world, where all peoples have access to all aspects of modern life, from the technological to the religious, there is no cultural hierarchy. It is just as important to study the Tajiks as the Italians. The study of some aspect of either Tajiks or Italian society, however, must be based on a thorough immersion in that society, even while it is framed by a coherent understanding of the larger world in which that society participates.

Notes

[1]For an excellent discussion of ethnic and civic nationalism, see Liah Greenfeld, *Nationalism* (Cambridge, Mass.: Harvard University Press, 1992).

Part III

Politics

Chapter 6

Common Knowledge:
Soviet Political Studies and the
Problem of System Stability

Thomas F. Remington

A wave of criticism and self-criticism has come over Sovietology. "Western Sovietology, so assiduously fostered over the past four decades, has done nothing to prepare us for the surprises of the past four years," charges Martin Malia.[1] Inability to anticipate the fall of communism represented "a dismal failure of political science," according to Adam Przeworski.[2] What did we miss? asks Donald R. Kelley.[3] Peter Zwick indicts scholars on three counts: they did not foresee communism's breakdown, they failed to explain why the changes occurred, and they are unable to discern the shape of things to come.[4] Theodore Draper, declaring that the mystery of Soviet communism is why it came to such an unexpected end, lays the blame for our excessive optimism squarely at the doorstep of Jerry Hough.[5]

Some, such as Malia and Richard Pipes, accuse Sovietology of misinterpreting the realities of the Soviet system by forcing them into the rationalistic and optimistic categories invented by Western social science. Pipes contemptuously dismisses Sovietologists by comparing them to an eighteenth-century Frenchman named Psalmanazar who won scholarly acclaim with his studies of an invented land called Formosa: "Playing scientists, they developed models which assumed that all states and societies were fundamentally identical because they were called upon to perform identical functions. . . . A good part of the Sovietological literature of the past 30 years has served us a Psalmanazarian Soviet Union: not totally invented, perhaps, but sufficiently deceptive to cause widespread disbelief once the true state of affairs was revealed."[6]

Others, such as Alexander Yanov, Alexander J. Motyl, Stephen F. Cohen, and Alexander Dallin, have blamed what they regard as the politicization of the field on observers' tendency to identify their purposes with the U.S. government's political needs and the prevailing "adversarial image" of the USSR in the United States.[7] Motyl adds that Sovietologists were lured too close to the press, preferring punditry to rigorous scholarship. But he also attacks Sovietologists for adopting a "sterile behavioralism" out of the need for academic respectability. What ecological niche for Soviet political studies is left, one might ask, if government, academe, and journalism are all corrupting influences?

A third set of critics accuse Sovietology of overlooking the state's multinational character by practicing "Sovietology in one country," to cite Motyl's sly phrase.[8] By neglecting the importance of ethnicity as a factor, they argue, Sovietology failed to grasp the threat nationalism posed to system stability. Ian Bremmer declares that "The Soviet Union has been viewed as a unified bloc, and many internal Soviet cleavages have been either dismissed or ignored" while only after the recent national explosion did the study of nationalities become significant.[9] Yet the bibliography of Western scholarly writing on Soviet nationality-related subjects included in the volume in which Bremmer's article appears contradicts his assertion: forty-five of the books cited were published in 1986 or before, and forty-one in 1987 and after. It is not self-evident that, as Bremmer claims, "the few scholars working on the Soviet periphery through this period were thus effectively marginalized."[10]

There is reason to fear, therefore, that as time passes, a set of self-serving myths about the field will become entrenched both in popular and in academic thinking unless they are squarely and objectively examined in the light of what in fact the literature on Soviet politics says. The present volume, and the workshop series out of which it grew, is a salutary attempt to link the past and future of Soviet studies by assessing the cumulative knowledge the field has bequeathed future researchers.[11]

I will contend here that many contemporary critiques of Soviet political studies miss the mark; some, such as Pipes, are completely wrong. There is in fact little mystery about what happened and why. Theories about the sources of stability and instability of the Soviet system have abounded for decades. Exactly when the necessary factors would combine to bring about the system's collapse was something that social scientists could no more have predicted than seismologists can say when the next great earthquake will strike along the San Andreas fault. Instead of blaming Sovietology for failing to predict a particular event—perestroika, coup, collapse—we should ask how well students of the Soviet political system understood the underlying tectonics. Those "pessimists" who predicted a Soviet collapse were not necessarily more insightful then those who did not, since some of those who did so have also confidently predicted many other events that have not come to pass.[12] In short, the pertinent criteria for evaluating Sovietological literature ought to be the quality and rigor of its reasoning.

As Peter Reddaway showed in a review of several recent works in the field,[13] many scholars identified severely destabilizing factors in the late Soviet period. Indeed, serious debate over the system's stability was a staple subject of theoretical discussion for decades. The problem has been that many fruitful leads were simply not followed up by systematic observation so as to permit the sharing and generalization of conclusions. Too often scholars sought a master key to the Soviet system, a single summary model for the system as a whole, rather than seeking or testing middle-range generalizations about particular aspects of the system's operation. As a result, the effects on the system itself of change over time and differentiation across regions were not sufficiently appreciated. The search for a general theory of Soviet politics may reflect the degree to which the regime itself presented the communist state as sui generis, allowing Sovietologists to pursue their studies in relative isolation from other branches of scholarship. The Bolsheviks treated their system as a self-interpreting text, the union of theory and practice, and outsiders have tended over time to follow their example. The central importance of socialist revolutionism to the subsequent evolution of the political system helps explain, through the force of inertia, the tendency to treat the system as the product of a distinctive theory. Still, if Sovietologists can be faulted for drawing upon a rather closed conceptual inventory derived from the system's Leninist roots, to which were added, in later decades, some behaviorally oriented Western concepts, the same intellectual inertia surely helps explain why so few social scientists outside the Sovietological community drew upon findings from Soviet studies in developing broader theories of comparative and international politics or political economy.

A particularly thorny problem for students of Soviet politics has been the relationship of the Soviet system to the tsarist past. In recent articles, Robert C. Tucker has chided the profession for neglecting the factor of Russian history and society in understanding Soviet politics.[14] He has consistently emphasized the need to recognize larger patterns in Russian history, particularly the cycle of state expansion followed by breakdown,[15] and he conjectures that the present period represents another phase of *smuty*, or internal "troubles" marking the transition from a collapsing state order to a new one. But although political scientists have been intensely concerned with the effects of change, they have resisted cyclical and dialectical theories in favor of linear and stage theories. The problem of the influence of Russian history, understood as a shorthand for a complex array of cultural and structural features, has been long debated, as Tucker observes, in studies of Soviet political culture. A long-standing question has been the degree to which the older political culture was irrevocably affected by both Soviet ideological indoctrination and contact with modernity.[16] This debate has taken a qualitatively new turn with the publication of results from several large-scale, rigorously implemented public opinion surveys. How conclusive their findings are about secular change in the distribution of values among the Soviet and post-Soviet population will become more evident as follow-up studies reveal the extent to which support for liberal democracy withstands social stress.

More problematic is the question of the relationship of the Russian prerevolutionary state to the Soviet system. The Soviet state may have been the "residuary legatee" of the Russian imperial state, to use Merle Fainsod's felicitous term, but it was not only that. The interests its power and wealth generated for its elite and populace increasingly diverged from those tied to Russia's own statehood. Our tendency to overlook this problem undoubtedly hindered our recognition that the fate of the Soviet regime was sealed when Russia turned against the union.

It is not the case that the field was misled by the application of social scientific concepts, whether derived from totalitarianism or modernization theory. Leading scholars of the totalitarian school employed an appropriate methodology for the analytical questions they raised given the origins of the system in a universalistic and mobilizing revolution. Totalitarianism, after all, was the only internally generated concept in Soviet studies, as Gabriel A. Almond and Laura Roselle have shown.[17] Some of the most rigorous and nuanced analyses both of the Soviet system and its dynamics were provided by scholars of the totalitarian school, who also called attention to trends that later empirical research placed greater emphasis on—the rising influence of the managerial elite and other groups, value shift in society, evolution of social structure and social cleavage, generational change and problems of nationality, the relationship of intelligentsia to political elite, and the corrosive effects of modernization and institutional decay. Therefore as the system evolved, pluralist and modernization perspectives complemented and built on the earlier literature addressing the tension among the competing elements of rationality, tradition, and power in the Soviet system.[18] Indeed, by comparison with the best of the earlier Kremlinology, much latter-day work seems derivative and impressionistic, as when, for example, writers used the tired device of citing "the mood in Moscow" as a datum on their return from their latest visits.

The most useful question we can raise in evaluating the scholarly legacy of Soviet political studies, it seems to me, is whether it yielded robust generalizations that expanded the common knowledge. To what extent has scholarship in Soviet political studies sought to make concepts and methods explicit and replicable, employ them systematically, and relate them to the study of other political systems? These are the criteria I shall try to use in this paper for evaluating the usefulness of our scholarly inheritance for future studies of politics in and among the successor states. To the extent that Soviet political studies to date have generated useful knowledge about the reciprocal influence of the old regime and its social and international environment, we may propose fruitful lines of inquiry for future studies of the successor regimes. How much do we understand about the distribution of power and other resources in the societies of the former Soviet Union, variation in the mobilization of demands, and evolution of institutional arrangements in politics and society? In the first part of this paper I will look back at the way the problem of the system's stability has been conceptualized in the past, in order to be able, in the second part of the paper, to propose avenues of research for the future.

Soviet Politics from X to Z

Analysts of Soviet politics working within the totalitarian paradigm demonstrated a considerable degree of sensitivity to the composition and interests of the political elite and its relationship to Soviet policy. In this sense they anticipated later research emphasizing the political, group, and bureaucratic influences upon regime behavior and the effects of social modernization on communist political institutions. A good example of such an analyst is Wolfgang Leonhard, who had the unique advantage of knowing the system from within. In *The Kremlin since Stalin* (1962), Leonhard was explicit about questions of theory and method. His method, Leonhard explained, comprised two sets of tasks: first, discovering the USSR's general line or policy (which includes identifying the major issues occupying the attention of policymakers, what changes in policy were being contemplated, and by what means they were to be carried out), and, second, studying changes in the membership of the most important ruling groups (i.e., the party, state, army, economy, and state security police). What groups are favored by the measures considered by the decision makers, and what effect will the appointments and dismissals of key individual policymakers have on future developments? Leonhard's focus is on the connection of power and policy. As the salience of issues changes, the influence of the group concerned with it rises or falls accordingly. And as the balance of forces changes among policymakers, so the outcomes of decision making will change. By the same token, policy change can itself affect the balance of power.[19]

Leonhard thus made the relationship between interest groups and the policy process central to his method of analysis. His theoretical model followed Milovan Djilas.[20] Leonhard identified five principal categories of groups that constituted the "new ruling class," each with policy tendencies reflecting corporate self-interest. This class had far more access to power than the population generally, whose material and social needs now, in the absence of terror, required more consideration than in the past but had little influence over policy. One of the roads not taken, it seems to me, was the lack of serious use of new class models in American studies of Soviet politics, in comparison with European scholars. On this point, for instance, T. H. Rigby has suggested that bureaucratic and new class approaches to the former Soviet system can now be revived, refined, and to some degree integrated with other approaches that have wider currency in contemporary studies of the Soviet and post-Soviet systems.[21]

Concern with the consequences of modernization for the Soviet system was a central issue for writers employing the totalitarian framework as well, some of whom specifically posed the question of whether totalitarian dictatorship could be sustained in an industrialized society. Merle Fainsod argued that the pluralization of authority among the functional groups that the regime fosters was reflected in factions within the Communist Party. It was possible that these groups would strengthen their position in Soviet society and ultimately succeed in building a constitutional order in which socialism was combined with political pluralism and multiparty democracy. But the probability of this outcome was low; the party would resist such a development and probably would be able to assert its political control over the elites whose power derived from technical authority. But to do so, the party would have to adapt and delegate authority, without allowing the industrial elite to "emerge as autonomous power groups." The party would also have to make good on its promises of improved political performance or face erosion of its power. Fainsod also noted, although only in passing, that social boredom was fatally weakening the party's legitimacy.[22]

Leonard Schapiro is an example of a scholar who emphasized leadership and central policy over change in society, a tendency cited as the "intentionalist fallacy,"[23] that is, an undue emphasis on personalities, ideas, and policies adopted at the center. Schapiro justified this perspective precisely because, in his view, the Communist Party of the Soviet Union, in contrast to other bureaucratic organizations, was exceptionally dependent for the direction of its policies on the personalities and values of its leaders.[24] For that very reason, significant change might be expected to occur once the older generation of party leaders gave way to a younger generation.

Zbigniew Brzezinski and Samuel P. Huntington, in their classic study of the American and Soviet political systems published in 1964, tended to emphasize the stability of both systems, in view of the proven capacity of each to innovate and adapt, albeit in very different ways. But they argued that, of the two, the Soviet system was the more likely to break down if the Communist Party leadership was unable to adapt itself politically and ideologically to the needs of later stages of modernization.[25] Huntington's contemporaneous essay on the tension between modernization and decay was quite confident about the Soviet system's success in balancing organizational articulation with the mobilization of popular participation, and in his important study of the development of single party regimes, he forecast the Soviet regime's evolution in the direction of such regimes as Mexico and Turkey.[26]

Brzezinski, however, grew more pessimistic about long-term prospects for the regime's stability. In his 1966 article, "The Soviet Political System: Transformation or Degeneration?" which launched a vigorous debate, he argued that the party had become an obstacle to further political development. Since, in his view, the 1970s would bring greater international tension, and given the near inevitability of growing claims by ethnonational elites in the union republics, Brzezinski concluded that the odds of a peaceful and evolutionary movement of the regime to a stable relationship with its environment were low.[27] He continued to take a pessimistic view about the Soviet regime's stability in light of the nationality cleavage. In an article in *Foreign Affairs* published at the beginning of 1990, he forecast the breakup of the USSR and other multiethnic communist states as a consequence of the destruction of class-based or other social attachments and the failure to instill a transcendent sense of nationhood across ethnic communities.[28]

The classic writings of scholars working in the totalitarianism tradition were thus indeed attuned to the effects of change in the domestic and international environment upon the regime. As early as 1947, in his X article, George Kennan suggested that "Soviet power, like the capitalist world of its conception, bears within it the seeds of its own decay, and that the sprouting of these seeds is well advanced."[29] If the regime's rulers were denied opportunities to suppress these tendencies through foreign expansion, they would ultimately bring about the collapse of the Soviet system. Not war and crisis, therefore, but the maturing of the internal contradictions of the system was the most probable of the possible causes of the system's ultimate demise. Perhaps Kennan foresaw more clearly than anyone else that it was the peculiar combination of modernization and decay which, under conditions of peace rather than war, would result in the system's breakdown.

Contemporary critics of totalitarian models in Sovietology are mistaken as well in their frequent assertion that those who employed the totalitarian model overlooked conflict within the system and overemphasized the role of ideology. The theoretical approach implied by Kennan's famous phrase—that the political personality of Soviet power was the product of ideology and circumstances—was made operational in the research of scholars such as Leonhard when they looked for clues about fluctuations in the regime's "general line." The general line represented a vector resulting from the interaction on policy making of political pressures generated by internal political dynamics and the country's international position and domestic environment. Once determined, the general line was removed from the arena of political debate, blessed doctrinally, and trumpeted and explicated throughout the country by being made the central element of current party propaganda. For this reason, policy could not be detached from the peculiar sphere of doctrinal authority and organizational control that constituted the party's ideological function. Study of ideological pronouncements revealed the play of factional, political, and interest group conflicts and tensions that, as T. H. Rigby noted, had been identified and analyzed by such early students of Soviet politics as Leonard Schapiro, Robert Conquest, and John Armstrong.[30]

There is therefore a direct line of succession linking the earlier generation of Kremlinologists, whose principal task was to explain the outcome of the policy-making process in terms of leadership competition, ideological value commitments shared by the party leaders, the drive for greater wealth and power, and the play of group pressures, with such latter-day students of Soviet elite level and leadership politics as Archie Brown, Peter Reddaway, T. H. Rigby, George W. Breslauer, John Patrick Willerton Jr., Jerry F. Hough, and Seweryn Bialer,[31] as well as to pioneering efforts to incorporate models and concepts from the family of pluralist models[32] such as those of H. Gordon Skilling and Franklyn Griffiths, Peter H. Solomon Jr., George Breslauer, Thane Gustafson, Valerie Bunce, Bunce and John M. Echols III, Blair Ruble, and many others,[33] to explain the influence of policy-oriented group alignments on regime decisions. It is a considerable exaggeration to claim, as David Lane does, that "in the early 1970s the study of class, nationalities, and pressure groups in the political process was regarded as marginal by most and even irrelevant by some Western commentators, who in their demonic black art of kremlinology focused narrowly on the 'outputs' of the political system."[34] It was, for example, in 1971 that Skilling and

Griffiths published the seminal volume *Interest Groups in Soviet Politics*, which itself grew out of several years of concerted scholarly attention to the influence of groups, tendencies, political subcultures, and social classes and strata upon regime behavior.

Let us consider the opposite critique, which claims that an artificial and misguided endeavor to fit Soviet politics to Western models led to our failure to foresee the system's collapse. How appropriate were concepts and methods developed for the analysis of democratic polities for understanding the distribution of authority and the processes of decision making in the USSR? How we answer this question will determine our current assessment of the degree of continuity between present and past and the validity and reliability of the legacy of Sovietological research. In retrospect Frederic J. Fleron Jr. and Erik P. Hoffmann's recent self-criticism seems reasonable. Denying that imported concepts had hindered understanding of Soviet political dynamics, they conceded that the attempt to develop conceptual frameworks before formulating hypotheses sometimes led to insufficient awareness of contextual factors in actors' behavior.[35]

However, as Fleron and Hoffmann show, when conceptual problems generated by comparative theory led to productive operational questions for analysis, the results generated important insights. They cite the useful findings about "cooptation" patterns in elite recruitment as a good example of the use of a modern analytic tool at a middle range of generalization, neither so abstract that the distinctive features of the Soviet party-state were overlooked, nor so case specific that comparability was lost. The question was how elite recruitment functioned in the Soviet system. Analysis of diverse career patterns of individuals revealed adaptive change in the political system over time. As Fleron and Hoffmann observe, the "cooptation" concept represented a useful conceptual alternative to the excessively abstract, insufficiently specified dichotomy of pluralism versus totalitarianism.

Some confusion arose from the temptation to leap across levels of analysis, to draw system-level inferences from local or sector-level analyses or vice versa. An example would be the discussion of "citizen participation" in the Soviet system. Inadequate specification of his pluralist model of Soviet politics led Jerry F. Hough to generalize too broadly from the restricted forms of political competition and interest articulation that research revealed to exist at both elite and mass levels. Hough went so far as to suggest that in degree and kind of participation, ordinary citizens in the USSR had roughly the same capacity to influence government as their Western counterparts. Emphasizing the parallels between patterns of direct citizen participation in Soviet and

Western societies, he qualified his comparison only by remarking that the "nuances in the similarities and differences are beyond our knowledge."[36] Unjustified inferences, yielding faulty macrolevel interpretations from limited microlevel observations, could have been challenged and corrected had the field been more methodologically self-conscious. Inappropriate characterizations of the system's nature could have served heuristic purposes had we given more attention to specification and testing of theory rather than the invention of new labels and categories.

To some extent, the weakness of the middle ground between the "concept-stretching" looseness of some interpretations of the Soviet system and highly detailed descriptions of particular institutions or leadership periods reflects the gap between the two cultures of area studies and cross-national aggregate comparativism. This issue was addressed directly by Jack Snyder in 1988, who called for building bridges between the idiothetic and nomothetic approaches or, in his terms, between the holistic and positivist schools. The holistic approach interpreted behavior in the context of historical, cultural, and other factors that were identified in a frequently ad hoc and idiosyncratic factor. Since many factors bore on a given phenomenon, it was difficult to offer useful predictions of the future, but past behavior could often be reconstructed in rich detail. The future was "underdetermined," while explanations ex post facto tend to be "overdetermined," in Snyder's phrase.[37] Yet Snyder proposed that scholarship seek to overcome the two cultures by, for instance, recasting a holistic explanation as an "if, then" proposition to be tested by a case study or case comparison. His position is echoed by some recent treatments of the case method in comparative politics.[38]

Moved by a related frustration with the overuse of self-referential, nonfalsifiable concepts for describing the regime, some scholars rejected the search for a grand concept of the Soviet system. Several, in fact, denied that there was any such thing as a single Soviet system. Alfred G. Meyer argued that changes in political regime had been so deep across Soviet history that the concept of a succession of different political systems was preferable to that of a single system evolving.[39] Stephen Cohen and Jerry Hough warned against imagining that the outcome of a particular historical conjuncture had followed inevitably from some initial set of Leninist practices and doctrines. Cohen quoted Robert Tucker to the effect that what we carelessly call "the Soviet political system is best seen and analyzed as an historical succession of political systems within a broadly continuous institutional framework."[40] Jerry Hough argued that the Soviet system, like any system, was open to a variety of possible futures and contained elements that could be synthesized in a variety of regime types. Its stability, therefore, was partly a matter of how the observer conceptualized the system.[41]

I find two problems with this position. The first is that it begs the question of what it is that brings about major changes in structures and processes of power. Saying that history does not move teleologically or deterministically does not mean that we should abandon the search for general propositions about causal forces in politics. Second, it soft-pedals the problem of distinguishing the system from the type of regime that ran it. The defining elements of the system were in fact constant across leadership periods, including the party's monopoly on several crucial political processes as well as the state's monopoly ownership of the major means of production. The new institutionalists in Soviet, post-Soviet, and East European studies have only been rediscovering what elites and scholars from the region always knew: that property ownership and political power are intimately tied with the pattern of their relationship defining distinctive properties of the state socialist system. Now that both the Communist Party's political monopoly and the state's property monopoly are broken, one can speak of a change of system. Regimes in previous periods were linked by the continuity of efforts to build, consolidate, advance, and rationalize a model of state socialism originally developed by the Bolsheviks. But to hold this view is, of course, to take seriously the regime's socialist identity.

George Breslauer broke the impasse between those searching for a general model of the system and those denying that there was any system worth speaking of by formalizing alternative conceptualizations of the relationship between ruling elite and society and by linking these to the problem of building and maintenance within the ruling elite.[42] He distinguished regime type from system: the latter was unlikely to break down (since to imagine its doing so conjures up notions of the elimination of Communist Party rule, which in 1978 and long afterward seemed quite impossible); the former was more than likely to change, as it had in the past. Breslauer described the general pattern of regime-society relations in the Brezhnev era as "welfare-state authoritarianism," a kind of implicit compact between regime and society that, as he rightly suspected, might not outlive the Brezhnev era itself. The terms of the contract invited empirical investigation and could safely replace the shark-hunt-like search for the "correct" model of the "system," Breslauer suggested. Change in the terms of the contract would depend upon changes in the alignments within the ruling elite and shifts in its relations with groups and interests in society. Breslauer called attention to the possibility of learning, or self-correcting, responses to policy outcomes and to the importance of compromise and bargaining, that is, coalition building within the political elite, as alternative explanations to models that assumed winner-take-all power games among opposing elite factions.[43]

For Breslauer, therefore, system stability depended upon how much adaptive change the governing regime would be able to make in the distribution of power and other resources to preserve the support of key groups. But unlike Martin Malia, Zbigniew Brzezinski, Bartlomiej Kaminski, Janos Kornai, and other pessimists, who argued that the state socialist system by its nature exhausted its capacity for long-term development more quickly than it could rebuild it, Breslauer expressed guarded optimism about the regime's stability, in large measure because of the importance of leadership in transforming the regime. Breslauer noted that a capable leader could turn crisis to advantage by creating an atmosphere of urgency for new political arrangements favoring a different coalition. So long as the political regime included new claimants and adopted rational policies, there was no necessary reason for the system to fail. Indeed, Breslauer challenged as ethnocentric Richard Lowenthal's Parsonian supposition that only proceduralism in a democratically organized polity could withstand the challenges to regime legitimacy that might arise as economic performance declined.[44]

A number of studies, however, called attention to the sea change in the value system of the Soviet population in the postwar era and implicitly challenged the view that support for liberal democratic and market institutions was specific to a Western European cultural community. On the basis of the Soviet Interview Project, Brian Silver found younger age cohorts and groups with higher educational levels to be more supportive of individual over collective rights and called attention to the "apparent disaffection of the educated class as a whole." In the same volume, Donna Bahry noted that for those cohorts with no firsthand experience of the Stalin period, "expectations would seem to have outpaced regime performance."[45] Several recent surveys in the USSR itself have confirmed the existence of a significant body of support for democratic values.[46] At a more global plane, a number of writers have reaffirmed the validity of key premises of modernization theory. Lucian Pye, for example, argues that because of the interaction between nation-states and an information-dense and financially integrated world society, "forces of modernization have made it harder for political willpower to mobilize and dominate."[47] Ronald Inglehart and Scott Flanagan have clashed over the nature of the "cultural shift" that is at work as a consequence of the cognitive mobilization brought about by modernization—whether the shift is from a "materialist" to a "postmaterialist" or an "authoritarian" to a "libertarian" value set—but both have analyzed multinational cross-sectional survey data to find impressive correlations between levels of national prosperity and value change.[48]

Value change at the mass level alters the character and structure of demands and expectations and renders larger populations available for movements of protest, particularly when the structure of sanctions and opportunities for collective action changes.[49] How did Sovietology conceptualize the impact of value change and rising expectations on the social contract? Were new social cleavages forming, or were old ones (including the dual Russia of state and society, or working class, or nationality) becoming more salient?

Considerable Sovietological debate surrounded the question of whether the effect of modernization on ethnonational communities would ultimately undermine Soviet rule. In his pioneering 1966 textbook, Frederick C. Barghoorn called attention to the importance of the success of the integration of distinct ethnonational populations for the viability of the Soviet regime: "The consensus of informed opinion is reflected in the carefully qualified findings of [Alex] Inkeles and [Raymond A.] Bauer that the nationality composition of the Soviet Union is unlikely, . . . under normal conditions, to be decisive in determining the regime's long-range stability." Barghoorn went on, however, to cite Alexandre Bennigsen and Richard Pipes, who argued that modernization would strengthen national consciousness among ethnic minorities and sharpen their resistance to the Russian-dominated Soviet communist regime.[50] The implicit question was whether modernization might upset "normal conditions."

Some scholars emphasized the rise of new national elites and forms of nationalism that were overlaid on old grievances as a consequence of modernization and predicted that the assimilationist politics of the center would exacerbate nationality-based claims against the center.[51] Others, however, stressed intrinsic and systemic limits on ethnonational mobilization.[52] Change in the center's willingness to suppress national movements reduced the external constraints on collective action, however, and allowed ethnic separatism to overwhelm countervailing integrationist forces.[53] Estimates of the system's stability in the face of these countervailing forces thus depended on the observer's assumptions about the strength of the incentives and sanctions available to the center to preserve the loyalty of the rising national elites and in turn provide them with the necessary arsenal of inducements to maintain loyalty and suppress opposition among their populations. On this point, we will no doubt see sharp disputes for years to come between those who believe that, by comparison to most of the world's multinational states, the old regime's nationality policy worked rather well and that it was destroyed only by the inept reform policies launched by Mikhail Gorbachev and those who believe that the awakening and intensification of nationality-based grievances created dynamics that the old regime could not ultimately have contained.[54]

More important, however, the Soviet pattern of modernization and decay intensified ethnic consciousness even among the *Staatsvolk*, many of whom came to consider themselves the most disadvantaged and exploited of nationalities. This was precisely the trend noted by Gail Lapidus in 1984, who observed, "The rise of Russian nationalism poses a strategic problem rather than one of management: its impact could be decisive for the system as a whole." If resentment toward the exploitation of Russia for the sake of preserving the union were to become politically salient, it could disrupt the precarious balance of power and status among the republics.[55] Lapidus's insight was prescient. Although the Russian republic as such was the least studied of any of the union republics,[56] its relationship to the union is critical to understanding the instability of the Soviet system. The union failed because of the demand by elites coalescing at the level of the Russian republic—which in 1990 united the democratic and conservative wings of the republic's elite—to reappropriate for a revived Russia the instruments of statehood that Russia had lent to the federal union at the dawn of the Soviet era. To this end they joined their cause successfully to a mass-level repudiation of the power and privilege of the Communist Party ruling elite as expressed through a series of elections, referenda, strikes, and other collective acts of protest. By destroying the all-union control structures, Russia deprived itself of the only means by which it could have preserved a union, since power then passed into republic-level party or opposition forces in the other republics.

But we are ahead of ourselves. Crucial as an understanding of the changing aspirations and values of the population at large was once the regime began to liberalize, it was at least as important to understand how and why the elite chose to undertake a reform course. The theory of the social contract offered guidance on this point, stipulating that the makeup and policy of a regime must be related to the political coalition it represented. In order to specify present and possible alternative regime coalitions, the analyst had to investigate the policy interests and available resources of the likeliest claimants to power.[57] One hypothetical model of development that Breslauer identified derived from Alexander Yanov's emphasis on the industrial managers as a prospective political force. Their rise to power, Yanov argued, would yield a pragmatic, Western-oriented, rather nationalistic and authoritarian regime, which would be devoted to modernization and hostile to the Communist Party's incompetent political domination.[58] In view of the recent prominence of the industrial lobby in Russia and Ukraine, and the tendency over the last few years for state industrial managers to acquire de facto, and now, increasingly, de jure property rights over their enterprises, Yanov's observations were prescient, if somewhat impressionistic. Linked to a line of analysis that goes back to Djilas and Leonhard and forward to the new institutionalism,[59] it stressed the tight relationship between the structure of ownership and control and the distribution of political power. Although research on the Soviet economy had long called attention to the influence of powerful regional, ministerial, and enterprise interests, where actual planning was "a world of special deals . . . customized to serve the needs and requirements of each side,"[60] the industrial technostructure itself was at most regarded as a latent interest and not a contender in the political arena. Now, however, the organization of associations and parties representing state industry and private entrepreneurs creates a political arena much closer to that of Asian and Latin American systems and lends itself to the application of models of bargaining and representation developed in those contexts. Moreover, strategic interaction models can be applied at several levels of the state hierarchy, including the restructuring of property rights within enterprises,[61] and lead prospectively to the application of corporatist models of interest representation.

The notion of the social contract has had a fruitful run. It led to consideration of the problem of legitimacy and its relation to performance as Gorbachev introduced a more differentiated incentives structure. Peter A. Hauslohner, for instance, argued that the decline in economic performance from the late 1960s to the early 1980s was a product of the Brezhnev-era contract and was therefore a function of political strategy rather than system structure. The radical measures undertaken by Gorbachev to restore growth would therefore engender greater differentiation between winners and losers, which would in turn contribute to sharper social tensions.[62] However, as the reform program faltered, Linda Cook found that the early challenge Gorbachev posed to the implicit compact between regime and working class had been blunted and turned back by a combination of worker protest and bureaucratic resistance.[63]

Likewise, Janine Ludlam argued that the old contract was not adequate for new claimants, particularly expanded strata of skilled workers and young professionals, or for the needs of running an "emerging postindustrial society"; hence reform was responding by opening up the participatory arena.[64] This opening up was actually benefiting the party by improving its competitiveness, although many in the party resisted the change. It is hardly fair to single out any particular authors for faulty predictions, especially when they bravely exposed them to the test of history. Moreover, the notion that expanding the political arena would result in increasing the CPSU's legitimacy was the accepted view among a number of the optimists,[65] but still it was startling to encounter the idea in an article published in 1991, when not only the Eastern European cases could have been profitably considered but, after all, Soviet election results were in from the 1989 and 1990 races. There was little sense of crisis in Ludlam's article despite the rise of sharp opposition to reform, Gorbachev's desperate efforts to form a coalition of hard-liners, and the broad front of retreat from liberalization in economic, political, and nationality policies.

Still, notwithstanding Peter Reddaway, who charged that Sovietologists went wrong by positing some sort of social contract between party and people that provided a "firm basis for evolution toward a better socialist future,"[66] it was not the social contract model itself that was responsible for excessively optimistic predictions but the failure to specify the model's terms for a given political regime and its implications for regime-society relations in a period of severe pressure, high uncertainty, and high fluidity of alignments. By 1991 it would have been possible to base conjectures about how readily popular expectations could be managed by the party leadership, and whether the party itself could be controlled by Gorbachev, on empirical data rather than simply the conventional wisdom.

In the late 1970s and early 1980s, however, not only reliable data, but accepted instruments for measuring and evaluating the deterioration in system performance, were scarce. Nonetheless, accumulating indications of decay were in fact recognized. Gail Lapidus, in her contribution to a major 1983 volume surveying the character and direction of pressures on the Soviet system in the post-Brezhnev era, identified five broad trends that could lead to social and political crisis if not arrested: stagnation in living standards, declining opportunities for upward mobility, unfavorable demographic trends, intensifying ethnic nationalism, and declining civil morale. Synthesizing evidence from both hard and "soft" sources, she concluded that Leonid Brezhnev's successors would be forced to confront a conjunction of several profound system-level problems simultaneously. Outbreaks of social unrest at the mass level were therefore likely, but insofar as the regime was resolved to maintain power even at the cost of high coercion, she considered that a regime collapse was only a remote possibility. Likelier was a turn to a more authoritarian line.[67] Although the specific prediction turned out to be wrong, the identification of the underlying "tectonics" was amply borne out by events in the latter half of the decade.

As pressure from the domestic and international environment grew, the question of the character and likelihood of reform came to occupy a central position in Soviet political studies, particularly given the imminence not just of leadership succession but of a much broader generational turnover. Seweryn Bialer, Timothy J. Colton, Jerry Hough, and a number of other authors asked whether reform would have a destabilizing impact on the system.[68] Bialer's *Stalin's Successors* (1980) came the closest to representing a consensus interpretation of the mature Soviet political system that the field has produced. Carefully enumerating sources of system-level stability both in the present and in the decade of "stringency" to come, Bialer contended that major reforms were being readied and were likely to be enacted given the coincidence of the coming leadership succession with a wider generational turnover. Although he agreed with Brzezinski and other pessimists that the system exhibited tendencies toward decay, he believed that through crisis and reequilibration it tended to increase in rationality over the long run.[69] Appropriately cautious on the question of system stability, Bialer and Colton both tied the strength of popular dissatisfaction to expectations and reference points for evaluating the system's performance. Both conjectured that if performance problems began to accumulate while popular expectations about change started to rise quickly, the system's stability would be endangered. Colton emphasized that economic disorder was so serious that it had the capacity to bring the system down if it were not reversed or if efforts at reform made matters worse.[70] Rather than regarding the system's stability and legitimacy as products of a constant relationship between populace and regime, these scholars treated them as dynamic products of the interaction of values and expectations. A sudden rise in expectations of improvement coupled with a rapid drop in favorable evaluations of regime performance might bring about a tipping phenomenon in which discontent could spread rapidly and the regime's stability evaporate. The question was whether reform could achieve gains in performance to outstrip the explosion of demands they would surely stimulate.

Pessimists argued that gains could not outstrip demands, citing both economic and political arguments. Given the "fused" character of the state socialist systems, Bartlomiej Kaminski argued, bursts of development use up reserves of human and physical capital more quickly than they can be replenished, and therefore the path of development in such systems leads to "economic self-strangulation."[71] "The institutional arrangements encourage crises-generating actions while at the same time blocking recuperative actions. Development under state socialism unavoidably leads to the exploitation of growth factors without simultaneously creating reserves that could be tapped in the future."[72] This result occurs because blockages in information flow and bureaucratic monopoly over collective action encourage authorities to ignore symptoms of crisis, and the capacity of the system to improve productivity and rationality in response to reform measures is limited. Reform invites further intensification of administrative levers to rectify resulting imbalances. Bargaining between firms and ministries upsets plans while neutralizing any efficiency gains. Therefore the system is not basically reformable, in contrast to open systems. Kaminski's position is similar to that of Janos Kornai, who concluded from analysis of the results of partial reform that ultimately only either bureaucratic or market coordination is possible and that halfway solutions bring about peculiar combinations of the worst features of each—inefficiency,continuing inequalities, inflation, shortages, and stagnation. He stresses, of course, that the market mechanism in capital resources and in labor works only to the extent that barriers to mobility are minimal.[73]

The political contradictions of the Soviet system worked, as well, to turn deep reform destabilizing, according to the pessimists. Malia argued that the "structural logic of the Soviet system prevents radical reforms from remedying its defects and condemns them only to aggravate the systemic crisis they were intended to alleviate." This result occurs because ultimately the system is a Communist Party dictatorship that is incompatible with the rule of law, political pluralism, and market competition. The leaders cannot share power with outside groups; they can only surrender it or defend it by force.[74] In his *Foreign Affairs* article published at the same time, Zbigniew Brzezinski argued that the national awakening of the non-Russians made the Soviet state untenable, particularly in view of the rejection of communist rule by Eastern Europeans.[75] He repeated his earlier arguments that national antipathies and grievances had been exacerbated by communist rule, while cross-cutting social attachments that might mitigate ethnic loyalties had been destroyed.

As had been the case with older models of the Soviet system, however, the tendency to view the Soviet system as something sui generis militated against comparisons between Gorbachev's reforms and other system-transforming periods of reform that might have facilitated evaluation of alternative forecasts. But unfortunately, the literature on radical reform is thin compared to that on revolution, as Michel Oksenberg and Bruce Dickson observed.[76] Among the few rarely cited attempts systematically to identify the conditions of successful reform are Gabriel A. Almond, Scott C. Flanagan, and Robert J. Mundt's *Crisis, Choice, and Change* (1973), and Samuel P. Huntington's 1981 lecture to South Africa, "Reform and Stability in a Modernizing, Multi-Ethnic Society."[77] Sovietologists' main source of theoretical inspiration for evaluating reform's prospects was earlier Russian and Soviet experience.[78] In all fairness, the pace and radicalism of change under Gorbachev—both leadership-initiated change and the accelerating popular mobilization—made it difficult simply to keep pace with events, much less to analyze their systemic implications. Data now deluged scholars in such quantities as to overwhelm the infrastructure for absorbing and analyzing them. Descriptive narratives and commentary, often focusing on Gorbachev's policies, tended to crowd out more systematic investigations of the ways the system itself was changing in the distribution of interests and power across sectors and regions as a consequence of the reforms.[79]

At times the preoccupation with Gorbachev led analysts of both optimist and pessimist persuasions to exaggerate his power. Jerry Hough's provocative essays suggesting that Gorbachev had orchestrated nationality dissent in order to stimulate Russian support for radical economic reform are the most prominent example,[80] and they have received a good deal of criticism.[81] However, whether Gorbachev was given blame for chaos or credit for democratization, writers sometimes focused on him to the exclusion of those with whom he shared power. For example, Marshall I. Goldman argued that Gorbachev had all the power he needed from the beginning: his capacity to purge the Politburo and force through the policy changes he wanted were ample proof of that.[82] Goldman therefore assumed that Soviet policy under Gorbachev reflected Gorbachev's own overconfident faith in reform. Even though he showed a capacity to learn from mistakes, Gorbachev's basic strategy of effecting deep political and economic change while preserving the socialist model was doomed. For Goldman, the only contenders seem to be Gorbachev and the "system," and the system finally won. The relevant question would therefore be how Gorbachev managed to engineer a vast program of economic and political liberalization during the nearly seven years in which he held power—let alone stay in power. Goldman's analysis of the problems of the economy is weakened by his oversimplified understanding of the political process, which assumes a rather undifferentiated bureaucratic machinery facing a leader whose political power is unchallenged but who cannot overcome the mute and faceless resistance of numberless self-interested bureaucrats. This frequently encountered conception is unfortunate given the rich literature on the way coalitions in Soviet leadership were formed.[83] In many cases, studies of Gorbachev's leadership could usefully have focused less on Gorbachev's "views" (what did Gorbachev think, and when did he think it?) and instead probed further to weigh the resources and agendas of Gorbachev's shifting sets of allies and enemies. Such, for instance, was Peter Reddaway's method at the end of 1990 when he concluded that Gorbachev had run out of potential allies and was suffering from an irreversible decline in authority.[84]

Of course there were attempts to devise testable propositions about the consequences of radical reform for the survival of the Soviet system. Early in Gorbachev's tenure, Timothy Colton outlined four categories of actors besides Gorbachev himself whose support or neutrality would be important factors in the success of economic reform. Relating Gorbachev's turn toward cultural and political liberalization to his frustration in introducing economic reform, Colton called attention to the likelihood that economic and political change would be "out of phase" with one another. Political decompression would reduce the authority Gorbachev enjoyed among both supporters and opponents of reform before he could bring about substantial change in economic behavior.[85] In my own writing on ideology and communication, I contended that ideological control served an essential function for elite integration. Therefore glasnost had important consequences for political control. The early Gorbachev coalition united those who sought to use glasnost to enforce discipline and authority and those who linked it to political liberalization. As glasnost expanded, that coalition would become unstable. Since ideological liberalization was achieved by reducing the ability of powerful bureaucratic interests to invoke party ideological controls over expression and organization, Nina Andreeva was justified in interpreting glasnost as a challenge to socialist ideology "both in form and content" because it was doubtful that political pluralism was compatible with communist rule.[86]

In an essay written before but published after the August coup, David D. Laitin presented an ambitious theory of ethnonational mobilization based on the historical pattern of elite incorporation, which sets out predictions about likely outcomes of center-republican tensions. Although his insistence on the need to differentiate patterns of the central control and cooptation across republics and of intra-elite cleavages within them is well taken, it is clear that Laitin underestimated the force of separatism, particularly at the mass level, given the rise of counterelites capable of ethnic outbidding.[87] A rival hypothesis on the union's stability that proved to fit the data better was suggested by Anatolii Lukianov: "Without Party leadership, the federation would fall apart."[88] Another example of an explicit "if/then" statement was Thane Gustafson's comment in a 1988 symposium that Gorbachev's reforms constituted a test of two competing hypotheses about neotraditionalism: "If Ken Jowitt was correct, and neotraditionalism is a corrupt form of Leninism, then Gorbachev's reformist strategy is reasonable and could succeed. If Andrew Walder was right that neotraditionalism is the essence of Leninism, then Gorbachev is bursting wide open the entire working basis of the communist authority system. Not only is he going to fail; he is going to blow the whole country wide open."[89] In this case, of course, a variety of other explanations for the outcomes of reform could have been proposed with equal plausibility; the very concept of neotraditionalism was too hazily conceptualized in the first place to allow much credence in this "test." But the point is that while many concepts characterizing the system at the macrolevel were proposed, many fewer were recast as falsifiable predictions. As a result, the field is littered with colorful but self-referential metaphors for a system that no longer exists.

Degrees of Vulnerability

At the opening of his book on Soviet trade unions, Blair Ruble cites Raymond Bauer's dictum that "it is axiomatic in the field of Soviet Studies that one is never right; he is only wrong with varying degrees of vulnerability."[90] The premise of this review has been that the best measure of the value of Soviet political studies as a branch of social science—rather than as punditry or policy advice—is not whether a particular conjecture was right or not but whether, right or wrong, it was useful in advancing shared knowledge of how the system operated. Some theories that were wrong were more useful than some that proved right because they forced ideas to confront empirical data. But to have heuristic value, an idea's real-world implications had to be thought through and assigned observable "objective correlatives" that allowed others to judge how it measured up against reality. Some studies that reached the right conclusions did not allow replication or refutation because they were based on intuition.

It is shameful to treat the literature of Soviet political studies as a species of scholarly fraud. The mechanisms by which power was generated and policy made were surprisingly well understood, considering the enormous lengths to which Soviet leaders went to conceal them. Excellent case studies analyzed decision making in terms of the interests, positions, and resources of individual and organizational actors. Studies of processes such as the circular flow of power, clientelism, political socialization, and authority building made lasting contributions to our understanding of the physiology of the old regime, while the literature on the CPSU, state structure, trade unions, local government, the mass media, economic decision making and administration, the military, and other structures have left us with lasting knowledge on its anatomy. Scientific survey research, both among emigrants and, increasingly, among the host population, has demonstrated major changes in the structure of values and beliefs among the Soviet population over time. Some of the latter-day criticisms of the Sovietological literature are far more politicized and "Psalmanazarian" than the research they purport to describe.

Odnako, some self-criticism is clearly in order. I believe it is the case that the common knowledge of Sovietology can be faulted for a theoretical bias in the direction of stability. As Donald Kelley suggested, there was "a tacit assumption about the continuing nature of Soviet politics, a sort of conventional wisdom that informed and seemed to give predictive continuity."[91] As we have seen, the most careful discussions of the problem of Soviet stability accurately outlined the pathways that could result in collapse given the necessary combination of circumstances. But they assigned this eventuality a lower probability than some combination of reform, crisis, and reequilibration. Historians and political scientists retrospectively searching for the explanation of the system's fall will surely debate for decades how much to weight intrinsic flaws in the system's design as opposed to gross miscalculations by the Gorbachev leadership. Certainly to read into the extraordinary sequence of events from 1985 through 1991 some sort of inevitability would be wrong. Yet, in view of the multiple and simultaneous processes of system collapse throughout the European communist world, the safest line of reasoning would probably run as follows: deep economic and political reform in the Soviet Union was becoming increasingly needed, and likely, as the 1980s wore on; the resistance of the tightly integrated institutional structure of the Communist Party state to policy changes enacted by a reformist leadership required Gorbachev to initiate ever more radical measures that ultimately subverted both party and union power, depriving him of any chance of forming a lasting political coalition. Therefore, as a systems model would suggest, any of several possible historical paths would probably have led to the same outcome, although the specific historical probability of any one of them taken alone is rather low. To say this is to echo Jerry Hough, who, in 1979, outlined a variety of scenarios for the future and observed that "while such possibilities—and others like them—must each individually be of fairly low probability, collectively the chance that something 'unexpected' will take place is fairly significant."[92] On the other hand, Hough, like most other scholars cited in this paper, overestimated the system's resilience.

We have already recalled Adam Przeworski's comment that a cancer patient is more likely to die of pneumonia or another opportunistic infection than of cancer. We might also recall the deacon's "wonderful one-hoss shay" in the poem by Oliver Wendell Holmes, which was so perfectly made that no one part would wear out first—therefore the whole carriage broke down simultaneously. If there is anything like a similarly high degree of complementarity in the structures of the communist system, under which the Communist Party's political monopoly and the "new class's" monopoly on the right to manage state productive property are closely interdependent, then we would venture to predict that the "state capitalist strategies" of China and Vietnam cannot be sustained. Either the diffusion of property rights among local political elites and new private entrepreneurs will bring about a critical confrontation with the Communist Party's political monopoly, or defense of that monopoly will force a reversion to coercive, command economy methods. Such a prediction emphasizes the bounded and systemic nature of communist society over the specific and local features of its history and culture. It assumes that the political system cannot accommodate the demands for power and wealth made by new claimants, whether ethnic or not, without surrendering power because in the "mono-organizational society" all rights to shares of public goods are controlled from a single source. When the political center is itself divided and one wing allies with groups outside the regime, the regime cannot turn to repression to preserve itself without risking a more general civil war. These choices and alliances have been modeled in the form of matrices of choices and payoffs by Adam Przeworski;[93] his "games of transition" are useful simplifications of the vastly more complex interactions that, in the Soviet case, would need also to be simulated for each of the union republics as well.

The year 1991 brought about a breakdown of the Soviet system along two dimensions: the disintegration of the union, and the end of Communist Party power. These changes qualify for even the most restrictive definitions of system change. Yet the old search for continuity and change is not over. The game has changed, but many of the players are the same. In Central Asia, Martha Brill Olcott has argued, Communist Party elites did not face a popular independence movement and, thanks to their skill in constructing independent political identities and machines, have protected themselves from any serious regime change.[94] Even before the system collapsed, regional and bureaucratic elites throughout the European communist world were working to secure themselves new rent-seeking opportunities, profiteering from their privileged positions and creating new forms of property without markets. We will need to understand the resources they commanded under the old system to follow their adaptation to the current anarchic environment. An enormous amount of fieldwork will be needed before we have a clear picture of trends and patterns; some has already begun, and much is being learned from studies of the equivalent processes in Eastern Europe.[95] We have barely begun to identify the nascent lines of political articulation of the new-old interests, trade union structures clinging to power through their continuing control over the state welfare funds fighting the independent unions, state enterprise directors and new commercial elites, the old kolkhoz sector versus new private farmers, the oblast and krai leaderships against the bureaucratic nationalists of the ethnic republics. The new politics is deeply conditioned by the distribution of power, interests, and preferences under the old regime, the resources at both elite and popular levels of the system, and the relationship of the political system to its domestic and political environments. And these factors must now be tracked both in comparative perspective as well as in depth in separate republics and regions.

Still, there are limits to continuity: the Kremlinologists' search for the general line is over with the end of Communist Party rule. The political systems of the newly independent states now must be understood as intrinsically similar to those of other authoritarian and democratizing political systems. The most categorical statement along these lines comes from Adam Przeworski, who discomfits area specialists from both camps with his pronunciamento: "The East has become the South."[96] But Przeworski contradicts himself since he would also argue that the East was the South all along. Communism did not represent, essentially, a different regime type from the bureaucratic-authoritarianism of Latin America and other states. To be sure, the communist system had characteristic features—for example, the command economy was unreformable,[97] on which point he appears to agree with the X-to-Z school. Likewise he suggests that the economic crisis of the Latin American world was brought about by a path different from that of Eastern Europe, where there had been a structural crisis requiring a change of system to resolve.[98] Still, as in Latin America, the transition today in Eastern Europe (and it is not clear how applicable he means his analysis to be to the successor states of the USSR) is likely to be a question of vacillation between participatory and technocratic-authoritarian impulses as a series of strong interests negotiate pacts. Surely Przeworski's comparisons are useful in calling attention to important and underexplored similarities between "East" and "South," in particular the vulnerability of the state to pressure from large enterprises and the organized managerial elite in communist as in Latin American regimes, and more broadly since he invites students of communist systems to bridge the scholarly gaps separating them from other branches of comparative politics.

Przeworski's approach is an elite-dominated one employing rational choice models; as George Tsebelis concedes, such models are most productive when restricted to arenas where the number of players is limited and their identities and goals are known, and where the rules of the interaction are known both to the actors and the observers.[99] Because studies of transition processes will require both "from above" and "from below" perspectives, however, we are in greater need than ever of lines of research that can link mass-level and elite-level dynamics, for example through analysis of elections and the study of institutions.[100] An example is the adoption of new constitutions, laws on elections, and laws on property in the newly independent states. We need case studies analyzing the influence of different electoral systems on the behavior and strategies of parties, on the translation of votes into parliamentary seats, and on the formation of governing coalitions in the republican legislatures, as well as comparative studies tracing similarities and divergences in the development of the successor states. Institutional studies will focus on the legislatures themselves, the courts, regional and local government, and the reconstruction of executive authority in presidencies, prefectures, and bureaucracies. Conscious of the enormous advances that have been made both in survey research and in the renewed attention to institutions, political studies in the post-Soviet phase will be both more comparative than their predecessors and more rigorous in the formalization of concepts and methods.

Yet even though the old rationale for treating the object of study as a political system sui generis (that it was the product of socialist revolution whose nature reflected an alternative theory of social and political organization) has disappeared, the prospects for the integration of post-Soviet political studies into the wider scholarly discourse face a new threat. There are indications that the fragmentation of the Soviet state is contributing to the fragmentation of scholarship in the field, as scholars become identified with "their" parts of the old empire. Hints of the tensions between the former Soviet nationalities may already be detected in some writings by scholars. Apologias for the national causes of various newly independent states pass in some quarters for scholarship. Unless scholars in the post-Soviet field themselves actively enforce canons of objectivity, rigor, and methodological self-consciousness, the field might enter a new era of self-imposed parochialism.

Notes

An earlier version of this paper was published under the title "Sovietology and System Stability," *Post-Soviet Affairs* 8, no. 3 (1992): 239–69. The comments of the journal's editor, George W. Breslauer, are gratefully acknowledged. The present article has benefited from the discussion of participants in the Kennan Institute Workshop "Rethinking Soviet Studies," held October 9, 1992. I wish also to express appreciation for the research assistance of Moshe Haspel in the preparation of this paper.

[1] Z [Martin Malia], "To the Stalin Mausoleum," *Daedalus* 119, no. 1 (1990): 297.

[2] Adam Przeworski, *Democracy and the Market: Political and Economic Reforms in Eastern Europe and Latin America* (Cambridge: Cambridge University Press, 1991), 1.

[3] Donald R. Kelley, review of Tsuyoshi Hasegawa and Alex Pravda, eds., *Perestroika: Soviet Domestic and Foreign Policies* (London: Sage Publications, 1991); Ronald J. Hill and Jan Ake Dellenbrant, eds., *Gorbachev and Perestroika: Towards a New Socialism* (Aldershot: Edward Elgar, 1989); Uri Ra'anan and Igor Lukes, eds., *Gorbachev's USSR: A System in Crisis* (London: Macmillan, 1990); Martin McCauley, ed., *Gorbachev and Perestroika* (London: Macmillan, 1990); in *Soviet Studies* 44, no. 2 (1992): 349.

[4] Peter Zwick, "The Perestroika of Soviet Studies: Thinking and Teaching about the Soviet Union in Comparative Perspective," *PS: Political Science and Politics* 24, no. 3 (1991): 461.

[5] Theodore Draper, "Who Killed Soviet Communism?" *New York Review of Books*, June 11, 1992, 7.

[6] Richard Pipes, "Russia's Chance," *Commentary* 93, no. 3 (1992): 33.

[7] Alexander Yanov, "Is Sovietology Reformable?" in *Reform in Russia and the USSR: Past and Prospects*, ed. Robert O. Crummey (Urbana: University of Illinois Press, 1989), 257–76; Alexander J. Motyl, *Sovietology, Rationality, Nationality: Coming to Grips with Nationalism in the USSR* (New York: Columbia University Press, 1990); Stephen F. Cohen, *Rethinking the Soviet Experience: Politics and History since 1917* (New York: Oxford University Press, 1985); Alexander Dallin, "Bias and Blunders in American Studies on the USSR," *Slavic Review* 32, no. 3 (1973): 560–76.

[8] Alexander J. Motyl, "'Sovietology in One Country' or Comparative Nationality Studies?" *Slavic Review* 48, no. 1 (1989): 83–88.

[9] Ian Bremmer, "Reassessing Soviet Nationalities Theory," in *Nation and Politics in the Soviet Successor States*, ed. Ian Bremmer and Ray Taras (Cambridge: Cambridge University Press, 1993), 12.

[10] Ibid.

[11] Another such effort is the journal *Post-Soviet Affairs* 8, no. 3 (July–September 1992), which is devoted to three articles discussing Sovietology's achievements and failings. Still another serious review of the literature is Frederic J. Fleron Jr. and Erik P. Hoffmann, eds., introduction to *Post-Communist Studies and Political Science: Methodology and Emperi-*

cal Theory in Sovietology (Boulder, Colo.: Westview Press, 1993), 3–23. The articles in these three collections differ in their final judgments as to the adequacy of the Sovietological literature, but all attempt to review it conscientiously rather than to caricature it for polemical purposes.

[12]On optimists versus pessimists, see George W. Breslauer, "Thinking about the Soviet Future," in *Can Gorbachev's Reforms Succeed?* ed. Breslauer (Berkeley: Center for Slavic and East European Studies and the Berkeley-Stanford Program in Soviet Studies, 1990), 1–34; Thomas F. Remington, ed., "Regime Transition in Communist Systems: The Soviet Case," *Soviet Economy* 6, no. 2 (1990): 160–90.

[13]Peter Reddaway, "The End of the Empire," *New York Review of Books*, November 7, 1991, 53–59.

[14]Robert C. Tucker, *Political Culture and Leadership in Soviet Russia* (New York: Norton, 1987); Tucker, "What Time Is It in Russia's History?" in *Perestroika: The Historical Perspective*, ed. Catherine Merridale and Chris Ward (London: Edward Arnold, 1991), 34–45; Tucker, "Sovietology and Russian History," *Post-Soviet Affairs* 8, no. 3 (1992): 175–96.

[15]Tucker, "Sovietology and Russian History," 193.

[16]For example, Stephen White, *Political Culture and Soviet Politics* (London: Macmillan, 1979); Archie Brown, ed., *Political Culture and Communist Studies* (Armonk, N.Y.: M. E. Sharpe, 1984); James R. Millar, ed., *Politics, Work and Daily Life in the USSR* (Cambridge: Cambridge University Press, 1987); Moshe Lewin, *The Gorbachev Phenomenon: A Historical Interpretation* (Berkeley: University of California Press, 1988; expanded ed., 1991); James L. Gibson, Raymond M. Duch, and Kent L. Tedin, "Democratic Values and the Transformation of the Soviet Union," *Journal of Politics* 54, no. 2 (1992): 329–71; Jeffrey W. Hahn, "Continuity and Change in Russian Political Culture," *British Journal of Political Science* 21, no. 4 (1991): 393–421; Arthur H. Miller, William M. Reisinger, and Vicki L. Hesli, eds., *Public Opinion and Regime Change: The New Politics of Post-Soviet Societies* (Boulder, Colo.: Westview, 1993); Ada W. Finifter and Ellen Mickiewicz, "Redefining the Political System of the USSR: Mass Support for Political Change," *American Political Science Review* 86, no. 4 (1992): 857–74.

[17]Gabriel A. Almond and Laura Roselle, "Model Fitting in Communism Studies," in *Politics and the Soviet System*, ed. Thomas F. Remington (London: Macmillan, 1989), 206.

[18]Barrington Moore Jr., *Terror and Progress—USSR: Some Sources of Change and Stability in the Soviet Dictatorship* (Cambridge, Mass.: Harvard University Press, 1954); Jerry F. Hough, *The Soviet Prefects: The Local Party Organs in Industrial Decision-Making* (Cambridge, Mass.: Harvard University Press, 1969); Jeremy R. Azrael, *Managerial Power and Soviet Politics* (Cambridge, Mass.: Harvard University Press, 1966); Frederick C. Barghoorn, "Soviet Russia: Orthodoxy and Adaptiveness," in *Political Culture and Political Development*, ed. Lucian W. Pye and Sidney Verba (Princeton: Princeton University Press, 1965), 450–511; Barghoorn, *Politics in the USSR* (Boston: Little, Brown, 1966).

[19]Wolfgang Leonhard, *The Kremlin since Stalin*, trans. Elizabeth Wiskemann and Marvin Jackson (New York: Praeger, 1962).

[20]Milovan Djilas, *The New Class* (New York: Praeger, 1957).

[21]T. H. Rigby, "Reconceptualizing the Soviet System," in *Developments in Soviet and Post-Soviet Politics*, ed. Stephen White, Alex Pravda, and Zvi Gitelman, 2d ed. (London: Macmillan, 1992), 300–319.

[22]Merle Fainsod, *How Russia Is Ruled*, rev. ed. (Cambridge, Mass.: Harvard University Press, 1965), 592–97.

[23]Mark von Hagen, "The Stalin Debate and the Reformulation of the Soviet Past," *Harriman Institute Forum* 5, no. 7 (1992): 1–12.

[24]Leonard Schapiro, *The Communist Party of the Soviet Union* (New York: Vintage Books, 1960), 590.

[25]Zbigniew Brzezinski and Samuel P. Huntington, *Political Power: USA/USSR* (New York: Viking, 1964).

[26]Samuel P. Huntington, "Political Development and Political Decay," *World Politics* 17, no. 3 (1965): 386–430; Huntington, "Social and Institutional Dynamics of One-Party Systems," in *Authoritarian Politics in Modern Society: The Dynamics of Established One-Party Systems*, ed. Huntington and Clement H. Moore (New York: Basic Books, 1970), 3–47.

[27]Zbigniew Brzezinski, "The Soviet Political System: Transformation or Degeneration?" *Problems of Communism* 15, no. 1 (January–February 1966): 1–15, reprinted in *Dilemmas of Change in Soviet Politics*, ed. Brzezinski (New York: Columbia University Press, 1969), 1–34.

[28]Zbigniew Brzezinski, "Post-Communist Nationalism," *Foreign Affairs* 68, no. 5 (1989–90): 1–25. See also Brzezinksi, *The Grand Failure: The Birth and Death of Communism in the Twentieth Century* (New York: Scribner's, 1989).

[29]X [George F. Kennan], "The Sources of Soviet Conduct," *Foreign Affairs* 25, no. 4 (July 1947): 566–82, reprinted in *Soviet Foreign Policy: Classic and Contemporary Issues*, ed. Frederic J. Fleron Jr., Erik P. Hoffmann, and Robbin F. Laird (New York: Aldine de Gruyter, 1991), 324.

[30]Rigby, "Reconceptualizing the Soviet System."

[31]Archie Brown, "Gorbachev: New Man in the Kremlin," *Problems of Communism* 34, no. 3 (1985): 1–21; Brown, "The Soviet Political Scene: The Era of Gorbachev?" in *Gorbachev and the Soviet Future*, ed. Lawrence W. Lerner and Donald W. Treadgold (Boulder, Colo.: Westview, 1988), 21–43; Brown, "Political Change in the Soviet Union," *World Policy Journal* (1989): 469–501; Brown, ed., *Political Leadership in the Soviet Union* (Bloomington: Indiana University Press, 1989); Peter Reddaway, "The Quality of Gorbachev's Leadership," *Soviet Economy* 6, no. 2 (1990): 125–40; Reddaway, "End of the Empire"; T. H. Rigby, "Stalinism and the Mono-Organizational Society," in *Stalinism: Essays in Historical Interpretation*, ed. Robert C. Tucker (New York: Norton, 1977), 53–76; George W. Breslauer, *Khrushchev and Brezhnev as Leaders: Building Authority in Soviet Politics* (London: Allen & Unwin, 1982); Breslauer, "From Brezhnev to Gorbachev: Ends and Means of Soviet Leadership Selection," in *Leadership Change in Communist States*, ed. Ray Taras (Winchester, Mass.: Unwin Hyman, 1989), 24–72; John Patrick Willerton Jr., "Patronage Networks and Coalition Building in the Brezhnev Era," *Soviet Studies* 39, no. 2 (1987): 175–204; Willerton, *Patronage and Politics in the USSR* (Cambridge: Cambridge University Press, 1992); Jerry F. Hough, *Soviet Leadership in Transition* (Washington, D.C.: Brookings Institution, 1980); Hough, *Soviet Prefects*; Hough, "Gorbachev Consolidating Power," *Problems of Communism* 36, no. 4 (1987): 21–43; Hough, *Russia and the West: Gorbachev and the Politics of Reform* (New York: Simon & Schuster, 1988); Seweryn Bialer, *Stalin's Successors: Leadership, Stability, and Change in the Soviet Union* (Cambridge: Cambridge University Press, 1980); Bialer, *The Soviet Paradox: External Expansion, Internal Decline* (New York: Knopf, 1986); Bialer, "Gorbachev's Program of Change: Sources, Significance, Prospects," in *Gorbachev's Russia and American Foreign Policy*, ed. Bialer and Michael Mandelbaum (Boulder, Colo.: Westview, 1988), 231–99; Bialer, "The Yeltsin Affair: The Dilemma of the Left in Gorbachev's Revolution," in *Politics, Society, and Nationality inside Gorbachev's Russia* (Boulder, Colo.: Westview, 1989), 91–120.

[32]Almond and Roselle, "Model Fitting in Communism Studies," 211.

[33]H. Gordon Skilling and Franklyn Griffiths, eds., *Interest Groups in Soviet Politics* (Princeton: Princeton University Press, 1971); Peter H. Solomon Jr., *Soviet Criminologists and Criminal Policy: Specialists in Policy-Making* (New York and London: Columbia University Press, 1978); Breslauer, *Khrushchev and Brezhnev as Leaders*; Thane Gustafson, *Reform in Soviet Politics: Lessons of Recent Policies on Land and Water* (Cambridge: Cambridge University Press, 1981); Valerie Bunce, "The Political Economy of the Brezhnev Era: The Rise and Fall of Corporatism," *British Journal of Political Science* 13, part 2 (1983): 129–58; Bunce and John M. Echols III, "Soviet Politics in the Brezhnev Era: 'Pluralism' or 'Corporatism'?" in *Soviet Politics in the Brezhnev Era*, ed. Donald R. Kelley (New York: Praeger, 1980), 1–26; Blair Ruble, "The Applicability of Corporatist Models to the Study of Soviet Politics: The Case of the Trade Unions," *Carl Beck Papers in Russian and East European Studies*, no. 303 (Pittsburgh: University of Pittsburgh Russian and East European Studies Program, 1983).

[34]David Lane, *Soviet Society under Perestroika*, rev. ed. (London and New York: Routledge, 1992), xiii.

[35]Frederic J. Fleron Jr. and Erik P. Hoffmann, "Sovietology and Perestroika: Methodology and Lessons from the Past," *Harriman Institute Forum* 5, no. 1 (1991).

[36]Jerry F. Hough and Merle Fainsod, *How the Soviet Union Is Governed* (Cambridge, Mass.: Harvard University Press, 1979), 318.

[37]Jack Snyder, "Science and Methodology: Bridging the Methods Gap in Soviet Foreign Policy Studies," *World Politics* 40, no. 2 (1988): 176.

[38]See, e.g., David Collier, "New Perspectives on the Comparative Method," in *Comparative Political Dynamics: Global Research Perspectives*, ed. Dankwart A. Rustow and Kenneth Paul Erickson (New York: HarperCollins, 1991), 7–31.

[39]Alfred G. Meyer, "The Soviet Political System," in *The USSR after 50 Years: Promise and Reality*, ed. Samuel Hendel and Randolph L. Braham (New York: Knopf, 1967), 39–60, reprinted in *The Soviet Polity in the Modern Era*, ed. Erik P. Hoffmann and Robbin F. Laird (New York: Aldine, 1984), 753–70.

[40]Cohen, *Rethinking the Soviet Experience*, 54.

[41]Hough and Fainsod, *How the Soviet Union Is Governed*, 558.

[42]George W. Breslauer, "On the Adaptability of Soviet Welfare-State Authoritarianism," in *Soviet Society and the Communist Party*, ed. Karl W. Ryavec (Amherst: University of Massachusetts Press, 1978), 3–25; Breslauer, *Five Images of the Soviet Future: A Critical Review and Synthesis* (Berkeley: Institute of International Studies, University of California, 1978).

[43]Breslauer, *Khrushchev and Brezhnev as Leaders*; Breslauer, "Is the Soviet System Transformable? The Perennial Question," in *Dilemmas of Transition in the Soviet Union and Eastern Europe*, ed. Breslauer (Berkeley: Center for Slavic and East European Studies and the Berkeley-Stanford Program in Soviet Studies, 1991), 1–14.

[44]Breslauer, *Five Images of the Soviet Future*, 40.

[45]Brian D. Silver, "Political Beliefs of the Soviet Citizen: Sources of Support for Regime Norms," in *Politics, Work and Daily Life in the USSR*, ed. Millar, 122–27; Donna Bahry, "Politics, Generations, and Change in the USSR," in ibid., 95. See also Lewin, *Gorbachev Phenomenon*; Gail Warshofsky Lapidus, "State and Society: Toward the Emergence of Civil Society in the Soviet Union," in *Politics, Society, and Nationality inside Gorbachev's Russia*, ed. Bialer, 121–48.

[46]Hahn, "Continuity and Change in Russian Political Culture"; James L. Gibson and Raymond M. Duch, "Emerging Democratic Values in Soviet Political Culture," in *Public Opinion and Regime Change: The New Politics of Post-Soviet Societies*, ed. Arthur H. Miller, William M. Reisinger, and Vicki L. Hesli (Boulder, Colo.: Westview, 1993), 69–94; Gibson, Duch, and Tedin, "Democratic Values and the Transformation of the Soviet Union"; Ronald Inglehart, "Democratization in Advanced Industrial Societies" (paper presented at the annual meeting of the Midwest Political Science Association, Chicago, April 1992).

[47]Lucian Pye, "Political Science and the Crisis of Authoritarianism," *American Political Science Review* 84, no. 1 (1990): 9.

[48]Ronald Inglehart, *Culture Shift in Advanced Industrial Society* (Princeton: Princeton University Press, 1990); Inglehart, "Democratization in Advanced Industrial Societies"; Scott C. Flanagan, "Value Change in Industrial Societies," *American Political Science Review* 81, no. 4 (1987): 1303–19; Flanagan, "Changing Values in Advanced Industrial Societies," *Comparative Political Studies* 14, no. 4 (1982): 403–44; Flanagan and Huo-Yan Shyu, "Culture Shift and the Transition to Democracy: The Case of Taiwan" (paper presented at the annual meeting of the American Political Science Association, Chicago, September 1992); Flanagan and Aie-Rie Lee, "Economic Development and the Emergence of the Authoritarian-Libertarian Value Cleavage" (Florida State University unpublished paper, photocopy, 1992).

[49]Sidney Tarrow, "'Aiming at a Moving Target': Social Science and the Recent Rebellions in Eastern Europe," *PS: Political Science and Politics* 24, no. 1 (1991): 12–20; Guillermo O'Donnell and Philippe C. Schmitter, *Transitions from Authoritarian Rule: Tentative Conclusions about Uncertain Democracies* (Baltimore and London: Johns Hopkins University Press, 1986).

[50]Barghoorn, *Politics in the USSR*, 80.

[51]Teresa Rakowska-Harmstone, "The Dialectics of Nationalism in the USSR," *Problems of Communism* 23, no. 3 (1974): 1–22.

[52]Gail Warshofsky Lapidus, "Ethnonationalism and Political Stability: The Soviet Case," *World Politics* 36, no. 4 (1984): 355–80, reprinted in *The Soviet Nationality Reader: The Disintegration in Context*, ed. Rachel Denber (Boulder, Colo.: Westview, 1992), 417–40; Alexander J. Motyl, *Will the Non-Russians Rebel? State, Ethnicity, and Stability in the USSR* (Ithaca: Cornell University Press, 1987).

[53]Bohdan Nahaylo and Victor Swoboda, *Soviet Disunion: A History of the Nationalities Problem in the USSR* (New York: Free Press, 1990).

[54]On this point, note the diametrically opposing positions taken by two contributors to a recent volume on nationality politics in the late Gorbachev period. Ian Bremmer declares flatly that "Soviet citizens never came to feel that a Soviet nation existed. . . . On the whole, Soviet policies of integration met with failure." "Reassessing Soviet Nationalities Theory," 18–19. In the following chapter, Victor Zaslavsky remarks that Soviet nationality policy failed because of the collapse of the command economy; by itself, nationality policy "was one of the most successful social policies of the Soviet regime." "Success and Collapse: Traditional Soviet Nationality Policy," in *Nation and Politics in the Soviet Successor States*, ed. Bremmer and Taras, 29–30. The latter position recalls the remark by Adam Przeworski that most cancer patients die of pneumonia; that is, various "opportunistic" social phenomena arise in response to the general weakening of the system. *Democracy and the Market*, 1. In this sense, those who agree with Zaslavsky would argue that the nationality policy worked so long as the center continued to deliver an adequately balanced stream of rewards for compliance and penalties for resistance via regional elites, and it

failed when the rewards dried up and the penalties became hollow. This is not the place to settle this fundamental question, only to note for the record that it was a significant issue in the Sovietological literature.

[55]Lapidus, "Ethnonationalism and Political Stability," 420.

[56]There have been a number of excellent articles dealing with the relationship between Russian national identity and Soviet politics. See Roman Szporluk, "Dilemmas of Russian Nationalism," *Problems of Communism* 38, no. 4 (1989): 16–23; Szporluk, "The Imperial Legacy and the Soviet Nationalities," in *The Nationalities Factor in Soviet Politics and Society*, ed. Lubomyr Hajda and Mark Beissinger (Boulder, Colo.: Westview, 1990), 1–23; Frederick C. Barghoorn, "Russian Nationalism and Soviet Politics: Official and Unofficial Perspectives," in *The Last Empire: Nationality and the Soviet Future*, ed. Robert Conquest (Stanford: Hoover Institution Press, 1986), 30–77; John Dunlop, "Language, Culture, Religion, and National Awareness," in *Last Empire*, ed. Conquest, 265–89; Dunlop, "Russia: Confronting a Loss of Empire," in *Nation and Politics in the Soviet Successor States*, ed. Bremmer and Taras, 43–72. Until very recently there have been no works discussing the politics of *Rossiiane* (citizens of the Russian republic, as opposed to *russkie*, or members of the ethnic Russian nationality) in Soviet society or that of the Russian republic within the union besides Edward Allworth, *Ethnic Russia in the USSR: The Dilemma of Dominance* (New York: Pergamon Press, 1980). See the recent work by Dunlop, *The Rise of Russia and the Fall of the Soviet Empire* (Princeton: Princeton University Press, 1993).

[57]Gabriel A. Almond, Scott C. Flanagan, and Robert J. Mundt, "Crisis, Choice, and Change in Retrospect," *Government and Opposition* 27, no. 3 (1992): 345–67.

[58]Alexander Yanov, *Detente after Brezhnev: The Domestic Roots of Soviet Foreign Policy* (Berkeley: Institute of International Studies, University of California, 1977).

[59]Simon Johnson and Heidi Kroll, "Managerial Strategies for Spontaneous Privatization," *Soviet Economy* 7, no. 4 (1991): 281-316; Joel S. Hellman, "The Revenge of the Past: Building Market Institutions in Soviet-Type Economies" (paper presented at the annual meeting of the American Political Society Association, Chicago, September 1992).

[60]Ed A. Hewett, *Reforming the Soviet Economy: Equality versus Efficiency* (Washington, D.C.: Brookings Institution, 1988), 207–8. Cf. Donna Bahry, *Outside Moscow: Power, Politics and Budgetary Policy in the Soviet Republics* (New York: Columbia University Press, 1987); Bahry, "The Union Republics and Contradictions in Gorbachev's Economic Reform," *Soviet Economy* 7, no. 3 (1991): 215-55.

[61]Michael Burawoy and Kathryn Hendley, "Between Perestroika and Privatization: Divided Strategies and Political Crisis in a Soviet Enterprise," *Soviet Studies* 44, no. 3 (1992): 371-402; Hendley, "Legal Development and Privatization in Russia: A Case Study," *Soviet Economy* 8, no. 2 (1992): 130–57.

[62]Peter A. Hauslohner, "Gorbachev's Social Contract," *Soviet Economy* 3, no. 1 (1987): 54-89, reprinted in *Milestones in Glasnost and Perestroyka: Politics and People*, ed. Ed A. Hewett and Victor H. Winston (Washington, D.C.: Brookings Institution, 1991), 31–64.

[63]Linda J. Cook, "Brezhnev's 'Social Contract' and Gorbachev's Reforms," *Soviet Studies* 44, no. 1 (1992): 37–56.

[64]Janine Ludlam, "Reform and the Redefinition of the Social Contract under Gorbachev," *World Politics* 43, no. 2 (1991): 284–318.

[65]E.g., Lewin, *Gorbachev Phenomenon*.

[66]Reddaway, "End of the Empire," 59.

[67]Gail Warshofsky Lapidus, "Social Trends," in *After Brezhnev: Sources of Soviet Conduct*

in the 1980s, ed. Robert F. Byrnes (Bloomington: Indiana University Press, 1983), 125–85.

[68]Bialer, *Stalin's Successors*; Bialer, "The Political System, in *After Brezhnev*, ed. Byrnes, 1–67; Bialer, *Soviet Paradox*; Timothy J. Colton, *The Dilemma of Reform in the Soviet Union* (New York: Council on Foreign Relations, 1984; rev. and expanded ed., 1986); Jerry F. Hough, *Opening Up the Soviet Economy* (Washington, D.C.: Brookings Institution, 1988); Hough, *Soviet Leadership in Transition*; Hough, *Russia and the West*.

[69]Bialer, *Stalin's Successors*, 138–39, 301.

[70]Colton, *Dilemma of Reform in the Soviet Union*, 1st ed., 79.

[71]Bartlomiej Kaminski, *The Collapse of State Socialism: The Case of Poland* (Princeton: Princeton University Press, 1991), 5.

[72]Ibid., 112.

[73]Janos Kornai, "The Hungarian Reform Process: Visions, Hopes, and Reality," in *Remaking the Economic Institutions of Socialism: China and Eastern Europe*, ed. Victor Nee and David Stark, with Mark Selden (Stanford: Stanford University Press, 1989), 32–94; Kornai, *The Road to a Free Economy: Shifting from a Socialist System* (New York: Norton, 1990); Kornai, *The Socialist System: The Political Economy of Communism* (Princeton: Princeton University Press, 1992).

[74]Z [Malia], "To the Soviet Mausoleum," 322, 333.

[75]Brzezinski, "Post-Communist Nationalism," 15–16.

[76]Michel Oksenberg and Bruce Dickson, "The Origins, Processes, and Outcomes of Great Political Reform: A Framework for Analysis," in *Comparative Political Dynamics*, ed. Rustow and Erickson, 235–37.

[77]Gabriel A. Almond, Scott C. Flanagan, and Robert J. Mundt, eds., *Crisis, Choice, and Change: Historical Studies of Political Development* (Boston: Little, Brown, 1973); Samuel P. Huntington, "Reform and Stability in a Modernizing, Multi-Ethnic Society," *Politikon* 8, no. 2 (1981): 8–26, also published as "Reform and Stability in South Africa," *International Security* 6, no. 4 (1982): 3–25.

[78]See, e.g., Crummey, ed., *Reform in Russia and the USSR*; Brown, "Soviet Political Scene"; Peter H. Juviler, "Prospects for Perestroika: New Goals, Old Interests," in *Gorbachev's Reforms: U.S. and Japanese Assessments*, ed. Juviler and Hiroshi Kimura (New York: Aldine de Gruyter, 1988), 21–48; William E. Odom, "How Far Can Soviet Reform Go?" *Problems of Communism* 36, no. 6 (1987): 18–33.

[79]Among the numerous examples of Gorbachev studies that could be cited are Stephen White, *Gorbachev in Power* (Cambridge: Cambridge University Press, 1990); White, *Gorbachev and After* (Cambridge: Cambridge University Press, 1991; rev. ed., 1992); Richard Sakwa, *Gorbachev and His Reforms, 1985–1990* (New York: Prentice Hall, 1991); Jerry F. Hough, "Gorbachev's Endgame," *World Policy Journal* (1990): 639–72; Hough, "Gorbachev Consolidating Power"; Brown, "Gorbachev"; Brown, "Soviet Political Scene"; Brown, "Political Change in the Soviet Union"; Brown, *Political Leadership in the Soviet Union*; Thane Gustafson and Dawn Mann, "Gorbachev's First Year: Building Power and Authority," *Problems of Communism* 35, no. 3 (1986): 1–19; Gustafson and Mann, "Gorbachev's Next Gamble," *Problems of Communism* 36, no. 4 (1987): 1–20; John Gooding, "Gorbachev and Democracy," *Soviet Studies* 42, no. 2 (1990): 195–231; Gooding, "Perestroika as Revolution from Within: An Interpretation," *Russian Review* 51, no. 1 (1992): 36–57.

[80]See, e.g., Jerry F. Hough, "The Politics of Successful Economic Reform," *Soviet Econ-*

omy 5, no. 1 (1989): 3–46; Hough, "Gorbachev's Politics," *Foreign Affairs* 68, no. 5 (1989–90): 26–41; Hough, "Gorbachev's Endgame."

[81]Draper, "Who Killed Soviet Communism?"; Reddaway, "End of the Empire."

[82]Marshall I. Goldman, *What Went Wrong with Perestroika* (New York: Norton, 1991), 111.

[83]Dennis Ross, "Coalition Maintenance in the Soviet Union," *World Politics* 32, no. 2 (1980): 262–69; Breslauer, *Khrushchev and Brezhnev as Leaders*; Breslauer, "From Brezhnev to Gorbachev"; Jiri Valenta, *Soviet Intervention in Czechoslovakia: Anatomy of a Decision* (Baltimore: Johns Hopkins University Press, 1969).

[84]Reddaway, "Quality of Gorbachev's Leadership."

[85]Timothy J. Colton, "The Politics of Systemic Economic Reform," *Soviet Economy* 3, no. 2 (1987): 145–70, reprinted in *Milestones in Glasnost and Perestroyka*, ed. Hewett and Winston, 87–88.

[86]Thomas F. Remington, *The Truth of Authority: Ideology and Communication in the Soviet Union* (Pittsburgh: University of Pittsburgh Press, 1988); Remington, "Gorbachev and the Strategy of Glasnost," in *Politics and the Soviet System*, ed. Remington, 56–82; Remington, "A Socialist Pluralism of Opinions: Glasnost' and Policy-Making under Gorbachev," *Russian Review* 48, no. 3 (1989): 277, 304.

[87]David D. Laitin, "The National Uprisings in the Soviet Union," *World Politics* 44, no. 1 (1991): 139–77.

[88]Quoted in Gail Warshofsky Lapidus, "Gorbachev and the 'National Question,'" *Soviet Economy* 53, no. 3 (1989): 201–50, reprinted in *Milestones in Glasnost and Perestroyka*, ed. Hewett and Winston, 226.

[89]Quoted in Ed A. Hewett, Thane Gustafson, and Victor H. Winston, "The 19th Party Conference," *Soviet Economy* 4, no. 2 (1988): 103–36, and 4, no. 3 (1988): 181–222, excerpted in *Milestones in Glasnost and Perestroyka*, ed. Hewett and Winston, 130.

[90]Blair Ruble, *Soviet Trade Unions: Their Development in the 1970s* (Cambridge: Cambridge University Press, 1981), 1.

[91]Kelley, review of of Hasegawa and Pravda, *Perestroika*, Hill and Ake Dellenbrandt, *Gorbachev and Perestroika*, Ra'anan and Lukes, *Gorbachev's USSR*, and McCauley, *Gorbachev*, in *Soviet Studies* 44, no. 2 (1992): 350.

[92]Hough and Fainsod, *How the Soviet Union Is Governed*, 570.

[93]Przeworski, *Democracy and the Market*; Przeworski, "The Games of Transition," in *Issues in Democratic Consolidation: The New South American Democracies in Comparative Perspective*, ed. Scott Mainwaring, Guillermo O'Donnell, and J. Samuel Valenzuela (Notre Dame, Ind.: University of Notre Dame Press, 1992), 105–52.

[94]Martha Brill Olcott, "Central Asia's Catapult to Independence," *Foreign Affairs* 71, no. 3 (1992): 112.

[95]Hellman, "Revenge of the Past"; Johnson and Kroll, "Managerial Strategies for Spontaneous Privatization"; Hendley, "Legal Development and Privatization in Russia"; Burawoy and Hendley, "Between Perestroika and Privatization"; David Stark, "Coexisting Organizational Forms in Hungary's Emerging Mixed Economy," in *Remaking the Economic Institutions of Socialism*, ed. Nee and Stark, with Selden, 137–68; Stark, "Privatization in Hungary: From Plan to Market or from Plan to Clan?" *East European Politics and Societies* 4, no. 3 (1990): 351–92; Stark, "Path Dependence and Privatization Strategies in

East Central Europe," *East European Politics and Societies* 6, no. 1 (1992): 17–54; Jadwiga Staniszkis, *The Dynamics of the Breakthrough in Eastern Europe: The Polish Experience*, trans. Chester A. Kisiel (Berkeley: University of California Press, 1991).

[96]Przeworski, *Democracy and the Market*, 191.

[97]Ibid., 124.

[98]Ibid., 140.

[99]George Tsebelis, *Nested Games: Rational Choice in Comparative Politics* (Berkeley: University of California Press, 1990), 32–38.

[100]See, e.g., Timothy J. Colton, "The Politics of Democratization: The Moscow Elections of 1990," *Soviet Economy* 6, no. 4 (1990): 285–344; Robert T. Huber and Donald R. Kelley, eds., *Perestroika-Era Politics: The New Soviet Legislature and Gorbachev's Political Reforms* (Armonk, N.Y.: M. E. Sharpe, 1991).

Commentary:

The Record of Soviet Studies

Gabriel A. Almond

Thomas F. Remington is eminently right in his reply to the critics of the Sovietologists, who fault them for failing to forecast or anticipate the collapse of the Soviet Union, "that instead of blaming Sovietology for failing to predict a particular event—perestroika, coup, collapse—we should ask how well students of the Soviet political system understood the underlying tectonics." We cannot expect more of political science than we expect of geology, or meteorology. Donna Bahry also argues in her remarks at the session, not published, that the critiques of Sovietology underestimate the growing sophistication of the Soviet field over the decades—its absorption of ideas and methods from the social sciences, its resourcefulness, and its accumulation of insight under conditions of information scarcity.

What was Sovietology telling us about the structure and process of Soviet politics on the eve of the Gorbachev revolution? As an outside observer, I am sure that I do not do justice to the research and interpretive output of Soviet studies, but it appears to me that the basis of Soviet legitimacy was pretty well understood by Sovietologists by the 1970s. The various studies of political culture and public opinion in the Soviet Union and Eastern Europe that appeared in the 1970s already pointed to the wide disparity between the normative political culture and the operative political culture. János Kádár's slogan, "He who is not against us is with us," represented an extreme case of apathy and alienation, but in none of the European communist countries (including the Soviet Union) was there anything approximating general, positive support of normative regime and system characteristics. Apathy, along with diffuse patriotism and an acceptance of collectivism, was the general picture given by the discipline; and it seems to have been relatively accurate, foretelling the resistance to entrepreneurship and the egalitarianism of contemporary Russian popular attitudes.

The strength of ethnicity and nationalism and the failure of the communist program of containing and assimilating ethnicity within the Marxist-Leninist framework were clearly recognized in a substantial literature. The importance of age and generation in effecting subcultural differences in the Soviet elite was widely appreciated.

Modernization theory applied to the Soviet Union had forecast the creation of an educated, literate, and technically competent intelligentsia with "impulses" toward participation in a civil society. I use the term "impulses" advisedly. Those Soviet researchers who pioneered in the study of public opinion, communication, and political participation in the Soviet Union can point to their work under the most difficult of conditions, with a great deal of pride. Their use of social science theories and approaches—Martin Malia to the contrary notwithstanding—illuminated the Soviet landscape rather than obscured it.

Soviet political processes—as Remington demonstrates—were quite well understood, and the application of concepts and models drawn from the political science literature had produced constructive results. The polemic over pluralism, corporatism, bureaucratism, clientelism, and the like gave intellectual life to the discipline and broke the monopoly of the totalitarian model. It introduced some of the creative playfulness of science into what otherwise would have been a dull, repetitive, and insightless discipline. The case studies of public policy that came out of these model-fitting exercises were beginning to provide a reliable picture of how the Soviet system worked.

Remington is right when he argues that Sovietology understood the "tectonics" of Soviet and Eastern European politics rather well. And Donna Bahry draws our attention to the fact that by the mid-1980s political science research on the Soviet Union had gone far beyond the early stress on Kremlinology and leadership politics to encompass, among others, empirical studies of societal trends, nationality policy and practice, local politics, political participation, and the characteristics of the media.

Hindsight suggests one failure in the discipline, although it would be an exaggeration to speak of it as a failure. Let us say, simply, that implications of this pattern were not fully appreciated. It may be that in the post-Stalin era there was a tendency to downplay the continued dependence of the system on the will and capacity of its elites to use force as a control, and to use it sufficiently to get the job done. Backing up this systemic use of force was the need for faith in the normative correctness of the ideology among the elite to justify this use of force. The treatment of dissidents in the Soviet Union and elsewhere was an indicator of this will to use force and the strength of ideological conviction within the Soviet Union itself. Various acts of suppression in East Germany, in Poland, in Hungary, and spectacularly in Czechoslovakia in 1968 were intermittent examples of the will to maintain, if not to extend, international gains. The invasion of Afghanistan was intended to be a similar use of force, not only specifically focused on the situation there but as a general signal of international intentions and capabilities.

The release of dissidents and refuseniks, the rehabilitation of Andrei Sakharov, and the withdrawal from Afghanistan in the early years of the Gorbachev administration perhaps ought to have alerted Sovietologists not only to the liberalizing aspects of these events, but also to the lessening of the will to employ force among the Soviet elites and an attenuation of the ideological underpinnings of this will to use force.

Robert Dahl, in his *Polyarchy*, proposed the axiom that the survival or transformation of authoritarian regimes depends on elite calculations of the relative costs of suppression and toleration on the one hand, and nonelite and mass calculations of the costs of dissent relative to the costs of obedience on the other.[1] Giuseppe di Palma uses Dahl's axiom in explaining transitions from authoritarian rule, including Eastern European patterns.[2] Soviet and communist politics were telling us, from the beginning of the 1980s on, that ideological conviction was becoming diluted among the communist elites and that there was consequent increasing ambivalence with regard to the use of force. Mikhail Gorbachev and his reformers did not understand the workings of their own system. They assumed more cohesion, more ideological commitment, than was actually there, thinking that it was possible to institute and stabilize a socialist pluralism under the aegis of a reformed Communist Party. Once the process of deconcentration was set in motion, there was no point at which a legitimate and effective reformed, restructured, and open system could be maintained without appreciating the kind and degree of coercion that would be required to maintain it. To contain Poland after Solidarity would have required major military action. Secessionary tendencies in places like Georgia and Lithuania would also have required major surgery. Without conviction of the full righteousness of the communist system, the costs of suppression had gone out of sight. The loss of coercive will had affected the very instruments of coercion themselves.

These judgments can be made after the fact. Neither the hard-nosed nor the soft-nosed Sovietologists anticipated the outcome. Indeed, in these historical processes, given the importance of individual personalities and of chance concatenations, we may along with Guillermo O'Donnell and Philippe Schmitter speak of these events as having been "underdetermined,"[3] so that in principle no one could have predicted them. Perhaps the hard-nosed ones were most oblivious of the significant transformations taking place, reducing everything, as they tended to do, to an ineradicable totalitarianism. The soft-nosed ones underestimated the importance of coercion in the maintenance of Soviet power.

Rather than being misled by it, Sovietologists may have erred on the side of the underuse of the general literature of political science. Let me give you an example. Sovietologists seem to have neglected those parts of modernization and development theory that dealt with state and nation building. Some of the ideas in this literature might have proven useful to Soviet and Eastern European historians and social scientists. For example, the possibility that Gorbachev's glasnost and perestroika would set in motion a process of dissolution of the Soviet empire might have been seriously entertained in the light of theories advanced in the work of Dahl, Charles Tilly, Dankwart Rustow, Lucian Pye, Leonard Binder, and my own work. It was generally argued in that work that state and nation building had to precede democratizing processes. Dahl deals with this theme in some detail in *Polyarchy*.[4] Rustow, in "Transitions to Democracy," sets nation building as the problem that has to be solved before a democratizing process can be set in motion.[5] Lucian Pye in his essays on "National Identity" and "Legitimacy" advances similar arguments.[6] In the first edition of *Comparative Politics: A Developmental Approach*, Bing Powell and I make a similar point.[7] State and nation building are not reconcilable with democratizing processes, as Tilly and his collaborators point out in *The Formation of National States in Western Europe*.[8] They arise out of and precipitate primordial commitments, create an unstable security environment, and provoke violent clashes not amenable to pragmatic bargaining processes. If they occur simultaneously with democratizing processes, they will tend to swallow them up. This was the conventional wisdom of comparative politics as early as the 1970s. Yet if I am not mistaken, the literature dealing with the Gorbachev years, when all of these intractable ethnicities and nationalisms were coming to the surface, did not place the Soviet case in the context of this literature of state and nation building.

Among the criticisms of Sovietology was one by Adam Przeworski alleging that the Soviet Union had been mistakenly judged to be "modernized" society but of an "eastern" variety. He advances the argument that the "East has become the South," and indeed was always "South" in the sense of underdevelopment.[9] I agree with Remington that this metaphor does not contribute to our understanding of the Soviet development and democratization problem. The Soviet population was not a third world population; it was an educated and skilled population. Soviet society was not overmobilized and underinstitutionalized in Samuel P. Huntington's terms;[10] it was overinstitutionalized in the sense of agencies of control and suppression and underinstitutionalized in the sense of political input structures and civil society. The problem of development in these societies is how to cope simultaneously with institutional dismantling and "mantling" in a turbulent ethnic and international situation. This juncture is what makes the transitions in Eastern Europe such novel and difficult problems.

There is nothing in the bag of cases treated in the contemporary "transitions" literature—the work of O'Donnell and Schmitter, Diamond, Linz and Lipset, di Palma, and Huntington—that is anything like the transition from communism. Nevertheless, this literature deserves a careful reading by the successor discipline of Sovietology. The notion of a bargaining process between the new and the old elites, of providing relatively soft landings for old power groups, of guarantees and of pacting, and of the generally underdetermined character of these processes may have the same relevance for democratization in Eastern Europe, as they have had in Southern Europe, and as they are now having in some East Asian and Latin American countries.

Notes

[1]Robert Dahl, *Polyarchy: Participation and Opposition* (New Haven: Yale University Press, 1971), 15.

[2]Giuseppe di Palma, *To Craft Democracies* (Berkeley: University of California Press, 1990), 9.

[3]Guillermo O'Donnell and Philippe Schmitter, *Transitions from Authoritarian Rule* (Baltimore: Johns Hopkins University Press), 65.

[4]Dahl, *Polyarchy*, chap. 3.

[5]Rustow, "Transitions to Democracy," *Comparative Politics* 2, no. 3 (1970): 350.

[6]Lucian Pye, "Identity and Political Culture," *Crisis and Sequences in Political Development*, ed. Leonard Binder et al. (Princeton: Princeton University Press, 1971), 112.

[7]Gabriel A. Almond and G. Bing Powell, *Comparative Politics: A Developmental Approach* (Boston: Little Brown, 1966), 314.

[8]Charles Tilly, ed., *The Formation of National States in Western Europe* (Princeton: Princeton University Press, 1975).

[9]Adam Przeworski, *Democracy and the Market: Political and Economic Reforms in Eastern Europe and Latin America* (Cambridge: Cambridge University Press, 1991), 191.

[10]Samuel P. Huntington, *The Third Wave: Democratization in the Late 20th Century* (Norman: University of Oklahoma Press, 1991).

Chapter 7

Beyond Soviet Studies:
The New Institutional Alternative

Scott A. Bruckner

Rational Choice and Institutions in
Positive Political Economy

The study of institutions has recently made a resurgence within the discipline of political science, particularly among political economists who work in the rational choice tradition. The current fascination with the role that institutions play in structuring political interactions finds its roots in the field of economics, where a few scholars departed from the neoclassical model and began to ask about the *costs of exchange* and the *role of information* in economic transactions.

The notion of costly economic exchange traces back to the work of Ronald H. Coase on the origins of the modern firm.[1] Cleaving to the assumption of the neoclassical model in economics that consumers and producers are rational (i.e., wealth-maximizing and cost-minimizing), Coase wondered, in particular, why economic agents would choose to organize their exchanges hierarchically in a firm—a seemingly costly action—rather than through what was traditionally viewed as a costless domain for economic transactions—the market. He presumed that the answer to this question had to lie in certain costs associated with using the market that were overlooked by the standard microeconomic models. Accordingly, Coase hypothesized that firms are organized to reduce the costs of market exchange, including costs of discovering relevant market prices and of negotiating and concluding separate contracts for each exchange transaction.

This move was pathbreaking for two reasons. First, Coase's hypothesis departed from the traditional neoclassical assumption that economic exchange is costless. It thereby introduced into the study of economics the influential notion of *transaction costs*.[2] In the most general sense of the term, transaction costs are the costs that arise when individuals exchange ownership rights to economic assets and enforce their exclusive rights to those assets. Transaction costs might emerge from any of a number of activities associated with such an exchange, including the search for information about price and product quality, bargaining, making contracts, monitoring the behavior of contractual partners, enforcing contracts and collecting damages in the event of a contractual violation, and protecting property rights. The significance of the assumption of positive transaction costs is that it provides a potent explanation for market failure; to the extent that transaction costs are exceedingly high, exchange will not occur among rational economic agents.

Second, the presumption that there are positive costs incurred with every economic transaction created a rationale for studying, among other factors that make transactions costly, the problem of acquiring *information* in exchange. Briefly, this latter development represented a break with a second neoclassical assumption—that individuals have full information—by assuming that "all human endeavors are more or less constrained by our limited and uncertain knowledge . . . about our own productive and exchange opportunities . . . [and] about how other people and even we ourselves are likely to behave."[3] This assumption brought with it two logical expectations. First, because information began to be treated theoretically as a valuable commodity, it was expected that people would be willing to pay for it, sometimes dearly. Second, when information is limited, individuals would be expected to devise solutions that increase the information available to them so that they can complete desired exchanges. Coase argued, for instance, that the economic firm is one such solution. It is important to understand that the neoclassical paradigm does not deny the importance of information to exchange; it merely assumes away the problems that can ensue from information shortages. The new direction introduced by Coase was to consider explicitly the effect of limited information on the behavior of economic agents.

These advances—the notions of positive transaction costs and incomplete information—opened up a line of inquiry into both the causes and consequences of different forms of organization (or institutional arrangements) for structuring economic exchange. It is this line of inquiry that constitutes the core of *neoinstitutional economics*.[4]

The neoinstitutional agenda in economics has resonated well with a number of the issues and problems that political scientists, and especially political economists, have been studying. It is not surprising, then, that it found its way into the study of politics. As in the field of economics, the new institutionalism has developed in political science and political economy around three assumptions. First, actors are presumed to be rational egotists. Second, politics is assumed to be equivalent to a set of transactions, the completion of which involves costs for the parties to the transaction and, frequently, for outsiders as well. Third, the information that is available to individual transactors is rarely, if ever, complete, perfect, or certain. It is worth reviewing each of these three assumptions as they have been employed in the study of politics and political economy.[5]

In positive political economy, political systems are assumed to be comprised of rational, egoistic agents, usually identified as individuals, groups, classes, or sectoral interests. The assumption of rationality states that these agents seek to maximize *expected* utility across a set of consistently ordered objectives. They will make choices that are calculated to bring them as close as possible to a preferred outcome in the most efficient (i.e., least costly) manner available. The assumption of egoism implies that actors' preferences are based on assessments of their *own* welfare and not that of others. Actors are not by nature altruists. Being rational egoists, they are expected to respond to the incentives and constraints provided by their environment in ways that are calculated to enhance their well-being, however defined.

There are two aspects of the rationality assumption that are worth noting. First, the fact that rational actors are presumed to be *self*-interested does not preclude them from undertaking altruistic actions. Moreover, the assumption of rationality will not be invalidated if a rational actor chooses to behave selflessly. However, if rational actors evince altruistic behavior, it is assumed that they do so only because of self-interested concerns (e.g., "I give blood because it makes me feel generous—*a feeling that I value*"). Second, it is not the case that rationality implies the pursuit of exclusively material or economic interests.[6] The assumption states only that individuals pursue *whatever* goal or goals they have by the best means available. Hence the assumption of rationality can be useful even in noneconomic domains.

The idea that politics can be viewed in terms of transactions is perhaps most evident in the study of cooperation and coordination problems, which has occupied a central place in positive political economy.[7] The understanding that cooperation and coordination may be problematic emerges from the assumption that political systems are comprised of rational, self-interested agents, each pursuing his or her own particular interests and goals. The problem for these agents is that, because they live and interact with others, they do not pursue these interests and goals alone. In fact, unless these agents are uncommonly powerful and influential, getting what they want usually means that they will have to bargain with and adjust to the actions of others who may have very different preferences and goals. Realizing some gain, then, almost always depends to a greater or lesser extent on what other agents want and do.[8] In addition, what other agents choose to do may not simply impede one's progress toward a goal; it can cause one considerable harm.[9] Thus, to achieve goals, political agents frequently have to anticipate and respond to the interests, goals, and intentions of those with whom they are transacting.

Anticipating a transaction partner's interests and intentions is no longer presumed to be a simple or costless task, however. The new institutionalism assumes that individuals rarely will have full information either about the conditions they are confronting or about the true underlying motivations and performance capabilities of their transaction partners. This assumption has lent extremely useful insights to research on social interactions. Specifically, it introduces into the study of politics the expectation that before a transaction will be completed the parties to it will attempt to get as much information as possible about each other.

Two logical implications follow from this expectation. First, gathering information can be quite costly. In fact, the task can sometimes be so difficult that it promises to diminish the gains an individual expects from the transaction beyond the point where the exchange is still minimally attractive to that individual. As a result, the transaction (or cooperative solution) will not occur.[10] This implication offers a potentially powerful explanation for puzzling instances of behavioral rigidity when, for example, a government or a nation-state fails to take advantage of what to outside observers appears to be obvious opportunities for advantageous change.

Second, where the costs of information gathering do not outweigh the anticipated benefits from a transaction, political agents will be expected to take steps to increase the information they have about others' future actions (and, therefore, about the likelihood of cooperation or coordination that leads to a preferred outcome). One way to increase information about others' future actions is by devising institutions. Very simply, institutions are understood in the neoinstitutional literature to be "the rules of the game in a society or, more formally, . . . the humanly devised constraints that shape human interaction."[11] Institutions may take many forms. In politics they are usually devised as constitutions, which define the property and behavioral rights in a society and procedural rules for structuring all types of exchange. In addition, institutions will involve some mechanism for enforcement and/or for monitoring the behavior of those operating within them.

Three important aspects of the neoinstitutional view of institutions and institution building are worth noting. First, institutions determine the opportunities in a society (or more narrow group) by explicitly limiting the choice set available to those who operate within them. In this manner they increase certainty about what others will or can do and, thereby, make both cooperation and coordination possible. Second, institutions are assumed to be costly to create. Likewise, to the extent that they provide valued regulation to political, economic, and social exchange, they also will be costly to dismantle. Consequently, old institutions are expected to persist beyond their usefulness. This does not mean that new institutions will never be created. It does suggest, however, that not only will political agents be slow to respond to changes in overriding incentives or in the relative gains they earn from extant structures but also that the shape of new institutions will be influenced to a large extent by the structure of old ones. Finally, in the neoinstitutional approach there is no presumption that institutions are necessarily efficient. They will frequently be created or captured to serve the interests of those with power and wealth. The preferences and goals of these actors may not always be consistent with the national welfare. As a result, institutions will often be seen to have suboptimal consequences for the societies in which they exist.[12]

The new institutionalism has been useful for political scientists in four respects. It provides a means for understanding the emergence of cooperation and coordination in conditions where these outcomes would not otherwise be expected. Consequently, it has helped the field's practitioners to understand seemingly costly rigidities in the behavior of a range of agents, including individuals, governments, nation-states, and class and sectoral interests. On the other hand, it also provides insights into the problems, pace, and direction of change when it does occur. Finally, by emphasizing the role that institutions play in responding to individuals' concerns about cost and their need for information, it has helped to account for the choice of certain forms of organization over others, including structures of property rights.

These issues are all raised by the transition currently under way in the former Soviet Union and also by the protracted period of stagnation in Soviet politics. In the next section I will review several applications by political scientists of the new institutional assumptions to these two settings.

Applications to the Soviet Union and to Its Successor States

Employing the assumptions of the new institutionalism, a few political scientists have recently begun to study the problems of rigidity and transition in the communist and postcommunist states. These applications have provided new insights into the functioning of Soviet-type systems and have helped to conceptualize the dynamics of reform in the emergent successors to them. In this section I will review some of the methods used and issues addressed by these applications. I will be gin by looking at how the problem of stagnation in the former Soviet Union might usefully be treated in neoinstitutional terms. Specifically, I will use this first example to provide a detailed explication of how a neoinstitutional argument might be constructed. I will then look more briefly at some of the issues raised by reform efforts both in the Soviet Union and in its successor states from the new institutional perspective.

CONSTRUCTING A NEOINSTITUTIONALISM ARGUMENT: THE CASE OF SOVIET STAGNATION

Suppose we were interested in examining the puzzling evolution of property rights in the former Soviet Union.[13] In particular, we might want to understand why, despite the fact that the Soviet economy suffered considerably from state ownership of all productive assets and state management of production, it was not until the 1980s that the issue of reassigning property rights on a massive scale began to be confronted head-on by public officials. Presuming that the government can affect the net wealth of a community by redefining the structure of property rights,[14] we might investigate this problem by focusing on public officials in the former Soviet Union and asking why they adhered for so long to a system of property rights that virtually devastated the Soviet economy.

In devising an answer to this question, we could begin by making three assumptions about public officials in the former Soviet Union. First, let us assume that these decision makers are rational egoists. Second, we will assume that the highest value for Soviet decision makers is assigned to job tenure. As long as holding office is instrumental to the realization of any preferences top leaders may have concerning policy, the most important personal political problem facing policymakers is how to improve or, at a minimum, retain position in the leadership. Accordingly, decision makers' choices will be influenced by the interest to stay in office. Third, let us assume that Soviet decision makers have incomplete information about their co-workers' "types" and, therefore, about their preferences as well. Further, we assume that the Soviet decision maker in our model is aware that his co-workers have incomplete information about him; he is also aware that his co-workers know that he has incomplete information about them.

To complete our model we would also note that the environment in which Soviet public officials interacted was seriously underregulated. Specifically, tenure of office for decision makers was not predetermined, authority relationships were not institutionalized, and formal legal constraints on the pursuit of self-interest by public officials did not exist.

Thus the key actors in our model are rational, self-interested decision makers whose interactions are underregulated and who pursue extended job tenure with incomplete information about each other's types. Given these assumptions, we could hypothesize that coalition building by these decision makers will produce policy rigidity, including policy about property rights. Let us examine the logic underlying this hypothesis.

Coalitions are cooperative endeavors by distinct interests that are designed to produce mutually valued objectives. Decision makers, who might otherwise act in opposition to each other, will join together in an alliance to realize some gain that can only be obtained through cooperation. While the gains that a winning coalition promises may be highly desired, cooperation to realize them may not be an easy venture. In forming a coalition with sufficient power to rule (or to challenge and defeat the existing governing coalition), prospective participants will necessarily be concerned about allying with those who genuinely intend to support the proposed coalition's compromise position. In particular, a prospective coalition member would want to know that his or her efforts at compromise and short-term sacrifice in the interest of long-term gain for the collective will be reciprocated by the coalition partners. This determination is difficult to make when public officials, as we have assumed, have incomplete information about a potential coalition partner's type.

The problem this situation presents for coalition building rests with the expected cost of being deceived by a coalition partner. Being on the losing side of a cooperative bargain means suffering some harm. In a ruling coalition of A and B, for instance, if A reneges on her promise to support some of B's policy positions (which she certainly has an incentive to attempt), B will have no influence on policy outcomes. As a result, B's policy preferences remain unrealized. If B expected this behavior from A, B would be better off on his own.[15] The problem for B, whose role in government depends on cooperation with A, is to find a way of being certain that A will be a fair coalition player.

The difficulty that these two coalition players face may be surmounted if both expect to interact for an indefinite period, as would presumably be the case in a ruling (as opposed to an issue-specific) coalition. Under these conditions, B might threaten to never cooperate with A again if A violates the agreement (i.e., B might employ a *trigger strategy*). If B defects forever, A has a lot to lose; mutual defection jeopardizes both the coalition and the advantages (e.g., a role in policy making) that the coalition brings. Such threats might well deter A from any violation.[16]

But it is important to note that a threat to employ a trigger strategy in order to initiate cooperation may not be credible under conditions in which the expected costs of being deceived by a coalition partner are very high. In the above example (the *coalition game*), threats to punish might lead to cooperation if the two politicians expect to interact for an indefinite period *and* the expected cost of a single failure is relatively tolerable. Politician B would be willing to adopt a trigger strategy in a repeated game with A (i.e., he is willing to put himself at risk by initiating cooperation) if he is able to tolerate a defection by A without suffering much damage.

But what if we assume that these anticipated costs are very high? It is not difficult to imagine a situation in which defection might mean the cooperator's elimination from the game. Josef Stalin's early coalition partners, many of whom were never heard from again after falling victim to the dictator's deception, are classic examples. Under these conditions threats to retaliate against defection may not be sufficient to get the players cooperating in an iterated game. The strategy that promotes cooperation in iterated plays breaks down under these conditions since the players know that the loser will not have a chance to retaliate. Therefore, threats to meet defection with defection in order to initiate and sustain cooperation are not credible.

Cooperation under these conditions, although anomalous, is not an impossible feat. However, when the consequences of being deceived by an opponent are dire, cooperation hinges on a fairly high degree of certainty about what an opponent intends to do. In particular, a politician would need to be able to distinguish those who would cheat from those who are genuinely interested in the gains from cooperation. The problem here is that a politician with incomplete information who is interested in cooperation has difficulty determining what her opponents' true intentions are. While she may believe that there are others who share her interests, she equally believes that there are those who will take advantage of her desire to cooperate. Thus, in a population of opportunists and cooperators, the politician faces the problem of reliably distinguishing the former from the latter.

One solution to this problem is *signaling*. Signals are activities or attributes of individuals that, by design or by accident, alter the beliefs of or convey information to others. An antiabortion stance, for instance, may serve as a signal of right-wing reliability in American politics and may cause its receivers to expect that the signaler will advocate other right-wing policies.

A politician with incomplete information about her opponent's preferences will look for signals from that opponent prior to a risky encounter with him. Where politician B is uncertain about A's preferences, a signal from A will likely affect B's beliefs about A's probable actions. Moreover, if A knows that B is uncertain about her, A may strategically employ a signal that will affect B's beliefs to A's advantage. In a game in which cooperation is unlikely but the gains from repeated cooperation are attractive, A might invest in acquiring a signaling reputation that leads B to believe that she is a "cooperator." Cooperation thereby becomes possible.[17] By unfailingly championing the "right-to-life" cause, for instance, the American politician can earn for herself a reputation that will encourage right-wing constituents to vote for her.

While signals permit joint action toward a common goal in high-risk environments in which information is incomplete, they can have the unintended side effect of producing rigid behavior. Indeed, signals that provide highly valued gains in such settings will tend to become stable. Someone who benefits from signaling will be loath to deviate from the signal, fearing that any such action might damage his favorable reputation and thereby deprive him of the gains that consistent signaling provides.

If we wanted to apply this argument to the case of rigid property rights in the USSR, we might begin by examining the scramble by the Soviet elite to fill the power vacuum created by Stalin's death. In this effort it is generally agreed that Soviet leaders seemed committed to one vital task: enhancing individual job security by curbing the brutal and costly competition for power and position that had previously characterized elite behavior. While reducing competition in favor of a cooperative leadership arrangement may have been preferred by most, the underinstitutionalized environment in which the elite interacted made cooperation among otherwise political rivals a highly risky endeavor. In a system in which political challenges were invariably job threatening and had been known to be life endangering, central politicians would only agree to coalesce and control their use of competitive tactics when they could be certain that their opponents intended to do the same.

We might, then, propose that Soviet politicians came to rely on ideology or, more specifically, the *language of Marxism-Leninism* to signal commitment to, and thereby build, a ruling coalition after Stalin's death. The use of Marxist-Leninist language to present and discuss policy issues both in public and in private would logically be an ideal way for a Soviet leader to credibly commit to a coalition of his peers. As representatives of Marxist- Leninist institutions, leading Soviet politicians derived both power and legitimacy from the existence and perpetuation of those institutions. Consequently, in coalescing with their peers, Soviet central decision makers would specifically have wanted to know that potential coalition partners did not intend to work toward dismantling Marxist-Leninist institutions.

Using the language of Marxism-Leninism as a verbal signal would help Soviet politicians to distinguish those genuinely committed to cooperation from potential challengers. By cleaving to this signal politicians, wittingly or not, would be contributing to the perpetuation of the institutions from which leaders gained their power. To the extent that all policy proposals and discussions are couched in Marxist-Leninist language, the risk that these institutions would be fundamentally altered or dismantled would be considerably reduced. On the other hand, deviations from the language of Marxism-Leninism would reveal a politician's inclination to challenge the polity's constitutive institutions and, therefore, the group's security. The unilateral introduction of a novel idea is itself a signal—intended or not—that the innovator is no longer happy with or willing to be bound by respect for extant institutions.

As the argument developed above proposes, however, this verbal signal would be expected to have the side effect of producing rigid behavior. To the extent that signaling enabled competitive politicians in the Soviet Union to increase their job security by building a ruling coalition, we would expect these politicians to be reluctant to deviate from the signal. Moreover, in later periods, we would expect this rigidity to be reinforced by the strong disincentive faced by coalition members against forming any alternative coalition with a group of challengers. A rational decision maker who thought about defecting would know that the existing coalition was providing certain rule, while a prospective coalition had only the probability of ruling. That probability would be, among other things, a function of other prospective members' types, which, as we have assumed, are unknowable. Because of his preference for certain rule, a prospective defector would have little incentive to unite with a new group. Thus the existing coalition, as well as the verbal signaling on which it depended, would remain intact.

Additionally, we would expect the concern about preserving the coalition to have a similar effect on policy, including policy about property rights. If our model is correct, coalition members should give preferred treatment to policies that are consistent with the ideology signal and avoid those that represent change. Even in the face of evidence suggesting that policy on property rights is ineffective or harmful, policymakers will be expected to eschew proposals that policy be significantly amended. In conditions of suspicion and insecurity one can never be certain whether innovativeness represents a sincere attempt to improve the common position or an opportunistic attempt to defect; it should, therefore, be avoided.[18]

For this case, to determine whether rigid and costly ideas about property rights resulted as the unintended consequence of the attempt to preserve the post-Stalin coalition, we would want to demonstrate that, while it may have become increasingly evident to Soviet Politburo and Secretariat members that ideas about centralization as an efficient industrialization program were misguided, concerns about being excluded from the coalition prevented the public expression of these doubts, the introduction of alternative policy proposals, and, therefore, the healthy evolution of these ideas and policies. We could proceed by examining Soviet elite statements about economic planning (especially where the need for policy adjustment was widely recognized or where proposals for change from outside the group were introduced)[19] during periods when the independent variable (the coalition) was both present and absent. Material could be collected from interviews with policymakers and policy advisers in the USSR, from recently available archival materials, and from published sources that include Soviet policy journals, government and party newspapers, and Communist Party of the Soviet Union congress material. In addition, a survey of academic opinion on the matter might be conducted to determine what type of ideas were available to policymakers had they sought them out. This survey would attempt to learn whether innovative ideas (i.e., those beyond the Marxist-Leninist set) were present at all in the USSR during the term of the coalition.

One of the primary benefits of such an argument, at least from the viewpoint of the new institutionalism, is that it is generalizable. What I have proposed, quite simply, is that cooperation under conditions of extreme uncertainty or information poverty will produce rigid behavior. Elite coalition building in the Soviet Union is just one case for evaluating the usefulness of this argument. We might also apply it to the commitment to economic liberalism in the United States, a commitment that has persisted despite the fact that some fundamental interests in the country were no longer served by it.[20] Or we might want to explain the persistence of the caste system in India in terms of a signaling problem. In that case, we could propose that a consistent public demonstration of support for the caste system ensures one's economic livelihood. Accordingly, we would expect all rational economic agents in that political economy to engage in it. Moreover, we would not expect these agents to condemn the system despite the high cost they suffer from sanctions preventing the substitution of low- for high-caste labor. Since everyone is signaling, no one interested in condemning the caste system can be certain whether there are others in the country who share such views (recall our assumption of incomplete information). Not wanting to be the first, and perhaps the only one, to speak against it, the potential defector remains silent, and the system is perpetuated.[21]

Let us now examine other conceptual issues that are raised by reform efforts in the Soviet and post-Soviet period from the new institutional perspective.

THE NEW INSTITUTIONALISM AND REFORM IN THE SOVIET UNION
AND ITS SUCCESSOR STATES

While empirical applications of the new institutional agenda are becoming more numerous, studies of the Soviet successor states that are informed by this perspective are still relatively few.[22] Their small number may be due, on the one hand, to the dearth of specialists on the region who are trained in the methods of this approach and, on the other, to the inaccessibility of the region to nonarea specialists who are familiar with the theory.[23]

Nonetheless, events in the communist and postcommunist worlds have produced a wealth of empirical cases of the types of problems that the new institutionalism addresses. In the Soviet period, as we have begun to see in the preceding section, the resistance to reform is quite amenable to neoinstitutional analysis. In the post-soviet era, the shift away from familiar structures of central control in favor of novel market institutions, recurrent attempts at reforming extant political practices and institutions, and the wholesale redefinition of systems of property rights have injected a considerable degree of uncertainty into the conduct of politics and economics in the new states of the former Soviet Union.[24] Those who have begun to study the postcommunist states from the perspective of the new institutionalism have been interested in learning how, under these extreme conditions of uncertainty, the various processes of reform—conceptualized as cooperation and/or coordination problems—can be (or are being) completed. Additionally, the post-Soviet states provide ample material for research on the ways in which uncertainty affects the pace and direction of the transitions, as well as the shape assumed by the institutions that develop out of them.

In addressing these questions, scholars working from neoinstitutional assumptions have noted that reform efforts in the Soviet Union and in the post-Soviet states raise three important conceptual issues. The first of these—the problem of making *credible commitments*— emerges from the interest in privatization evinced in varying degrees by the governments of the region. The second problem—designing new forms of *governance structures*—results from the state's inability to play its traditional role of third party enforcer and the corresponding need by economic and political agents to institute reliable procedures for regulating their daily transactions. Finally, the problem of *path dependence*, which refers to the influence of extant structures on the development of new institutions, is raised both by the resistance to change characteristic of the Soviet period and by the convoluted patterns of political and economic transition that have been evident in the effort to depart from Soviet-era institutions.

Credible Commitment

As the former socialist states grapple with ways to put their economies onto productivity-increasing paths, a prominent course of action that they have embarked on is to transfer previously state-owned property to private hands.[25] One prevailing expectation that motivates this drive is that privatization will encourage long-term investment that in turn4 promises to stimulate economic growth. The success of this reform strategy, however, hinges on a high degree of certainty for investors that both private property and investments will be protected from political change and/or predation by the state. To the extent that an investor is uncertain about the future security of her assets, she will not be inclined to make the kinds of long-term investments that are an essential component of sustained national economic growth. Instead, the entrepreneur will engage in activities that promise only her own short-term enrichment, regardless of their impact on the national welfare.[26]

The problem that the emphasis on the short term poses for governments in the post-Soviet states that have articulated privatization strategies is to find a way of increasing investor confidence in the government's commitment to keep the local investment environment healthy. In particular, these regimes must find a mechanism for *credibly committing* to long-term respect for private rights of ownership and private earnings from investments.

For a number of reasons, this task will not be simple. First, having emerged from a system that demonstrated little respect for either private interests or ownership, most citizens of the new states will understandably be wary of government guarantees to protect newly granted rights. Second, the likelihood of severe economic hardship in the near term will make it extremely tempting for leaders to maintain popular support by redistributing wealth away from those sectors that are making the greatest contribution to economic growth in the direction of more needy sectors.[27] The expectation of this type of response, of which there has already been some evidence in Russia, will cause potential investors seriously to discount leaders' commitments to refrain from intervening in the economy. Third, the implementation of reform programs has involved numerous stops and starts as politicians have attempted to correct policy mistakes and reverse undesirable effects of initial policies. Such erratic behavior makes it very difficult for a government to acquire a reputation for commitment to any policy line, let alone one that emphasizes a difficult transition toward sustained respect for private property. Finally, there are probably few citizens of the post-Soviet states who would be willing to wager on the long-term stability of their respective governments. Prospective investors will undoubtedly bear in mind that a regime professing commitment to private property today may be replaced by one that repudiates that pledge tomorrow.

Whether and in what manner the governments of the postcommunist states can make credible commitments to sustained market reform remain open questions. Recent research on these issues has relied on game theory methods to uncover equilibrium[28] governance forms that will allow leaders to address future problems without threatening entrepreneurs' beliefs in the security of their private property rights. From the vantage point of game theory, a government's commitment to a certain set of property rights is credible to prospective investors only if it emerges as a stable product of strategic interaction. Thus, as Daniel Diermeier and his colleagues explain, "*Secure* property rights are neither granted solely by the state, nor seized by private actors; they emerge as an equilibrium outcome of the interaction of powerful groups."[29]

This inquiry has tended to focus on one particular governance structure—constitutions—as efforts have been made to articulate a positive theory of constitutionalism. Underlying this effort is the recognition that constitutions can reduce uncertainty about current and future decision rules and, thereby, help to coordinate the actions of political and economic agents. As a result, they can play (and in the West have played) an important role in facilitating economic development.[30] A positive theory of constitutionalism would recognize that credible commitments to markets require constitutional limits whose written constraints prove binding in practice. The goal of theorizing, then, is to understand the conditions under which respect for constitutional provisions by public officials and private citizens emerges as an equilibrium outcome. The answers to this question will tell us not only about the issue of credible commitment but also about the broader problem of how stable state institutions develop.[31]

Governance Structures

The new institutionalism leads us to expect that, in the absence of third party enforcement, most transactions will not be completed. This issue is particularly salient in the new states of the former Soviet Union where traditional state-backed structures for enforcing agreements are widely recognized as feeble. Law enforcement agencies, for instance, have neither adequate material resources nor effective legislative backing to contain the outbreak of crime. In a number of regions they have been superseded by a thriving mafia that (often forcefully) sells protection for steep prices.[32] State adjudicative institutions are no better off. Despite their newfound independence, the courts have become far too cumbersome, costly, and unpredictable to serve as reliable arbiters of contractual disputes. Justices (and even lawyers) remain untrained in basic market economics, making them unqualified to preside over cases emerging from alleged contractual violations and other issues related to the functioning of the market. More fundamentally, though, the lack of an effective law enforcement agency means that justices may be virtually powerless to enforce their rulings.

Nonetheless, as a number of empirical studies and less formal news reports have documented, there is a relatively large residual of fulfilled contracts; trading occurs daily as markets seem to function more or less effectively. In the presence of a weak central authority, the assumptions of the new institutionalism would lead us to ask why transactions are being completed. In answering this question, we would logically hypothesize that alternative governance structures have emerged to regulate the behavior of economic and political agents in the market. Because these structures increase certainty about the outcome of transactions, agents are more willing to enter into exchange arrangements.

One recent study has systematically examined this hypothesis by using the case of commodity exchanges in Russia.[33] The specific problem in this instance, according to the study's author, Timothy Frye, is that the institutional design of Russian commodity exchanges provided small compensation to traders and brokers for weak state regulation. Transactions on the exchanges were opaque, dispute resolution procedures were weak, and recurrent trading was discouraged. These characteristics of the commodity exchanges did little to encourage contract compliance. Indeed, incentives to violate contractual provisions (to behave *opportunistically*, in the language of the new institutionalism) were remarkably strong.

Given the interest on the part of brokers and traders in completing transactions, one would expect that they would rely less frequently on the commodity exchange in favor of other methods for structuring their transactions. In investigating this hypothesis, Frye discovered that traders and brokers were either not completing transactions or were employing a number of alternative arrangements outside the exchange to regulate their trades. These arrangements have taken several forms: the use of economic hostages (e.g., deposits of money or goods that would be forfeited in the case of a contractual breach); relational contracting (in which transactors forgo the search for optimal contracts in favor of trading—usually inefficiently—with well-known and trusted partners);[34] vertical integration, in which trades are organized hierarchically, as in an economic firm or large enterprise, rather than horizontally through the market; and the employment of private third party enforcers, agencies of which have proliferated in Russia.

The study of governance structures, like that of credible commitment, will help to reveal insights into both the processes of and choices made about state building and development in general, and in the successor states to the Soviet Union in particular. In examining governance structures, two things are worth noting. First, these inquiries need not be restricted to economic transactions. They can usefully be focused on the development of political institutions as well. We might, for instance, examine the choices that legislators in the parliaments of the new states make to structure their interactions and to ensure overall compliance with political bargains (i.e., long- and short-term coalition building). Second, it is useful to recall that, as I noted earlier, governance structures will be designed to serve the interests of those who choose to operate within them. As a result, they will neither necessarily be efficient nor satisfy the needs of the nation as a whole. The approach, therefore, should lead us away from rigid expectations that current reform efforts in the former Soviet Union always (if ever) will have positive developmental effects, either economically or politically.

Path Dependence

From the post-Stalin era to the present, reform efforts in the former centrally planned economies have been characterized by two pronounced traits. First, in the Soviet period, attempts to move grossly inefficient methods of economic management and organization in more rational directions either resulted in immediate failure or, where they were not instantly stifled, were followed by significant and protracted backsliding that ultimately reversed whatever forward movement was initially achieved. Second, in the post-Soviet era, there has been considerable variation in the pace, direction, and results of the reform efforts under way both in the successor states to the Soviet Union and in the countries of Eastern and Central Europe. However, even where reform has had a marked degree of success, initial expectations of a relatively rapid, linear, and smooth transition have rarely been realized. The reform process everywhere has been marked by fierce struggle and frequent reversals, and, in many instances, it has produced forms of ownership and exchange that have left the intended beneficiaries of change—the mass—worse off.

Reform in Soviet-type systems and in their emergent successors raises questions not only about the divergent patterns of growth and development of societies, polities, and economies more generally, but also about the survival of political economies with persistently poor performance. These two issues lie at the core of neoinstitutional analyses, many of which have tried to understand why some states have been more successful at development while others seem to consistently lag behind.[35] The effort to address these questions has hinged on a presumption that the institutional matrix of societies, polities, and economies is a significant factor affecting their respective growth and development patterns. The institutional makeup of a political economy can provide strong incentives to maintain the status quo (i.e., it can suppress the urge to reform) and also constrain the path of change when it does occur. This dynamic is captured in the new institutional literature by the concept of *path dependence*.[36]

The notion of path dependent development refers to a process in which an existing institutional structure provides increasing returns to, and imposes transaction costs on, organizations, groups, and individuals operating within it. These costs and returns shape decisions and strategies about altering the current institutional matrix. For example, organizations, groups, and individuals that benefit from the current institutional matrix will understandably have a strong incentive to ensure that efforts to alter it are defeated (i.e., that "today's institutions are around tomorrow").[37] Not only will this effort to maintain the status quo affect the pace of change; it will also affect its path. Attempts to redefine the current institutional structure will involve struggle, bargaining, and compromise with interests that are empowered by current institutions.[38] In this manner, transformations spurred by the intro-

duction of new elements are in most instances characterized by adaptations, rearrangements, permutations, and reconfigurations of current
institutional forms.[39]

Two closely related expectations emerge from path dependent
analysis. First, we would expect that the process by which societies,
polities, and economies arrive at current structures matters for the content of future choices. Put simply, where you choose to go depends to a
large extent on where you are coming from. Second, because the current institutional matrix constrains the set of future possible equilibria,
we would expect that different distributions of resources will result in
differential patterns of development.

One recent study demonstrates extremely well the usefulness of
path dependent analysis for understanding trends in the Soviet and
post-Soviet economies. "Breaking the Bank," by Joel Hellman, traces
the peculiar and theoretically unanticipated manner in which private
firms have emerged in Russia by examining the influence of existing
structures of incentives and constraints on the development of private
commercial banks.[40]

The focus of the argument is the role of bureaucrats in the formation
of market-oriented firms. Challenging conventional depictions of bureaucrats as a force obstructing market reform in centrally planned
economies, Hellman argues that as the "center" becomes increasingly
unable to direct the use of state-owned assets and to govern all transactions in the economy, a large set of residual rights of control over state
assets is effectively placed in the public domain. In an attempt to fulfill
their obligation to meet centrally imposed plans and contracts, bureaucrats capture those rights and initiate new forms of economic organization—what Hellman refers to as "firms." The new firms are designed to
act as agents of the bureaucrats in meeting centrally imposed obligations; they are not created intentionally to promote the shift toward
marketization. But the newly created firms and their managers have interests of their own and eventually attempt to break the ties to their
founding bureaus to pursue profit- and rent-seeking opportunities in
the emerging market. Thus economic organizations that were originally created to assist bureaucrats in fulfilling their nonmarket functions evolve into market-oriented entities that appropriate state assets
as private property in the process.

In sum, Hellman proposes that bureaucrats, in adapting to the increasing uncertainty about and new opportunities for meeting centrally imposed obligations, create institutions that allow them to continue to fulfill their functions, but that, virtually unwittingly, they *also
create institutions that eventually propel the establishment of markets*. The

path of market reform in Russia, according to this account, is determined largely by the existing structure of power (the power and interests of rent-seeking bureaucrats) rather than by any concern for economic efficiency. Market-oriented firms emerge out of the individual decisions and strategic interactions of bureaucrats and the economic agents they create.

One of the most interesting issues raised by the transition under way in the former Soviet Union is the shape that new institutions will assume. The importance of path dependent analysis in addressing this issue is that it emphasizes the influence of existing structures on possibilities for new ones. The assumptions of path dependent arguments remind us that the collapse of communism is not tantamount to the creation of an institutional vacuum.[41] Moreover, it cautions against discussions about "market-building" and "democratization" in the Soviet successor states that tend to focus on transitional paths and outcomes that may be precluded from the post-Soviet context. Path dependence suggests that we focus on vestiges of the old order, including multiple patterned relationships,[42] which not only persist but also form the stuff out of which a new order will be constructed.

Conclusion

What I have tried to offer in this chapter is a survey of a relatively novel approach to the study of politics and political economy in the former Soviet Union: the new institutionalism. In doing this, I have been guilty of distilling a rich and complex body of literature down to a form that might be distasteful for those positive political scientists who work within it. Additionally, I have not been able to cover all the issues that this approach addresses; nor have I been able to review all of the studies that embrace this approach. I have tried, however, to compensate for these faults by providing numerous references to additional surveys and applications of the literature. I hope that readers will explore these.

The focus that I have chosen for this chapter represents only one alternative among what may be numerous directions for political scientists to pursue in the emerging field of post-Soviet studies. My intention in conducting a survey of the new institutionalism has been to encourage post-Sovietologists to consider how it can offer a number of new and useful concepts to guide their research. The task for theorists working with the assumptions of the new institutionalism is to convert these concepts into testable hypotheses; this process has only just begun. Because events in the former Soviet Union resonate extremely well with the new institutional agenda, post-Sovietologists are well positioned to continue this task. The reassessment currently under way in the field of post-Soviet studies presents an extraordinary opening for practitioners to make an important contribution to this literature's development.

Notes

I would like to thank Susan Bronson, Joel Hellman, and Robert Monyak for their comments on an earlier draft of this essay. I also benefited from discussions with Timothy Frye about applications of the approach outlined below to reform in the Soviet successor states.

[1]See the pioneering studies by Ronald H. Coase, "The Nature of the Firm," *Economica* 4 (1937): 386–405; Coase, "The Problem of Social Cost," *Journal of Law and Economics* 3, no. 1 (1960): 1–44. The question about the origins of the firm was reexamined and answered differently more than thirty years later by Armen A. Alchian and Harold Demsetz, "Production, Information Costs, and Economic Organization," *American Economic Review* 62, no. 5 (1972): 777–95. For an alternative view, also see Oliver E. Williamson, *Markets and Hierarchies: Analysis and Antitrust Implications* (New York: Basic Books, 1975); Williamson, *The Economic Institutions of Capitalism* (New York: Basic Books, 1985). An extremely useful survey of this issue can be found in Thráinn Eggertsson, *Economic Behavior and Institutions* (New York: Cambridge University Press, 1990), esp. chap. 6.

[2]The following definition is distilled from Eggertsson, *Economic Behavior and Institutions*, 13–32.

[3]Jack Hirshleifer and John G. Riley, *The Analytics of Uncertainty and Information* (New York: Cambridge University Press, 1992), 1. This is an outstanding survey of developments in the economics of uncertainty and the economics of information. Also see the pioneering work in this area by George J. Stigler, "The Economics of Information," *Journal of Political Economy* 69, no. 3 (1961): 213–25. The role of information has also received extensive treatment in modern game theory, which examines the impact of different information environments on individuals' behavior and interactions. For a survey of this literature, see Eric Rasmusen, *Games and Information: An Introduction to Game Theory* (Oxford: Basil Blackwell, 1989); David M. Kreps, *A Course in Microeconomic Theory* (Princeton: Princeton University Press, 1990).

[4]Throughout this chapter I will use "new institutionalism" and "neoinstitutionalism" to refer to the same body of assumptions.

[5]Terry Moe has written most explicitly about transferring concepts from neoinstitutional economics to the study of politics and political economy. While he has been one of the strongest advocates for employing insights from neoinstitutionalism, he also has cautioned about the potential problems that can ensue from directly borrowing from another discipline. These cautions are well worth reviewing. See, for example, Terry Moe, "The New Economics of Organization," *American Journal of Political Science* 28, no. 4 (1984): 739–77.

[6]This narrow definition of interest has frequently been raised by critics of the approach in order to question its utility outside the domain of economics in general, and in the study of politics in particular. Jeffry Frieden has addressed this criticism quite well in *Debt, Development, and Democracy: Modern Political Economy and Latin America, 1965–1985* (Princeton: Princeton University Press, 1991), esp. chap. 1. For an excellent general defense of the rational choice approach, see George Tsebelis, *Nested Games: Rational Choice in Comparative Politics* (Berkeley: University of California Press, 1990), chap. 2.

[7]The distinction between cooperation and coordination is developed in the literature on modern game theory. To *cooperate* refers to some act an individual undertakes *against his or her own self-interest* that generates some benefit for others. Because of the rationality assumption, it is expected that individuals will usually cooperate only when they expect that others will cooperate as well. The *prisoner's dilemma game* is the best known theoretical representation of this problem. When several individuals want to achieve one of a number of good outcomes, but are having difficulty doing so, they are suffering from a *coordination problem*. Difficulty in achieving a good outcome may result because the individuals are unable to communicate their preferences to each other or because they disagree about which of the several good outcomes is best. Two games that are frequently used to represent this problem are the *assurance game* and the *battle of the sexes*. For more on the distinction between cooperation and coordination problems and the games that are used to represent them, see any basic text on game theory. As they specifically relate to the study of institutions, see Randall L. Calvert, "The Rational Choice Theory of Social Institutions: Cooperation, Coordination, and Communication" (University of Rochester, November 1992, photocopy).

[8]This is what is meant in the literature on game theory by the term *strategic interaction*.

[9]The *prisoner's dilemma* and *chicken games*, for instance, capture this situation of strategic interaction extremely well.

[10]In economics, this situation is referred to as an instance of *market failure*.

[11]Douglass C. North, *Institutions, Institutional Change and Economic Performance* (New York: Cambridge University Press, 1990), 3.

[12]For example, see the argument about distributional coalitions in Mancur Olson, *The Rise and Decline of Nations: Economic Growth, Stagflation, and Social Rigidities* (New Haven: Yale University Press, 1982). Also see North, *Institutions, Institutional Change and Economic Performance*.

[13]The following theoretical framework is adapted from my own research. See Scott A. Bruckner, "The Strategic Role of Ideology: Exploring the Links between Incomplete Information, Signaling, and 'Getting Stuck' in Soviet Politics" (Ph.D. diss., University of California, Los Angeles, 1992).

[14]A redefinition of property rights, for instance, can increase national wealth by introducing the prospect of increasing individual wealth. This expectation will enhance individual incentives to produce. Privatizing production, then, should, *ceteris paribus*, enhance output (both qualitatively and quantitatively) and, as a result, generate a source of state revenue.

[15]Modeling this situation in terms of a prisoner's dilemma game, we would note that, despite the fact that B is unable to realize his policy preferences in either cell DD or cell DC, B's expected payoff from mutual defection (DD) is higher than what he expects to receive from being deceived by A (DC), because presumably there are costs associated with being "shafted" by a coalition partner. These might include being seen as a wimp by his constituents and other potential coalition partners, alienating other potential coalition

partners who would never ally with anyone who cooperated with A, being disappointed as a result of A's deception, and so on.

[16]When players enter into a repeated interaction they are interested in maximizing their payoffs during the entire period of the interaction. Where B threatens to respond in kind to a defection by A, A will compare the gains she receives from a defection today with her potential gains from continued cooperation. As long as the discounted present value for A of repeated cooperation exceeds the best that she can get from defecting in a single round, cooperation is an equilibrium outcome.

[17]The constraint imposed by reputational concerns on behavior is important to this outcome. Actors who consistently send signals that indicate an intention to cooperate will continue to reap the rewards that coordinated arrangements provide. On the other hand, those who develop reputations as defectors will subsequently find it impossible to realize the benefits of collectively produced gains. Someone who is caught cheating on one occasion creates the presumption that he may do so again (i.e., he develops a bad reputation), obviously limiting his future opportunities.

[18]Under these conditions innovative ideas will only emerge if there is an expectation that other members of the group will be supportive of them. But this information remains unknown because of the concern for maintaining a reputation as a group supporter; nobody wants to be first in challenging old ideas (and presumably the personnel who are believed to support them) by introducing new ones.

[19]We might, for instance, carefully examine the content of Evsey G. Liberman's proposals for economic reform against the form in which Aleksei Kosygin, as the carrier of these ideas to the leadership, presented them to his peers.

[20]Judith Goldstein has raised this point in "A Reexamination of American Trade Policy: An Inquiry into the Causes and Consequences of Protectionism" (Ph.D. diss., University of California, Los Angeles, 1983). Also see Goldstein, "Ideas, Institutions, and American Trade Policy," *International Organization* 42, no. 1 (1988): 179–218.

[21]On this problem, see Timor Kuran, "Preference Falsification, Policy Continuity and Collective Conservatism," *Economic Journal* 97, no. 387 (1987): 642–65; George Akerlof, "The Economics of Caste and of the Rat Race and Other Woeful Tales," *Quarterly Journal of Economics* 90, no. 4 (1976): 599–617.

[22]With funding from the National Science Foundation, a workshop was convened at UCLA in January 1992 and February 1993, in part, to remedy this situation. Participants included graduate students and junior and midcareer faculty, each of whom was required over the course of the workshop to develop a proposal applying the new institutional literature to any aspect of the postcommunist transition. The principal investigators for the workshop were Ronald Rogowski, UCLA, Department of Political Science; Jeffry Frieden, UCLA, Department of Political Science; and Matthew Evangelista, University of Michigan, Department of Political Science.

[23]By inaccessibility I mean that they lack the requisite language skills and familiarity with the research terrain that have enabled Soviet area specialists to conduct effective research in the former Soviet Union.

[24]Valerie Bunce makes this point emphatically. "Leaving Socialism: A Transition to Democracy," *Contention* 3 (1993): 35–47. Also see Vladimir Popov, "Soviet Economic Reforms: Possible Difficulties in the Application of Public Choice Theory," *Journal of Comparative Economics* 15 (1991): 304–24.

[25]The following section draws on ideas presented in three studies of the postcommunist states and two more general discussions of credible commitment. The former include Daniel Diermeier, Joel Ericson, Timothy Frye, and Steve Lewis, "Credibility and Commitment: The Case of Property Rights" (Wallis Institute of Political Economy, University of Rochester, March 24, 1993, photocopy); Joseph E. Stiglitz, "Theoretical Aspects of Privatization: Applications to Eastern Europe" research paper IPR22 (Institute for Policy Reform, Washington, D.C., September, 1991); Barry R. Weingast, "The Economic Role of Political Institutions" research paper IPR46 (Institute for Policy Reform, Washington, D.C., September, 1992). The two general studies of the problem are, Barry R. Weingast, "The Role of Credible Commitments in State Finance," *Public Choice* 66, no. 1 (1990): 89–97; Douglass C. North and Barry R. Weingast, "Constitutions and Commitment: Evolution of Institutions Governing Public Choice in 17th Century England," *Journal of Economic History* 69, no. 4 (1989): 803–33.

[26]In this manner, the entrepreneur reduces her own prospects for long-term gain but, more important, minimizes her personal risk of suffering large losses. One example in the former Soviet Union is asset stripping by managers of state-owned enterprises in the early stages of the Russian privatization drive. For an interesting treatment of this phenomenon in Russia, see Joel S. Hellman, "Breaking the Bank: Bureaucrats and the Creation of Markets in a Transitional Economy" (Ph.D. diss., Columbia University, 1993).

[27]This point is made by Weingast, "Economic Role of Political Institutions," 2–3.

[28]An equilibrium outcome is one in which each individual agent is doing as well as it can for itself given the actions of other agents. Consequently, to the extent that there is no change in the institutional framework that defines the options of the individuals involved and links their actions, the outcome is stable. For a nontechnical discussion of the topic of equilibrium, see Jon Elster, *Nuts and Bolts for the Social Sciences* (New York: Cambridge University Press, 1989), 101–12.

[29]Diermeier et al., "Credibility and Commitment," 9–10, emphasis added.

[30]See North and Weingast, "Constitutions and Commitment"; Weingast, "Economic Role of Political Institutions"; and Diermeier et al., "Credibility and Commitment."

[31]Weingast, "Role of Credible Commitments in State Finance," 92.

[32]From the perspective of the new institutionalism, this development is suboptimal but not completely unfortunate or unexpected. In the absence of state institutions that can provide oversight, regulation, and enforcement of contracts, the various regional mafia provide vital third party enforcement and, thereby, facilitate economic transacting.

[33]Timothy Frye, "Caveat Emptor: Institutions, Credible Commitment, and Commodity Exchanges in Russia," in *Institutional Design*, ed. David L. Weimer (Boston: Kluver Academic Publisher, forthcoming).

[34]For a wonderful empirical study of the emergence of relational contracting in China, see Dorothy Solinger, "Urban Reform and Relational Contracting in Post-Mao China: An Interpretation of the Transition from Plan to Market," *Studies in Comparative Communism* 22, no. 2–3 (1989): 171–85.

[35]For instance, this is the focus of North, *Institutions, Institutional Change and Economic Performance*.

[36]The concept of path dependence was first introduced in the field of economics to account for the persistence of suboptimal paths of technological advancement. See Paul David, "Clio and the Economics of QWERTY, "*American Economic Review* 75, no. 2 (1985): 332–37. David's argument demonstrated that technological developments, once begun

on a particular track, could lead certain technological solutions to win out over others, even when these solutions are less efficient than the abandoned alternatives.

[37]North, *Institutions, Institutional Change and Economic Performance*, 93.

[38]Certain strands of the literature on path dependent development will also stress the constraints imposed on reform by the existing stock of knowledge and technology associated with current institutions. See, for example, Peter Murrell, "Conservative Political Philosophy and the Strategy of Economic Transition," *East European Politics and Societies* 6, no. 1 (1992): 3–16.

[39]David Stark, "Path Dependence and Privatization Strategies in East Central Europe," *East European Politics and Societies* 6, no. 1 (1992): 20–22.

[40]Hellman, "Breaking the Bank."

[41]This point is made emphatically by Stark, "Path Dependence and Privatization Strategies." See also Philip G. Roeder, *Red Sunset: The Failure of Soviet Politics* (Princeton: Princeton University Press, 1993), which addresses the issue of the Soviet system's inability to reform itself by focusing on institutionalized rules of behavior.

[42]For an example of these persistent relationships, see Solinger, "Urban Reform and Relational Contracting."

Part IV

Economics

Chapter 8

Rethinking Soviet Economic Studies

James R. Millar

My assignment is to initiate a discussion among economists trained primarily as specialists on the Soviet centrally planned economy about the future of the field and of those trained in the area. It is important, first, I believe, for our rethinking to be based upon an empirical description of the profession. In 1980, I described the various generations of Soviet economic specialists through 1978 in an attempt to assess the prospects for replacement of senior scholars.[1] The first section below is devoted to updating and revising that report to include the latest generation (V).

Second, I propose to update a survey I conducted in 1973 that was designed to elicit from scholars in the field of Soviet economics a subjective evaluation of what areas needed more, or less, work.[2] The survey was based upon one that had been published earlier in the *Journal of Economic Literature* for the economics profession as a whole. I shall also examine what subfields have been receiving the attention of specialists and how that pattern has been affected by perestroika and the August 1991 putsch.

Third, I shall draw upon a report that several colleagues (Dan Berkowitz, Joe Berliner, Paul Gregory, and Susan Linz) and I prepared for the House Permanent Select Committee on Intelligence evaluating the economic products of the Central Intelligence Agency's Soviet division (SOVA) between 1970 and 1990.[3] The purpose was to address questions that had been posed about the failure of the CIA to predict the collapse of the Soviet system. As we all failed to predict this event, it seems material for us to ask ourselves, too, how well we did as Soviet economic specialists.

In the final section I consider several hypotheses about the future of the specialty and its specialists. In particular, I set out the challenge to individuals trained in area studies from two kinds of interloper: those from mainstream economics and those from the successor states of the USSR. I also raise questions about the relevance of the comparative economics paradigm in the future.

The Generations of Soviet Economic Specialists

As I pointed out in 1980, the field of Soviet economic studies is very recent and thus relatively young. It is also still quite small as subfields in economics go. In 1980, for example, I was able to identify 128 specialists (since approximately 1930) who had received Ph.D.'s in the field and been active at some time in their careers in Soviet economic studies. In 1980, almost all were still alive and still working actively in the field. Soviet economy specialists were counted from the date of their receipt of a Ph.D. in the field (with the exception of the first generation). About 76 are members of what I called the fourth generation, or generation IV, that is, scholars who received their doctorates between 1969 and 1978. I have now identified another 61 new specialists who received doctorates between 1979 and 1988, generation V by my criteria. This yields a grand total for generations I through V of 253 specialists (see appendix A), and, by my best estimate, all but about twenty are still active in the field (at least intermittently). Thus, the total existing stock of specialists is relatively youthful, for a little more than one-third received their Ph.D.'s since 1969. Moreover, prior to 1949, only 6 or 7 American economists elected to specialize in the field: Peter Swanish (Chicago, 1930); Lazar Volin (Michigan, 1931); Arthur Z. Arnold (Columbia, 1937); Abram Bergson (Harvard, 1940); D. Gale Johnson (Iowa State, 1945); Joseph Kershaw (Columbia, 1948); Chee-Hsein Wu (Harvard, 1948). Naum Jasny, Wassily Leontief, and Alexander Gerschenkron, of course, brought their expertise from abroad.

Generation I trained the great bulk of Generation II. By my count, the second generation numbered 39 individuals. Thirteen were trained by Abram Bergson at Columbia and Harvard. Gerschenkron trained seven at Harvard during these years, and 3 others (Holland Hunter, Gardener Clark, and Edward Ames) received Ph.D.'s at Harvard under other auspices. Thus, Gerschenkron and Bergson dominated the production of Soviet specialists between 1949 and 1958, and Harvard and Columbia together produced about half of the total. Only about sixteen Ph.D.'s were awarded elsewhere. The second generation assumed most of the remaining premier academic posts in the field, notably Yale, Berkeley, Chicago, Cornell, Princeton, Tufts, Brandeis, Illinois, Wisconsin, and Indiana, and most have remained in these posts throughout their careers. In fact the field has been remarkable for lack of mobility.

Generation III, who received doctorates between 1959 and 1968, differed from Generation II in several significant respects. It was the first generation recruited following the launching of *Sputnik I*. Ford Foundation Foreign Area Fellowships helped to finance graduate study in the area, and Office of Education grants began to be made regularly in support of the development of Russian and East European Centers; they help to explain the growing proportion of Ph.D.'s produced outside the Columbia-Harvard axis. Generation III was the first to have access to a growing stock of official Soviet postwar economic data series, and it benefited from de-Stalinization in other ways as well, notably freer and more sophisticated economic discussions among Soviet economists. Generation III was the first also to have the opportunity to conduct firsthand observation in the Soviet Union under the U.S.-USSR Cultural Exchange Program, although not many did more than visit on a short-term basis.

By comparison with the generations on either side, generation III was placed disproportionately in academic positions, thanks to boom times in the academy generally as well as in the demand for Soviet economic specialists as international tensions increased. Consequently, the placement of members of this generation was only somewhat inferior to that of generation II. Many were placed in major research institutions such as Duke, Hebrew University, Illinois, Indiana, Maryland, Pennsylvania, and Pittsburgh, or in quality undergraduate colleges near major research libraries, such as Wellesley, Boston College, Brandeis, and Windsor.

My main concern in 1980 was with the placement and prospects of generation IV, that is, with those who received their degrees between 1969 and 1978. The seventy-six members of this generation raised almost by one-third the total number of Soviet economic specialists in the country. The bulge is readily apparent in figure 1. Generation IV had a

● FIG. 1. Ph.D.'s in Soviet Economics, 1949–1978
SOURCE: SEE APPENDICES A AND B

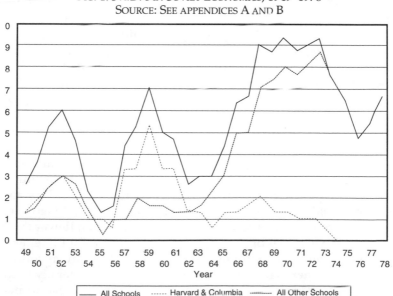

much more diverse provenance than either II or III. Approximately one-half (twenty-four) of generation II and about 40 percent (19) of generation III were produced by Harvard and Columbia combined. These two schools produced only 6 Ph.D.'s between 1969 and 1978, and no single school produced more than 7 during this decade. The great diversity of generation IV Ph.D.'s by institution of origin is clear from table 1. In this respect, generation V (1979–88) is very similar. Columbia and Harvard accounted for about 6 Ph.D.'s of a total of some 61. Thirty-four different institutions produced at least one Ph.D. between 1969 and 1978, as opposed to twenty-nine institutions for 1979–88 (as opposed to 20 different institutions for 1959–68). Over the twenty-year period, 1969–88, Ph.D.'s in Soviet economics were awarded in 47 different institutions. About 20 institutions produced only one Ph.D. in the twenty-year period; 18 that produced at least one Ph.D. in generation IV produced no member of generation V. The average output was about one and one-half per decade per school, but Berkeley produced 14, Duke 9, Michigan 8, Northwestern and Pennsylvania 7 each, and Columbia and Harvard 6 each.

The diversity of institution of Ph.D. origin is in part a measure of the success of Office of Education grants in spreading the "wealth." It also reflects the sensitivity of students (and perhaps faculty) at Harvard, Columbia, and other top economics departments to the filling of the best placement opportunities by previous generations. Furthermore, it is a measure of excess capacity, for the Ph.D. represents a license to replicate oneself at any Ph.D.-granting institution. Generations IV and V more than doubled the Ph.D.-granting capacity of the field. They were also placed disproportionately in nonacademic jobs.

Generally speaking, the academic placement of generation IV was inferior to that of either II or III. Inferior placement was attributable partly to the fact that economics departments have rarely hired more than one Soviet specialist; more than two is unheard of. Consequently, generations II and III skimmed off the best placements and remained in place until only very recently. Initial placement in academia is either lateral (at best) or downstream (more ordinarily). Given the institutions of origin, the placement of the bulk of generations I and V is about what one would expect normally to occur regardless of subfield of economics. The retirement of senior members of generation II over the last few years, however, has opened up new opportunities for placement at top-ranked institutions. Most of these have been filled by members of generation V rather than IV because replacement has generally been at the entry level. Generation IV has not, therefore, been able to move "upstream" in any significant degree. In this sense, generation V has

TABLE 1
PH.D.'S IN SOVIET ECONOMICS BY SCHOOL BY DECADE

Universities	1969–78	1979–88	Total
American	3	1	4
Arkansas	1		1
Berkeley	7	7	14
Boston College	1	1	2
Boston		1	1
Brown	1		1
Chicago	1	1	2
Columbia	2	4	6
Cornell	1		1
Davis		1	1
Duke	4	5	9
Georgetown	1		1
George Washington	3		3
Harvard	4	2	6
Houston		2	2
Illinois	2	2	4
Indiana		3	3
Johns Hopkins	2		2
MIT	3	2	5
University of Miami		1	1
Michigan	6	2	8
Michigan State	2		2
Minnesota	1	1	2
Missouri, Columbia	1		1
New Hampshire		2	2
New School for Social Research		1	1
New York	2		2
North Carolina		4	4
Northwestern	1	6	7
Notre Dame	1		1
Ohio State	2	2	4
Oklahoma	1		1
Oregon	1		1
Pennsylvania	5	2	7
Purdue		1	1
Rand Graduate Institute		1	1
Rochester	1		1
Southern California		1	1
Southern Illinois	1		1
SUNY, Buffalo		1	1
Syracuse		1	1
Tufts	1	1	2
Virginia	2		2
Washington	2	2	4
Washington State	1		1
Wisconsin	5		5
Yale	4		4

been placed in a wider range of departments of economics measured by academic quality than IV, and the same seems to be holding for generation VI on the basis of early returns.

The motivation for my earlier study of the generations of Ph.D.'s in the field of Soviet economics was mainly to explore whether the senior members of generation II would be replaced, for the consensus at the time was that they would not and that the field would eventually expire. As I pointed out at the time, subfields in academia are like trees: they die from the top down. Failure to replace top positions will ultimately cause the field to die away. Ironically, because placement is downstream, the last generation could be the largest ever, but placed at institutions that by scholarly convention cannot resupply the top. Because the Soviet field grew from the top down, the replacement problem was evident in the late 1970s as one of replacing specialists at Harvard, Yale, Columbia, Berkeley, Chicago, Indiana, Wisconsin, Michigan, and a few others. The situation looked quite bleak in 1980 because the flow of new Ph.D.'s was declining (see figure 1), particularly at the top institutions that had produced the bulk of generations II and III and had traditionally supplied these schools.

The production of Ph.D.'s in Soviet economics peaked in 1972 and declined steadily throughout the period of détente. For reasons that are not entirely clear, a new surge of production occurred in the 1980s (see figure 2).

FIG. 2. PH.D.'S IN SOVIET ECONOMICS, 1969–1991
3-YEAR MOVING AVERAGE
SOURCE: SEE APPENDIX B

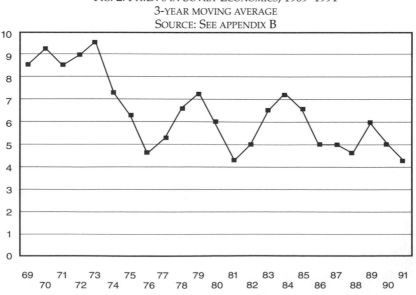

Year

This surge may have been partly a reaction to forecasts of doom and gloom for the profession and perhaps even my 1980 article, which indicated what needed to be done to preserve the field. Senior members of the field and certain foundations worked together to generate a new crop of Ph.D.'s. It is also possible that the renewal of the cold war generated renewed interest at all levels. Finally, the emigration of many former Soviet citizens to the United States during the 1970s may have contributed a bit to the surge, too. In any event, the new surge peaked out in 1985, and the earlier downward trend in the number of Ph.D.'s produced was reestablished. Once again, the rate of output has declined to only four or five per year.

On the brighter side, however, several major schools have recently replaced senior specialists (notably Harvard, Columbia, Yale, Indiana, Pittsburgh, Haverford, Tufts), and several have created new positions altogether (notably Stanford and Brown). Most of these appointments have been made at the junior level, and generations V and VI have benefited disproportionately from these developments. Thus we are not in as great a danger, as we thought we might be in 1980, of losing the capacity to produce Ph.D.'s in the top institutions. The field is in much less danger today of dying from the top down, assuming that the new hires achieve tenure.

As I pointed out in 1980, the danger was, and still may be, real, for there are examples of subfields disappearing altogether from academic economics. The original American "institutionalist" movement of the 1920s and 1930s has faded irrevocably and almost completely from the academic scene. When the "giants" of this movement, such as Wesley Mitchell, J. M. Clark, and Carter Goodrich of Columbia, John R. Commons of Wisconsin, Morris Copeland of Cornell, and Clarence Ayres of Texas retired, they were not replaced, and downstream institutions have continued the process of nonreplacement, as their disciples have themselves retired. Many institutionalists trained in their intellectual traditions remain in departments of economics today, but the truncation of the academic prestige and power pyramid has led inevitably to the gradual erosion of the field. The end of institutionalism as a subdiscipline is essentially certain at this time. A distinct but related process eliminated Marxism as a living economic subdiscipline during the 1950s.

The field of Soviet economics may have missed this bullet for the present, but it may have caught another from an unexpected quarter: the career choice and placement implications of the collapse of the Soviet bloc and the abandonment of central planning both in the former Soviet Union and in Eastern Europe. There are three clear and present dangers to the maintenance of a distinct field. First, the field seems always to have been vulnerable to the possible end of the cold war. It has always been driven at least partly by the intelligence community. The output of Ph.D.'s declined during most of the Khrushchev years and again during Richard Nixon's détente of 1972–79 (see Figures 1 and 2). Just before détente officially ended in 1980, a highly placed Soviet economist (at the Academy of the Social Sciences, Communist Party of the Soviet Union) pointed out to me the asymmetry of area studies in the USSR and the United States in this respect. "When tensions are high between our two countries," he explained, "study of the American economy contracts here. In your country it is just the other way around." The end of the cold war does seem likely to have an adverse effect on the production of "area" Ph.D.'s in the United States, both because the strategic threat has declined and because of the disappearance of a unique type of economic structure to study and to compare with market economies. And, of course, the study of the American economy and of market economics is flourishing in the successor states of the USSR.

Second, the field of Soviet and East European economics is being invaded from two sides. Mainstream economists, who had displayed little interest in the economies of Eastern Europe because of language and institutional barriers and a lack of interest in modeling command economies, are now pouring into the field. The problem of the transition from central planning to a market economy is intellectually interesting to them, and their command of both theoretical and policy models applicable to market economies gives them the confidence to step forward as analysts, consultants, and even participants in the transition process. In addition, many of their students are getting hands-on experience and preparing dissertations in the field on aspects of the transition process. Meanwhile, students, young economists, and even some older policymakers in Eastern Europe and the successor states of the Soviet Union are busily learning Western economics and gaining seat-of-the-pants experience conducting economic policy. We Soviet economic specialists have lost our monopoly and will have to compete with a growing number of such "interlopers" and "upstarts."

Third, the fragmentation of the Soviet bloc is mirrored in the fragmentation of the subject matter of the field. Where there was once the model of a centrally planned economy that could be modified to describe the various Eastern European economies, now we have a spectrum of economies diverging at different rates and in somewhat differing directions from the Soviet model, and the same thing is happening among the newly independent states of the old Soviet empire. This disintegration cannot but fracture the intellectual coherence of the field. Moreover, the smaller new economies are likely to be neglected in

American institutions in the same way that most of the economies of the old Eastern Europe were. There is no way one scholar can cover the field (about twenty-five separate economies now, and still counting), but no institution is likely to hire more than one, or at best, two economic specialists in this area.

The irony is that the invasion from mainstream economics and the development of local, native upstart economists is likely to give the field, for a few years at least, better coverage and perhaps higher quality analysis than we have had in the past, but this very process (dialectically?) may obliterate the field as a distinct entity. After all, what can we call ourselves today? Even if we describe ourselves as specialists on the "transition process," the implication is that we are ourselves as transitory as the phenomena we are describing. Thus the field is prospering from greater attention in both East and West, but the continuation of the specialty as a distinct subfield of economics is in serious jeopardy.

The Changing Subject Matter of the Field

The early generations of Soviet economic specialists were able to carve out large chunks of virgin territory. Most of their work was empirical and descriptive, but informed wherever possible by standard economic theory. One thinks of Abram Bergson's work on Soviet wages as a model that combined a theoretical analysis of socialist wage formation and an empirical exploration of the structure of actual wages, a model that his students generally emulated (see, for example, David Granick's dissertation on Soviet management, or Herb Levine's on central planning). Bergson's national income study for Rand Graduate Institute employed a number of his students and provided their dissertation topics as well (see the dissertations, for example, of Richard Moorstein, Abraham Becker, or Jerzy Karcz). Gerschenkron's students also developed a wide range of essentially empirical studies, including Joe Berliner's study of management based on the Harvard Refugee Project, Donald Hodgman's investigation of industrial production indices, and Frank Holzman's study of Soviet taxation. The difference between generations II and III was mainly one of degree, with the latter having access to a larger stock of official data and more open Soviet sources and a narrowing of research topics as the territory began to be worked more intensively. Generally speaking, however, generations II and III were preoccupied with the collection and assessment of a wide assortment of data on the Soviet economy from a mass of Soviet sources that were difficult to locate and niggardly with what data were presented and afforded incomplete descriptions of data series, institutional arrangements and economic behavior generally.

After 1958, the research situation improved significantly. A gradual expansion in regular publication of economic handbooks, census data, and historical data made many standard types of Western economic research increasingly feasible, and generations IV and V were not obliged to spend such a large proportion of their time in data collection as did previous generations. In fact, until very recently, no member of generations IV or V would have considered constructing or reconstructing an industrial production index, national income series, input-output tables, or any other standard social accounting measure for the Soviet economy. Where these figures were missing or considered unreliable, the field expected government or federally funded agencies to undertake the task of estimation, reconstruction, or evaluation. These tasks were no longer regarded as of intrinsic scholarly interest.

As a result, generations IV and V were free to utilize the increased availability of economic data and descriptions of economic institutions and processes to focus on problems that were more conceptual, internationally comparative, or technically more sophisticated and rigorous, a direction that was reinforced by the propagation of mathematical and statistical model building in the profession as a whole. Indeed, tenure was best assured by undertaking rigorous analyses of statistical data and/or of simulations. Throughout the period 1969–88 these two generations focused heavily upon analyses of the Kosygin (and subsequent) managerial reforms of the late 1960s and 1970s. Mathematical models of the Soviet economy became popular in the early 1970s. Some were designed to analyze the impact of various managerial rules on enterprise behavior, again reflecting the influence of the enterprise reform discussions. Others were macroeconomic models designed to explore macroeconomic relations within the Soviet economy or, more frequently, external impacts of, for example, increased international trade or of the Organization of Petroleum Exporting Countries (OPEC). Through the 1970s and early 1980s, however, the most popular topic was Soviet foreign trade and aid, reflecting a heightened interest within mainstream economics thanks to the floating of the dollar and the increased significance of trade to the Soviet Union in the acquisition of grain and technology. But it is difficult to characterize in any simple way the publications of generations IV and V, prior to 1986, because of the wide spectrum of interests generated by the equally wide variety of institutions of origin and of mentors as the field expanded in size and geographical spread over these years. This expansion was to change radically and quickly with the coming of perestroika and the subsequent abandonment of central planning and the old economic ministries.

One measure of the degree of change may be seen in table 2. It is based upon two surveys. The first was conducted in 1973. Donna Bahry and I designed it to ascertain whether there were "significant discrepancies between the existing distribution of scholarly effort and the judgments of active scholars in the field as to what the allocation ought to be."[4] In effect, we sought to develop a subjective demand curve for new research in the field of Soviet economics. The questionnaire consisted of fifty-one topics based upon the list of subdisciplines maintained by the *Journal of Economic Literature*. Respondents were asked to indicate for each topic whether in their judgment the topic should receive more (M) or less (L) attention from economists specializing in the study of the USSR and Eastern Europe or whether they thought the allocation of effort to this area of investigation was about right (R). In the presentation in table 2, the responses to the Eastern European portion of the questionnaire are not shown. The respondents were all of the economists in the field who could be identified by means of the 1971–77 membership directory of the American Association for the Advancement of Slavic Studies (AAASS) as holding a Ph.D. and/or teaching position at the instructor or higher level, and/or research post in the field, plus other economists known to the authors but not listed in this directory. There were ninety-four economists on the panel, of whom fifty-two responded.

The 1992 panel was drawn from the pool of Soviet economic specialists described in my 1980 article on generations of economists in the field, plus those identified subsequently for this essay. The total mailing was sent to fifty-eight individuals, of whom thirty-two have replied to date. The questionnaire was identical to the 1973 survey, except that it excluded Eastern Europe and referred to the Commonwealth of Independent States (CIS).

The results of the two surveys are presented in table 2. For each survey date, responses are arranged along the stub according to rank order of "More minus Less" (M-L) responses for 1973 respondents. It is obvious that much has changed since 1973. (Too bad that I did not think of repeating the survey in 1983 or so.) The most drastic changes in rank order are presented in table 3, where the top ten increases and decreases are displayed. The decline of interest in theories of economic planning, east-west trade, intrablock economic relations, economics of peace/disarmament, and war/defense economics is not surprising. The decline in econometrics (planimetrics) may merely reflect the influence of the parenthetical item, but the other declines are more difficult to interpret with confidence. Let me suggest that the sharp fall in re-

TABLE 2
WHICH FIELDS IN SOVIET ECONOMIC STUDIES NEED MORE (LESS) ATTENTION? 1973 AND 1992

Field	1973					1992				Change
	(1) Total	(2) Right	(3) More	(4) Less	(5)* Rank	(6) Total	(7) Right	(8) More	(9) Less	(10)* Rank	Cols. 5-10
Technological change	40	6	33	1	1	25	9	15	1	12	-11
Income distribution and distribution theory	44	7	34	3	2	29	8	20	1	10	-8
Regional and urban economics	36	9	25	2	3	26	10	9	7	29	-26
Money, credit, and banking	35	12	22	1	4	31	3	28	0	1	+3
Fiscal policy	32	8	22	2	5	29	2	25	2	3	-2
Intrabloc economic relations	38	11	23	4	6	29	6	9	14	39	-33
Income policies	30	7	21	2	6	25	11	9	5	25	-19
Human resource economics	34	10	21	3	8	29	18	8	3	22	-14
Monetary theory policy	32	9	20	3	9	29	6	22	1	7	+2
East-West trade	40	17	20	3	9	28	9	9	10	35	-26
Regional and local finance	32	9	20	3	9	30	3	26	1	2	+7
Industrial organization	33	9	20	4	12	30	4	23	3	8	+4
Applied econometrics	32	6	21	5	12	29	8	13	8	22	-10
Industry studies	36	13	19	4	14	27	11	13	3	16	-2
Health, education, welfare	31	12	17	2	14	29	14	11	4	18	-4
Income and employment theory	32	11	18	3	14	26	6	17	3	12	+2
International economics	35	13	18	4	17	27	11	14	2	15	+2
Agricultural economics	36	12	19	5	17	25	14	7	4	27	-10
Economic fluctuation and stabilization policies	30	5	19	6	19	30	4	22	4	11	+8
Environmental economics	37	12	19	6	19	32	6	24	2	5	+14
Economic history	34	11	18	5	19	30	14	8	8	34	-15
Welfare programs/applied welfare economics	34	6	20	8	22	26	6	17	3	12	+10

Public finance	38	16	17	5	22	31	6	25	0	3	+19
Price formation	49	13	24	12	22	27	6	14	7	18	+4
Economics of peace/disarmament	29	9	16	4	22	29	8	9	12	37	-15
Economic systems	40	19	16	5	26	58	13	6	39	38	-12
Statistical methods	36	16	15	5	27	26	9	10	7	27	0
Theories of economic planning	41	14	18	9	28	30	6	2	22	51	-23
Natural resources, land economics	30	17	11	2	28	28	12	11	5	20	+8
Consumer economics	33	16	13	4	28	26	13	7	6	33	-5
Econometrics (planimetrics)	38	13	17	8	28	25	7	4	14	45	-17
Population	33	19	11	3	32	25	16	2	7	39	-7
Economics of property rights	30	12	13	5	32	30	8	21	1	8	+24
History of economic thought	35	15	14	6	32	29	12	3	14	46	-14
War/defense economics	34	12	15	7	32	28	7	5	16	46	-14
Statistical data	37	19	13	5	32	30	8	22	0	5	+27
Planning and reform	44	15	18	11	37	28	10	10	8	29	+8
Social accounting	35	14	13	8	38	26	12	9	5	25	+13
Wage formation	34	18	10	5	38	26	14	7	5	29	+9
Transportation economics	28	10	11	7	40	24	8	5	11	41	-1
Research methodology	28	7	12	9	41	27	11	9	7	29	+12
Labor economics	32	20	7	5	42	27	13	10	4	20	+22
Economic geography	22	12	6	4	42	24	11	6	7	35	+7
Price and allocation theory under socialism	47	22	13	12	44	29	9	7	13	41	+3
Historical antecedents of communist economic systems	27	12	8	7	44	26	8	5	13	44	0
Production functions	35	13	11	11	46	27	6	4	17	48	-2
Economic development	36	13	11	12	47	30	9	16	5	17	+30
Welfare economics	33	8	12	13	47	26	11	10	5	22	+25
Radical economics	24	5	9	10	47	25	6	0	19	50	-3
Growth theory	37	14	7	16	50	29	6	8	15	43	+7
Economic convergence	33	10	6	17	51	27	5	2	20	49	+2

*Rank order More minus Less

SOURCE: for 1973, Donna Bahry and James Millar, "An Evaluation of Research Opportunities and Allocations in Studies of the Soviet and East European Economies," ACES Bulletin 17, no. 1 (1975): 93–96.

TABLE 3
RANK ORDER CHANGES IN FIELDS IN SOVIET ECONOMIC STUDIES,
1973–1992

	Top Ten Increases		Top Ten Decreases
+30	Economic development	-33	Intrabloc economic relations
+27	Statistical data	-26	East-West trade
+25	Welfare economics	-26	Regional and urban economics
+24	Economics of property rights	-23	Theories of economic planning
+22	Labor economics	-19	Income policies
+19	Public finance	-17	Econometrics (planimetrics)
+14	Environmental economics	-15	Economic history
+13	Social accounting	-15	Economics of peace/
+12	Research methodology		disarmament
+10	Welfare programs/applied	-14	Human resource economics
	welfare economics	-14	History of economic thought
		-14	War/defense economics

gional and urban economics, income policies, economic history, and history of economic thought reflect trends in the field of economics proper over the twenty-year period rather than anything peculiar to Soviet economic specialists.

On the up side, the results certainly do reflect developments peculiar to Soviet economic studies. The relevance of economic development, statistical data, welfare economics, economics of property rights, public finance, labor economics, social accounting, and research methodology for the economies of the CIS is clear, and the prominence of these eight areas here runs counter to what is currently most popular in mainstream economics. These areas represent the need to reconceptualize the field and to develop a more satisfactory data base under the rather chaotic current conditions of transition both from Soviet socialism to the market and from the empire to its component parts. The other two items—environmental economics and welfare programs/applied welfare economics—are clearly important problem areas in the successor states of the USSR.

The rank order of fields needing study today (the 1992 survey) differs radically from the kinds of dissertations new P.h.D.'s were writing in the late 1980s and early 1990s, and many of these recent members of the profession are being obliged to change their research area radically before getting much in the way of publications out of their dissertations, a shift that puts them in some peril for achieving tenure. The problem is vividly revealed in table 4, which lists dissertation titles of sixteen young scholars who compose the first members of generation

VI. This is just a small sample of the collapse of the field's intellectual capital stock that accompanied the fall of the Berlin Wall. The cost may prove to be disproportionate for the young, nontenured members of the profession because they have so little time to retool. On the other hand, the young should be able to retool more rapidly than the older members of the profession. Evidence that the members of generation VI who are still in the pipeline are getting the message about a change in priorities in the field may be seen in the topics that were presented in 1992 to the Eighth Annual Workshop on Soviet and East European Economics, organized by Herb Levine and Rick Erikson (see table 5). The list also reveals the potential importance of "native" scholars in the pool of future specialists.

TABLE 4

TITLES OF DOCTORAL DISSERTATIONS IN SOVIET ECONOMIC STUDIES
1989–1991
(generation VI)

1989

"Technical and Allocative Efficiency in Soviet Communication"
"Product Planning in the Soviet Union"
"Economic Reform: A Comparison of the Polish and Hungarian Experiences"
"Public Policy and Income Distribution in Yugoslavia: A Case of Arrested
  Market Reform"

1990

"Political Economy of Price Reform in the Soviet Union"
"Return to the Market: Subsidies in the Process of Transition"
"Essays on the Fiscal Aspects of Economic Reforms in Developing and
  Socialist Countries"
"Marketing and Supply Response in Lithuanian Agriculture"
"A Comparative Applied Economic Analysis of Soviet Foreign Trade: An
  Intra-Industry Approach"
"Perestroika: The Soviet Political Economy in Transition"

1991

"Incentive Problems in the Management of Soviet-Type Economies: A
  Theoretical Study of the Ratchet Effect"
"Essays on the Transition from a Centrally Planned Economy to a Free Market
  Economy"
"The Formation and Demise of Market Socialism under the Soviet New
  Economic Policy, 1921–1929"
"Managerial Reasoning Styles: A Cross-Cultural Comparison"

1992

"Re-Assessment of East German Industry at the Time of the Currency Union"
"The Soviet Black Market in Hard Currency"

TABLE 5
PARTICIPANTS AND TOPICS IN THE EIGHTH ANNUAL WORKSHOP ON SOVIET
AND EAST EUROPEAN ECONOMICS, 1992

Michael Blackman, University of Pennsylvania, "Indigenous Development of the Private Sector in the Former Soviet Union"

Annette Brown, University of Michigan, "Risks and Wages in the Private Sector: Evidence from Estonia"

Ruth Cooper, University of California at Berkeley, "Fuel Use and Emissions in the USSR"

Ben DeDominicis, University of Pittsburgh, "The International Monetary Fund and Liberal Democratic Polish Institutions"

Dietrich Earnhart, University of Wisconsin, "The Property Rights Model Applied to Water Resource Institutions in the Transitional Economics of Eastern Europe"

Tomasz Inglot, University of Wisconsin, "Social Policy Development under Communist Rule and Its Impact on Political and Economic Transformations in Contemporary Eastern Europe"

Daniel Kahn, Columbia University, "Towards a Theory of Property Rights and Financial Markets"

Evan Kraft, State University at Salisbury, Maryland, "The Role of Soft Budget Subsidies in Investment Finance in Yugoslavia: A Model with Estimates for 1986–87"

Yevgeny Kuznetsov, Cornell University, "On an Optimal Asset Holding under High Uncertainty and Depressed Aggregate Demand"

Bryan Roberts, Massachusetts Institute of Technology, "Welfare Consequences of Price Liberalization in Eastern Europe"

Huizhong Zhou, Western Michigan University, "Behavior of State Enterprises in a Hybrid Economy with Market Imperfection"

Lev Freinkman, Academy of Economy for the Council of Ministers, Russia, "Unbalance on the Wholesale Industrial Market in the USSR in the 1980s"

Sergei Kokovin, Russian Academy of Sciences, Siberian Institute of Mathematics, "Equilibrium in Soviet-Type Imperfect Markets"

Gleb Koshevoy, Russian Academy of Sciences, Moscow, "Mixed Economy with Two Currencies"

Andrei Kovalev, Central European University, Prague, "The New Russia and the Arms Trade"

Vladimir Matveenko, Central European University, Prague, "Dynamic Analysis of Externalities: Applications to the Problems of the Russian Economy"

Vladimir Mau, Institute of Economic Policy, Moscow, "Social and Economic Processes under Nonstable Political Conditions"

Pawel Milobedzki, University of Gdansk, Poland, "Behavior of Polish State-Owned Enterprises during the Transition to a Market Economy"

Eszter Muranyi, Central European University, Prague, "Income Tax Evasion, Labor Supply—Implications for the Hungarian PIT System"

Seppo Ruoho, Lappeenranta Institute of Technology, Lappeenranta, Finland, "The Problems of Measurement of Soviet Economic Growth during the Period 1961–1990"

Igor Tsukanov, Institute of World Economy and International Relations, Moscow, "Foreign Investment into the Russian Energy Sector"

The field of what used to be Soviet economic studies is undergoing a radical change in structure. Many once prominent topics, such as modeling reforms of central planning and comparative economic systems, are no longer viable current topics. Others, such as intrabloc trade, have been redefined and are much changed in significance. Most important, however, to my mind, is the fact that the changes have left the field without an intellectual center of gravity. The old socialist economies are breaking up into pieces that have primarily only their past histories and an intention to develop a Western-style mixed economy in common. To the extent that the field was focused upon centrally planned economies, or Soviet-type economies, and I think it was mainly so focused, the field today is adrift. Much of our previous capital stock has been severely depreciated. Knowledge of Russian language no longer provides entry as it did previously throughout the old empire for research purposes. And the fact that essentially all of the newly independent states claim to be moving toward mixed, capitalistic economies means that our primarily descriptive subfield of economics is going to be overshadowed by the essentially theoretical and prescriptive approach of mainstream Western economics. The aim increasingly is to tell policymakers in the economies of Eastern Europe and the newly independent states how to reform and manage their economies, how to transform them into market economies. There is doubtless a place for those of us with institutional knowledge of centrally planned economies in the short run, during the transition, but not thus after. In short, the changes in priorities that have been revealed above imply with a high degree of certitude the end of a special field in economics devoted to this area of the world. It still may be covered, and covered well, with the help of mainstream "interlopers" and local native "upstarts," but a special field devoted to a geographically defined area studies is, I suggest, doomed.

Requiem for Soviet Economic Studies

From the outset there has been considerable tension between the discipline of economics and Soviet and East European economics, a field defined by geographical and system-type criteria. All area studies programs have encountered this tension with most of the social science disciplines, and the discipline of economics is perhaps the most resistant of all, especially to a geographical focus. The field of area studies was founded on an anthropological foundation. The unit of study and analysis was culture, and cultural relativity was the main guiding principle for research. This approach presupposed that a society's culture, or any component, such as the economy, could be understood or analyzed successfully only by those who were steeped in the culture broadly defined to include language, literature, history, and unique social institutions, and in its relation to other components. Hence the approach stressed the need to use "native informants" as sources of information or, absent native informants, the need for the investigator to be immersed in the culture through language training, general education, and participant observation in order to simulate a native informant to the extent possible.

Where an anthropologically based area studies is culture bound and holistic in method, economics aspires instead to a body of theory that is universal in application and timeless in relevance. That is, economics has modeled its scientific aspirations upon physics, and its practitioners are understandably impatient with the notion that culture or holism should be perceived as potential constraints upon analysis. I describe the relation between area studies and the discipline of economics above as involving a certain tension. In truth, the conflict is irreconcilable because it is based on mutually contradictory methodological assumptions. The best one can hope to do is to minimize the conflict by clouding the issue. For those of us trained in Soviet economic area studies, the conflict can no longer be disguised because members of the cultures we have been studying now explicitly assert the intention to abandon their unique, culturally bound economies. Native informants not only want to build a Western-style mixed economy, they want to learn Western economic theory as well! Ironically, from the area studies perspective, they will clearly have a comparative advantage in the analysis of their own economies because of their language skills and their familiarity with the local cultures.

Soviet area studies has also been descriptive, where mainstream economics prefers prescriptive optimizing models. Comparative economic systems is a descriptive subdiscipline, and the existence of the Soviet-type socialist economy provided the main descriptive model for comparison with capitalism. The two were seen as representing the opposite ends of a spectrum, separated by a smooth transition curve of mixed cases. Recent experience belies such a smooth transition curve and raises a question about whether the two alternatives are, in fact, on comparable historical footing. The question is, will the Soviet command economy fare better historically as an economic archetype than has National Socialism? My best guess is that comparative economic systems will be a victim of the collapse of Soviet socialism. The new paradigm for this region of the world economy is almost certainly going to be economic development, with an appropriate emphasis upon institution building for formerly centrally planned economies. This approach is suitably theoretical and prescriptive and thus compatible with mainstream economics.

For the immediate present, however, most of us who have already been trained and nurtured by Soviet and East European economics and in comparative economic systems may find ourselves at a comparative disadvantage as analysts, consultants, and policy advisers. Our experience studying the Soviet and Eastern European economies did not prepare us as policy advisers. Although we did comment upon reform efforts and even occasionally proposed certain solutions to the problems we viewed, it was not our job to help make the Soviet-type economy work better. Table 6 shows, however, that a number of practicing specialists have already made their own personal "transitions" in their research agendas. I take this list as support for the proposition that the new paradigm is economic development and that the field as we have known it will die more or less quietly.

TABLE 6
CURRENT RESEARCH TOPICS OF PRACTICING SPECIALISTS IN SOVIET
ECONOMIC STUDIES, 1992

★ Determining the ownership structure of the economies in transition—"Privatization by Contractual Arrangements"
★ Enterprise behavior during transformation in Czechoslovakia, Hungary, Poland
★ Voucher privatization in Czechoslovakia
★ Inflation stabilization where policymaker is learning about effects of monetary policy on economy while carrying out said monetary policy
★ Collapse of effort in cooperatives as participants discover the weaknesses of the system
★ Transition in (reforming) socialist federal states (or collapsing federations)—theoretical approaches
★ Fiscal federalism—theory and applications for the former Soviet Union and Czechoslovakia
★ Modeling the opportunity costs of maintaining inefficient firms and industries during the transition from the socialist command economy, and weighing them against the direct costs of unemployment in determining an appropriate structural adjustment policy
★ An elasticities approach to estimating excess demand in price-controlled markets
★ Privatization of Russian farms
★ Macroeconomics of stabilization
★ Credit process in Russia—effect of the current state of the financial system on enterprise behavior and the general importance of capital markets
★ Survey of the perestroika era

TABLE 6 (CONTINUED)
CURRENT RESEARCH TOPICS OF PRACTICING SPECIALISTS IN SOVIET
ECONOMIC STUDIES, 1992

★ Soviet budgets, especially urban
★ Welfare economics and market socialism
★ Monetary policy in the former Soviet Union
★ Comparative regional development in the socialist countries of Eastern Europe
★ Soviet common property resource management practice—the case of the fishery
★ Reforming socialist agriculture, especially Russian policies
★ Changes in statistical organizations in the Commonwealth of Independent States
★ Proponents and critiques of market under the New Economic Policy
★ Capital markets and financial issues in economies in transition
★ The evolution of local public finance in the Soviet Union
★ Territorial decentralization of political power and the liberalization of the economy—Estonia and Leningrad/St. Petersburg
★ Convertibility
★ Theoretical aspects of the transition from socialism
★ New approaches to the study of comparative economic systems
★ Issues involved in defining and measuring inflation during the transition period
★ Role of informal activities in the reform
★ Unemployment in the former Soviet Union
★ Barriers to innovation—development and diffusion of new technology
★ Defense conversion—impact on quality, employment, wages, and prices
★ Joint venture—impact on economic performance
★ Transfer of environmental technology, United States to the Commonwealth of Independent States
★ Russian labor market in transition
★ Privatization in Russia and Poland—comparative study

In view of this conclusion, it seems appropriate at this point to have a few kind words said in memoriam. It is usual for these affairs to have someone sum up the accomplishments of the one being buried. As a matter of fact, Soviet social science studies in general and Soviet economic specialists in particular have been singled out for sharp criticism for failure to predict the breakdown of the Soviet system and the collapse of the economy. Certain U.S. senators have used this juncture as an opportunity to bash the U.S. intelligence service for its failure, and certain established academics trained in Russian-Soviet history and the humanities use it as evidence of the failure of social science generally as a methodology. I have, therefore, attached as an appendix an extract from a report that several of us (Berkowitz, Berliner, Gregory, Linz, and myself) produced in 1991 for the House Permanent Select Committee on Intelligence evaluating the economic products of the CIA, primarily SOVA, between 1970 and 1990 (including classified reports).

As a standard for evaluating how well the CIA carried out its intelligence duties, we took the performance of the academic Soviet economics profession as a whole. Thus our evaluation of the CIA involved an evaluation of the profession simultaneously. Our fundamental conclusions were, first, that no one in the field predicted, or even entertained as a possible scenario, the collapse of the Soviet economy and the abandonment of central planning in favor of a capitalist-type economy. No one. Some have claimed to have done so, but every case I have seen involves either ex post interpretation or selective self-quotation. (I will be interested to see whether this gathering will be able to document an accurate forecast or scenario.) Second, the economic system was not overthrown by popular demand. The collapse was initiated from above, and as such was an extremely low probability event—so low, in fact, that no one even entertained it as a credible limit for a predictive range of outcomes. The two concluding paragraphs of the report read as follows:

> The profession did identify the more probable outcomes, like "muddling down," and some of the less probable outcomes, like the adoption of market socialism. But it did not foresee the possibility of one particular outcome, that the Party would be destroyed by the hand of the Party leader himself. In that sense the whole profession failed.
>
> Had that scenario been put forward for consideration, it would no doubt have been generally considered as of extremely low probability, and properly so. Low-probability events do occur, however, and the occurrence of such an event does not signify that those who judged that event to be improbable were wrong. Prophets are expected to foresee the most improbable events, but social scientists do not have that power, should not be expected to have that power, and should be criticized when they claim to have that power. Good social science may be wrong, but it should be wrong for the right reasons. Only prophets should never be wrong.[5]

Notes

I would like to thank my research assistant, Julijana Budjevac, for assistance in compiling the data for this article.

[1] James R. Millar, "Where Are the Young Specialists on the Soviet Economy and What Are They Doing?" *Journal of Comparative Economics* 4 (1980): 317–29.

[2] Donna Bahry and James R. Millar, "An Evaluation of Research Opportunities and Allocations in Studies of the Soviet and East European Economies, "*ACES Bulletin* 17, no. 1 (1975): 89–96.

[3] James R. Millar, chair, and Daniel M. Berkowitz, Joseph S. Berliner, Paul R. Gregory, and Susan J. Linz, "An Evaluation of the CIA's Analysis of Soviet Economic Performance, 1970–1990," a report prepared for U.S. Congress, House Permanent Select Committee on Intelligence, November 18, 1991. An extract appears in appendix C.

[4] Bahry and Millar, "Evaluation of Research Opportunities," 89.

[5] Millar et al., "Evaluation of the CIA's Analysis," 46.

Appendix A

Soviet Economists,
Generations I, II, III, IV, V, and VI

Generation I: Before 1949

Wassily Leontief (USSR)
Alexander Gerschenkron (Austria)
Naum Jasny (USSR)
Peter Swanish (Chicago, 1930)
Lazar Volin (Michigan, 1931)
Arthur Z.Arnold (Columbia, 1937)
Abram Bergson (Harvard, 1940)
D. Gale Johnson (Iowa State, 1945)
Joseph Kershaw (Columbia, 1948)
Chee-Hsein Wu (Harvard, 1948)

Generation II: 1949–1958

Holland Hunter (Harvard, 1949)
M. Gardener Clark (Harvard, 1950)
Edward Ames (Harvard, 1952)

Bergson

David Granick (Columbia, 1951)
Henry H. Ware (Columbia, 1951)
Edward Janssens (Columbia, 1951)
John P. Hardt (Columbia, 1955)
Richard Moorstein (Columbia, 1956)
John M. Montias (Columbia, 1958)
Egon Neuberger (Harvard, 1958)

George J. Novak (Columbia, 1958)
Lynn Turgeon (Columbia, 1958)
A. David Redding (Columbia, 1958)
W. Donald Bowles (Columbia,1958)
Abraham S. Becker (Columbia, 1958)
James H. Blackman (Columbia, 1958)

Gerschenkron

Donald R. Hodgman (Harvard, 1951)
James F. Coogan (Harvard, 1952)
Franklyn D. Holzman (Harvard, 1952)
Gregory Grossman (Harvard, 1953)

Alexander Erlich (New School, 1953)
Joseph S. Berliner (Harvard, 1954)
Robert W. Campbell (Harvard, 1956)

Other

Mikhail V. Condoide (Ohio State, 1949)
Chris D. Calsoyas (Berkeley, 1949)
Phillip M. Raup (Wisconsin, 1950)
Vladimir Katkoff (Ohio State, 1950)
Robert A. Johnston (Northwestern, 1951)
John M. Letiche (Chicago, 1952)
Stanley H. Cohn (Chicago, 1952)
Robert Holloway (Stanford, 1952)

Nicholas Spulber (New School, 1952)
Morris Bornstein (Michigan, 1952)
Rush Greenslade (Chicago, 1953)
Raymond P. Powell (Columbia, 1953)
Gertrude Schroeder (Johns Hopkins, 1953)
George Murphy (Washington, 1957)
Ted Osgood (Yale, 1957)
Benjamin Ward (Berkeley, 1958)

Generation III: 1959–1968

Bergson

Warren W. Eason (Columbia, 1959)
Jerzy Karcz (Columbia, 1959)
Norton T. Dodge (Harvard, 1960)
Jack Minkoff (Columbia, 1960)
Leon Smolinski (Columbia, 1960)
Herbert S. Levine (Harvard, 1961)
Marshall I. Goldman (Harvard, 1961)

Nicolas DeWitt (Harvard, 1962)
Janet G. Chapman (Columbia, 1964)
Barney Schwalberg (Harvard, 1966)
Charles E. Butler (Harvard, 1966)
Leonard Kirsch (Harvard, 1967)
Alan Brown (Harvard, 1967)
Gur Ofer (Harvard, 1968)

Other

John S. Hoyt (American, 1959)
Arkadius Kahan (Rutgers, 1959)
Glen A. Smith (Stanford, 1959)
Vladimir Bandera (Berkeley, 1960)
James H. Blackman (Columbia, 1960)
Judith Thornton (Harvard, 1960)
Murray Yankowitch (Columbia, 1960)
Zinowij L. Melnyk (Michigan State, 1961)
Bertrand N. Horowitz (Minnesota, 1962)
Richard Moorsteen (Columbia, 1962)
Frederic L. Pryor (Yale, 1962)
Vladimir G. Treml (North Carolina, 1963)
Earl Brubaker (Washington, 1964)
Andrzej Brzeski (Berkeley, 1964)
Harold J. Noah (Columbia, 1964)
Frank H. Sargent (George Washington, 1965)
James R. Millar (Cornell, 1965)

Alan Abouchar (Berkeley, 1965)
Carl B. Turner (Duke, 1965)
Francis M. Watters (Berkeley, 1966)
Wolodymyr Klachko (New York, 1966)
Joyce E. Pickersgill (Washington, 1966)
Walter J. Klages (Alabama, 1967)
Marvin R. Jackson Jr. (Berkeley, 1967)
David W. Conklin (MIT, 1967)
Francis W. Rushing (North Carolina, 1967)
Michael Bradly (Cornell, 1967)
Martin Weitzman (MIT, 1967)
Charles K. Wilbur (Maryland, 1967)
Elizabeth J.M. Clayton (Washington, 1968)
Curtis H. Knight (Indiana, 1968)
Paul Marer (Pennsylvania, 1968)
Carmelo R. Mesa-Lago (Cornell, 1968)

Generation IV: 1969–1978

Robert E. Athay (American, 1969)
Terence E. Byrne (Brown, 1969)
James R. Carter (Oregon, 1969)
Edward G. Dolan (Yale, 1969)
Rachel E. Golden (Columbia, 1969)
Paul Gregory (Harvard, 1969)
John M. Martin (Washington, 1969)
Wayne W. Sharp (Michigan State, 1969)
Yasushi Toda (Harvard, 1969)
Robert C. Stuart (Wisconsin, 1969)
Phillip M. Weitzman (Michigan, 1969)
Arthur W. Wright (MIT, 1969)
Michael R. Dohan (MIT, 1970)
George Gorelik (Berkeley, 1970)

Phillip Grossman (American, 1970)
Norman Kaplan (Chicago, 1970)
Martin J. Kohn (Yale, 1970)
Michael E. Manove (MIT, 1970)
Joseph A. McKinney (Michigan State, 1970)
William Moskoff (Wisconsin, 1970)
Robert B. Skurski (Wisconsin, 1970)
Jean-Michael Beillard (Notre Dame, 1971)
Joseph Brada (Minnesota, 1971)
Norman E. Cameron (Michigan, 1971)
Ralph A. Fulchino (Georgetown, 1971)

Generation IV: 1969–1978 *(continued)*

Edward A. Hewett (Michigan, 1971)
Stephen Sacks (Berkeley, 1971)
Martin C. Spechler (Harvard, 1971)
Manuel R. Agosin (Columbia, 1972)
Robert Dalton III (Missouri, Columbia, 1972)
Donald W. Green (Berkeley, 1972)
Corinne A. Guntzel (Illinois, 1972)
Leo Yong-Gol Kim (George Washington, 1972)
Volkmar Liebscher (Southern Illinois, 1972)
Carl H. McMillan (Johns Hopkins, 1972)
Steven Rosefielde (Harvard, 1972)
Christine Wollan (Illinois, 1972)
James A. Younker III (Northwestern, 1972)
Scott Boaz (Arkansas, 1973)
John P. Bonin (Rochester, 1973)
Antonio M. Costa (Berkeley, 1973)
John C. Evans (Tufts, 1973)
John Farrell (Wisconsin, 1973)
Alice C. Gorlin (Michigan, 1973)
Peter J. Grandstaff (Duke, 1973)
Sergei S. Kasakow Jr. (Washington State, 1973)
David P. Levine (Yale, 1973)
George C. Logusch (New York, 1973)
Shannon R. Brown (Berkeley, 1974)
Darius J. Conger (Oklahoma, 1974)
Murray Feshbach (American, 1974)

Barbara G. Katz (Pennsylvania, 1974)
John P. Lewis (Ohio State, 1974)
Roman Senkiew (Virginia, 1974)
James R. Thornton (Cornell, 1974)
John H. Wilhelm (Michigan, 1974)
David H. Howard (Virginia, 1975)
Laurie R. Kurtzweg (Duke, 1975)
Craig L. Moser (Ohio State, 1975)
Arthur L. Moses (Duke, 1975)
Andrew Feltenstein (Yale, 1976)
Kenneth R. Gray (Wisconsin, 1976)
Jeffrey Miller (Pennsylvania, 1976)
James P. Murray (New York, 1976)
Peter Murrell (Pennsylvania, 1976)
Joseph Pelzman (Boston College, 1976)
William N. Turpin (George Washington, 1976)
Michael Marrese (Pennsylvania, 1977)
Sheldon T. Rabin (Johns Hopkins, 1977)
Marc Rubin (Pennsylvania, 1977)
Clark J. Chandler (Michigan, 1978)
Harold S. Gardner (Berkeley, 1978)
James W. Gillula (Duke, 1978)
Michael D. Harsh (Washington, 1978)
George D. Holliday (George Washington, 1978)
Andris Trapans (Berkeley, 1978)

Generation V: 1979–1988

Daniel Bond (North Carolina, 1979)
Richard E. Ericson (Berkeley, 1979)
Gene D. Guill (Duke, 1979)
Lyle D. Israelson (MIT, 1979)
Silvana Malle (Berkeley, 1979)
Poong Rhee (Illinois, 1979)
Merle W. Shoemaker (Syracuse, 1979)
Jeffrey Summers (Purdue, 1979)
Lenore S. Taga (Berkeley, 1979)
Robert A. Walker (Southern California, 1979)
Michael L. Wyzan (North Carolina, 1979)
Bruce M. Everett (Tufts, 1980)

David M. Kemme (Ohio State, 1980)
Susan Linz (Illinois, 1980)
John S. Pitzer (American, 1980)
Matthew J. Sagers (Ohio State, 1980)
Anna S. Kuniansky (Houston, 1981)
James B. Streets (Michigan, 1981)
Karen M. Brooks (Chicago, 1982)
Lorrie Jo Brown (Washington, 1982)
Richard C. Harmstone (Columbia, 1982)
Susan G. Jacobs (Duke, 1982)
Victor Kamedrowsky (North Carolina, 1982)
Wolfram Schrettl (Boston, 1982)

Generation: V 1979–1988 (Continued)

Keith W. Crane (Indiana, 1983)
Yoo Soo Hong (Northwestern, 1983)
Blaine E. McCants (Duke, 1983)
Judith A. R. McKinney (Indiana, 1983)
Ebrahim Sheibang (Indiana, 1983)
Robert S. Whitesell (North Carolina, 1983)
Voytek Zubek (SUNY, Buffalo, 1983)
Michael Aleexev (Duke, 1984)
David P. Apgar (Rand Graduate Institute, 1984)
Paul A. Goldberg (Columbia, 1984)
Barry W. Ickes (Berkeley, 1984)
John Parsons (Northwestern, 1984)
Ernest Raiklin (New School for Social Research, 1984)
Huizhong Zhou (Northwestern, 1984)
Stuart S. Brown (Columbia, 1985)
Vladmir Kontorovich (Pennsylvania, 1985)
Robert B. Koopman (Boston College, 1985)
Heidi A. Kroll (Berkeley, 1985)

Kent H. Osband (Berkeley, 1985)
Helen T. Otto (Houston, 1985)
Steven Popper (Berkeley, 1985)
Lung-Fai Wong (Minnesota, 1985)
William Liefert (Michigan, 1986)
Elisa B. Miller (Washington, 1986)
Janet Mitchell (Northwestern, 1986)
Perry L. Patterson (Northwestern, 1986)
Pedro F. Pellet (University of Miami, 1986)
Barry Kotlove (Davis, 1987)
Mark A. Prell (MIT, 1987)
Daniel Berkowitz (Columbia, 1988)
Jeanine D. Braithwaite (Duke, 1988)
Michael Hemeseth (Harvard, 1988)
Nicholas Kozlov (New Hampshire, 1988)
John Litwack (Pennsylvania, 1988)
Michael A. Murphy (Northwestern, 1988)
Yassaman Saadatmand (New Hampshire, 1988)
Michael Spagat (Harvard, 1988)

Generation VI: 1989–1992
(incomplete)

Greg Brock (Ohio State, 1989)
Gary Krueger (Wisconsin, 1989)
Christopher Martin (Berkeley, 1989)
Benjamin Slay (Indiana, 1989)
Andrew Boone (Houston, 1990)
Joshua D. Charap (Pennsylvania, 1990)
Abu Faij Dowlal (Southern California, 1990)
Mihaljek Dubravko (Pittsburgh, 1990)
Mark R. Lundell (Berkeley, 1990)
Jehoon Park (Ohio, 1990)
Gisela M. Esoe (Ohio, 1991)
Clifford G. Gaddy (Duke, 1991)
Thomas Richardson (Columbia, 1991)
David Sedik (Berkeley, 1991)
Alina Zapalska (Kentucky, 1991)
Helga Hessenius (Berkeley, 1992)
Anna Meyendorff (Berkeley, 1992)

Appendix B

Number of Graduates, Soviet Economic Studies, 1948–1992

1948–1968	1969–1992
(SUPPORTING DATA FOR FIGURE 1)	(SUPPORTING DATA FOR FIGURES 1 AND 2)

1948: 2	1969: 12
1949: 3	1970: 9
1950: 3	1971: 7
1951: 5	1972: 10
1952: 8	1973: 10
1953: 5	1974: 8
1954: 1	1975: 4
1955: 1	1976: 7
1956: 2	1977: 3
1957: 2	1978: 6
1958: 9	1979: 11
1959: 5	1980: 5
1960: 7	1981: 2
1961: 3	1982: 6
1962: 4	1983: 7
1963: 1	1984: 7
1964: 4	1985: 8
1965: 4	1986: 5
1966: 5	1987: 2
1967: 10	1988: 8
1968: 5	1989: 4
	1990: 6
	1991: 5
	1992: 2

Appendix C

Extract from "An Evaluation of the CIA's Analysis of Soviet Economic Performance, 1970–1990"

Interpretive Reporting

Apart from reports on defense expenditures, as noted above, the review committee has formed a generally favorable opinion of the quality of the CIA's interpretive reports on the Soviet economy. As was indicated earlier, the CIA's reports on the growth of GNP and its components (excepting the defense component) during the 1980s were generally accurate and informative. We believe that the CIA's clients received timely and reasonably accurate information also on the slowing rate of growth and the increasingly tough allocation decisions that Soviet leaders would face in the resulting resource crunch. There were, however, some significant "misses" too. Most significantly, the CIA failed to foresee that perestroika and glasnost and certain policy blunders would lead to the sharp decline of the economy and to the breakup of the Soviet Union at the end of the 1980s. The question we explore in what follows is just how good were the CIA's interpretive reports relative to those of the profession of Soviet specialists at large?

The short answer is that the CIA was not significantly better or worse than academic specialists. Both academic and agency analysts had mixed records, and the bottom line reveals that neither anticipated the intensity of potential ethnic separatism or even considered the possibility that the communist party would lose legitimacy completely and that the Soviet political and economic system would disintegrate. It perhaps should be said that neither did Gorbachev and his advisors.

It needs to be underscored at the outset that the actual course of events between 1988 and 1990 in the USSR was, even in hindsight, a low probability outcome. The problem for forecasters is that low probability events do nonetheless occur, and there is an indefinite number of low probability outcomes to consider. No forecaster can represent such possible outcomes as anything other than as of low probability. This offers no basis for criticism and illustrates the review committee's preference for scenario style analysis of a range of possible future events of differing likelihoods, for it allows policy makers at least to consider the ramifications of several low as well as high probability outcomes.

Regarding the CIA's success in forecasting, on the positive side, the 1977 analysis of trends and prospects that has been referred to previously ("Soviet Economic Problems and Prospects," ER 77-10436U) is an impressive piece of analysis. It correctly identified 1976 as a critical inflection point in growth trends and projected accurately the potential long-run consequences of the slowdown. Several subsequent studies, notably two in 1981 (ER 81-10009 and ER 81-10023), elaborated this theme helpfully. The report entitled "Soviet Perceptions of Economic Prospects" (ER 81-10018) spelled out very neatly the rising Soviet concerns about energy resources, planning and management deficiencies, and consumer welfare, all of which pointed to the need for a new growth strategy—one based upon intensive growth. Gertrude Schroeder's analysis of the futility implied by the "treadmill of reform" (Sov 82-10068) was right on the mark. Despite growing economic problems, no genuine economic reform was in fact taking place. Her subsequent analysis of "The Slowdown in Soviet Industry, 1976–82" (Sov 83-10093), which was based on a series of CIA industry studies that were particularly well-chosen, is widely recognized as a major contribution to our understanding of the causes and intractability of Soviet stagnation. Another 1983 report, "USSR: Policy Toward the Consumer" (Sov 83-10202), provided an excellent interpretation of the problems posed by excess demand, forced saving and the way in which the Soviet leadership had become ensnared in its own economic illogic. These reports illustrate the very best in economic analysis and forecasting and compare favorably with the best academic analyses of the period.

Some analytic products do not fare as well in retrospect. The National Intelligence Estimate for 1982 ("The Soviet Challenge to US Security Interests"), for example, portrays the USSR as aggressively confronting the United States in the Third World and as prepared to maintain the growth of its defense establishment at all costs. The growing economic stresses and strains receive little recognition in the analysis. One report (Sov 84-10017) that did confront directly the larger implications of the slowing rate of economic growth proved to have been wrong in retrospect:

> . . . [T]he period of continued low level of growth that we project through 1990 should not be taken as a harbinger of economic collapse. . . . It [is] more accurate [to say that] our projection depicts a difficult and stressful period for a large, if inefficient, economy.

As we shall see, academic specialists were not noticeably better in interpreting the ultimate consequences of the growth slowdown. But it is important to note also that the essence of this report is still informative:

that a stressful period is being entered. Most students of the Soviet economy believed at that time that the Soviet economy would continue to "muddle through."

Joseph Berliner, for example, explored four possible scenarios for economic change (Reactionary, Conservative, Radical and Liberal), and ended his contribution to *The Soviet Economy: Toward the Year 2000* (1983 edited by Levine and Bergson) with:

> I conclude that the prospects for change in the system of planning and management depend upon the performance of the economy under the Conservative Model. If the growth rate should stabilize at a level that may be low but that nevertheless exceeds the incentive threshold, that model will be retained and the century will limp quietly to its end. Chronic cases do not normally evoke extreme measures. Only acute attacks, like depressions or rebellions, galvanize a society into such measures. If the Conservative Model cannot stabilize the growth rate even at that low level, the accumulation of social and political pressures will propel the leadership into either the Reactionary or the Liberal Model. Both are likely to improve the performance of the economy, but the greater potential lies with the latter. If the counsels of political prudence prevail, however, the lot will fall to the former.

Berliner's look into the future is more satisfying than the previous forecast because it is based upon alternative scenarios, but it still missed including the actual outcome because there was none that assumed the collapse of the communist party. The Radical Model was a model of market socialism, not the repudiation of socialism.

Seweryn Bialer contributed a summary, concluding chapter to the same volume. He concluded: "In sum, we can anticipate no fundamental changes in the Soviet Union during the 1980s despite intense and divisive discussions concerning economic reforms, a number of organizational policy initiatives, experimentation with the economic structure, and significant political conflict." Bialer and Joan Afferica argued in *Foreign Affairs* at about the same time (Winter 1982/83) against the notion that the US had acquired a degree of leverage over domestic Soviet developments because of the deterioration of the economy. They declared this a "worst case" analysis:

> That severe economic stress will provoke political collapse may be a possible outcome in the next decade, but it is nonetheless an unlikely one. What generations have wrought with so much sacrifice, cruelty and conviction will not change radically under

pressures of economic decline or leadership instability. The Soviet Union is not now nor will it be during the next decade in the throes of a true economic crisis, for it boasts enormous unused reserves of political and social stability that suffice to endure the deepest difficulties. The Soviet economy, like any gigantic economy administered by intelligent and trained professionals, will not go bankrupt. It may become less effective, it may stagnate, it may even experience an absolute decline for a year or two; but, like the political system, it will not collapse.

And Bialer was of essentially the same opinion three years later in *The Soviet Paradox. External Expansion, Internal Decline* (1986).

Analyzing the circumstances facing the Andropov regime, Walter Laqueur ("What We Know About the Soviet Union," *Commentary*, 1983) conceded the seriousness of the political and economic problems, but he argued that "a modern dictatorship has powerful instruments with which to assuage, to suppress protest, to postpone the day of reckoning for a very long time." Although he granted the existence of an economic crisis, he dismissed it as a possible cause of fundamental change in the Soviet system: "The long and short of it is that the Soviet economy will muddle through."

Richard Pipes (in *Survival Is Not Enough*, 1984) also failed to entertain the possibility that the party and economic bureaucracy might be completely dismantled. He cited Chalidze and Djilas approvingly, "That reforms are conceivable only as a result of major internal and external setbacks, that they will come about only when the *nomenklatura* concludes that they are the price it must pay for its survival." Pipes himself considered and discussed only "what kind of reform can one expect from the Soviet leadership?" Even this was a low probability outcome in his view. How much more so must have been the actual course of Soviet history since 1988.

Our purpose is not to single out individuals for criticism, but to document our contention that highly qualified academic scholars shared with those who worked for SOVA an assumption that the Soviet Union, despite its visible problems, remained fundamentally sound in the early and middle 1980s. Many other scholars could be cited in support of this thesis. The review committee's criticism of the work of SOVA in this connection is not for failing to see what essentially no one saw, but for its occasional failure to present its speculations in the form of explicit alternative scenarios with probabilities attached to each.

A July 1984 SOVA report, "Policy Implications of the Slowdown in Soviet Economic Growth" (Sov 84-10104), was particularly categorical in dismissing the possibility of radical change in the Soviet Union, and it may indeed have generated some of the criticism the CIA has received for its reports on the Soviet economy. The authors conclude that:

> [T]he chances are low that, by 1990, the growth slowdown will precipitate . . . unrest . . . or compel [a] shift to a decentralized socialist market economy. . . . The slowdown is not likely to lead Moscow to forgo major weapons programs. . . . [N]or is it likely to substantially increase economically based Western political leverage, [or] drive the leadership to accept arms control agreements. . . .

In conclusion, the report states that the "chances are low" that the economic slowdown will:

- Precipitate . . . widespread popular unrest in the USSR.
- Pave the way for either significant liberalization or a Polish-style militarization of the regime.
- Bring to power a leadership group with significantly different foreign policy aims.

The authors also conclude that "Moscow's economic problems, while serious and intractable, do not threaten the continued existence of the Communist political system."

A 1986 report, "Domestic Stresses in the USSR" (Sov 86-10017X), provided a similarly conservative view of possible changes in the Soviet social system, but it was more successful in considering the alternatives. Like most Western analysts outside the US Government, the authors concluded that major systemic changes were unlikely. Rather, what was expected was "vigorous reform," a slight increase in legal private activity, a shift in the balance of domestic political power to the KGB and an expanded role for the party. Overall, they concluded: "we expect that Gorbachev's political position will remain strong and the USSR . . . is likely to see some improvement in system performance over the next few years." More radical reform (a "new NEP") was rated a low probability scenario because it would be "risky and controversial." A move toward greater repression was viewed as of low probability also and would result only out of leadership "desperation." Most probable was a "No surprise-free future," that is, "further unconventional leadership changes and surprises appear probable." We consider this a model report under the circumstances of uncertainty that prevailed at the time it was prepared. It is not only informative, it also pointed in the correct direction and represents a good forecast.

The 1987 NIE report, entitled "Whither Gorbachev: Soviet Policy and Politics in the 1990s," is also a solid piece of work in our opinion. This was the first general assessment of perestroika and glasnost, and the report stated that they contained the "potential" to change the USSR as radically as Stalin had done in his time. The main question was whether or not Gorbachev had, or could, concentrate sufficient power in his hands to do so. This was a very valuable and timely analysis. (Incidentally, the director of NSA dissented from this conclusion.) The report concludes that:

1. the most likely outcome of the Gorbachev reforms would be the rejuvenation of the existing system;
2. there was a small chance (perhaps 1 in 3) to effect true systemic reform;
3. a neo-Stalinist outcome was even less likely; and
4. "the odds of a turn toward democratic socialism, featuring a more radical push for a market economy and a pluralistic society will remain virtually nil under any circumstances."

Finally, and significantly, the report concludes: "We believe he [Gorbachev] recognizes he is pursuing a potentially dangerous course but is determined to try—even at the risk of failure—rather than accept the status quo."

The review committee believes that this is as good a report as its clients can hope to receive about a society in flux. Even those American scholars who were forecasting "gloom and doom" for the Soviet economy were not more accurate in their appraisals. Marshall Goldman, for example, in *Gorbachev's Challenge* (1987), was dubious about the likelihood of success of Gorbachev's early reforms, anticipating "improvements and improved productivity, but not the breakthrough Gorbachev seems eager to achieve." Goldman expected the Soviet leadership to continue to "experiment," and he speculated that "It is conceivable that the Soviets will adopt the Chinese approach, but it does not seem likely. Instead, the Soviet Union will probably continue to look to East Germany as a model of reform, making a marginal and even radical change here and there, and to operate much as it did in past periods of reform." After considering the possibility of radical reform, Goldman decided that:

> The odds are that, given the resistance his reforms will face, and the risks a really radical reform entails, he [Gorbachev] will opt for the more conservative route.
>
> Short of some unexpected catastrophe, the Soviet economy is unlikely to come close to collapse, but without some equally unex-

pected transformation neither is it likely to improve its standing among the world's economic leaders. In the end, Gorbachev, like his predecessors, will probably have to settle for an economy that has to rely more on its natural riches than on its creative potential.

Finally, as late as 1988, Ed Hewett (in *Reforming the Soviet Economy: Equality versus Efficiency*) considered a middle course of reform as the most likely. He ruled out as very low probability both his "success scenario," where "everything works as planned" and both qualitative and quantitative goals are met, and his "failure scenario," which is essentially a "muddling through" outcome, not a collapse. The remaining alternatives, "high growth" and "high quality," appear to have been equally probable in Hewett's view. Thus, even at this late date, so perceptive a student of the Soviet economy as Ed Hewett was still working within the old framework of analysis, one essentially the same as Gertrude Schroeder's in the "treadmill of reform."

We conclude, therefore, that the CIA's interpretive reporting was at least as good as any competitor. There were some notable successes, and some notable misses, but overall the CIA's reports have been of high quality, timely and useful to policy makers. We believe it would be unreasonable to expect otherwise unless CIA analysts were privy to critical secret sources. This does not appear to have been the case.

The CIA's assessment in the early 1980's, which was shared by the scholarly community generally, was that there was a very "low probability" that the system would collapse from popular unrest or from internal strains. Subsequent events have not proven that assessment to have been wrong, contrary to what many critics now assert. The system in fact did not collapse from internal strains, and there was no public unrest. It collapsed for another reason that no one foresaw; namely, the cumulative sequence of events that culminated in the dissolution of the Party by the very man who had been elected five years earlier to lead the Party and had no intention at that time of contributing to its dissolution.

Note

This report was submitted on November 18, 1991, by the Permanent Select Committee on Intelligence: James R. Millar, professor and director, Institute for Sino-Soviet Studies, George Washington University and Review Committee chairperson; Daniel M. Berkowitz, assistant professor of economics, University of Wisconsin—Madison; Joseph S. Berliner, professor emeritus of economics, Brandeis University; Paul R. Gregory, professor of economics, University of Houston; and Susan J. Linz, associate professor of economics, Michigan State University. Pages 38–46 are presented here.

Commentary:

The Future of Soviet Economic Studies

Christopher Clague

The first question that occurred to me in reading James Millar's paper was whether the focus of the discussion should be on the future of the field or the future of the specialists in Soviet economic studies. These are two very different questions. It seems undeniable that a good part of the intellectual capital of many of the specialists in the field has been suddenly reduced in value, inasmuch as the world is now much less interested in how the centrally planned economies actually functioned and how that system might be made to function better. On the other hand, the discipline of economics, among others, is confronted with a whole new set of questions relating to the collapse of communist central planning and political control. These questions are intellectually fascinating and of supreme practical importance to the millions of people in the formerly socialist economies, as well as to the rest of the world. It seems to me that the topic for scholarly discussion should be how to approach these new questions rather than on the academic prospects for the existing specialists in the field.

What should happen to Soviet economic studies? How should the intellectual orientation of the field be changed? It should be emphasized that my remarks on these questions are those of an outsider, one who has not studied the bulk of the literature with which members of this group are familiar. My fields have been international trade and economic development, with a recent interest in New Institutional Economics. Like many outsiders, I have in the last couple of years done some reading (and a little writing) on the problems of the transition from a socialist to a market economy.

I have been struck by the extraordinary intellectual challenge of coming to grips with the collapse of communism and the emergence of new institutions in the formerly socialist societies. The task of understanding these phenomena draws on developments in economics and other social sciences in the last couple of decades: the analysis of cooperation, conventions, and institutions, even culture; transaction cost economics and the economics of (asymmetric) information; organization theory; and collective action and political economy. But the ongoing events in these societies offer tremendous opportunities for further development and reformulation of these theories. The collapse of communism offers opportunities for deeper understanding of the nature of capitalism.

It follows that there will probably be a flood of research on formerly socialist economies by persons who are not specialists in the study of these societies. In this respect the study of these societies will become like many other fields in economics, such as economic development or international finance, where much of the research is done by people who work on other topics as well. Such fields do not constitute a tightly knit community in the way that Soviet economic studies has in the past.

Despite this likely fragmentation of the area of study, it seems to me that a field such as economic problems of formerly socialist economies has a good deal of intellectual coherence. An advantage of such a field is that it would cover not only societies making a successful transition to a market economy but those in transition to something else. Such an area would make sense as a subject of comprehensive examination in economics graduate schools and as an area in departments to be staffed by the faculty. My feeling is that the transitions to a market economy are likely to be sufficiently slow to give this field a substantial lease on life.

In the long run, I think Professor Millar is correct that Soviet economic studies will disappear as a separate field, provided that these societies do eventually make the transition to a market economy. In that event, the study of Eastern European and Central Asian economies will become like the study of the economies of Europe, Latin America, Africa, and South Asia. These are not areas in which American academic economists tend to specialize, but of course many nonacademic economists specialize in these areas and in particular countries in these areas.

I am not fully in agreement with Professor Millar's characterization of the difference in orientation between mainstream economics and comparative economic systems. The distinction in my mind is not between descriptive and prescriptive, but rather between descriptive and theoretical. There are many areas in mainstream economics in which the models are used to guide empirical research rather than primarily to make prescriptive statements.

Finally, I agree with Professor Millar that the Soviet economics profession should not be blamed for failing to predict the collapse of communism, which took everyone, including its participants, by surprise. What I think is a more serious charge is that the profession of economics failed to predict the degree of economic disruption accompanying the attempted transition to a market economy. The difficulty of creating the institutions of a market economy, and in particular the difficulty of privatizing the large state enterprises that dominated the formerly communist economies, was greatly underestimated by most economists who considered these issues in the early days of the collapse of communism.[1] I think the lack of appreciation of the institutional foundations of capitalism impeded our understanding of the nature of transitions from socialism to a market economy. By the same token, the varied experiences of the formerly communist societies afford a fascinating opportunity to study institutional change and its path-dependent features.

Notes

[1] These ideas are developed at greater length in Christopher Clague and Gordon Rausser, eds., *The Emergence of Market Economies in Eastern Europe* (Cambridge, Mass.: Basil Blackwell, 1992).

Commentary:

An Untenured Perspective on the Death of Soviet Economic Studies

Thomas J. Richardson

As I read Jim Millar's piece last fall, I began to feel that I ought to dress in black for the October 1992 meeting at the Kennan Institute. His eulogy for the now dead field of Soviet economic studies was naturally rather unsettling. What was surely good fortune for the world as a whole—the end of the USSR and, by extension, the cold war—was bad news for me and for members of my generation.[1] As a distinct field, Soviet economic studies, like its namesake, was to go the way of the dodo bird.

Millar's paper is in part an update of a 1980 piece that quite frankly influenced my own career choice.[2] The shortage of Soviet studies economists that he depicted, coupled with generous institutional support, in the form of Foreign Language in Area Studies (FLAS) and Social Science Research Council (SSRC) fellowships, and tremendous moral and intellectual support from members of generations III, IV, and V,[3] motivated and enabled me to work in this area. As I finished my dissertation, the countries of Eastern Europe had their revolutions. And when I went on the job market in early 1990, as a specialist on economic planning, I was asked everywhere I went what I would do now that Soviet-style planning was doomed. I replied confidently that the reform process would proceed fitfully and that I did not expect the Soviet Union to have a "normal" market economy until sometime after I had achieved tenure.

What Happened?

I stand by that statement, but much depends on how one defines "normal." Millar is right in his central point—that the fundamental difference between the Soviet economic system and the mixed, market-oriented economies of the rest of the world is disappearing, with profound consequences for those of us who specialized in the institutions and problems of that system. In 1980 Millar worried that Soviet economic studies would die from the supply side, and so supply side measures were taken to ensure that did not happen. Today, he is convinced that it will die from the demand side.

But perhaps the rumors of our intellectual passing are somewhat exaggerated. Certainly there will be demand for academic work on the economies of that part of the world, even after the transitory upsurge of interest associated with the reforms is over. Most large research institutions offer courses on the economies of one or more of the other areas of the world—Africa, China, Japan, Latin America, and South Asia. There is no reason to think that the same will not be true for Eastern Europe and the former Soviet Union. Moreover, research questions of great interest to the economics profession will remain on the table of Russian and former Soviet studies well into the next century. The volume of work already in print on the relative merits of shock therapy and its consequences, for example, suggests that our field has not yet died.

Millar would argue, I believe, that it is the special position of Soviet area studies in the geography of foundation and government support which is surely on the wane. National security concerns induced much greater demand for work on the Soviet economy than for the economies of the other areas, and with the end of the cold war, that demand is lessened. But it has not gone to zero. On the contrary, as the spring 1993 aid package developed by the Clinton administration and the other Group of Seven countries indicates, there is still considerable concern that adversarial relations between Russia and the West are not henceforth impossible to conceive. That the West has a stake in Russia's future hardly needs emphasis, but the flip side of the aid coin is the possibility of failure, in which case national security will again stimulate demand for specialists on this part of the world.

Yet even in the worst case, should Russian become hostile to American and Western interests, it is exceedingly unlikely that Russia will again adopt socialist institutions.[4] The economies of Russia and the other former Soviet republics are certainly becoming much more like those of the rest of the world; some nationalists may continue to believe in a form of Russian particularism, but in economics they will be wrong. Thus, while demand for specialists on planning has suffered a severe and adverse shock, demand for labor economists, public finance specialists, industrial organization specialists, and especially development and macroeconomists willing and able to work on this part of the world has boomed. In the past, very few of us went into macroeconomics, feeling, perhaps correctly, that in the planned system all economics was fundamentally microeconomics. Now that is changed, and one can concentrate on any subfield of economics and find useful ways to apply it to the former USSR.

There has always been a bit of tension among us about whether we are comparative systems or Soviet area studies specialists.[5] With the death of socialism,[6] this tension should wane. There is obviously less now to compare, but I have always felt that somehow more fruit might be yielded by contrasting the economies of relatively more similar countries (the United States and Sweden, for instance) rather than those that seem utterly different. More to the point, without the mind-bending task of truly understanding socialism to distract us, we have no reason not to integrate our work much more completely into the mainstream of the economics profession.[7]

What Is to Be Done?

Therefore, those of us who were trained to work on the planned Soviet economy now have two options. First, we can retrain to some extent, or simply brush up on the work in fields closer to the mainstream of economic thought. Or we can go back with a fresh eye to work on the problems of the planned economy, now that it is extinct. There is a whole range of terribly interesting issues to explore, now that access to data and archives has opened up. I have in mind debates like the David Granick–Michael Keren exchange on whether Soviet industrial ministries face a ratchet effect,[8] or perhaps that between the "shortage" (Janos Kornai) and "disequilibrium" (Richard Portes et al.) schools.[9]

Those who pursue the economic history route will not face much competition from interlopers and natives of the former USSR, as these will be driven to work on more contemporary issues. There is thus much work to be done in economic history, but most of it will be important for solid intellectual reasons, not for national security reasons. I would hope, therefore, that this research would not suffer overmuch in the competition for grants and funding by comparison with "sexier" research on topical issues of current economic reform.[10]

Those who work on contemporary problems *will* face competition, both from economists without an area studies pedigree and from Russians, Ukrainians, and others who themselves are retraining to work as real economists. As economists, however, we should welcome this competition, for if as a profession we believe in anything it is competition. Competition certainly will raise the quality of research we do, as in my view it already has.[11] Moreover, there are few faster ways to win professional attention than to point out and correct the mistakes of one's famous colleagues.

Millar therefore exaggerates the decline we are likely to face. True, there is no "field" of Latin American or African or South Asian economics, but there is demand for courses on those areas and for research un geographically defined economic issues. And perhaps the luxury afforded by the security-induced demand for our work led to a bit of the soft budget constraint behavior we noted in the Soviet economy.

Moreover, demand has expanded significantly in one area. The international economic organizations (International Monetary Fund, World Bank, European Bank for Reconstruction and Development) are hiring a number of Soviet area studies economists. The numbers are not large in absolute terms, but in a field as small as ours, they are noticeable. And while these opportunities may be only a temporary demand shock, they will certainly have some long-run consequences.[12] Thus, at least until these organizations (and others, like the U.S. Agency for International Development and the United Nations Development Program) build up a stock of institutional knowledge adequate to their needs, the language and cultural background of area studies specialists will have value.

In another, more subtle way, the death of Soviet economic studies could be a good thing. It is clear that, during the cold war Soviet studies received, relative to studies of other areas of the world, relatively more funding. To some extent the same thing was true of the flow of individuals to the field. Some of those who were attracted to the study of Soviet economy because they detested or admired socialism will now go elsewhere. Those who have an intrinsic intellectual interest in that part of the world, in its culture and issues, will be drawn to it as before.

Conclusion

To summarize, I strongly believe that the field of Soviet and former Soviet area studies is changing rather than dying. Some of us will continue to work on socialist economic institutions and problems, on issues that I believe have enormous and enduring intellectual, if historical, interest. Others of us will work on current problems of economic reform—or the lack of it—in the former USSR. National security considerations will continue to stimulate demand in this area, as will the needs of the international economic organizations.

But in either case, one will need to make one's work speak to the interests and tastes of the economics profession as a whole. Our work should address the various subdisciplines (labor, public finance, industrial organization, macroeconomics) with which economists who focus on other areas of the world have long concerned themselves. Consequently the interdisciplinary committees that fund research on this part of the world may need to be particularly understanding in the face of increasing economic jargon, mathematics, and statistical rigor.

Notes

[1]Generation VI, in Millar's genealogy. Much of what I have to say applies as well to at least the untenured portion of his generation V.

[2]James R. Millar, "Where Are the Young Specialists on the Soviet Economy and What Are They Doing?" *Journal of Comparative Economics* 4, no. 4 (1980).

[3]Including Jim Millar, I might add.

[4]Socialist rhetoric may be useful to politicians in that part of the world, but material balance planning and institutions like Gossnab are not likely to reappear.

[5]See the papers on "What Is Comparative Economics?" *Comparative Economic Systems* 31, no. 3 (1989): 1–32.

[6]"Actually existing" socialism, to distinguish it from the intellectually less troubling imaginary varieties.

[7]As an aside to noneconomists, I should note that this means our work will become more mathematical and technical. While this shift may distress some who fear they will not understand what economists do (and reinforce their belief that what we do is not terribly relevant to the "real world"), it is worth remembering that area studies economists have typically been seen as being toward the low-tech, and therefore low-prestige, end of the profession. Reforming the whole discipline, consequently, to make it less mathematical and more "relevant," is a task area studies–types, in particular, are not well equipped to do, even if they wanted to.

[8]David Granick, "The Ministry as the Maximizing Unit in Soviet Industry," *Journal of Comparative Economics* 4, no. 3 (1980): 255–73; Michael Keren, "The Ministry, Plan Changes, and the Ratchet Effect in Planning," *Journal of Comparative Economics* 6, no. 4 (1982): 327–42.

[9]See, for example, the survey by Jozef van Brabant, "Socialist Economics: The Disequilibrium School and the Shortage Economy," *Journal of Economic Perspectives* 4, no. 2 (1990): 157–75; or the book by Christopher Davis and Wojciech Charemza, eds., *Models of Disequilibrium and Shortage in Centrally Planned Economies* (London: Chapman and Hall, 1989).

[10]There may also be some scope for foundation support to preserve the electronic and paper records of planning data from Gosplan and Gossnab archives. After all, a thousand years from now historians will look back at what may well turn out to be the world's longest and most complete experience with national economic planning, and we will have been remiss if we do not undertake to preserve the empirical legacy of the Soviet economic experiment.

[11]Similarly, I find the animosity toward economists like Jeffrey Sachs who are working on Russian economic reforms to be utterly misplaced. While one might disagree with him on scholarly or professional grounds, it is absurd to argue that, as an interloper who knows no Russian, he has no place in our midst. He is at this point certainly more knowledgeable about the Russian economy than are most of us.

[12]It is worth pointing out as well that, for the most part, in these institutions one is prohibited from working on one's own country, meaning that Americans can work on Russia easier than Russians can work on Russia.

Part V

Foreign Policy

Chapter 9

The State of the Field: Soviet Foreign Policy

David Holloway

During the cold war, Soviet foreign policy was a matter of obsessive concern to the United States. The government spent considerable resources to discover the motives and purposes of that policy, while the press gave extensive coverage to U.S.-Soviet relations. In spite of this interest, the study of Soviet foreign policy never held a central place in political science as that field developed in American universities in the years after World War II. Those in comparative politics often regarded it as less interesting than research on the Soviet system itself, and international relations specialists, too, often viewed it as marginal. The study of Soviet foreign policy occupied an uneasy position between two poles of attraction: the demand for explanations and interpretations of current Soviet policy and for advice on U.S. policy, and the desire to be part of the discipline of political science. It was this context that shaped the academic study of Soviet foreign policy in the United States.

With the collapse of the Soviet Union and the creation of fifteen independent states in its place, the study of Soviet foreign policy—and of post-Soviet foreign policies—has entered a wholly new period. The events of recent years have set off a process of reassessment, of which this volume is a part. One element of this reassessment is retrospective: why did Sovietologists fail, by and large, to predict the collapse of the system? A second element is future oriented: what should now happen to the field of Soviet studies, and should its relationship to academic disciplines be redefined? Should there indeed be such a field, even if it is renamed post-Soviet studies?

This reassessment is taking place at the same time as a similar reappraisal in the study of international relations, the academic field to which the study of Soviet foreign policy is perhaps most closely linked.[1] That reappraisal, too, has been prompted by the end of the cold war and the collapse of the Soviet Union. Should international relations theory have predicted those events? Does international relations theory provide an adequate explanation for the end of the cold war? Are the dominant forms of international relations theory adequate for the post–cold war world? The study of Soviet foreign policy finds itself, therefore, at the intersection of two fields—Soviet studies and international relations—both of which are engaged in introspection and redefinition.

There is no longer a Soviet foreign policy but a whole cluster of states seeking to consolidate their statehood and to define their interests and their policies. The study of the foreign policy of the Soviet Union retains considerable historical and theoretical interest, however. Clearly no adequate understanding of the cold war will be possible without an examination of the Soviet role on the basis of archives that are now beginning to open up. Besides, much of the midlevel theorizing in international relations—about deterrence and crisis management, for example—drew on a particular reading of the cold war. It is possible, therefore, that more detailed research on U.S.-Soviet interactions during the cold war will change our understanding of deterrence and crisis management, not only in relation to specific events but also in theoretical terms, such as, for instance, the conditions in which deterrence is effective.

Retrospection is only one part of the problem, however. It is also necessary to consider how the field of post-Soviet international relations will develop. Before looking at the new directions in which the study of Soviet foreign policy and post-Soviet international relations might develop, I shall offer an impressionistic, and doubtless idiosyncratic, survey of the study of Soviet foreign policy since World War II.

Soviet Foreign Policy Studies in the Cold War

The dominant school of international relations in the United States since World War II has been realism. The modern version of realism, heir to the European tradition of realpolitik, was self-consciously propagated from the late 1930s on as an antidote to Wilsonian idealism and a reaction to the failed British and French policy of appeasing Adolf Hitler.[2] Realism stressed that international politics was about power and about the use of power by states to pursue their national interests. To fail to recognize this, to believe that world opinion or international agreements alone would maintain peace, was to fall prey to a dangerous illusion. As the wartime cooperation between the United States and the Soviet Union broke down, realism became firmly established in the United States as the prevailing approach to the theory of international relations.

The dominant model of the Soviet system in American political science after World War II was totalitarianism. This model came in various forms, but, whatever the form, it drew a parallel between the Soviet Union and Nazi Germany and contrasted those states with the liberal democracies of the United States and Britain. The totalitarian model pointed to the destruction by the state of civil society and to the ideological character of the ruling party. Most versions of totalitarianism stressed the ideological and expansionist character of the state's foreign policy and in particular the Soviet drive to further the cause of world revolution.[3]

The single most influential American piece of writing on Soviet foreign policy combined the central arguments of the realist and totalitarian models, though it mentioned neither term. In his Long Telegram from Moscow in February 1946 (and his subsequent "X" article, "The Sources of Soviet Conduct," which appeared in *Foreign Affairs* in July 1947) George F. Kennan argued that the basic problem facing the United States was to contain an expansionist and uncooperative Soviet state. The Soviet Union, he wrote, was by its very nature "committed fanatically" to the belief that it could have no permanent modus vivendi with the United States and that Soviet power could be secure only if the international authority of the United States was broken. Kennan was trying to remove what he saw as illusions about the prospects for U.S.-Soviet cooperation. His Long Telegram made an enormous impact in Washington, which was frustrated by its dealings with Moscow and puzzled by Soviet unwillingness to cooperate, especially in view of the U.S. atomic monopoly. Kennan's argument was seen in Washington as a coherent explanation for the deterioration in U.S.-Soviet relations; it was, moreover, an explanation that placed the blame squarely on the Soviet Union.[4]

Realist theory and the totalitarian model combined to provide a powerful analysis of the Soviet Union and to point to the kind of policy that the United States should pursue. The Soviet Union was an inherently expansionist power with which it would be impossible for the United States to cooperate. The United States should therefore use its power and that of its allies to contain Soviet expansion; the Soviet Union would be forced to turn in upon itself and to change, and then cooperation might become possible. Kennan was later dismayed by the way in which the policy of containment became militarized, but containment, which assumed that power was the chief currency of international relations and that the Soviet Union was an expansionist state, continued to provide a framework for U.S. policy until the 1980s.[5]

Within that framework, however, there was considerable room for debate and disagreement. The title of Kennan's *Foreign Affairs* article defined one of the central questions: what were the sources of Soviet conduct? Some scholars argued that the Soviet Union, like other states, pursued its national interests in the context of the international balance of power.[6] Others, like Kennan, pointed to the ideological sources of Soviet policy. It became one of the staple questions of research to ask whether Soviet foreign policy was driven by ideology or national interest. Put more broadly, the question was whether Soviet foreign policy should be explained in terms of the (totalitarian) nature of the Soviet state or in terms of the balance of power in the international system.[7]

In this context the role of the international communist movement in Soviet policy proved to be one of the most important topics for research. The Soviet Union was no "mere" state but the self-proclaimed head of a movement that would lead the world to communism. Its relations with other communist states, and especially with foreign communist parties, were a vital area of research, not only for the purposes of American policy but because it was in such relations that the tension between state-centered realpolitik and revolutionary goals could most profitably be examined.[8] There was plenty of scope for such research. The 1948 break between Josef Stalin and Josip Broz Tito provided an important object of study. Nikita Khrushchev's attack on Stalin at the Twentieth Party Congress in February 1956 had profound repercussions on the international communist movement, as did the Soviet suppression of the Hungarian Revolution later that year. The rift with China, which began to become apparent at the end of the 1950s, provided further evidence of disarray.[9] These splits showed that the international communist movement could no longer be viewed merely as an instrument of Soviet policy. They suggested that ideology was losing its appeal inside the Soviet Union and abroad. They also supported the realist contention that international politics is primarily about states, not about ideologies or revolutionary movements.

Two interesting analyses of the relationship between external and internal influences on Soviet foreign policy were published in 1963. Marshall Shulman argued, in *Stalin's Foreign Policy Revisited*, that by 1952 Stalin had come to realize that his attempts to enhance Soviet power had provoked the West to adopt policies that harmed the Soviet Union and he therefore moved toward a policy of peaceful coexistence, with the aim of encouraging interimperialist contradictions among the Western powers.[10] Robert Tucker, on the other hand, argued in *The Soviet Political Mind* that Stalin remained adamantly opposed to the idea of a relaxation of international tension and it was only Stalin's death that opened the way to a shift in foreign policy.[11] Shulman's argument fitted the classic realist conception of international relations, with the Soviet Union adjusting its policy to the shifting balance of power. For Tucker, Stalin was the decisive factor in explaining policy, which changed only when he died.

The dichotomy between external and internal influences on Soviet foreign policy is rather crude, and most Sovietologists were of course aware that there was an interplay between these factors. The influence of ideology did not exclude the operation of the balance of power; ideology could be understood as affecting the way in which Soviet leaders viewed the international system and thus as interacting with the balance of power to shape Soviet policy. One of the central questions to emerge in the 1960s was whether the Soviet leaders' conception of international relations was changing. William Zimmerman's influential *Soviet Perspectives on International Relations* explored changes in the Soviet understanding of international relations by examining the concepts and terms used in Soviet writings.[12] Zimmerman concluded that, with the emergence of international relations as a legitimate field of study in the Soviet Union, Soviet specialists were adjusting the way in which they conceived of the international system. They were beginning to move from Leninist to realist categories that emphasized the role of the state as the primary actor in international politics. Zimmerman argued that this shift showed that the role of ideology in Soviet foreign policy was declining.

The study of Soviet writings about international relations and foreign policy became increasingly popular from the late 1960s on, as those writings became more numerous.[13] The journals of the Ministries of Foreign Affairs and Defense and of the various institutes of the Academy of Sciences could be examined for the assumptions they embodied about international relations and for the analyses they provided of specific issues. There were debates in these journals and clear evidence of disagreement. It was difficult, however, to know precisely where these writings fitted into the overall policy-making process. Western scholars understood that there were serious restrictions on what could be published, but they knew that some Soviet academics wrote memoranda for the leadership and assumed, with some reason, that what was being published reflected, to some degree at least, discussions in official circles. Some authors argued that reading Soviet sources was a distraction and that a better analysis could be obtained by examining the balance of power and deducing Soviet interests and likely Soviet actions from that.[14] This was not the dominant view, however, among students of Soviet foreign policy, most of whom believed it was essential to look not only at the balance of power but also at the way in which that balance was interpreted by the Soviet leadership.

Realization that the role of ideology was declining was not the only reason that the dichotomy between ideology and national interest was abandoned. The concept of national interest, too, came under increasing criticism in the field of international relations. If the national interests cannot be specified, except in the most general sense (survival, economic well-being, military power, etc.), how can specific policies be explained in terms of the pursuit of national interest when alternative courses of action can be construed as serving that interest? National interest was increasingly regarded by students of international relations as a problematic concept. In response to this difficulty, a new formulation of realism, known as structural realism or neorealism, found favor. This approach focused not on the interests and motives of states but rather on the constraints imposed on states by the distribution of power in the international system.[15]

This shift had important consequences for the study of international relations in the United States. Unlike classical realism, neorealism did not claim to explain the foreign policies of particular states. It thus opened the way to different approaches to the analysis of foreign policy. Some of these were more or less compatible with realism: cognitive psychology, for example, could help to explain how decision makers perceived the international system and acted on their perceptions, but it did not question the assumption that their decisions were shaped by their understanding of the external environment; nor did it challenge the idea that there were external constraints and balances, even if those might be misperceived.[16] Other approaches—notably bureaucratic politics—challenged the realist conception of the state as a rational, unitary actor and shifted attention to domestic politics.[17]

Developments in the field of international relations had consequences for the study of Soviet foreign policy. Most scholars had focused on a set of questions that sprang rather naturally from realism and from the totalitarian model of the Soviet state. Was the Soviet Union a different kind of state? Was it driven by ideology or national interest? Would it adapt to the existing balance of power? Would its policy become more moderate? These questions were all related to realist theory and also relevant to U.S. policy. Students of Soviet foreign policy by and large saw their role not as contributing to international relations theory but rather as analyzing Soviet foreign policy; they were consumers rather than producers of theory. Their analyses drew on sources that were far from satisfactory and were usually based on realist or totalitarian assumptions.

In some ways Soviet foreign policy studies were well suited to the new directions in the study of international relations. Some scholars, like Zimmerman, had paid serious attention to the conceptual prism through which leaders viewed the international system. The study of foreign policy concepts remained an important topic for research, and it became especially topical when Mikhail Gorbachev began to propagate the "new thinking." Students of Soviet foreign policy began to explore the idea of learning and the way in which states learn how to conduct themselves vis-à-vis other states.[18] Other scholars had looked closely at leadership politics (Kremlinology) to explain policy as the outcome of the struggle for power.[19] Leadership politics, too, remained an important topic for research. Domestic politics—the struggle for power, institutional arrangements and interests, and coalitions of political interests—was used to explain both the continuity of policy under Leonid Brezhnev and the changes that took place under Mikhail Gorbachev.[20]

The shift from classical to structural realism took place at about the same time that the totalitarian model was losing its popularity.[21] Sovietologists began to criticize the model for obscuring important aspects of Soviet politics and to focus on the emergence of interest groups, on bureaucratic politics, and on the decentralization and dispersion of power in the Soviet state. The influence of this shift is evident in a collection of essays, *The Domestic Context of Soviet Foreign Policy*, published in 1981.[22] These essays took a differentiated view of Soviet policy making and did not assume that policy was determined by the essential nature of the system. Though it never completely lost its influence, the framework that totalitarianism had provided for the analysis of Soviet policy was no longer dominant after the late 1960s.

There were, however, ways in which the new developments in international relations theory did not fit easily with the study of Soviet foreign policy. Neorealism abstracted from the policies of individual states to focus on the structure of the international system and on the constraints that structure imposed on states. Neorealists shared with students of Soviet foreign policy an interest in the behavior of states in the cold war. But neorealism was not especially interested in the specifics of foreign policy. Classical realism had dovetailed neatly with the kind of contemporary diplomatic history that dominated the study of Soviet foreign policy.[23] Neorealism did not fit quite so well.

In the 1970s there was a growing gap between international relations theory and the study of Soviet foreign policy. Those who were primarily interested in international relations theory steered clear of the Soviet Union: if they were structural realists, the specific character of the Soviet state was of no special interest to them; if they were interested in decision-making approaches, why work on the Soviet Union, when the kind of information needed was so difficult to come by?

Those whose primary interest was the Soviet Union did not always find developments in international relations theory very helpful. This disjunction had partly to do with training and the methodological predilections it instilled. Students of Soviet foreign policy were often committed to "thick description" rather than more positivist conceptions of international relations.[24] Most of them believed it was crucial to study how the Soviet leaders understood the world, whereas international relations specialists sometimes recommended that the decision-making process be treated as a "black box" and inferences drawn from the process's inputs and outputs. Positivists argued that theories could be tested by observing behavior. Many students of Soviet foreign policy took the view that behavior was not unambiguous and that it was essential to try to understand the meaning of actions from the actor's point of view.

The new approaches to the study of foreign policy (bureaucratic politics and organization theory, for example) often required, for successful application, more and richer evidence than could be gained about Soviet decision-making procedures and processes. There was a difference between applying these models and theories to the United States or to historical cases like the outbreak of World War I, for which the evidence was extensive and rich, and using them to examine Soviet foreign policy making, for which the evidence was sparse. There was the danger that assumptions would be made about bureaucratic interests, for example, when the relationship between organization and interests in the Soviet system was poorly understood. Theories might be used to generate "facts" rather than to organize and make sense of rich evidence (for example, the commander in chief of the Strategic Rocket Forces *must* have thought that . . .). Some students of Soviet foreign policy were skeptical, moreover, about applying theories developed on the basis of American experience (e.g., bureaucratic politics) to a different institutional context.[25]

It became a commonplace to say that the gap between international relations theory and Soviet foreign policy studies was a bad thing, and several scholars published papers exhorting students of Soviet foreign policy to make more use of theoretical developments in the field of international relations.[26] Not all the advice was good—nor did the authors always follow their own advice—but the general point they made was surely a good one: that studies of Soviet foreign policy would benefit from greater theoretical self-awareness. The effect of these strictures became apparent in the 1980s and 1990s when studies of Soviet foreign policy paid greater attention to theoretical developments in the field of international relations.

This brief review has looked at Soviet foreign policy studies in relation to international relations theory. It would have been possible to review the field by linking it to the history of the cold war and the questions that that history raised: the extension of Soviet control over Eastern Europe, the death of Stalin and the policy of peaceful coexistence, the rift with China, détente, the military rivalry with the United States, and so on. The relationship between real events and foreign policy studies was very close. So, too, was the relationship between the cold war and international relations theory. The dominance of realism was buttressed by the central place of the U.S.-Soviet rivalry in world politics.

How successful was the field of Soviet foreign policy studies? The answer depends on the criterion one uses to make a judgment. If the field is judged in terms of its contribution to international relations theory, then it has not been terribly successful, for reasons already discussed. If the criterion is whether the field was able to make sense of Soviet policy and give a general picture of where that policy was headed, the answer is probably that it did fairly well. At any rate, no great surprises have emerged to show that the analyses written— granting the wide disagreements in interpretation—were completely wrong. But the field did well only up to a point, and that point was the end of the cold war. Soviet studies did not foresee that the cold war would end in the way it did or that the Soviet Union would collapse. Nor did international relations theory predict the end of the cold war. That failure has sparked considerable debate in Soviet studies as well as in the field of international relations.

The End of the Cold War

In the early 1980s the Soviet Union, although militarily stronger than it had ever been, was in relative decline. Brezhnev had let serious social and economic problems slide close to the point of crisis without attempting serious reform. Moreover, the buildup of Soviet military power had not led to commensurate gains in foreign policy; indeed it had worsened Soviet relations with all the major powers. All this was more or less clearly understood by students of the Soviet Union at the time, although in retrospect it appears that the Soviet Union's problems were more severe than most Western specialists thought.

It was not clear, however, how the Soviet Union would respond to the situation in which it found itself in the early 1980s. Edward Luttwak argued that the Soviet Union would use its military power to make an irreversible strategic gain by attacking China.[27] A group of eminent American Sovietologists concluded in 1983 that the post-Brezhnev leadership would muddle through, making minor adjustments to the system but putting off reform.[28] Some scholars argued that the post-Brezhnev leadership would in all probability turn to reform at home and to accommodation with the West abroad.[29] No one, however, predicted in the early 1980s that ten years later the cold war would be over and the Soviet Union no more.

When Gorbachev took over as general secretary in March 1985 it soon became evident that he would inject new vigor into the Soviet leadership, but it was not clear how far he wanted to go—or would be able to go—in the direction of economic reform or a new foreign policy. New ideas were soon being put forward, and younger people advanced, but it was not clear to Western observers what these would lead to. The "years of stagnation" had instilled in many Sovietologists—as in many Soviet citizens—a cynicism and wariness about the prospects for reform, and the signs of change were therefore treated with caution.

As the "new thinking" was elaborated, it became clear that the conceptual underpinnings of Soviet foreign policy were changing. Students of Soviet foreign policy appreciated the importance of this change because, by and large, they had taken seriously the conceptual prism through which Soviet leaders had viewed the world.[30] (Western political leaders, notably Margaret Thatcher, were perhaps even quicker to see that Gorbachev would introduce significant changes into Soviet policy.) As Soviet policy shifted on important issues such as the war in Afghanistan and intermediate-range nuclear forces in Europe, it became evident that a fundamental change was taking place in Soviet policy and in U.S.-Soviet relations. Gorbachev's speech to the United Nations General Assembly in December 1988, in which he announced that he was reducing the Soviet armed forces by 500,000 troops, was a dramatic sign that the "new thinking" would have practical consequences for the armed forces, too.

Whatever doubts and hesitations may have remained in Western minds were swept away by the revolutions of 1989 in Eastern Europe and by the Soviet Union's relinquishing of control over the region. These events took everyone by surprise. It had been apparent that there was a crisis of rule in Eastern Europe, but the crisis was chronic, and no one in the mid-1980s had predicted that the Soviet Union would forgo its control over Eastern Europe and acquiesce in the unification of Germany within the North Atlantic Treaty Organization (NATO).

One reason why these events were so surprising is that the dominant theoretical approaches to international relations and to Soviet politics deflected attention away from system change. Neorealism focused on the functioning of the international system, not on the problem of system transformation. When changes in the international system were discussed, it was generally in connection with war.[31] A change in the system would take place only if power were redistributed (from a bipolar to a multipolar system, for example), and a rapid redistribution would be accompanied by a major war. Nuclear weapons seemed to rule out such a war; they certainly made a major war something to be avoided. When John Lewis Gaddis argued in 1985 that the cold war should be seen as the "long peace," an unusually stable period of international relations,[32] no one challenged his thesis by arguing that the cold war would soon come to an end.

While systemic theories treated the international system as stable, theories of foreign policy decision making diverted attention away from the issue of system change by focusing on specific events and specific aspects of Soviet foreign policy. International relations theory thus reinforced a tendency, implicit in much of the work on Soviet politics, to treat the Soviet Union as a normal, functioning system and to ignore a more dynamic analysis that would examine the "contradictions" of the system and the pressures for change.

The end of the cold war, which is variously said to have taken place between 1987 and 1991, has now become the focus of an intense debate in the field of international relations as well as in Soviet studies. Critics of realism, and more especially of neorealism, have argued that it cannot explain the end of the cold war and that this failure proves its inadequacy as a theory of international relations.[33] The critics' most important argument is that the shift in Soviet foreign policy cannot be explained in terms of a shift in the international distribution of power because no such redistribution took place. In other words, the basic causal variable in realist theory did not change, yet the international system was transformed; hence realism is invalidated, or at least has nothing useful to say about the end of the cold war. Alternative causes for the shift in Soviet policy have been suggested: transnational networks, which injected new ideas into the Soviet political system; Gorbachev's own personality; domestic political competition; learning by the Soviet leadership. Many people have also argued that declining economic performance was a primary impetus for Gorbachev's policies, but it is difficult to distinguish this argument from realism, because economic decline weakened the Soviet Union's position in the international system.

Realists have made several responses to this criticism. One is that the end of the cold war does not constitute a valid test for theory because it is a "mere data point":[34] it cannot invalidate theories that claim only to predict patterns of behavior. This is a debatable point, but even if it is accepted, it calls into question the relevance of a theory that cannot explain one of the most important changes in the international states system in the twentieth century.

A more convincing realist response is to provide a realist account of what happened: the Soviet Union was in decline relative to the United States and other major powers, and Gorbachev's understanding that this was so impelled him to embark on new policies. It is also plausible to argue that one reason for Soviet decline was the burden imposed on the economy (the level of expenditure plus the command-administrative system that made that level possible) by its foreign and military policies. Hence the effort to arrest decline involved a reorientation of foreign policy. Such an account does not explain everything and can, of course, be combined with other factors, domestic and transnational, to explain the particular course that Soviet foreign policy took in the 1980s.[35]

This kind of realist explanation raises two important questions, however. The first has to do with the Soviet system itself. The debate among international relations theorists neglects questions that have been central to the Soviet studies debate. Were decline and collapse inevitable? Were they the consequence of fundamental flaws in the Soviet system? Or were they path dependent, the consequence of decisions that, if they had been different, could have led to a different outcome?[36] This debate is certainly related to the end of the cold war and the collapse of the Soviet Union, because the "loss" of Eastern Europe is difficult to explain without reference to the crisis of Soviet-type systems. The Soviet Union had used military force in Eastern Europe in 1956 and 1968 to prevent the erosion of its control. To have used force in the same way in the late 1980s would have destroyed the prospects for reform within the Soviet Union and put an end to Soviet efforts to improve relations with other countries. The Soviet Union was caught in a trap: to prevent the loss of control in Eastern Europe, it would have to turn its back on perestroika, which was motivated, in part at least, by the desire to enable the Soviet Union to remain a powerful state. It was the incompatibility between the efforts at reform and the old policy toward Eastern Europe that provided the context for the Soviet decision not to use force in 1989. This conclusion suggests that no satisfactory explanation of the end of the cold war and the collapse of the Soviet Union is possible without taking the specific character of the Soviet system into account.[37]

The second issue has to do with the concept of power, which occupies a central place in realist theory. Critics of realism have argued that Soviet power did not decline in the late 1980s because the Soviet Union still had the same armed forces in 1991 as it had had in 1985; hence there was no decline in Soviet power. But this argument is simplistic. In explaining how power affects policy, the important question is how power is understood by the policymakers. It is clear that Gorbachev did not believe that the Soviet Union's ability to remain a great power depended only on its military forces; it also depended, among other things, on its economy and on its capacity to generate new technology. If, however, we have to examine how power is perceived to understand its effects on foreign policy in particular cases, then we are forced, as William Wohlforth has pointed out, into historical analysis.[38]

Future Directions

The end of the cold war and the collapse of the Soviet Union have opened up two areas of research of enormous interest and importance. The first is the history of the whole Soviet experience, including its foreign policy; the second is international relations after the breakup of the Soviet Union.

If political scientists suffered from the lack of information about Soviet policy making during the cold war, historians of Soviet foreign policy were disadvantaged by their inability to use Soviet archives. The history of Soviet foreign policy had to be written on the basis of published documents, defectors' accounts, and the memoirs of those non-Soviet political leaders and diplomats who dealt with the Soviet Union. Non-Soviet archives were of great importance, especially for the prewar years and World War II, but increasingly for the cold war, too. Among other historians, E. H. Carr used them to explore the history of the Comintern; Jonathan Haslam to study Soviet foreign policy in the 1930s, Vojtech Mastny to analyze Soviet policy in World War II, and William Taubman to examine Stalin's postwar policy toward the United States.[39]

It will now be possible to examine Soviet foreign policy in all its various aspects in quite a different way. The study of Soviet foreign policy will not be tied intimately to the conduct of the cold war, and this should allow for more dispassionate analysis, less affected by the push and pull of policy debates and political loyalties. New sources are becoming available as the Russian archives open up, and they will make it possible to tackle on a deeper and more serious level many of the issues that have been raised in the study of Soviet foreign policy. What role did ideology play? What was the balance between ideology, realpolitik, and personality in Soviet foreign policy? How were decisions made? What calculations lay behind different policy moves? What was the relationship between Communist Party and government instruments of foreign policy? What was the relationship between domestic politics and foreign policy? Access to new sources will not remove controversy—and we do not know how open the archives will become—but it will provide a much more solid foundation from which to argue. The gaps in our knowledge will not be filled all at once. We have much richer evidence on the Soviet side for the end of the cold war than for its beginning, for example.[40]

The questions to be asked deal not only with the specifics of Soviet policy and the mechanisms of policy making. There are some very broad questions about the relationship between the Soviet Union and the outside world. What were the effects on the international system of the creation of a powerful revolutionary state? How did the international system cope, and how was mutual adjustment achieved? What led to the end of the cold war and the collapse of Soviet control over Eastern Europe? Was it a consequence of imperial overstretch, resulting from domestic politics or from a long-term failure to understand how the international system operated? Was it the result of a crisis of the Soviet system that spilled over into foreign policy? Or was it a result of interdependence and transnational influences that altered the Soviet leaders' conception of their interests?

The problem of writing the history of Soviet foreign policy is not merely a question of filling in gaps in what has been written so far. It is a matter of reconstructing the history from two different angles: from the vantage point of the international system, which will involve looking at the Soviet Union in the context of the international system of the twentieth century; and from the Soviet side, which will mean situating decisions and policies in their Soviet context. These are both interesting challenges.

Most historians are not concerned with theoretical questions of the kind that interest political scientists, or at least they are not concerned with them in the same way. But they inevitably have to ask what kind of state the Soviet Union was and to make assumptions about the determinants of its foreign policy. They have to take a position on the role of ideology in foreign policy, for example. The sensibility of the political scientist may differ from that of the historian, but it would be useful to have a greater dialogue between historians and political scientists on the Soviet Union's foreign relations.[41]

The second major area of research is the effect on international relations of the breakup of the Soviet Union and the formation of fifteen new states. Many of the issues raised by this new state of affairs fall outside the normal purview of international relations theory. This is partly because the things that international relations theory tends to take for granted—states and interests, for example—are themselves problematic in this context. New institutions are being created, new identities formed, and new interests defined. Besides, some of the states that have been formed are riven by ethnic disputes and may not exist in ten years' time. The foreign relations of the post-Soviet states are thus bound up with the processes of state building taking place within those states. In Russia, for example, there is sharp debate about the place that Russia occupies and ought to occupy in the world, about national identity and national interests. What effect will the outcome of this debate—or rather what effect will this continuing debate—have on Russia's foreign policy? The analysis of international relations and foreign policies is an interesting, but also a difficult, problem in this fluid and inchoate, but probably also formative, period.

Post-Soviet international relations raise many interesting questions for research. There is great scope for cooperation and collaboration between historians and political scientists interested in international relations and comparative politics and also between generalists and those with a special interest in Soviet and post-Soviet affairs. This cooperation ought to be fostered. At a time when state borders have shown themselves to be permeable and changeable, it is hardly wise to allow disputes over the boundaries between disciplines and subdisciplines to limit or hamper research.

Notes

[1]See, for example, Pierre Allan and Kjell Goldman, eds., *The End of the Cold War: Evaluating Theories of International Relations* (Dordrecht: M. Nijhoff, 1992); Richard Ned Lebow and Thomas Risse-Kappen, eds., *International Relations Theory and the End of the Cold War*, forthcoming; John Lewis Gaddis, "International Relations Theory and the End of the Cold War," *International Security* 17, no. 3 (1992–93): 5–58.

[2]E. H. Carr, *The Twenty-Years' Crisis, 1919–1939* (London: Macmillan, 1940); Hans Morgenthau, *Politics among Nations: The Struggle for Power and Peace* (New York: Knopf, 1948).

[3]Hannah Arendt, *The Origins of Totalitarianism* (New York: Harcourt, Brace, 1951); C. J. Friedrich and Z. K. Brzezinski, *Totalitarian Dictatorship and Autocracy* (New York: Frederick A. Praeger, 1956).

[4]On the Long Telegram, see George F. Kennan, *Memoirs, 1925–1950* (Boston: Little, Brown, 1967), 271–97, 547–59; X [Kennan], "The Sources of Soviet Conduct," *Foreign Affairs* 25 (July 1947): 566–82.

[5]John Lewis Gaddis, *Strategies of Containment* (New York: Oxford University Press, 1982).

[6]See, for example, Barrington Moore, *Soviet Politics—The Dilemma of Power: The Role of Ideas in Social Change* (Cambridge, Mass.: Harvard University Press, 1950).

[7]A related issue also received attention: what were the elements of continuity and discontinuity between the foreign policies of imperial Russia and the Soviet Union—in other words, how far did Marxism-Leninism shape foreign policy? See Ivo J. Lederer, ed., *Russian Foreign Policy* (New Haven: Yale University Press, 1962).

[8]In this chapter I am looking at American debates, but reference should be made to the contribution made by European Marxists to the study of Soviet foreign policy. Critics from the left were quicker than others to see the Soviet Union as a great power that had betrayed its revolutionary heritage. These authors were well versed in, and sympathetic to, Marxism, and therefore sensitive to the relationship between foreign policy and domestic politics. Many of them, like Isaac Deutscher, took their cue from Leon Trotsky's analysis of Josef Stalin's betrayal of the revolution. See Deutscher, *Stalin: A Political Biography*, rev. ed. (New York: Oxford University Press, 1967). Paolo Spriano, *Stalin and the European Communists* (London: Verso, 1985), is a particularly good analysis of the relationship between Soviet state interests and the communist movement. A collection of essays edited by Egbert Jahn, *Soviet Foreign Policy: Its Social and Economic Conditions* (London: Allison and Busby, 1978), examines Soviet foreign policy in the context of the development of the Soviet system as a whole.

[9]See, for example, Adam Ulam, *Titoism and the Cominform* (Cambridge, Mass.: Harvard University Press, 1952); Zbigniew Brzezinski, *The Soviet Bloc: Unity and Conflict* (Cambridge, Mass.: Harvard University Press, 1960); William E. Griffith, *The Sino-Soviet Rift* (London: George Allen and Unwin, 1964).

[10]Marshall Shulman, *Stalin's Foreign Policy Revisited* (Cambridge, Mass.: Harvard University Press, 1963).

[11]Robert Tucker, *The Soviet Political Mind* (New York: Praeger, 1963).

[12]William Zimmerman, *Soviet Perspectives on International Relations* (Princeton: Princeton University Press, 1969).

[13]This tradition was strong and effective in the study of Soviet military thought. See Raymond Garthoff, *Soviet Strategy in the Nuclear Age* (London: Atlantic Books, 1958); Herbert Dinerstein, *War and the Soviet Union* (New York: Frederick A. Praeger, 1959); Thomas W. Wolfe, *Soviet Strategy at the Crossroads* (Cambridge, Mass.: Harvard University Press, 1964).

[14]See, for example, Edward Luttwak, *The Grand Strategy of the Soviet Union* (New York: St. Martin's Press, 1983).

[15]The classic statement of this theory is Kenneth N. Waltz, *Theory of International Politics* (New York: McGraw-Hill, 1979).

[16]See Robert Jervis, *Perception and Misperception in International Politics* (Princeton: Princeton University Press, 1976).

[17]The most influential work was Graham Allison, *The Essence of Decision* (Boston: Little, Brown, 1971).

[18]George Breslauer and Philip Tetlock, *Learning in U.S. and Soviet Foreign Policy* (Boulder, Colo.: Westview, 1991). For some critical comments, see Matthew Evangelista, "Sources of Moderation in Soviet Security Policy," in *Behavior, Society, and Nuclear War*, ed. Robert Jervis et al. (New York: Oxford University Press, 1991). Critics pointed out that there is no universally accepted theory of learning that can be applied to the study of foreign policy making; nor is there any objective criterion for deciding when a state has indeed learned—that is, drawn the correct lessons—except by seeing how things turn out.

[19]Robert Conquest, *Power and Policy in the USSR* (London: Macmillan, 1961); Carl A. Linden, *Khrushchev and the Soviet Leadership, 1957–1964* (Baltimore: Johns Hopkins University Press, 1966).

[20]Harry Gelman, *The Brezhnev Politburo and the Decline of Detente* (Ithaca: Cornell University Press, 1984); Jack Snyder, "The Gorbachev Revolution: A Waning of Soviet Expansionism," *International Security* 12, no. 4 (1987–88): 93–131.

[21]See Carl J. Friedrich, Michael Curtis, and Benjamin R. Barber, *Totalitarianism in Perspective: Three Views* (New York: Praeger Publishers, 1969).

[22]Seweryn Bialer, ed., *The Domestic Context of Soviet Foreign Policy* (Boulder, Colo.: Westview, 1981).

[23]Probably the most widely read study of Soviet foreign policy was Adam Ulam, *Expansion and Coexistence*, 2d ed. (New York: Holt, Rinehart and Winston, 1974), which was written by a historian (though a professor of government) who paid little attention to what was happening in the field of international relations theory.

[24]Clifford Geertz, "Thick Description: Towards an Interpretive Theory of Culture," in Geertz, *The Interpretation of Cultures* (New York: Basic Books, 1973), 3–30.

[25]For a shrewd discussion of these issues, see Alexander Dallin, "The Domestic Sources of Soviet Foreign Policy," in *Domestic Context of Soviet Foreign Policy*, ed. Bialer, 335–408.

[26]William Welch and Jan F. Triska, "Soviet Foreign Policy Studies and Foreign Policy Models," *World Politics* XXIII, no. 4 (1971): 704–33; Arnold L. Horelick, A. Ross Johnson, and John D. Steinbruner, *The Study of Soviet Foreign Policy: A Review of Decision-Theory-Related Approaches*, Rand Report R-1334 (Santa Monica, Calif.: Rand Corporation, December 1973); Jack Snyder, "Richness, Rigor, and Relevance in the Study of Soviet Foreign Policy," *International Security* 9, no. 3 (1984–85): 89–108; Snyder, "Science and Sovietology: Bridging the Methods Gap in Soviet Foreign Policy Studies," *World Politics* XL, no. 2 (1988): 169–93.

[27]Luttwak, *Grand Strategy of the Soviet Union*.

[28]Robert F. Byrnes, ed., *After Brezhnev: Sources of Soviet Conduct in the 1980's* (Bloomington: Indiana University Press, 1983).

[29]In my *The Soviet Union and the Arms Race* (New Haven and London: Yale University Press, 1983), I argued that there was "a great deal to suggest that the 1980s will be a major turning-point in Soviet politics: the change of leadership, economic difficulties and foreign policy problems all point towards this" (176). I argued that there was a strong probability of far-reaching reform, but also a chance that the opportunity to reform would not be taken. In the interests of honesty, I should note that I argued that while accommodation and reform were likely, retreat and collapse were not.

[30]See, for example, Robert Legvold, "Revolution in Soviet Foreign Policy," *Foreign Affairs* 68, no. 1 (1988–89): 82–97, and my "Gorbachev's New Thinking" in the same issue, 66–81.

[31]See Robert Gilpin, *War and Change in the International System* (Cambridge: Cambridge University Press, 1980).

[32]John Lewis Gaddis, "The Long Peace: Elements of Stability in the Postwar International System," in Gaddis, *The Long Peace* (New York: Oxford University Press, 1987), 215–45.

[33]See, for example, Janice Goss Stein, "Political Learning by Doing: Gorbachev as Uncommitted Thinker and Motivated Learner"; Thomas Risse-Kappen, "Ideas Do Not Float Freely: Transnational Coalitions, Domestic Structures, and the End of the Cold War"; Rey Koslowski and Friedrich V. Kratchowil, "Understanding Change in International Politics: The Soviet Empire's Demise and the International System"; Richard Ned Lebow, "The Long Peace, the End of the Cold War, and the Failure of Realism," all in *International Organization* 48, no. 2 (1994): 155–84; 185–214; 215–48; 249–78.

[34]A senior International Relations Specialist quoted in Lebow, "Long Peace," 251–52.

[35]I draw here on an excellent article by William Wohlforth, "Realism and the End of the Cold War," *International Security* (Winter 1994–95). One of the criticisms made of realism in the current debate is that it is indeterminate, because changes in the international distribution of power cannot explain the scope and direction of Gorbachev's foreign policy. At the very least, the argument goes, other factors have to be taken into account—domestic politics or Gorbachev's personality, for example. This is not a strong argument against realism, because realism does not claim to provide an explanation for each state's foreign policy.

[36]See, for example, Alexander Dallin, "Causes of the Collapse of the USSR," *Post-Soviet Affairs* 8, no. 4 (1992): 279–302; Martin Malia, "Leninist Endgame," *Daedalus* 121, no. 3 (1992): 57–75.

[37]As Coit Blacker makes clear in his *Hostage to Revolution: Gorbachev and Soviet Security Policy, 1985–1991* (New York: Council on Foreign Relations Press, 1993).

[38]This is a central argument in William Wohlforth, *The Elusive Balance: Power and Perception during the Cold War* (Ithaca: Cornell University Press, 1993).

[39]E. H. Carr examined the Comintern in his multivolume history of the Bolshevik Revolution and in his *The Twilight of the Comintern, 1930–1935* (London: Macmillan, 1982). Jonathan Haslam's three volumes on the 1930s are *Soviet Foreign Policy, 1930–33* (New York: St. Martin's Press, 1983); *The Soviet Union and the Struggle for Collective Security in Europe, 1933–39* (London: Macmillan, 1984); *The Soviet Union and the Threat from the East, 1933–41* (Pittsburgh: University of Pittsburgh Press, 1992). Vojtech Mastny looks at Soviet wartime policy in *Russia's Road to the Cold War* (New York: Columbia University Press, 1979). William Taubman, *Stalin's American Policy* (New York: W. W. Norton, 1982), focuses chiefly on the cold war.

[40]On the end of the cold war, see, for example, S. F. Akhromeev and G. M. Kornienko, *Glazami marshala i diplomata* (Moscow: Mezhdunarodnye otnosheniia, 1992); A. S. Cherniaev, *Shest' let s Gorbachevym* (Moscow: Progress, 1993). Nevertheless, new evidence on the early stages of the cold war is coming to light. See Sergei Goncharov, John Lewis, and Xue Litai, *Uncertain Partners: Stalin, Mao, and the Korean War* (Stanford: Stanford University Press, 1993); David Holloway, *Stalin and the Bomb: The Soviet Union and Atomic Energy, 1939–1956* (New Haven and London: Yale University Press, 1994).

[41]Lynn Eden, "The End of U.S. Cold War History? A Review Essay," *International Security* 18, no. 1 (1993): 174–207.

Part VI

Culture

Chapter 10

The Relentless Cult of Novelty; or, How to Wreck the Century: Rethinking Soviet Studies

Nancy Condee

This essay organizes its task around three questions. First, how do we resituate "Soviet studies," now an altered object, into the university structure in a way that serves our redefined needs? Second, how do we proceed with "real-time research"—scholarship contemporary to our own lives—as we leave the Soviet period behind us? And third, how do those of us who study both Soviet and contemporary Russian culture avoid simply reinventing the established alliances of Soviet studies but also separately strengthen new alliances with our colleagues in what is loosely referred to as cultural studies? This last question is not an endorsement of cultural studies, which hardly awaits our endorsement; it is an endorsement of survival within the university system. The ways we might rethink Soviet studies are themselves less important than—in fact, will largely be shaped by—the alliances we maintain. And, inevitably, those alliances will shape our scholarship in ways we do not yet recognize.

Resituating Soviet Studies

I begin these remarks on Soviet studies with a brief mention of my own history and position in the field. My assumptions that subsequently surface will then be evident from the outset.

Sputnik went up in 1957. Enrollments in high school Russian language courses reached their peak in 1965.[1] Many of us who went to high school in the 1960s—as indifferent to *Sputnik* as we were at sixteen—studied in high schools where Russian was offered. The educational reforms of this period reflected the common concern that U.S. students might occupy second place to those we then called "the Russians"; studying the language was considered, presumably, to be one way of addressing that concern.

I studied Russian through the late 1960s and 1970s, the major stretch of what the profession of Russian literature calls the "Malik years," the years of stabilization and consolidation inside the field of Russian literature. Outside the field, but elsewhere in academia, these were years of destabilization and deconsolidation. The university students of the late 1960s and 1970s remember the political instability that they themselves brought, frivolously or not, into academia; they remember Vietnam not as the lead story on the nightly news but as the focus of campus activity, including protests (whether organized by idiots is unimportant to this discussion) and the National Student Strike, which briefly closed down many of the universities where we studied. Watergate was merely an afterthought that confirmed our beliefs about the system.

Faculty members of our Russian and Slavic departments, we can safely say, were not in the revolutionary vanguard of this university protest movement of the 1960s and early 1970s. And I do not think I speak only for myself in suggesting that, for this particular generation of future U.S. Slavists, these were years of intellectual schizophrenia. To paraphrase the early Karl Marx, we recited Evgenii Onegin in the morning, occupied the provost's office in the afternoon, and wrote compositions in the evening. I am no longer advocating this course of study; I am merely describing it.

While these activities might seem incompatible or even duplicitous to the casual American reader, I urge my colleagues to recall that we were Russian students. That is to say, there was a category within Russian culture that comfortably "housed" the contradictory activities of this double life and gave it coherence, even within our assigned classroom reading. This split consciousness, or double life, or *dvoeverie*, could be found both within a right-wing tradition and a left-wing tradition of Russian culture.[2]

Young U.S. Slavists who then went on to study in Moscow or Leningrad during the 1960s and 1970s encountered intellectual schizophrenia of a much larger order. There the daily schedule was different: we reviewed verbs of motion in the morning, toured the Lenin Museum in the afternoon, visited disaffected Soviet friends at night. This double life, too, had its own internal coherence: compositions were due the next morning; they had to include at least ten verbs of motion describing our visit to the Lenin Museum; anti-Soviet friends tirelessly rewrote the compositions, crossing out all the mistakes and discouraging irreverent excesses. They always lived close to the Lenin Museum, whoever they were. It was never a long distance from one to the other.

The capacity to feel comfortable operating within multiple, mutually antagonistic systems of thought became routine, whether in the American classroom with the conservative émigré language teacher or in the Soviet classroom with the teacher-informer. Survival within these conflicting systems depended specifically on not articulating publicly either one's own position or one's vision of how the system should work. Those who did so deserved our contempt and our questions about their true motives.

The reader, therefore, will forgive my discomfort. These remarks are made in spite of the suspicion that such utterances are gestic. Who knows how we shall in fact rethink Soviet studies? *Kak prikazhet barin, tak i budem dumat'*. Translated into the language of academia, we in the humanities, even more than those in social sciences, keenly feel the absence of maneuvering room within the university structure. The future depends as much on deans as brains, a small but significant typographic substitution.

It has been characteristic of our totalizing tendencies within Soviet studies to see our own history, like Josef Stalin's model vision, as monolithically constructed, a fortress against the Soviet threat. But as recent literature on the subject shows,[3] the fortunes of particular assumptions, methodologies, wisdoms, and interpretive models[4] have risen and fallen from one decade to the next by pressures both internal and external to the profession.

This new self-examination (metaresearch, perhaps, is more accurate) appears endless, overwhelming, self-perpetuating. Why are we rushing to explain to ourselves what we were doing all those years? Weren't we all here before? And yet, with all the unremitting quantity and uneven quality, the effort to particularize and discriminate within the field of postwar U.S. Sovietology, rather than to champion our side, is long overdue. The time has come when, polemics aside, "teaching the conflicts" of Soviet studies is a necessary stage in making sense of twentieth-century research on the Soviet Union.[5] This new focus is not a divisive act but one that makes explicit the assumptions of the field and holds them up for legitimate discussion. Scholars of twentieth-century Russian and Soviet culture have been slowest to initiate this process.

Literature departments, as one participant in Soviet studies, traditionally place the weight of the field on nineteenth-century literature, and in particular the long novel. My colleagues and I shall differ about the specifics, the reasons, and the wisdom of this practice, but I think we can agree on the century. It is not necessary to attack that orientation; it is high time, however, as we part with our own twentieth century, that we figure out better ways of studying that century, in particular the period from April 23, 1932, the date of the Central Committee's VKP(b) Resolution "On the Reformation of Literary-Artistic Organizations," to the demise of the Soviet Union in December 1991. Until now our century has run from 1900 to 1932 and from 1953 to 1964—that is, thirty-two years of culture and eleven years of trench warfare, adding up to forty-three. The remaining fifty years have not been thought worthy of attention.

To study the twentieth century adequately, we must set aside several long-standing assumptions. The first is the dominance of the "good art–good scholar" connection, which appears most often in the following dual instantiation: only good art is worthy of serious scholarship; since we all strive to be good scholars, we must look only at good art. I leave it to specialists of nineteenth-century culture to argue whether the "good art–good scholar" assumption might productively dominate in investigations of their historical period. It is no longer—and in fact has never been—a useful norm for research in twentieth-century culture.

We do not need, God forbid, to become social scientists to recognize how this assumption has imposed limitations, hobbling our work in twentieth-century culture. Do our colleagues in other fields only study nice nationalities? vital economies? model democracies? healthy environmental systems? Do we do justice to twentieth-century culture by teaching only its best moments? or, a mere variant, by teaching it as a set of binary opposites, "true" art and "false" art? Vital economies do not go unstudied simply because troubled economies are examined as well. If cultural degradation—that is to say, the "degradation" of the particular culture of late nineteenth-century Russia—is characteristic of the twentieth century, is not cultural degradation a compelling area of research?

A second hobbling assumption asserts that literature is the crowning medium of cultural expression and that other cultural activities organize themselves around the specific coherence that literature offers. Again, the nineteenth-century specialists will make their own choices, but for twentieth-century specialists it must by now be amply clear that an attempt to explain modernism, let alone later cultural movements, by restricting the examples to literature is a violation of modernism. It is akin to explaining childbirth using the standard male anatomical structure.

The irony is that in the Soviet Union, socialist realist theoreticians constructed this gravitational force field around literature (in particular the long novel) and administered other forms of cultural production around literature's false centrality. We in U.S. academia are guilty of the same enterprise. Scholars in twentieth-century culture must disengage from this practice. Adequate graduate-level training in the analysis of visual media is part of this process.

In making sense of Soviet culture, we must encourage research across all decades of this century, in particular the neglected ones: the

1930s, 1940s, and 1970s. For this expansion in both research and teaching we must have better access to examples of socialist realism: painting, sculpture, posters, film, and other visual material on slides, videodiscs, CD-roms, videocassettes, and other media. It is our responsibility to pursue this access. We do not need to like this police art, imposed for a half century from 1934 to roughly 1984; we need to ask interesting questions. As we do so, some of the good scholars studying good art may become better scholars studying worse art. This is a necessary stage in coming to terms with Soviet culture.

What is "Soviet culture"? Paralyzed between an ideological definition of Soviet culture (exclusively socialist realism) and a historical-geographical one (inclusive of the dissident tradition), the literature faculty's joke was that Soviet culture does not exist except as an oxymoron: what is Soviet is not culture; what is culture is not Soviet. Thus, 1932 was the "fateful year" after which our own research became divided into two paths: "Soviet" and "culture," two mutually antagonistic but interdependent concepts, a familiar tradition in Russian history. The attention we paid to one or the other concept defined our stature in the community of literary studies.

Although the following categories are not in fact as clear-cut as I shall present them here, existing scholarship on twentieth-century culture has tended to fall into three categories. The first is the set of texts that have been vital to our own education and teaching, namely, the large surveys of twentieth-century writers, including important works by Deming Brown, Edward J. Brown, Marc Slonim, and Gleb Struve.[6] The second are the lively, polemical texts of Herman Ermolaev, Maurice Friedburg, Abraham Rothberg, or Grigorii Svirskii, which intentionally participate in the very politics they also elucidate, covering the postwar period to 1976.[7]

A third category of research aspires neither to preserve established codes of literary scholarship nor to engage the enemy in polemics. The most important works here are by Katerina Clark, Vera Dunham, and Richard Stites.[8] Two of these scholars restrict their unconventional analysis to literature; the third, our *stiliaga* (bad boy) of Russian culture, looks at the broader arena of Russian culture, including urban songs, movies, the entertainment stage, and light reading. What these three scholars share is an unabashedly partial (in both senses of the term) view of twentieth-century culture with no particular engagement with the binary oppositions that have defined Soviet studies. Whoever they are, they are not "point men" either for high culture or for Western Sovietology.

My trichotomy breaks down when it attempts to integrate important examples of "hybrid scholarship" that have been crucial to the discussion of the intersection of Soviet culture and Soviet politics: Priscilla Johnson on Nikita Khrushchev and the arts; C. Vaughan James on socialist realism; and N. N. Shneidman on Soviet literature in the 1970s and the 1980s.[9] Johnson's work, while openly polemical against the Soviet leadership, includes an enormous number of useful transcripts, newspaper articles, political speeches, and other texts that chronicle the critical two years (1962–64) in which the Thaw ended. Her work addresses the conflicts in painting, music, and film as well as the literary arts. Not surprisingly, the Thaw has a different shape when these forms of cultural production are given broader discussion. James's volume, a revisionist critique of Soviet Marxism-Leninism, provides the only thorough English-language introduction to socialist realist theory. Shneidman combines an observance of scholarly codes with a valuable overview of the internal conflicts among the theoreticians of socialist realism. To the extent that all three scholars give serious attention to the power of "theory"—that is, the institutional rules enforced by the gulag—in shaping cultural production, they best support the kind of work that steps away simultaneously from the established codes of literary studies and the overinvested polemics of Sovietology.

The neglected decades (1930s, 1940s, 1970s) would benefit from more such research that is neither above the fray nor in the fray; a simple description of the fray is still needed. This description is the value, for example, of Sergei Chuprinin's three-volume (perhaps, one day, four-volume) collection of Thaw materials, which includes an invaluable chronicle of events.[10] It helps us make sense of the fray. Of enormous use as both reference and history would be a collection of Radio Liberty articles and news pieces on culture covering the stagnation (1964–85) and perestroika periods (1985–1991), with a long introduction situating them in the field. As Katerina Clark has pointed out, these are the kinds of research tools that would help us gain a deeper understanding not only of familiar landmarks (1932, 1934, 1937, etc.) but of unfamiliar ones as well. Another sorely needed volume is a serious treatment of socialist realism—not to legitimize or excoriate the beast but to examine the ways in which the idea, in all stages of theoretical debate and artistic application, shaped cultural production (including dissident, parallel, alternative, and postmodernist cultures) for more than half a century.

While it would be distracting to enumerate at length areas of "new"—that is, underdeveloped—research in Soviet studies, I cannot resist mentioning two. The first might be called anti-Soviet studies, or an examination of cultural texts that articulate a fuller range of positions in opposition to official policy. This writing is not the same thing as dissident literature as we have defined it up until now. We know very little, for example, about the opposition to Soviet power from the cultural *right* and the ways that opposition was inscribed in the texts of country prose writers.[11] Our long-standing history of ignorance and misperception in this area resulted, for example, in substantial misreadings of Valentin Rasputin's *Pozhar* (1985) in the early months of perestroika.

A second area of fruitful research is the aesthetics of totalitarian art. Where the totalitarian model may have failed political scientists as an adequate description of the actual political process, its brilliant array of "errors"—hyperpoliticization, one-sided moral superiority, unilinearity, resistance to change, facile comparisons with fascism, narrow focus on the leader and politics at the top, blindness on the national question, claims to explanatory completeness (I simply paraphrase the limitations cited by my own colleagues, Moshe Lewin and Ronald Grigor Suny, in this forum)—serve as an unintentionally perceptive guide to the cultural aspirations of totalitarian art. What sense to make of this I leave for another time.[12] If the *Slavic and East European Journal* can publish articles on the themes, motifs, symbols, and influences in the work of . . . , why can't it publish articles on the cultural codes of totalitarian art? Such articles would find a readership.

We would do well to evaluate—not at an institutional level but in our own minds—the unconscious criteria by which we select faculty from the fourth wave of Russian emigration. To suggest that we should reach a consensus is nonsense; to suggest that there are not patterns of hiring within each wave is, of course, also nonsense. A Slavic Department faculty whose native speakers were predominantly first wave had a very different departmental ecosystem, so to speak, from one whose native speakers were predominantly second wave or third wave. Those ecosystems were not reducible to generational or historical differences.

And just as there were different hiring practices, there was also a different range of "appropriate" professional activities for the Slavic Department émigré, not to mention different conceptions of literature, curricula, syllabuses, methodologies, examination and advising procedures, and so forth. I have no doubt that we will be uncomfortable addressing this issue. Is it unreasonable, for example, to expect the émigré faculty to publish regularly in leading professional journals, whether in Russia or in the United States, and also to run a well-organized class in verbs of motion?

I broach this difficult topic because of the new group of excellent

Russian scholars and writers—recently, if temporarily here in the United States—who work across established disciplines and modes of cultural production: Mikhail Epshtein, Mikhail Iampol'skii, Mark Lipovetskii, Tat'iana Tolstaia, Iurii Tsivian, Maia Turovskaia, Andrei Zorin, and others. We would benefit if they could find some place within our profession of academia, whether a full appointment or a position with alternating semesters in the United States and Russia. These accommodations will be negotiated by enterprising departments.

My remarks here so far address only implicitly the original question of resituating Soviet studies. I would like to conclude these recommendations—that we teach the conflicts, research the neglected decades, acquire greater access to culture of the socialist realist period, question the centrality of the nineteenth century and of literature, draw upon the strengths of the fourth wave, and so forth—with the following acknowledgment: the value of these recommendations for a redefined Soviet studies is largely contingent upon the extent to which we scholars of twentieth-century culture can establish greater legitimacy for our work within our own departments and discipline. As it now stands, we in twentieth-century culture often find ourselves to be the stepchildren both of the discipline and of area studies. This position explains why cultural studies (where very little time is wasted on establishing legitimacy) is a blessed alternative for many of us who work in twentieth-century culture. The Slavic department, our disciplinary home base, is too monolithic for its own good.

A different problem faces Soviet studies. Pulled in two administrative directions, Soviet studies might easily disband, its social science faculty assimilated into Western-oriented international studies, its humanities faculty assimilated into Western-oriented cultural studies. The survival of Soviet studies will depend on, first, its ability to reinvent a credible story about itself in the context of profoundly altered global conditions, and, second, its success in drawing on precisely those same university resources that might assimilate it. I myself do not foresee the demise of this academic "cluster," temporarily referred to as Soviet studies;[13] rather, I see us bringing in different strengths from the outside as a result of contact with other sets of colleagues.

What we call ourselves, therefore, may be of no small importance, however dull the topic is to us by now. The shortcomings are evident: "Soviet studies" implies that the world ends in 1991; "post-Soviet studies" implies that it begins in 1991; "Russian studies" is fraught with ethnic emphasis and geographic restrictions that many of us do not want. For many of us, it may be that "Russian and East European Studies," in all its retrograde glory,[14] serves our funding interests better than the alternatives. As an appellation, it brackets together three pairs of research interests: geographic (Russia and the newly independent European states), historic (pre- and post-1991), and disciplinary (social sciences and the humanities). True, it smacks of Russian imperialism; but will the project on Polish culture fare better if it is thrown into the competitive funding pool with American, British, and French projects? All of Eastern Europe will then become the "token discipline."

My own fear is this: academia is already comprised of two major institutions—not the obvious social sciences and humanities but two autonomous and self-integrated "entities," namely, international studies and cultural studies. International studies is the domain of what one colleague calls "big-picture model builders" without a trace of language competence or messy empiricism. Cultural studies is the refuge of disgruntled language and literature faculty unwittingly coopted from departments that, in the dean's view, "need" to shrink anyway. Within these two institutions, a battle of the giants is under way. The linoleum trembles. In international studies, giganto-machy plays out between and among Western-oriented economists and political scientists; in cultural studies, it is between English and history. In either case, the parole is "hegemony."

If any part of this analysis rings true, then we must assess our chances accordingly. Does Soviet studies become a peripheral curiosity or a line of communication between these two institutions? It is my guess that the altered Soviet studies will exist no longer as a meeting place for many disciplines but as one of several bridges between these two large institutions.

Real-Time Research: The Futurologists' Apprentice

While our colleagues in other disciplines, faced with the unexpected collapse of communism, describe what one scholar calls "a common obligation to examine how we collectively failed,"[15] we in culture have been shameless, denying any responsibility for foreseeing or not foreseeing the collapse of Soviet culture or even small pieces of it. Perhaps we deny responsibility because we were not permitted to don the futurologist's glasses very often. Or, perhaps, trained originally in literary studies, we come out of a discipline that traditionally looks backward from the present moment into cultural history, not forward into the future.[16] Given this difference, who cares whether we foresaw the collapse of Soviet culture? Its collapse affects how we proceed with our work, but it does not affect our credibility in the profession.

Research in the present moment—without this overweening element of "predictivity"—is not a more modest task than the predictive sciences; it is a more ambitious one, with greater accountability. Given the paucity of information and the difficulties of gathering materials in the Soviet Union, futurology was, for its worst practitioners, an easy, arrogant science. It was easier to predict the future than to describe the present. Now the opposite is true.

But futurology was not our principal battle within the field of contemporary culture. Coming out of a discipline without futurology, with no established tradition of contemporary studies, and with no institutionalized "rush for the instantaneous," as Moshe Lewin cautions in comments here, we who haved worked in contemporary culture more often encountered the trivialization of our work by comparisons with journalism.[17] By contrast, new support for our work in the contemporary came from cultural studies, with its at times overweening emphasis on the contemporary.[18]

Interdisciplinary Studies and Interdisciplinarity

How do area studies and cultural studies differ in their orientations? As one colleague points out, area studies receives more federal funding than cultural studies. Area studies is a set of related disciplines that often (though not exclusively) defines itself by spatial coordinates (Latin American studies, Asian studies); in cultural studies, the notion of "related disciplines" must be reinvented with each new enterprise. Area studies, like literature departments, respects the national treasures of culture yet plunders them for its own uses; cultural studies does not respect them, except as an anthropologist might respect a prize yam rack. Thus, *Doktor Zhivago*, a very different object in literature from what it is in area studies, is different yet again in cultural studies. If area studies strives to arrive at a fuller truth by bringing us together, cultural studies assumes a partial truth as the final assemblage of partial truths. If area studies has occasional doubts about what will be "curricularized," cultural studies has only doubts. It is not surprising, therefore, that cultural studies is more fraught with conflict even than area studies.

To my mind, however, the principal difference is that area studies is an interdisciplinary forum while cultural studies incorporates interdisciplinarity into the project itself. While area studies asks that we bring our established discipline to the round table,[19] cultural studies asks that we check it, dismantled, at the door. While area studies is interdisciplinary, cultural studies is "antidisciplinary."[20]

Cultural studies, with its traditions of Western, insular, left-wing oppositional culture,[21] is often an uncomfortable fit for Slavists, accustomed to an Eastern European, insular, right-wing oppositional culture. Moreover, given the history of attenuated contacts between Slavic and other foreign culture departments,[22] the reconfiguration of our faculties into (among other things) cultural studies makes us confront the ways in which Russian culture confounds some of the "accepted wisdom" of cultural studies. A proper development of this argument requires a separate article. My point here is that we Slavists have long been content not to join into conversations with our colleagues in Western European cultures, and they have been content not to listen. Since the fall of the Berlin Wall, this "parallel play" can no longer proceed as before.

If indeed the concept of area studies as an academic model is most compelling for the study of societies that are linguistically inaccessible or culturally distinctive (Asian studies, Latin American studies, and so forth), then scholars of Russian culture are faced with a familiar question that must be thought out anew: how European is Russia? Cultural studies is not an enterprise that promises better scholarship. It promises different misunderstandings, different mistakes, as well as some familiar ones, such as the proliferation of code words that ferret out the interlopers ("interventionist," for example, signals something a wee bit different in cultural studies from its implications in Soviet studies).

Yet, if we can rest assured that cultural studies—like area studies, like film studies, like feminist studies—surely attracts its share of idiots without threatening to deplete our own supply, then perhaps we can look anew at their discussions on the politics of "disciplinarity" and discover that they are engaged in an enterprise similar to our own here in this forum.

Russian and East European studies has a valuable and disruptive contribution to make in an enterprise that is itself creatively disruptive. It is a necessary, if contradictory, activity to examine both the death of Russia's vision of itself as a unique culture and the distinctive data that Russia contributes to the discussions of cultural studies: marginality, the myth of authorship, migrant cultures. We have something to say about the encroachments of U.S. popular culture, the coalescence of global culture, and biculturalism, whether Russian-Soviet or the more complex variety in the Baltic states. Russia's "distinctive material" includes class-differentiated culture in this post-"classless" society; the new Christianity of this post-"atheist" Russia; its long and entrenched traditions of essentialism in both gender and ethnicity;[23] and its politicization of text and canonicity (Pavel Medvedev, Andrei Platonov, and Mikhail Sholokhov merely begin the discussion). Russia's philosophical traditions, both elite and folk, complicate Western European traditions in ways that have not yet even been separated from Great Russian sentiment.[24]

At the same time, our own protracted but unfinished discussions within Soviet studies—the constituent features of sovietism, the fate of the Russian intelligentsia—could use some "airing out" in the larger arena of cultural studies. The "one culture or two" debate, with its very long beard,[25] confronts useful, if ignorant, questions from cultural studies—which "two"? émigré/Soviet? Soviet/Russian? Russian/transnational? box office/philanthropic?

These are relevant questions precisely because, however refined our "Soviet studies" research on Russia as it moves from an imposed culture to a national culture, we are less likely to notice the opposite flow: from national culture to imposed multinational culture, what (yes) jargon-laden cultural studies scholars call the tension between cultural autonomy and homogenization, national identity and global culture. Whether or not we study postcolonial marginalization within Western culture, we must at least ask ourselves whether we are not an example of it.[26]

Inescapably, cultural studies will also "air out" our discussions of what constitutes Russian culture. As a Sovietologist, one could get away with being apologetically Russocentric; it was, after all, our language of training. Now, with the collapse of the Soviet Union, we come to the awkward realization that we are poorly acquainted with Russian culture, that we have lost touch with it since the 1920s.[27]

It would be a shame if Soviet studies (as a title) stayed intact, and thus (as an enterprise) shrank to designate the short historical period of a particular region. Robert Daniels has cautioned us that "academic fashion and departmental politics have combined to question the interdisciplinary area studies concept, or confine it at most to history and language-literature."[28] Perhaps someone should warn fashion and politics that "history and language-literature" feel the centrifugal pull as much as anyone else. It may be that we shall meet less often, but have more interesting conversations.

Let me say in closing that I agree completely with my colleagues about the need for increased fieldwork, collaborative scholarship with Russians, emphasis on language competence, training in archival research, and retraining for all of us. These have always been opportunities we needed more of; they are one of the few respects in which we have stayed the same. The fact that we need them still does not diminish their urgency.

Notes

I was surprised to discover that the prose writer Aleksandr Solzhenitsyn and I happened coincidentally upon similar titles. See his excellent piece, "The Relentless Cult of Novelty and How It Wrecked the Century," *New York Times Book Review*, February 7, 1993, 3, 17. Perhaps we consulted with the same group of scholars. For my part, I would like to thank Bill Chase, Katie Clark, Dan Field, Helena Goscilo, Carol Leonard, Ron Linden, Jerry McCausland, Volodya Padunov, Scott Prater, and Fritz Ringer for conversations that helped to shape my thinking. They are in no way responsible for the views expressed here.

¹J. Thomas Shaw, "AATSEEL: The First Fifty Years," *Slavic and East European Journal* 35, [American Association of Teachers of Slavic and East-European Languages Golden Jubilee Issue] (1991): 117.

²Examples that come to mind include not only specific cultural figures such as Siniavskii-Tertz, I. A. Goncharov, and Azev and the multiple dual identities of V. I. Ulianov-Lenin, Josef Djugashvili-Stalin, V. M. Skriabin-Molotov, and others but also the larger conceptual parallelisms of paganism and Orthodoxy, party membership and Orthodox baptism, and so on.

³Recent publications include William E. Butler, Alexander Dallin, Dan E. Davidson, et al., "Restructuring Our Scholarship: An Open Forum," *American Association for the Advancement of Slavic Studies (AAASS) Newsletter* 29, no. 4 (1989): 1–10; Robert V. Daniels, "The State of the Field," *AAASS Newsletter* 3, no. 1 (1992): 1–3; Theodore Draper, "Who Killed Soviet Communism?" *New York Review of Books*, June 11, 1992, 7–8, 10, 12–14; Richard Ericson, "The Director's Corner: The Future of The Harriman Institute," *News from the Harriman Institute* 3, no. 1 (1993): 2–4; Frederic J. Fleron Jr. and Erik P. Hoffmann, "Sovietology and Perestroika: Methodology and Lessons from the Past," *Harriman Institute Forum* 5, no. 1 (1991): 1–7; Fleron, Hoffmann, and Edward W. Walker, "Whither Post-Sovietology?" *Harriman Institute Forum* 6, no. 6–7 (1993), Stephen R. Gaubard, ed., "The Exit from Communism," *Daedalus*, special ed. (Spring 1992); Robert Legvold, "The Director's Forum," *At the Harriman Institute* 5, no. 7 (March 15, 1992); Ronald H. Linden, "New and Old Needs," *AAASS Newsletter* 32, no. 5 (1992): 1–3; Stephen M. Meyer, "Key Questions for Soviet Studies," *Chronicle of Higher Education*, September 4, 1991, A-72; Alexander J. Motyl, *Sovietology, Rationality, Nationality: Coming to Grips with Nationalism in the USSR* (New York: Columbia University Press, 1990); Motyl, "Totalitarianism is Dead! Long Live Totalitarianism!" *At the Harriman Institute* 6, no. 1 (September 22, 1992); Alex Norsworthy, "The Poverty of Sovietology," *We/My*, May 18–31, 1992, 5; Benjamin Rifkin, "Professional Training for Slavists: Priorities for the Next Thirty Years," *AATSEEL Newsletter* 34, no. 4 (1992): 13; William Rosenberg, "'Traditional' Disciplines and the Changing Environment," *AAASS Newsletter* 32, no. 5 (1992): 3–4; Shaw, "AATSEEL"; Stephen White, "Slavists in New Times," *AAASS Newsletter* 31, no. 4 (1991): 1–2; Alexander Yanov, "Is Sovietology Reformable?" in *Reform in Russia and the USSR: Past and Prospects*, ed. Robert O. Crummey (Urbana: University of Illinois Press, 1989), 257–76; and, of course, Z [Martin Malia], "To the Stalin Mausoleum," *Daedalus* 119, no. 1 (1990): 295–344.

⁴I notice in the wording of the Ford Foundation grant that supported this research a marked absence of the word "model." Normally, social scientists do not talk without this word. Its absence here, I gather, signals a reluctance to reopen old arguments against the totalitarian model and an encouragement instead of a wider range of shared assumptions, less explicitly articulated in Soviet studies. Yet we have returned to the totalitarian

model in our work for this series because it is still useful as the most familiar example of the rise and fall of an idea. While I see its limitations as a model, it is a very effective metaphor. No doubt its defenders will take offense at that "disciplinary demotion" from political sciences to literary studies; nevertheless, my comments are meant to be complimentary. All of us in culture should have such professional success with our metaphors.

[5]The reference here is to Gerald Graff, *Beyond the Culture Wars: How Teaching the Conflicts Can Revitalize American Education* (New York: Norton, 1992), although, of course, relevant texts in Soviet studies would include such *Ur-texten* as Stephen F. Cohen, *Rethinking the Soviet Experience: Politics and History since 1917* (New York: Oxford University Press, 1985); Frederic J. Fleron Jr., ed., *Communist Studies and the Social Sciences: Essays on Methodology and Empirical Theory* (Chicago: Rand McNally, 1969); Erik P. Hoffmann, "The Soviet Union: Consensus or Debate," *Studies in Comparative Communism* 8, no. 3 (1975): 230–44; Jerry F. Hough, *The Soviet Union and Social Science Theory* (Cambridge, Mass.: Harvard University Press, 1977). See also Abbott Gleason, "'Totalitarianism' in 1984," *Russian Review* 43, no. 2 (1984): 145–59. No comparable body of texts exists in literary studies.

[6]Deming Brown, *Soviet Russian Literature since Stalin* (Cambridge: Cambridge University Press, 1978); Edward J. Brown, *Russian Literature since the Revolution,* rev. and enlarged ed. (Cambridge, Mass.: Harvard University Press, 1982); Marc Slonim, *Soviet Russian Literature: Writers and Problems, 1917–1967* (New York: Oxford University Press, 1967); Gleb Struve, *Russian Literature under Lenin and Stalin* (Norman: University of Oklahoma Press, 1971).

[7]Herman Ermolaev, *Soviet Literary Theories, 1917–1934: The Genesis of Socialist Realism,* University of California Publications in Modern Philology 69 (Berkeley: University of California Press, 1963); Maurice Friedburg, *A Decade of Euphoria: Western Literature in Post-Stalin Russia, 1954–64* (Bloomington: Indiana University Press, 1977); Abraham Rothberg, *The Heirs of Stalin: Dissidence and Soviet Regime, 1953–1970* (Ithaca: Cornell University Press, 1972); Grigorii Svirskii, *Na lobnom meste: Literatura nravstvennogo soprotivleniia (1946–1976)* (London: Overseas Publications Interchange Limited [OPI], 1979).

[8]Katerina Clark, *The Soviet Novel: History as Ritual,* rev. ed. (Chicago: University of Chicago Press, 1985); Vera S. Dunham, *In Stalin's Time: Middleclass Values in Soviet Fiction,* enlarged and updated ed. (Durham, N.C.: Duke University Press, 1990); Richard Stites, *Russian Popular Culture: Entertainment and Society since 1900* (Cambridge: Cambridge University Press, 1992).

[9]Priscilla Johnson, *Khrushchev and the Arts: The Politics of Soviet Culture, 1962–64* (Cambridge, Mass.: MIT Press, 1965); C. Vaughan James, *Soviet Socialist Realism: Origins and Theory* (New York: St. Martin's Press, 1973); N. N. Shneidman, *Soviet Literature in the 1970s: Artistic Diversity and Ideological Conformity* (Toronto: University of Toronto Press, 1979); Shneidman, *Soviet Literature in the 1980s: Decade of Transition* (Toronto: University of Toronto Press, 1989).

[10]Sergei Chuprinin, ed., *Ottepel',* 3 vols. (Moscow: Moskovskii rabochii, 1989–90).

[11]The few useful works in this area include John B. Dunlop, *The Faces of Contemporary Russian Nationalism* (Princeton: Princeton University Press, 1983); *The New Russian Nationalism* (New York: Nordland, 1985); Kathleen Parthe, *Russian Village Prose: The Radiant Past* (Princeton: Princeton University Press, 1992); Alexander Yanov, *The Russian New Right: Right-Wing Ideologies in the Contemporary USSR* (Berkeley: Institute of International Studies, 1978).

[12]Someday I will write, "The Totalitarian Model: A Sovietologist's Inadvertent Guidebook to Socialist Realism."

[13]How could Soviet studies die when, in literature departments, at least, it never really lived in the first place? It was the Soviet Union, not Soviet studies, that metaphorically "died," now affording us an unprecedented opportunity to study it. Like forensic pathologists, literary specialists put on their rubber gloves once the patient is deceased. Only then does the corpse become a legitimate object of research. I disagree, therefore, with Stephen White's comment that "it is difficult . . . to see much future for GDR studies." "Slavists in New Times," 1. Precisely now is an unusually good moment to do new work in the cabaret, theater, film, and other areas of cultural production in the German Democratic Republic.

[14]Or "Eurasian studies," if an institution develops that contact.

[15]This sentiment is likewise expressed or discussed in Draper, "Who Killed Soviet Communism?" 7; Fleron and Hoffmann, "Sovietology and Perestroika," 2–3; Z [Malia], "To the Stalin Mausoleum," 297; and the comments of James R. Millar, Thomas F. Remington, and Ronald Grigor Suny in this volume.

[16]The exception to this rule in literature is the topos of "future rebirth" that concludes many surveys of Soviet literature. See, for example, Slonim, *Soviet Russian Literature*, 349: "In the near or distant future, its vitality is sure to manifest itself in a free and meaningful rebirth." Slonim is, of course, correct, but this is not what interests me here.

[17]I have never understood why this comparison was unflattering. Journalism is a field with very different skills and higher salary expectations.

[18]Cultural studies is not per se concerned with the contemporary. Indeed, the University of Pittsburgh is an exception in this regard. See Colin MacCabe, "Editorial," *Critical Quarterly* 34, no. 3 [Special Issue on Cultural Studies at Pittsburgh] (1992): 1.

[19]This is precisely why twentieth-century scholarship in culture has worked at a disadvantage; the very tools we brought to the area studies forum are not our own but belonged to another era.

[20]See Cary Nelson, Paula A. Treichler, and Lawrence Grossberg, "Cultural Studies: An Introduction," in *Cultural Studies*, ed. Grossberg, Nelson, and Treichler (New York: Routledge, 1992), 2.

[21]If we take the Centre for Contemporary Cultural Studies at Birmingham to be the "genesis story" of cultural studies (and this point is certainly open to debate), then the formative texts charting its development are Richard Hoggart, *The Uses of Literacy* (New York: Oxford University Press, 1958); Louis James, *Fiction for the Working Man, 1830–1850* (Harmondsworth: Penguin, 1974); E. P. Thompson, *The Making of the English Working Class* (New York: Vintage, 1963); Raymond Williams, *Culture and Society, 1780–1950* (London: Chatto and Windus, 1958); Williams, *The Long Revolution* (London: Penguin, 1961). See also Graeme Turner, *British Cultural Studies: An Introduction* (New York: Routledge, 1992). A major U.S. text of this period is James D. Hart, *The Popular Book: A History of America's Literary Taste* (Berkeley: University of California Press, 1961).

[22]For an excellent overview of this history, see Peter Steiner, "Slavic Literary Studies Yesterday and Tomorrow," *Profession 87* (1987): 2–9.

[23]For an informed discussion on essentialism (feminist, feminine, female, and otherwise) as part of a larger examination of Russian women's writing, see Helena Goscilo, "Coming a Long Way, Baby: A Quarter-Century of Russian Women's Fiction," *Harriman Institute Forum* 6, no. 1 (September 1992): 1–7.

[24]I will mention in passing, because I hope other scholars will address this issue, the enormous need for the reprinting of such texts as James M. Edie, James P. Scanlan, and Mary-Barbara Zeldin, *Russian Philosophy*, 3 vols. (Knoxville: University of Tennessee Press, 1976); Thomas Riha, *Readings in Russian Civilization*, 2d ed. rev., 3 vols. (Chicago: University of Chicago Press, 1969).

[25]The liveliest discussion on this ancient theme remains Olga Matich with Michael Heim, *The Third Wave: Russian Literature in Emigration* (Ann Arbor, Mich.: Arbor, 1984).

[26]Some efforts have begun, for example, Greta Slobin's organization of "Postcommunism: Rethinking the Second World" at the Center for Cultural Studies, University of California at Santa Cruz, March 5–7, 1993.

[27]See Legvold, "Director's Forum," 1.

[28]Daniels, "State of the Field," 3.

Chapter 11

Cultural History and Russian Studies

Richard Stites

> The modern Middle East is not a center of great cultural achieve-
> ments, nor is it likely to become one in the near future. The study
> of the region or its languages, therefore, does not constitute its
> own reward so far as modern culture is concerned.
> —Morroe Berger

Cultural Imbalances

I begin with the rather negative term, "imbalances," to capture the
reader's attention. Cultural studies, as I envisage it, is something that is
all-embracing, studied partly for its own sake and partly for its relationship to other aspects of society. I believe that there is as yet no real
cultural studies of the USSR, its antecedents and its successors. Its
growth has been inhibited by two main aspects of our own culture—including our styles of scholarship: (1) the overweening investment in
payoff knowledge, driven mostly by Kremlinology, about power—especially central power—and strategy, a knowledge whose main if not
sole purpose is prediction; and (2) the fragmentation of disciplines that
deal specifically with culture. I shall first attempt a critique of our cultural approach, then set out something of an agenda for broadening
and enriching our study and teaching of Russian and related cultures.

Russian cultural studies has long been dominated, and still is, by
university literature departments. In the view of many teachers of that
subject in this country—not only émigrés and their students—their
field of study all but ceased to exist in 1917 except for the emigration
and selected "Soviet" period writers, mostly victims, martyrs, or dissidents. And for some others, literary scholarship has meant a close
analysis of selected texts from the canon. For those scholars and their
students, a four-way policy of exclusion has ensued: (1) the aesthetic
exclusion of noncanonical works (for example, popular fiction before
the Revolution) blocked out from the vision of students the vast bulk of
what people actually read on the grounds that it was worthless; (2) the
methodological exclusion in the once-prevailing practice of deep study
of certain master texts omitted many well-known Russian writers of
the nineteenth century from serious study; (3) the chronological exclu-

305

sion, practiced by those who, for political and/or aesthetic considerations, did not recognize Soviet works of socialist realism as a legitimate field; (4) the linguistic exclusion, derived from the relative nondevelopment of language study of the component nationalities of the USSR (or the Russian Empire), made it seem as though Russian culture was the only culture in that empire.

The result was an extreme narrowing of the study of the written products of the Soviet people over seventy years—to say nothing of the deep past—a period that produced millions of works. Add two more circumstances to this picture. One is the fact that other fields of culture—important for their own sake as well as for their intimate and eternal interaction with print culture—have been orphaned by the hierarchical structure of knowledge that prevails in most universities, a hierarchy that places the fine arts, theater, cinema, architecture, and other things in strict subordination to literary studies. The second is the fact that the popular, "lower" or more vulgar and mass-produced and mass-oriented genres of all these arts—in other words popular culture—have until recently been almost wholly neglected or ridiculed.[1]

If I may be graphic for a moment, imagine the culture of a multinational empire as a mountain range with a dozen peaks and scores of outcroppings and foothills. Visualize then hundreds of geologists studying intensively the snowy top of one of them in the belief that they are studying the whole range. Needless to say, there are many exceptions and qualifications needed for this sweeping metaphor. But any quick scanning of American Association for the Advancement of Slavic Studies (AAASS) members, jobs, positions, departmental activities, curricula, conference papers, and publishing patterns will confirm its general truth.

This is not to argue that those literary specialists have wasted their time or pursued irrelevant matters. The clustering at the top is not like ten thousand angels poised on the head of a pin because our Slavic scholars have produced magnificent works of analysis and have enriched and deepened our comprehension of big cultural questions—philosophical, religious, semiotic. Nor would I deny that related cultural disciplines have been inactive. One could assemble a library of American monographs in art history, architecture, theater, music, folklore, and cinema. But the library would be small, with many of its volumes written solely within the context of their own disciplines. The narrow disciplinary approach has the advantage of placing Russian cultural production in a comparative or world context and of applying rigorously the well-established rules of analysis that each discipline has developed. But this focus sometimes means neglecting the specifically Russian or other traditions that helped to shape the various arts. To my knowledge, there is no single modern work that treats synthetically all the arts and modes of cultural expression for any period of Russian history, and certainly none that grounds this cultural production in the historical, social, political, and intellectual context of the time.[2]

Take, for example, the reign of Alexander II (1855–81), an age of reform, of rapid intake of Western intellectual styles, and of turbulent radical activity. This was also the age of Fyodor Dostoevsky, Ivan Turgenev, Leo Tolstoy, and arguably a half-dozen other major writers and dozens of minor writers. It was the age of the insurgent group of painters called the Wanderers who defined Russian aesthetic norms for forty years. And it was the age of the Mighty Five (César Kyui, M. A. Balakirev, Aleksandr Borodin, Modest Musorgsky, and Nikolai Rimsky-Korsakov), the so-called national school of composition, as well as that of Russia's best-known composer, Piotr Ilich Tchaikovsky. Add to this the various turns taken in the history of architecture, theater, and popular entertainment, and we see at once what a fabulously opulent cultural epoch it was. And beneath it all flourished a whole range of middlebrow and popular genres in literature and all the arts. Is it not remarkable that no study of the cultural interaction in this period has ever been undertaken? And yet even a cursory glance at the periodical literature and the correspondence and memoirs of the time reveals a continuous interaction and mutual enrichment of creative figures and of their relation to the historic milieu in which they lived.

The Silver Age, the World of Art, the New Religious Consciousness—have all found able chroniclers, as have the cultural currents of the avant-garde in the Soviet 1920s. But who has been bold enough to stand forth and produce works of cultural synthesis that might reveal deeper meanings of those respective eras? And what I have said here can be said for every well-established period in Russian history up to the present moment. I believe that such integrated studies would teach us much about Russian and Soviet history that has remained a mystery. And I believe that the study of all the arts would enhance the study of each; that is to say, a macrocultural panorama would lead scholars to rethink and perhaps rewrite the history of individual arts and media in a given epoch.

All this theorizing is based on a philosophy of history that ascribes to a given period of human experience within a well-defined society a certain Zeitgeist—what William Shakespeare in *Hamlet* called "the very age and body of the time." Zeitgeist does not mean that the combination of social, political, and broad cultural exploration of a given epoch will always add up to "coherence" or unity. It may, on the contrary, indicate social and cultural diversity, confusion, ambivalence, conflict, and turbulence; it may even show us that what we once considered valid segments of periodization are really false and misleading. For example, it was widely held in the 1930s that Germany, in spite of social division and political polarization, had settled into a "normal life" in the late Weimar years, 1925–29. Siegfried Kracauer, by examining only one branch of cultural production—cinema—made a convincing case in the 1940s that the psychological schisms and fissures in Weimar Germany were insurmountable. Kracauer was faulted at the time for assigning too much weight to cinematic evidence, but later historians who examined the same period with attention (however selective) to the other arts tended to confirm his argument.[3]

What have historians of Russia been doing? In recent decades, our profession has been reshaped by a flood of works on social history dealing with workers, peasants, women of various classes, merchants, teachers, physicians, bureaucrats, and others. All this work has had great value in sensitizing us to the deeper realities of Russian life. It has added a rich and heavy ballast to our knowledge about the top without displacing that top: state, dynasty, military, diplomats, aristocracy, the intelligentsia, political leaders, and so on.

But at the same time, Russian historians have always been surrounded by "culture" because so many of the notable figures in Russian history were connected with culture; because all writers of survey histories mention culture as something important; because our colleagues in Russian literature are so visible and influential in the field of Slavic studies; and because cultural themes seemed to count for a lot in the glamorous media of television and movies or publications like the *New York Review of Books.* On the other hand, a feeling of inadequacy on this issue nagged many of us. For historians, culture, when treated at all, was consigned to a chapter at the end of a textbook section or a lecture tacked on to the end of a chronological division in the course. And what kind of culture? It was usually only literature (belles lettres), and if something else got attention it was almost overwhelmingly "high culture"—the fine arts, classical music, legitimate theater, art cinema. It is fair to say that most historians of modern Russia probably engaged with culture at three points: classic nineteenth-century novels and plays (Aleksandr Pushkin to Tolstoy and Anton Chekhov); the Silver Age in literature and the arts, flowing into the revolutionary avantgarde of the 1920s; and dissident or persecuted writers of fiction in the Soviet Union.

One reason perhaps (there are others) that social historians did not do much more than this to integrate culture into our studies is that they assumed it to be yet another elite activity like diplomacy, war, government, and enterprise. And, given the traditional limited definitions of culture, that is indeed what it was. Culture was high culture and only that (and is still so treated in most accounts) and was thus an adjunct of elite life, occasionally drawing interest when it intersected with politics. I believe that the wondrous growth of social history and the recent spurt of the history of popular cultures enable us to end the artificial divisions between "history" and "culture."

The works of Jeffrey Brooks, Fred Starr, Denise Youngblood, Katerina Clark, Régine Robin, Vera Dunham, and others have given us a clearer feeling for popular tastes and values. Their work certainly reinforced my own positive feelings for popular culture and my discomfort at the huge gulf between high and popular cultures (even though these cultures are more closely related than we sometimes admit) and at the elitism that it often produces among academics. I must confess also that I had become dissatisfied with some of the "new social history," not for what it contained but for what it often left out: blood, life, élan, feelings, emotions, human expressiveness, personal relations. Some of this social history was too latent or passive, treating masses of people as statistical objects. It seems to me that the study of popular culture gives life to social history and complements it perfectly, in a way that the exclusive focus on high culture heretofore has not been able to do.

Imperial Russia and Its Cultural Universes

The rough branches of study that I have been talking about now lie before us in a square made up of four separate blocks: elite history, high culture, social history, popular culture. I believe that these may be integrated by careful and thoughtful comparison of how culture is created and consumed in society and influenced by class, gender, ethnicity, geography, and other factors. I offer some very rough notes on questions about the relation of cultures to one another, to society, and to the state—that is, to "state culture" or political culture that might be the subject of future research, graduate and undergraduate courses, and even textbook surveys. Many of these questions invite collaborative effort among people from various disciplines.

What I have in mind are studies of the relationship among various realms of culture—state culture, urban high culture, folklife, "empire" or ethnic and frontier culture, revolutionary subculture, and urban popular entertainment—in, for example, imperial Russia. This inquiry into the relationship of all the major cultural streams should attempt to relate cultural institutions and artifacts to social identities. Although some of these realms have been studied in the past, there has been no attempt to look at them as a cultural system, an interlocking edifice of ideas, values, and images in which Russian people of all classes dwelled.

Urban high culture, certainly the best known of these, particularly in its literary production, was that of Europe introduced by Peter the Great in the eighteenth century, modified and enriched by Russian elements, and institutionalized in academies, philharmonic societies, theaters, urban salons, and on gentry estates. It was limited in consumption almost exclusively to the upper and upper middle classes in town and country. High culture ought to be studied as part of social history, which is a history of taste formation, expressiveness, the dynamics of audience as a community, the role of the arts in daily intercourse, the organizational side of cultural production and its politics, the power of elitism, its relationship to European models, and its overall function in the social identity and consciousness of those who made it and consumed it.

Let us take as a specific case the visual culture of the eighteenth century, adopted by Russia from Europe. Patrons and artists of that epoch made little or no distinction between "fine arts" (painting and architecture) and the so-called minor or decorative arts. Everything was decorative, and all the arts were integrated in whole ensembles. The most elaborate and luxurious of the palaces and manor houses were designed as complex but unified works of art in which painting, sculpture, architecture, landscaping, garden planning, furniture, interior decor, and objets d'art (faience, Meissen, chinoiserie, Gobelin tapestries, porcelain, tiles, marble) were coordinated and aligned, orchestrated like the timbres, notes, and chords of a piece of symphonic music. To this one must add costume, speech patterns, and choreographed and ritualized behavior and gestures that—seen against the visual backdrop—gave art its social meaning: the theatricalization of life. Traditional art history has tended to lift certain elements—especially the oil canvas—out of this artistic ensemble and to study it as a separate subject. But such a narrow and hierarchical approach to culture pulls one branch of art out of its living context, marks it as superior to all that surround it, and then presents Russian "art" as inferior to that of the West because only one of its component genres is held up for comparison.[4]

In turning to the art of the common people, folklore or folk culture, we run into a different problem. Historians of Russian fine art have often simply ignored its role in social life, while folklorists have more often claimed that their field of study takes us inside the peasant mentality. Like Maksim Gorky, whose famous utterances in the 1930s about folk literature marked the revival of recently deceased folklorism in the Soviet Union, they believe that the history of the Russian people is encoded in their folk culture. The well-known literary historian, William Harkins, recently misread the point of Gorky's statement in the preface to a new book on the subject by Frank Miller. Taking Gorky literally, Harkins states, correctly, that the historical epics associated with folk creativity (the epics and historical tales and poems) give a distorted and factually erroneous picture of the past. But what Gorky meant, I believe, is that the entire body of folk culture—folk ditties, songs, rituals, as well as the longer folk epics—contains an accumulated record of peasant attitudes that can be decoded through careful scholarship. The fact that even before Gorky died in 1936, the Stalinist use of folklore was transformed into "fakelore"—the artificial creation of government-sponsored propaganda couched in archaic and rustic formulas—does not change the validity of Gorky's comment and does not invalidate the effort of folklorists to unravel the inner life of the village world by examining its expressive modes.[5] I would note also that in studying the depth and scope of Josef Stalin's panegyric utopia, the analysis of posters, paintings, movies, busts, and parades glorifying and deifying the leader would gain much by adding the study of Soviet fakelore. It would show that pseudoculture gains in power of persuasion when framed in "authentic" forms.[6]

But even if one is skeptical about the utility of folklore as a source of peasant thought and feeling, there are other reasons for historians to engage it. The folklife of the vast peasant population, more ancient than all the rest, flourished largely independently of high culture until "discovered" in the early to mid-nineteenth century by intellectuals, ethnographers, and revolutionaries. These outsiders reacted in various ways to incorporate it into high culture, adapt it to urban entertainment, politicize it, or suppress it. The works of Pushkin and Nikolai Gogol, of Tchaikovsky, Borodin, and Rimsky-Korsakov cannot be fully understood outside the realm of folk motifs, and for some of them, many non-Russian motifs. Outdoor entertainment that played a great role in the public life of the urban masses and later indoor stage variations on it (*estrada*) drew freely from every level of cultural expression including that of the folk. Radical propagandists from the 1860s onward who sought the attention of workers and urbanized peasants were alive to the repertoires of folk songs and tales and tried to couch their populist, anarchist, or Marxist messages in a folkish idiom—a practice continued on through the Revolution.[7]

Finally, there were publicists of all political persuasions who looked upon folklore as the true expression of peasant life and precisely for that reason hoped to suppress it in the name of progress and European civilization. Their spiritual descendants were the antirural Bolsheviks who continued and escalated the assault on village culture in the 1920s until silenced by the prophets of Stalinist neofolklorism. Investigating the rescue operations on the remnants of folklife and folklore made by ethnologists and the assaults upon it by *Kulturträgers* and missionaries may take us beyond the brilliant work done by Richard Wortman on the psychological nexus between the populist intelligentsia and the common people and lead us further into the margins where overlapping, conflict, and social mimicry produced new forms of identity.[8]

The least studied of the rough categories I have suggested has been "empire" culture, where the Russian mainstream was reshaped by non-Russian ethnic elements, blossoming into frontier adventure, the poeticization of exotic lands, representations of empire, military iconography, the romance of the steppe, the imaging of Gypsies, cossacks, and "native peoples"—we as yet have no nondemeaning term for them—and the migration of all these elements from high to popular culture. All these topics can bring together the insights of historians, art historians, anthropologists, and literary scholars—to name just a few.[9]

Revolutionary subculture dated from the 1860s (or from the 1810s by Yury Lotman's reading of the Decembrists) and has had only fragmentary treatment by Soviet historians, who have largely idealized and heroized it but without examining its relation to the other cultures. It is interesting and revealing that nothing very much has been done about the cultural values and habits of nineteenth-century Russian revolutionaries except the obvious and endlessly repeated things about Nikolai Chernyshevsky, Nikolai Dobrolyubov, and others on literature.[10] What I have in mind is the study of revolutionary imagery, panegyric politics, radical emotionalism (as expressed for example in song), the culture of the underlife, and emerging atheist sensibilities. (Note that I do not treat religion as a separate aspect of culture in that it takes on vastly different ritualistic, devotional, and other forms depending on when and where it is examined.)

Urban popular entertainment became "modern" around 1900 with the import of technology (automobile, train, camera, cinema, gramophone, rotogravure presses) and soon outstripped in popularity almost all the rest. The new mass culture created with the help of the market and technology gave birth to new tastes, new notions of celebrity and fame, new ideas of ambition and hero worship, and a new cultural geography. One need not keep an eye constantly glued in the direction of

February 1917 to appreciate how much these innovations were modifying social relations and identities.[11]

Finally—but not necessarily most importantly—we come to political culture, including what Richard Wortman has called respectively, "legal culture" and "the scenarios of power"—political art, court ritual, dynastic style, and the mythology of the old regime. Out of the myriad studies of the Russian bureaucracy, monarchy, local administration, judicial procedures, and the doings of the State Duma and other bodies, one always gets a sense of a peculiar Russian manner of dealing with politics and statecraft. Perhaps a "cultural" approach to politics and institutions through the study of language, rhetoric, costume, gesture, artifacts, and chancery architecture can enlighten us further about the essence of the tsarist system and how it fit or did not fit into the other cultural systems of the vast empire.

In offering the preceding topics of study, my hope—a pedagogical agenda and research strategy for the profession—is that an integrated study of mutually interacting cultures within the nation can enrich our understanding of the whole society as well as bring once independently floating subjects into the mainstream of history.

Twentieth-Century Russia: Film and Music

In turning to the waning years of the tsarist period and the Soviet period with its aftermath, I wish to call attention to the pedagogical utility of the mass film or popular movie for historians and other scholars of Russian-Soviet culture and society. By focusing on cinema, I do not wish to abandon my belief in the importance of studying all the arts together in a given epoch (see my comments at the end of this section) but to speak concretely about movies as, arguably, the most influential of the popular arts in our century. The topic of film in the classroom is hardly new; panels have been talking for years about enriching courses through cinema and the other arts. But the practice has not yet reached many classrooms in Russian and Soviet history—to say nothing of literature or government—probably because the traditional method of using films has not proven very productive. In my observation during thirty years of teaching and talking to colleagues, that method has been usually to show the great classics of the silent screen from the 1920s and early 1930s—Sergei Eisenstein, V. I. Pudovkin, Dziga Vertov, and the others—and particularly revolutionary spectacles such as Eisenstein's *Battleship Potemkin* (*Brononosets Potemkin*, 1926), and films that seem to have direct political messages, such as the same director's *Alexander Nevsky* (1938), or, more recently, the jarring documentaries of the glasnost era. I hasten to add that great works of film art clearly have a place not only in the study of cinema culture but also in the history of cultural politics and aesthetic discourse. We will all continue to use them for appropriate purposes. And the value of "films of persuasion" or propaganda is self-evident.

I would argue, however, that such films are only marginally useful in understanding Russian-Soviet history and society. As recent Western scholarship has shown—and as the Soviet critics and the public have always known—the classics of Soviet cinema for the most part were not immensely "popular" either as huge box office successes or in expressing widely held values of the time.[12] This scholarship also shows that what people like in Russia is what they like almost everywhere and that what they liked in 1900 is what they still like in the 1990s—action, adventure, romance, melodrama, comedy—with of course plenty of local variation in time and place. Ideology and politics have had a much lower appeal, and artistic experiment even less—again with obvious exceptions. I might add here that the strict division between "art" or "serious" films on the one hand and entertainment movies on the other may be useful when gauging the intention of creators, but not for the final product in that both art and entertainment have produced shoddy films just as both have produced extremely good ones—quite apart from success in the market.

Extrapolating national or cultural values from popular movies is of course a problematic business filled with conceptual traps; it is not a simple operation, and we are far from a consensus about which values are actually reflected in or help shape popular culture. But the enterprise itself can reanimate some of those who are tired of the old conventions in using "film as history." Another reason for studying Soviet popular movies is that millions of Soviet people know and remember them, have felt deeply about them, and are more than willing to discuss them. This attachment rarely applies to the films of Eisenstein, Andrei Tarkovsky, Aleksandr Sokurov, and Tengiz Abuladze, which are justifiably treasured by the literati and intelligentsia—a tiny segment of the Soviet population.

Popular movies and popular culture in general can tell us more about a society in a given historical epoch than can works of high art. I hold no brief for abandoning high culture as a subject of study. On the contrary, it is essential to know it for its own sake as a precious treasury of a nation's creativity, as a counterforce and sometimes foe of the popular arts, and as their symbiotic partner. My purpose here is to suggest that popular movies can be made to speak to the student of history in the languages of their stories, acting styles, mise-en-scènes, and music in the cultural context of the era in which they were made and viewed.

Soviet popular movies are virtually unknown throughout the profession of Russian-Soviet studies. Part of the problem, of course, has been their relative unavailability compared to that of the classics for use in Western classrooms. But the birth of freedom in Russian cultural politics and the invention of the videotape and player have changed things dramatically. We are now able to introduce into our teaching the kinds of movies that have been genuinely popular for decades among Soviet people. To promote the pedagogical use and scholarly study of them, I will present a few brief remarks about the kinds of films that can be shown and the kinds of materials they contain that can be tied to historical themes—using the term "historical" in a wide sense. I will organize my remarks around four clusters of films and focus on a representative, only one of which (the second) is well-known outside the former USSR: *Be Still, My Grief* (*Molchi, grust, molchi*, 1918), *The Radiant Road* (*Svetlyi put* [also known as *Bright Path*], 1940), *Ivan Brovkin in the Virgin Lands* (*Ivan Brovkin tselinu*, 1956), and *Déjà vu* (*Dezha vyu*, 1989). The selection is limited and arbitrary, but it does range through the century and deals with several popular genres: salon melodrama, Stalinist fairy tale, the construction epic, and the gangster comedy. Each in its own way illustrates the possibilities of reading a film for the purposes of historical understanding. I can think of no other way to make my point clear than to discuss a few of these films in detail.

The prerevolutionary decade (1908–17) was one of civil violence and peasant disorder and of increasing urban crime and social misery, but also one of material progress—city tramcars, lavish restaurants, an influx of foreign culture, and an outpouring of popular culture that captivated mass audiences and challenged the traditional rule of fine arts and high culture. By 1910 Gypsy songs, nightclubs, the cabaret, music hall reviews, and a flood of detective and adventure stories and boulevard novels of sex and ambition dominated Russian urban entertainment. The cinema, born amid the swirl of the new popular culture, was a Moloch who consumed it all: folkloric themes and narrative styles, popular music, *estrada* (the popular stage), and fiction. The omnivorous pioneers of moviemaking would devour anything that would pull a film through a camera and tell a story. When ordinary materials ran out, they hired hacks to create scripts right on the set—exactly as was done on the meadows of Astoria and the backlots of Hollywood. The greed of the studio for profit was no greater than the greed of the public for more movies.[13]

The dominant genre—half of all films made—was the salon or "bourgeois" melodrama. Neya Zorkaya has analyzed a few hundred of these using a method resembling the classic work of the folklorist V.Ya. Propp, whose "morphology of the folktale" proclaimed the structural unity of all folktale plots. Most film melodramas bear the marks of standardized production—formulaic repetition, cardboard characters, psychological shallowness, and the absence of political content. Almost all are variants on a master plot about a "slave of passion" (the title of one of them). The idyllic life of a young girl, marred only by vague malaise, is disrupted by the appearance of a seducer; her passion for him gives way to disenchantment and, at the end, tragedy ensues (suicide, ruin, murder, vengeance). Several themes are linked constantly: money, power, leisure, boredom, the need for distraction, gambling and game playing among affluent men—the main game being seduction of a young and innocent woman. The conquered prey becomes a possession, a toy to be fondled for a while and then discarded. The victims are framed in a virtuous idyll—humble or opulent: in *Be Still, My Grief*, the poor doting wife of an aging alcoholic circus acrobat; in *Children of the Age* (*Deti veka*, 1915), the young mother, happily married to a poor bank clerk; in *A Life for a Life* (*Zhizn' za zhizn'*, 1916), two happy foster sisters. The victimizers dwell in obvious settings of social decadence: expensive parties, smoking, drinking, Gypsy entertainers.

These films are filled with social and sexual tension. The contrast between innocence constructed as poor or weak and evil constructed as rich and powerful is rendered by making urbane, cruel, and impeccably dressed matinee idols break the hearts and shatter the lives of beautiful women on screen. The female superstar, Vera Kholodnaya, appeared regularly as their victim. The former dancer with the sad, gray eyes animated the celluloid world she dwelled in, a world of tainted money, opulent restaurants, champagne picnics, luxury autos careening through the night, and illicit love ending in tragedy. Of the Kholodnaya pictures, *Be Still, My Grief*, directed by Petr Chardynin, was the last of the salon psychological melodramas, a ten-year anniversary film celebrating the birth of Russian cinema and—as critics noted—a reunion of all its clichés.[14] Chardynin played Lorio, the pitiful alcoholic circus clown whose physical injury is compounded by the loss of his wife. Circus—a popular theme in movies up into the 1930s—is here a symbol of the poverty and vulnerability of entertainment figures to the allure of money and the ruthlessness of the upper classes. Kholodnaya plays Pola, the young wife who is seduced by the charms of luxurious parties and attentive men and then destroyed. The process of decay is accompanied by the then-popular title song played on violin and guitar by the begging couple (unheard by modern ears, but generally performed live in the old movie houses).

Bolshevik officials and filmmakers detested films like *Be Still, My Grief* as frothy and unserious, attuned to the decadent leisure postures of the upper class, catering to the base instincts of man, paying excessive attention to sex, violence, and crime, lacking in moral uplift and correct political content, generally uneducational, and rooted in the search for profits. Like most elites, the Bolsheviks feared that "dark forces" dormant among the lower classes could be evoked by sitting in the darkened chamber of the commercial cinema. The Bolshevik critics also hated its "theateritis": the cinematography (called "Khanzhonkovism" by later filmmakers) of long takes, intermediate shots, and a stationary camera; and the acting style called "Delsartism," a repertory of exaggerated poses and gestures coded to emotions developed on the stage by the nineteenth-century Frenchman François Delsarte and taken into popular melodrama and then films. It was against this art that many of the great film masters of the revolution rebelled. But it was precisely this sort of entertainment film that the masses rushed to see before the revolution—and after it. In late 1921 when the first private movie house under the New Economic Policy opened its doors on Tverskaya Street, it showed *Be Still, My Grief* from morning to night to full houses. With the recent showings in Europe and the United States of prerevolutionary film, we now know that some of these films were masterpieces of cinematic art.[15]

It is more than probable that widely shown films like *Be Still, My Grief* generated angry feelings toward the upper classes. Hatred and collective indignation can be engendered by the popular media; war films alone are proof of this. If hostility already festers, it can be reinforced by a cultural product that tells viewers that the makers of the movie and the public share their feelings about social morality and its outward affects—raiment, scenery, and manners. It is no wonder that slicked hair and bowler hats, prime emblems of the slimy cinematic seducers, were angrily rejected, satirized, and even assaulted under the new Soviet regime. The privileging of classical motifs in architecture and furnishing in the mise-en-scène of the P. I. Chardynin and Evgenii Bauer films—classical busts, statuettes, columns, cornices, Grecian urns—were meant to signify perfection, beauty, and aesthetic honesty and to provide ironic contrast to the degraded values of their owners. But to the masses they may have been simply the emblems of excessive and needless luxury of the owning classes. These images may have deepened the "vandalistic" behavior of the riotous urban lower classes in 1917–18.[16] Thus the "bourgeois" films of the prerevolutionary era, while catering to mass tastes, in a sense helped feed radicalism; and the Bolsheviks thus owed the great movie tycoons a debt of gratitude for their unintentional assistance. In any event, films like *Be Still, My Grief* can enliven and even illuminate a whole range of discussions on topics such as new versus old art, Bolshevik censorship policies, the relationship between film and audience, and the role and function of architecture and decor in the old regime.[17]

The Radiant Road (released in a cut version in the United States as *Tanya*), the product of a wholly different cultural matrix, is the pinnacle of social and political fantasy in prewar Stalinist cinema.[18] It was the last in a series of stunningly successful and long-remembered prewar musical comedies starring Lyubov Orlova, directed by her husband Grigory Alexandrov, and with music by the master mass-song composer of the era, Isaac Dunaevsky—*Happy-Go-Lucky Guys* (*Veselye rebyata*, 1934), *Circus* (*Tsirk*, 1936), and *Volga, Volga* (1938). They offered a winning recipe of patriotism, cornball sentiment, spectacular cinematic effects, singable tunes, and celebration of the new Moscow. Forming the intriguing political-cultural context of these films were the easing up of the social mood in 1933–34, the sharpening of tension in 1935–36, the outward sloganizing of a "happy life," the murderous purges of 1936–38, the ascendance of the Stakhanovite mythology of production, the cultural representation of economic achievements and urban construction, and—twisting around all these—the spasmodic reordering of jazz and light music and the national campaigns to legitimize and foster a mass movement of amateur and folk culture.

In *Radiant Road*, the heroine Tanya (Orlova), a classical Cinderella with a smudged nose, rises through the textile industry to become a Stakhanovite superworker who can run hundreds of looms simultaneously and beat world records. Along the way, Tanya learns her letters and wins the love of a clean-cut engineer—a Soviet prince charming with a pipe and a briefcase. She makes the dreamed-of pilgrimage to Moscow and is decorated by the "peasant" President Kalinin in an opulent Kremlin palace. The finale contains a splendid visual treatment of the just-completed Agricultural Exhibition in Moscow, whose Central Pavilion resembled a castle. In one of the final shots the living couple is foregrounded in front of Vera Mukhina's statue of the male industrial worker, hammer in hand, and the female agricultural worker, sickle in hand—thus proclaiming gender equality and simultaneously assuring the male engineer the dominant role in this "equal" partnership.[19]

The movie asserts constantly that this plot is real life and not a fairy tale. In the finale, a chorus sings the aviation song "Ever Higher" (a colossal hit of the 1930s), which opens with the words: "We are born to make fairy tales come true." Indeed the film is roughly modeled on the rise of the then-famous female Stakhanovites, Evdokiya and Mariya

Vinogradova,[20] and Orlova studied intensively on the mill floor to prepare herself for the exploits she performed on screen. Orlova plays the victorious plebeian, as she had in *Happy-Go-Lucky Guys* and in *Volga, Volga*. Social mobility through the Soviet system, a breakthrough to "consciousness" with the help of a mentor (in this case, a female schoolteacher), and triumph over a languid bureaucrat—all the ingredients of socialist realism are present. But Alexandrov and his associates rise above the usual drabness of the master plot by use of the fantastic mise-en-scène at the conclusion, where monumental structure is framed by dream-filled billows in the sky. The uncut original (which I have not seen) has an automobile flying over the rooftops of Moscow![21] The fusion of the traditional fairy tale with metallic and mechanical furniture of modernity and with the official scenario for success accounts for the immense popular triumph of this movie—designed for and consumed by "the millions."

The Alexandrov-Orlova-Dunaevsky films can be analyzed and taught as stories of social mobility, as political mystification, as gender construction, or as musical entertainment—they were all of these. But one of the "stars" of these movies was Moscow, specifically the new Moscow construction that was represented as heroic and populist in the media. It is often argued that Stalinist architecture's celebration of state grandeur was only meant to underline the insignificance of the citizen on the street. But when a provincial woman in Moscow first gazed upon the newly finished Hotel Moskva—filmed from every angle in *Circus*—she exclaimed, "I do not know if this is a hotel or a fairy tale palace." Similarly the harbor building (or River Station) on the Moscow River, built to punctuate the completion of the Volga-Moscow canal, was meant to extend a dignified but warm welcome from the capital to newly arriving passengers from the hinterland. One of the final scenes of *Volga, Volga* shows the beautiful steamer *Josef Stalin* docked alongside this gleaming, white-columned edifice whose staircase leads up to the capital where the heroes find success and instant popularity for their amateur music.

In August 1939 the massive Agricultural Exhibition opened in Moscow and was visited by as many as twenty to thirty thousand people a day. It was a fairyland—in many ways resembling its contemporary, the New York World's Fair, in opulence and monumentality, with its domes, gothic buildings, fountains, broad walkways, a giant statue of Stalin, and the huge Mukhina ensemble.[22] These and other examples of Soviet construction and decor were deployed in the films of the 1930s not to depress and not only to impress but to enliven and animate the viewer with self-esteem and communal pride. Architecture and decor in these industrial melodramas have exactly the opposite function from what they had in the old regime melodramas: they are the status symbols of the upwardly mobile proletariat.

Ivan Brovkin in the Virgin Lands is a rustic musical that, aside from being a marvelous hour-and-a-half entertainment, summarizes and resolves several themes in the history of Soviet popular movies and marks a turning point in cultural history. It draws on two lines of scenic backdrop and social mood: the epic and the idyll. The epic of construction, a major theme in all genres of popular culture since 1917, but especially since 1928, romanticized physical labor, manual toil, and the realia of machinery against a backdrop of wilderness. During the Civil War, building something fast—such as a railroad—took on epic proportions, a fact celebrated with gorgeous cinematography in A. A. Alov and V. N. Naumov's *Pavel Korchagin* (1955), the best screen version of Aleksandr Ostrovsky's notorious novel *How the Steel Was Tempered*. In the first full sound film, Nikolai Ekk showed another example of railroad as salvation in the *Start in Life* (*Putevka v zhizn*, also known as *Road to Life*, 1931), about orphan boys in the 1920s. In the 1930s Sergei Gerasimov's *Komsomolsk* (1938), offered a camera study of deforestation and town building in the Soviet Far East. In these pictures, the act of cutting down and building up is endowed with a special pathos and poetics that proved irresistible over the decades and whose cinematographic style was incorporated into the wartime epic.

The idyll came later. In the 1920s, village life was often ridiculed in the popular arts. Folk dances, songs, and costumes were depicted as the archaic trappings of roach- and god-infested worlds of darkness— the great exception to this image of course being the work of Aleksandr Dovzhenko. But after collectivization, the new kolkhoz was romanticized as a confluence of the new and the best of the old—bicycles and hospitality, tractors and head scarves, brigades and peasant fertility. This theme blossomed in folk dance ensembles, paintings, operettas, novels, and films in the 1930s and 1940s and reached its apogee in Ivan Pyrev's famous *Kuban Cossacks* (*Kubanskie kazaki*, 1949), a cinematic kolkhoz operetta and a classic of the glossy, "conflictless" films of the late Stalin era. When tension between new and old was treated, the new was always vindicated—as in the most famous example, *Cavalier of the Golden Star*, a novel, an operetta, and Yuly Raizman's 1950 film starring Sergei Bondarchuk in one of his most wooden performances.

Ivan Brovkin was made in the midst of Nikita Khrushchev's Virgin Lands campaign, a drive to cultivate large tracts of land in the steppe between the Urals, the Caspian, and Siberia and in the Northern Kazakhstan. Although made only a few years after *Cavalier*, it gave the conflict a new resolution by treating the old village and the new sovkhoz equally. The former is symbolized by rural folkways, stubborn elders, and a bride who refuses to join her man on the cultivation sites beyond Orenburg. But this standard symbolic characterization—almost identical to that in *Cavalier*—is deployed with great tact and delicacy. The old village is captured in beautifully framed color shots resembling the picture postcards of rustic life that were mass-produced before the Revolution; and it is drenched in the sounds of lovely music of the popular songwriter, Anatoly Lepin. Out on the steppe, modernity springs forth from a semidesert under the hands and brains of the hero, his wise and kindly mentor, and a crew of young, idealistic, ethnically varied komsomols who tear open the earth and careen upon it in their iron victory chariots in a civic version of savage joy. The domestic scenes of gathering, home building, and planning are done in the painterly fashion of Stalinist socialist realism.

The marriage of epic and idyll is celebrated at many levels: the wedding scene that choreographs the disorderly and energetic folk dancing along a ruler-straight street laid out on the steppe; the accordions and birch twigs on the nuptial automobile; the return of the hero to claim his bride and their journey back to the steppe on a train. The director authenticates his movie with a direct quotation from the famous potato tactics scene in *Chapaev* (1934), here having Brovkin showing his sovkhoz chairman how tractors can be deployed more effectively. Brovkin (played by Leonid Kharitonov) is a younger, more vigorous, more credible version of Bondarchuk's cavalier of the golden star, and his triumph more humane. *Ivan Brovkin* is a proclamation of moral equality and coexistence between kolkhoz life, with all the cultural baggage it retained after collectivization, and new sovkhoz life with its clean bathrooms and electric light. The film illuminates that moment in Soviet history between the relentless Stalinist exaltation of new over old that prevailed from 1928 until the mid-1950s and the exaltation of traditional village values that has been under way for thirty years and more in the words of village prose writers, filmmakers, and intellectuals of many kinds.

The reader will note that I have ignored the obvious historical aspects of this film. One is its glossy treatment of the genuine hardships and shortcomings of the Virgin Lands campaign that were generally known then and have since been well documented; even the sugary memoirs of one of its chief organizers, Leonid Brezhnev, reveal more reality than does this film.[23] The lack of amenities, the ferocious blizzards that enveloped the steppe and snuffed out the lives of the unsuspecting; the surliness of the locals; the inability of Soviet plowshares to carve open the root-entangled sward of the ancient grassland—all are missing in the film. The other historical aspect is its obvious design as a mobilizing agent to recruit needed youth—particularly women and physicians (combined in one character in the movie as in real Soviet life)—out to the Virgin Lands. In this *Brovkin* resembles the great construction epics of the 1930s, both documentary and fiction films. What could be more obvious than either of these points? Frontiering and construction invite romanticism in cinematic treatment; they make for fun, "profit," and good ideology. The American boomtown, railroad, and oil field epics of the 1930s are hardly different in this regard.

At the present juncture in film history, we are faced with flux and the unpredictable. One of the main themes of agonizing debate among Soviet filmmakers is commercialism or "Hollywoodism" and its natural offspring: romance, adventure, sex, violence, crime, and all the rest. In the midst of this debate, and a clear product of the free atmosphere of glasnost, appeared the gangster-comedy film, *Déjà vu*. A direct instance of *amerikanizm* in movies, *Déjà vu* is a hilarious Odessa Studio production set in 1925 and advertised as having "American-style action." The plot of this manic parody of the gangster film—which recalls the cinematic gifts of Billy Wilder—revolves around a Chicago Prohibition war and a Polish-American hit man sent to Odessa to wipe out an informer. The foolery explodes in the shameless quotations from old James Cagney films (very popular in Russia in the 1940s), from *The Godfather*, and from *Potemkin* (the shooting of Eisenstein's staircase scene is woven into the chase), and the reactions of foreigners to Soviet life in the 1920s, elements of which still linger to this day, particularly in tourist hotels. The large audience at the Coliseum in Leningrad (where I viewed it in early 1990) never stopped laughing and almost convulsed at the shot of a mafioso with a Civil War machine gun pointed through a loft window—a direct quotation from *Chapaev*. The lurid depiction of the Odessa criminal underworld of bootlegging, American jazz, and sex during the New Economic Policy is an affectionate reminder of another age, a sharp commentary on the kingdoms of illegality that were flourishing in the USSR in 1989 (and still are), and a sidesplitting mockery of everything Soviet and communist in the early days of the Revolution.

Déjà vu seems to herald a new era or a return to the old era of I. A. Ilf and Evgenii Petrov. If Soviet filmmakers and audiences are capable of laughing at gangsters, they are also capable of taking them seriously—which none has yet done. The makers of *Déjà vu* are, in a sense, outsiders: the director, Juliusz Michulski, is a Pole; the film was made in Odessa—that once fertile and febrile pool of Jewish comedy, musical, and cinematic talent (comedians Mikhail Zhvanetsky and Vladimir Khenkin, band leader Leonid Utesov, songwriter Oskar Feltsman, director Mark Donskoy, among others). But "outsiders" have always gotten inside the cultural center and reshaped it and themselves. Students of Russian life will certainly learn more from films openly catering to the public taste than they will from the anti-Stalinist revisionist documentaries—some of them truly masterful as art—that have come to our shores in an endless stream.

These few remarks are meant to suggest that even artless films can quicken the art of historians and enlarge their vision. Although I have formed my remarks around four titles, I do not believe that textual analysis of individual films is the only or even the most fruitful device for the cultural historian. To understand society, people, institutions, mentalities, and identities in any given epoch—and then to explain how they change in a subsequent epoch—one might take a body of films on any given theme over a long period or a more varied body within a manageable period. In doing so, one has to come armed not only with a knowledge of history and cinema but of popular culture as well—songs, stories, myths, legends, cults; performing arts such as circus, cabaret, and variety stage (*estrada*); customs, gestures, and jokes. These are the treasury of symbols and codes, the keys to the value systems of those who create and consume them. Movies and the popular culture they encapsulate may not answer questions directly, but they are sure to generate many new ones heretofore unasked. It is not too extravagant to say that all of Soviet history could be rewritten and retaught on the basis of cinema and the other arts in order to uncover national moods and feelings. Those literary and high culture scholars who have looked upon Soviet culture as a vast wasteland might even discover in it something of value; and traditional Kremlinologists might even find in the history of Soviet people something other than robotic subjects of a despotic state.

Let me now turn briefly to music, the most neglected of all arts in terms of integrating it with other matters. The neglect has sometimes been based on ignorance of or indifference to music, but more often I suspect on the belief that music is apolitical and cannot be tied to historical-social phenomena. But even if one does not share Plato's belief in the ominous influence of certain kinds of music over the emotions and minds of the Republic's citizens, one can hardly deny that music and politics intersected many times in the Soviet period of Russian history and not just in the occasional political abuse of certain classical composers (the cases of Vano Muradelli, Dmitry Shostakovich, and Sergei Prokofiev are the best known). Political leaders who claimed to represent the moral concerns and artistic tastes and interests of the masses have brought under their scrutiny music of every sort: folk, popular, jazz, prerevolutionary, foreign, classical, and rock.[24] But there is more to it than direct political meddling; entire national moods can be shaped by and reflected in music, especially popular music.

In the United States, for example, scholars and listeners both know that the whole emotional structure of popular song changed drastically and permanently around 1940–41 with the onset of the war in Europe and then in the Pacific. As proof, one may examine the music of Richard Rodgers first in partnership with Lorenz Hart in the 1930s and then with Oscar Hammerstein in the 1940s. Anyone who has even an inkling of this body of music knows at once that the change in tone was fundamental—though few people noticed it at the time. The Rodgers and Hart team in the decade of depression and recovery had produced a corpus of sophisticated, bubbly, ironic—and eminently danceable—music. It went to the head like Cole Porter's bubbles in a glass of champagne; it moved the dancing parts of the body rather than the heart. It was sassy and irreverent and belonged in spirit to the music of the preceding decade. It was not "singing" music: the lyrics of Hart were too clever and "hip" and the melody line of Rodgers relatively complex. The lyrics of his later collaborator Hammerstein, on the other hand, were eminently singable, emotional, and accessible—and Rodgers's music fit the bill perfectly.

Can a war, or a similarly potent moment in national experience, effect such a shift in popular art and in popular taste? In this question we have the key to relationship of art to life. Many scholars have tried to tie art to the other modulations of history—social change, economic development, migration, even revolution. One of the most famous of these is the study by Arnold Hauser on *The Social History of Art*.[25] But his book, though rich in detail and adventurous in conception, is ultimately reductionist since it grounds major changes in artistic sensibility in the relations of production—in other words, in narrow Marxist categories. It is not a work to be dismissed because, although Hauser's answers may not satisfy, his questions are brave and relevant. Also, it cannot be denied that social and economic change—however effected—can have a profound impact upon cultural expression. Yet it is the sudden and profound political change—revolution and war for example—that really registers a modification in popular moods, and thus in culture and art. One can hardly deny that the 1790s in France witnessed a shift in artistic styles in almost every genre and every art. At the same time one must recognize that the classical revival of the mid-eighteenth century was continued, however politicized, by the great revolutionary painters and festival managers of the French Revolution.

The Bolshevik Revolution was exceptionally self-conscious in terms of its artistic expression, and its cultural history is well known. It generated a big musical war in the 1920s and early 1930s between pure "proletarian" composers, who wanted to banish every trace of popular commercialism from song, and ordinary consumers who wanted rhythm, fun, and pathos in their songs and dances. In the 1930s, Stalin's cultural managers ended this war by an eclectic and synthetic compromise: dance and novelty tunes were permitted but not sponsored; revolutionary songs would continue to offer the pathos of struggle and sacrifice; and a new genre of "mass song" would provide the joyful element. But the joy had to be collective, optimistic, and patriotic. Hundreds of sunny upbeat marches and songs were produced by the mass composers for young communists, children, shock workers, the military, tractor drivers, and every other community that was actively helping to build socialism. "March of the Happy-Go-Lucky Guys" was written for the Komsomol in 1934; "March of the Enthusiasts" accompanied the five-year plans. The biggest nonmovie hit was Matvei Blanter's "Katyusha" (1938), destined to achieve world fame during the war. The rocket mortar invented by A. G. Kostikov and first used in the Russo-Finnish War of 1939 was named after this song. Mass songs saturated the airwaves, film soundtracks, the stages, and the public parks; they were performed in solo, by dance bands, and by huge orchestras and choirs.

A Soviet Tin-Pan Alley composed of songwriters—mostly Jewish, many from Odessa—was assembled to produce mass songs in large numbers. Its acknowledged king was Isaac Dunaevsky, a legendary figure in the history of popular music in the USSR. Dunaevsky became the major mass song writer of the 1930s and 1940s and produced hundreds of songs until his death in 1955. He was also highly paid and honored throughout the country. A key to his success was precisely his lack of profundity or originality. His compositions, especially the film tunes, were (and still are) undeniably appealing, and they became enormous national hits in the 1930s. As mentioned above, he was the musical genius behind the great Alexandrov-Orlova musicals of that decade. *Happy-Go-Lucky Guys* launched Dunaevsky's famous "heart" into the hearts of millions, many of whom recognize it at once a half-century later. His songs from *Circus* were given massive distribution, and long before the movie reached the provinces radio listeners were singing them as if they were folk songs. The theme "Song of the Motherland" attained such stupendous popularity that it became the station signal of Radio Moscow for many years and was played on the Kremlin chimes until the 1950s. In the words of a former Soviet citizen, the music from *Circus* "helped stifle the shots that killed several generations of revolutionaries, it masked Stalin's ruthlessness and Great Russian chauvinism, and it presented to the world the benign face of an idealistic socialist state on the march."[26] At the same time it entertained millions of ordinary people.

But almost imperceptibly—first in the war years and then in the postwar era—Dunaevsky's popularity began to fade. Folk music rose into ascendance, heavily financed by the regime but also eagerly desired by the masses. On the urban scene, an idyllic, sentimental style of popular song rose as well, displacing the more urbane, town-anchored styles of the 1930s. The new force in popular music, Vasily Solovev-Sedoi, composed "Evenings Near Moscow" (known abroad as "Moscow Nights"), an elegiac celebration not of collectivized peasants, marching youth, or resolute Stakhanovites, but of innocent young lovers fondly courting in the forests outside the capital. Writers continued to compose songs of cities, but their works lacked the urban bite of earlier times, and none could compare to the popularity of Solovev-Sedoi's hit song. When its opening bars replaced those of Dunaevsky's in the Kremlin chimes, they signaled something about the burgeoning domestication and personalization of the revolution, the calming of energies, the privatization of life, and the curious shifting of gaze from the proletarian factories to the "woods outside Moscow" and to the great world of the Russian countryside beyond, a phenomenon that was matched in the emerging literary genre of "village prose."

Thus one of the effects of the great war was to make the personal a part of the national struggle, to establish a tie between historic Russia, its rural roots, and patriotism, and to legitimize private emotion. In doing so, the war fostered the sentimentalization of urban popular song and valorized country and folk music as an authentic expression of "the people" in a fashion that almost paralleled what happened in the United States at the same time. If the content and style of the American products differed clearly from the Russian (a difference arising not only from local cultural roots but also from the divergent experiences of the two nations in the war years), the shift in national mood was strikingly similar.

The National Republics and the Socialist States

What is needed for the ethnic minorities, constituent republics, and newly independent Russian states are separate, parallel studies of their cultural history to include (1) the high cultural, intellectual, religious, and spiritual traditions, including folklore and legend as well as ecclesiastical and theological history and that of popular devotion; (2) the deeply rooted and still surviving customs of everyday life and behavior, including family, gender, codes of honor, and work habits; and (3) the dominant modes of popular entertainment and use of leisure time, including socializing, reading, performance styles and attendance, radio and television, rituals and public ceremonies, styles of political discourse and interaction. These studies should be rooted in the pre-revolutionary past and move through the Soviet period with an eye as to what was truly indigenous, what was imported or imposed, and what was adapted from the dominant culture (Russian) and from neighboring cultures as well. And scholars should be alert to the fact that "adapted" or syncretic forms of culture—however unauthentic they may appear—can be an important, even dominant part of people's lives.

The cultural history of Eastern Europe has been particularly disserved. Is there any work that addresses the high, folk, and urban popular cultures of the Slavic, Magyar, Romanian, Baltic, and other peoples of this region in modern times; that analyzes the role of Gypsy music, coffeehouses, operetta, folk ensembles, Jewish storytelling styles, or a dozen other elements that were a visible and audible part of the environment; or that tells us how these elements were dealt with under the communist regimes; or about Sovietization and even Russification of certain cultural practices in the region? What could enliven more the history of this culturally rich and diverse region than to go beyond (though never omit) the details of anti-Titoism, collectivization and decollectivization, reform, repression, and power struggles of the era and delve into the politics and texture of culture at every level?

Conclusions

In the Chinese idiom, I am "throwing out a brick in order to attract jade," that is, laying out some rough and crude positions in the hope that others will refine them through experience and dialogue. But here I want to stress my insistence that reform does not necessarily entail the deletion or abolition of the things we have been doing up to now. It is rather an appeal to all the disciplines to address issues that often fall between the cracks because of the traditional and legitimate interests of our own fields; to work for inclusion of cultural expression and social behavior—including politics—into a unified discourse; to add new things to those we are already engaged in; to rethink those distressing geological (and ideological) faults that divide "old-fashioned" history from the new social history, highbrow from lowbrow, literature from the "other arts." I believe that this expansion can be accomplished by turning in the following directions:

1. Increasing the number of courses on "Russian civilization" and enlarging their scope by including all the arts (high and popular) in more or less equal measure, offering a sociology of taste by showing which genres appealed to which strata of society—and why—and explaining what political significance they had in various epochs of Russian history.

2. Encouraging research at all levels on the relationship between culture and other aspects of people's lives through direction of graduate theses and dissertations and the teaching of seminars and colloquia. Publishers have a nose for new research directions and can be pushed in those directions. Scholarly conferences in general and the AAASS in particular ought to encourage this agenda in its program committees; and it certainly ought to be more responsive to those scholars who wish to use video projectors and other audiovisual devices in their presentations.

3. Emphasizing oral as well as reading fluency in Russian in history and other fields outside literature and language. I should confess a strong bias here that I have developed after sitting on several granting bodies—a bias against those economists, political scientists, and other social scientists who believe that the languages and methods of their disciplines are a kind of Esperanto that can unlock crucial knowledge about any society without knowing a word of the actual language used in that society.

4. Amplifying the study of languages of the other republics and nationalities of the area. This amplification will not happen in our universities as long as the weight of research is in countable and standardized categories such as budgets, demography, or weapons systems. Scholars of such matters can convincingly argue (and have done so successfully) that the local language is not really essential—even though, ironically, the very best of them do take language seriously. Once local cultures are seen to be important in subcutaneous understanding of a society, study of the languages will automatically follow.

5. Multiplying by many factors our use of "media" in the classroom: art, music, cinema, and television. As I indicated above, the flowering of video culture among the general population here and in Russia, the unprecedented accessibility of musical cassettes, video, and film from Russia, and the recent interest by journals in reviewing

such material in addition to traditional book reviews have enhanced our awareness of the materials at hand. Now is the time to put them to use.[27]

6. Building on present curricula and disciplines, such as literature, history, and political science, by incorporating—perhaps modestly at first—elements of cultural life and cultural history through film, slides, readings, music, videos of performance art, always in conjunction with the familiar and traditional artifacts of one's own discipline. Let me give one more concrete example: one can now expand the parameters of teaching Aleksandr Pushkin's *Queen of Spades*, a remarkable literary classic of the early nineteenth century, by following up on a close reading and textual analysis of the story with listening to Piotr Ilich Tchaikovsky's opera and its libretto by his brother to examine the adaptations (or distortions) of the original, taking a critical look at Alexander Benois's illustrations for the 1905 edition of that work (and many other graphic examples are available as well), and then viewing two films, Chardynin's 1910 ten-minute version (closer to the opera), and Yakov Protazanov's forty-five minute version, more faithful to Pushkin. Both the films mentioned are now available on affordable videocassettes.[28]

One could enumerate hundreds of ways to integrate cultural matters and methods into other disciplines, especially but not only history. The problem is communicating them to the profession in a systematic and organized way. Two such enterprises in recent years have been extraordinarily successful. One was the series of Summer Seminars on Contemporary Literature and Popular Culture sponsored by the SSRC and led by Nancy Condee, Vladimir Padunov, Edward Brown, and Katerina Clark. They were held at American universities and in Russian centers and included graduate students and faculty from both nations. The other, sponsored by the National Endowment for the Humanities, was a Summer Institute on Art and Artifact in Russian History, led by George Munro and Alison Hilton at the Hermitage and the Russian Museum in the summer of 1992. The students were twenty-five to thirty American professors of various disciplines, with four American professors and a staff of Russian curators, restorers, archaeologists, historians, and art historians. More of these seminars are in the making. Catherine Evtuhov and Boris Gasparov held a two-week seminar in Smolensk (1993) and Kazan (1994) for twenty American and twenty Russian participants as part of a four-year program on Russian Culture and History in various mid-sized Russian cities and towns. The virtue of such programs is that they include a dominant element of cultural study and that they are held in the country being studied. How can we generate more of them? How can we energize the profession to take culture seriously?

Culture and social science have for too long dwelt in separate houses. The task of bringing them closer together must fall to history and literature, the disciplines in Russian studies with the broadest ambit, the most imagination, the longest experience, the heaviest demographic weight in the profession—though not perhaps the equivalent power and influence. Our job will be to open our eyes and ears, as well as our minds, to the images and sounds of the past and the present and then to reach out to other fields and to each other.

Notes

The epigraph, from Morroe Berger, is quoted in Edward Said, *Orientalism* (New York: Pantheon Books, 1978), 288.

[1]For exceptions see Gerald Smith, *Songs to Seven Strings* (Bloomington: Indiana University Press, 1984); S. F. Starr, *Red and Hot: The Fate of Jazz in the Soviet Union* (New York: Oxford University Press, 1983); Jeffrey Brooks, *When Russia Learned to Read* (Princeton: Princeton University Press, 1985); Richard Stites, *Russian Popular Culture: Entertainment and Society since 1900* (Cambridge: Cambridge University Press, 1992); and the works on fiction and society by Katerina Clark, *The Soviet Novel: History as Ritual* (Chicago: University of Chicago Press, 1981); Vera Dunham, *In Stalin's Time: Middleclass Values in Soviet Fiction* (Cambridge: Cambridge University Press, 1976); Hans Guenther, ed., *The Culture of the Stalin Period* (New York: St. Martin's Press, 1990); Régine Robin, *Socialist Realism: An Impossible Aesthetic* (Stanford: Stanford University Press, 1992); William Mills Todd, ed., *Literature and Society in Imperial Russia* (Stanford: Stanford University Press, 1978); and on cinema by Peter Kenez, *Cinema and Soviet Society, 1917–1953* (Cambridge: Cambridge University Press, 1992); Anna Lawton, *Kinoglasnost: Soviet Cinema in Our Time* (Cambridge: Cambridge University Press, 1992); Richard Taylor, *The Politics of Soviet Cinema, 1917–1929* (Cambridge: Cambridge University Press, 1979); Denise Youngblood, *Movies for the Millions: Popular Cinema and Society in the 1920s* (Cambridge: Cambridge University Press, 1992).

[2]There are, of course, various works that recognize the relationships among the arts in a given time, such as Theofanis Stavrou, ed., *Art and Culture in Nineteenth Century Russia* (Bloomington: Indiana University Press, 1983), but this is a multiauthored anthology spanning a whole century. The one single-authored example, James Billington, *The Icon and the Axe* (New York: Knopf, 1961), takes on all of Russian history and can offer no more than speculative, though stimulating, sketches from crucial periods of exceptional creativity.

[3]Siegfried Kracauer, *From Caligari to Hitler: The Psychological History of the German Film* (1947; Princeton: Princeton University Press, 1974). See also Peter Gay, *Weimar Culture: The Outsider as Insider* (New York: Harper and Row, 1968); Walter Laqueur, *Weimar* (New York: Putman, 1975).

[4]For alternate ways of looking at cultural production and settings, see Richard Wort-

man, *Scenarios of Power*, vol. 1 (Princeton: Princeton University Press, forthcoming); Stephen Baehr, *The Paradise Myth in Eighteenth Century Russia* (New Haven: Yale University Press, 1991); Priscilla Roosevelt, *The Culture of the Gentry Estate in Russia* (New Haven: Yale University Press, forthcoming); and James von Geldern, *Bolshevik Festivals* (Berkeley: University of California Press, 1993).

⁵For William Harkins's comments, see his preface to Frank Miller, *Folklore for Stalin: Russian Folklore and Pseudofolklore of the Stalin Era* (Armonk, N.Y.: M. E. Sharpe, 1990), ix. For an example of a historian—who has of course been challenged—using folk culture as a historical source, see Maureen Perrie, "Folklore as Evidence of Peasant Mentalité," *Russian Review* 48, no. 2 (1989): 119–43. Among the problems presented by the use of folklore are the great variations in time and place, the notorious difficulty in dating any particular version of a work, its fluid character as an oral tradition, and the ever-lurking problem of peasant irony and masking.

⁶Miller, *Folklore for Stalin*; Felix Oinas, ed., *Folklore, Nationalism, and Politics* (Columbus: Slavica, 1972); Eric Hobsbawm and Terence Ranger, *The Invention of Tradition* (Cambridge: Cambridge University Press, 1983). See also the recent fascinating article by the film scholar, Mikhail Yampolsky, "The Rhetoric of Representation of Political Leaders in Soviet Culture," *Elementa* 1, no. 1 (1993): 101–13.

⁷For three different perspectives on urban-rural cultural interaction, see Alison Hilton, *Russian Folk Culture* (Bloomington: Indiana University Press, forthcoming), Catriona Kelly, *Petrushka* (Cambridge: Cambridge University Press, 1989); Deborah Pearl, *Educating Workers for the Revolution* (Berkeley: University of California Press, forthcoming).

⁸Richard Wortman, *The Crisis of Russian Populism* (Cambridge: Cambridge University Press, 1967).

⁹A beginning has been made by Michael Khodarkovsky, *When Two Worlds Met* (Ithaca: Cornell University Press, 1992), a study of the Kalmyk frontier in early modern Russia. See also Thomas Barrett, "The Remaking of the Lion of Dagestan: Shamil in Captivity," *Russian Review* 53, no. 3 (July 1994): 353–66.

¹⁰Iurii Lotman et al., *The Semiotics of Russian Cultural History* (Ithaca: Cornell University Press, 1985). A brilliant and notable exception is Irina Paperno, *Chernyshevsky and the Age of Realism: A Study in the Semiotics of Behavior* (Stanford: Stanford University Press, 1988).

¹¹Louise McReynolds, *The News under Russia's Old Regime* (Princeton: Princeton University Press, 1992); Stites, *Russian Popular Culture*, chap. 1; Stephen Frank and Mark Steinberg, eds., *Cultures in Flux: Lower-class Values, Practices, and Resistance in Late Imperial Russia* (Princeton: Princeton University Press, 1994). Forthcoming is Hubertus Jahn, *Patriotic Culture in Russia during World War I*.

¹²Taylor, *The Politics of Soviet Cinema*; Youngblood, *Movies for the Millions*; Youngblood, *Soviet Cinema in the Silent Era* (Ann Arbor: UMI Research Press, 1985); Kenez, *Cinema and Soviet Society*. These books are excellent guides to popular films up to 1953. There is no comparable work as yet on the Khrushchev period. For the Brezhnev and Gorbachev eras, see Lawton, *Kinoglasnost*.

¹³S. S. Ginsburg, *Kinematografiya dorevolyutsionnoi rossii* (Moscow: Iskusstvo, 1963), massive and detailed; R. Sobolev, *Lyudi i filmy russkogo do-revolyutsionnogo kino* (Moscow: Iskusstvo, 1961), short and gossipy; Neya Zorkaya, *Na rubezhe stoletii: uz istokov iskusstva v Rossii 1900–1910 godov* (Moscow: Nauka, 1976), a masterly analysis of the function of movies in popular culture; Jay Leyda, *Kino* (London: Allen and Unwin, 1960), a Western perspective by a keen critic of art film. The recent collection, *Testimoni silenziosi: Film russi*

1908–1919/Silent Witnesses: Russian Films, 1908–1919, ed. Yury Tsivian et al. (Pordenone, Italy: Biblioteca dell' Imagine, 1989) is a gold mine of catalog data and commentary (in English and Italian) on the old silents (the Indiana University Press edition is identical to this one except that the title is reversed). About thirty of the films discussed in this book are now available on ten videocassettes (see n. 28).

[14]Tsivian, ed., *Silent Witnesses*, 478–84.

[15]The screenings that I know about took place beginning in 1989 in Pordenone, Italy, and in Munich, Paris, London, Los Angeles, and Washington, D.C., where, at the Library of Congress, about seventy were presented in the winter of 1992.

[16]See Richard Stites, "Iconoclastic Currents in the Russian Revolution," in *Bolshevik Culture*, ed. Abbott Gleason et al. (Bloomington: Indiana University Press, 1985), 1–24.

[17]For purposes of illustration, I have given only one example from the wealth of ideas on social relations, identities, mentalities, and ethnographic realia (including costume, gestures, interior decor, leisure habits) that can be detected from the vivid imagery of this body of films—even granting that seventy is a small sample of the two to three hundred surviving films and the approximately two thousand films made in the tsarist period, including those from private studios in 1918–19.

[18]For the background, see Richard Taylor, "Boris Shumyatsky and the Soviet Cinema in the 1930s: Ideology as Mass Entertainment," *Historical Journal of Film, Radio, and Television* 6, no. 1 (1986): 48–64.

[19]In Soviet iconology, the woman had come to be identified with the countryside and thus with a relatively nurturing role in society, in spite of her prominence in the urban work force, and the man with the city, the factory, the machine—and thus power. See Gail Warshofsky Lapidus, *Women and Soviet Society* (Berkeley: University of California Press, 1978); Richard Stites, *The Women's Liberation Movement in Russia* (Princeton: Princeton University Press, 1978).

[20]Lewis Siegelbaum, *Stakhanovism and the Politics of Productivity in the USSR, 1935–1941* (Cambridge: Cambridge University Press, 1988), 76, 80, 173, and passim for the realities behind the Stakhanovite mythology.

[21]A detailed analysis of this film by the late Maria Enzensberger will appear in Richard Taylor and Derek Spring, eds., *Stalinism and Soviet Cinema*. One ought to put this fairy tale motif in the context of world cinema of the 1930s: the Universum-Film-Ak-tiengesellschaft (UFA) musicals of the Nazi period, the Hungarian drawing room comedies, the "White Telephone" films of fascist Italy which drew on the former, the adventure fantasies and colonial epics of Alexander Korda in England, and Hollywood, which of course possessed its share of Central European dream makers and fantasists: Ernst Lubitsch, Billy Wilder, Ferenc Molnár, Michael Curtiz (Kertesz Mihaly, earlier an agitprop film director for Béla Kun's Soviet regime), and the lesser-known storytellers, Melchior Lengyel and Lajos Biro.

[22]Milka Bliznakov, "Architecture as Decorative Art" (unpublished manuscript); Vladimir Papernyi, *Kultura "dva"* (Ann Arbor: Ardis, 1985). A Western visitor to Moscow in 1936, Kurt London, after lamenting the vulgar array of porticoes, parapets, cornices, and friezes of Hotel Moskva (then used for delegations of workers and peasants), cites this explanation of its decor from a Soviet citizen: "These people, who very often only live in poor huts, are to see that the greatest luxury is thought fit for their reception. They are to return home with the feeling that they are citizens of a great and wealthy country. That increases their self-respect and strengthens their allegiance to a regime which affords them such princely hospitality." *Seven Soviet Arts* (London, 1937), 259–61.

[23]L. I. Brezhnev, *Trilogy: Little Land, Rebirth, the Virgin Lands* (1978; Moscow: Progress Publishers, 1980), 231–398.

[24]See Starr, *Red and Hot*; Stites, *Russian Popular Culture*.

[25]Arnold Hauser, *The Social History of Art*, 2 vols. (New York: Knopf, 1951).

[26]Mark Kuchment in *Soviet Observer* (January 26, 1989), 4.

[27]*American Historical Review, Russian Review, Soviet Union,* and *Slavic Review* have introduced film and video reviews.

[28]*Early Russian Cinema: Films before the Revolution Now on Video*. Ten VHS videos; 28 films. Milestone Film & Video, 175 West 96th Street, New York, N.Y. 10025; telephone (212) 865-7449. Price: $29.95 each, $250.00 for the set of ten. My review of the set appeared in *Russian Review* 53, no. 2 (1994): 285–95.

Contributors

GABRIEL A. ALMOND Professor Emeritus of Political Science, Stanford University

SCOTT A. BRUCKNER Associate, Associates in Rural Development, New York

MICHAEL BURAWOY Professor of Sociology, University of California, Berkeley

CHRISTOPHER CLAGUE Director of Research, Center for Institutional Reform and the Informal Sector, and Professor of Economics, University of Maryland

NANCY CONDEE Associate Professor of Slavic Languages and Literatures, University of Pittsburgh

DAVID HOLLOWAY Co-Director, Center for International Security and Arms Control, and Professor of Political Science, Stanford University

MOSHE LEWIN Professor of History, University of Pennsylvania

JAMES R. MILLAR Director, Institute for European, Russian, and Eurasian Studies, and Professor of Economics, George Washington University

MARTHA BRILL OLCOTT Professor of Political Science, Colgate University, and Senior Fellow, Foreign Policy Research Institute

DANIEL ORLOVSKY Professor of History, Southern Methodist University

THOMAS F. REMINGTON Professor of Political Science, Emory University

THOMAS J. RICHARDSON Assistant Professor of Economics, Yale University

BLAIR A. RUBLE Director, Kennan Institute for Advanced Russian Studies, Woodrow Wilson International Center for Scholars

RICHARD STITES   Professor of History, Georgetown University

GALE STOKES   Professor of History, Rice University

RONALD GRIGOR SUNY   Alex Manoogian Professor of Modern Armenian History, University of Michigan, Ann Arbor

KATHERINE VERDERY   Professor of Anthropology, Johns Hopkins University

REGINALD E. ZELNIK   Professor of History, University of California at Berkeley

Index

21, 269; data for, 276; diplomatic history and, 275; Eastern Europe and, 21; economic factors in, 280; Gorbachev and, 275, 286n35; history of, 281, 282; ideology and, 272–73; independent states and, 8, 269, 270, 282, 286n35; international relations studies and, 8, 269–70, 273–77, 279–81, 282–83; neo-realism and, 278–79; organization theory and, 276; realism and, 271–75; research questions for, 272; socialism and, 40, 273, 274; Stalin and, 272–73; structural realism and, 279–81
Foucault, Michel, 7, 50
free trade, 88, 90, 91
French Revolution, 150, 324–25
Friedburg, Maurice, 293
Frieden, Jeffry, 219n22
Friedrich, Carl, 108
Frye, Timothy, 212, 213

Gaddis, John Lewis, 279
Gasparov, Boris, 329
Georgia, 115, 119, 120, 122, 125, 128, 139, 151, 195
Gerasimov, Sergei, 320
Gerbner, George, 15, 16
German Democratic Republic, 303n13
Germany, 69, 95, 278, 308
Gerschenkron, Alexander, 226, 233
Gitelman, Zvi Y., 117, 121
glasnost, 73, 135, 178, 257, 322
Goble, Paul, 133n50
Gogol, Nikolai, 311
Goldhagen, Erich, 114
Goldman, Marshall L., 177, 257
Goodrich, Carter, 231
Gorbachev, Mikhail: Afghanistan and, 195; collapse of Soviet Union and, 23n12; domestic politics and, 120, 172, 173, 195, 275; East Germany and, 38, 52; foreign policy of, 275, 286n35; glasnost and, 73, 135, 257; leadership by, 21, 47, 178; miscalculations by, 180; *1989* revolution and, 17–18; personality of, 279; political goals of, 20, 40, 257, 278, 280, 281; power of, 174, 177, 256; reform policies of, 51–52, 177, 179, 196; rhetoric of, 7, 43
Gorky, Maksim, 311

Gosplan archives, 266n10
Gossnab archives, 266n10
Granick, David, 233, 264
Great Reforms, 18
Greenfeld, Liah, 15
Green Menace, 125
Gregory, Paul R., 258
Griffiths, Franklyn, 166, 167
Gustafson, Thane, 166, 179

Hammerstein, Oscar, 324
Harkins, William, 311
Hart, Lorenz, 324
Harvard Project on the Soviet Social System (Harvard Refugee Project), 107, 111, 112, 233
Harvey, David, 42, 43, 52
Haslam, Jonathan, 281
Hauser, Arnold, 324
Hauslohner, Peter A., 173
Hellman, Joel, 14, 23n11, 215
Herzen, Aleksandr, 54
Hewett, Ed, 258
Hilton, Alison, 329
historical studies: analogy in, 79, 90; anthropology and, 122; area studies and, 128; change and, 168; cultural studies and, 121, 306–9, 310–12, 329; determinism in, 15; of Europe, 154; events in, 57; focus of, 13, 153, 180, 281, 308–9; frameworks for, 79; of Germany, 59, 68; ideology in, 60, 67, 106; issues of, x, 3, 152; modernization theory and, 79; perspective in, 282; prediction and, 17–19, 244–45; retrospect in, 77; of Russia, 7, 58; social history and, 65, 116; social sciences and, 5; sources for, 121, 147, 266n10, 281; of Soviet Union, 10, 56, 88, 161, 266n10; specialization in, 59; synthesis and, 62; uses of, 22n4
history: continuance of, 59, 73, 78; cultural dimension of, 61, 62, 87, 138, 149, 327; nature of, 6; social, 67, 107, 110, 308–9; uniqueness in, 87, 93
Hobsbawm, Eric J., 127
Hodgman, Donald, 233
Hoffmann, Erik P., 167
Holloway, David, 7, 8, 23n6
Hollywood, 332n21